DATE DUE	

DEBATE

Mariann Fedrizzi

Randy Ellis

 SOUTH-WESTERN
CENGAGE Learning

Australia • Brazil • Japan • Korea • Mexico • Singapore • Spain • United Kingdom • United States

SOUTH-WESTERN
CENGAGE Learning

Debate, 1st Edition
Mariann Fedrizzi and Randy Ellis

Editorial Director: Jack W. Calhoun

Vice President/Editor-in-Chief: Karen Schmohe

Executive Editor: Eve Lewis

Senior Developmental Editor: Enid Nagel

Editorial Assistant: Anne Kelly

Marketing Manager: Linda Kuper

Content Project Management: Pre-PressPMG

Technology Project Manager: Lysa Kosins

Senior Manufacturing Buyer: Kevin Kluck

Production Service: Pre-PressPMG

Senior Art Director: Tippy McIntosh

Cover and Internal Design: Kim Torbeck,
Imbue Design

Cover Image: ©Getty Images

Permissions Acquisition Manager/Text: Mardell
Glinkski-Schultz

Permissions Acquisition Manager/Photo:
Deanna Ettinger

For product information and technology assistance, contact us at
Cengage Learning Customer & Sales Support, 1-800-354-9706

For permission to use material from this text or product,
submit all requests online at **www.cengage.com/permissions**
Further permissions questions can be emailed to
permissionrequest@cengage.com

ExamView® is a registered trademark of eInstruction Corp. Windows is a registered trademark of the Microsoft Corporation used herein under license. Macintosh and Power Macintosh are registered trademarks of Apple Computer, Inc. used herein under license.

© 2008 Cengage Learning. All Rights Reserved.

Library of Congress Control Number: 2009941309

Student Edition ISBN-13: 978-0-538-44966-3

Student Edition ISBN-10: 0-538-44966-7

Annotated Instructor's Edition ISBN-13: 978-0-538-45039-3

Annotated Insrtructor's Edition ISBN-10: 0-538-45039-8

South-Western Cengage Learning
5191 Natorp Boulevard
Mason, OH 45040
USA

Cengage Learning products are represented in Canada by Nelson Education, Ltd.

For your course and learning solutions, visit **school.cengage.com**

Printed in the United States of America
1 2 3 4 5 6 7 8 9 13 12 11 10

Amber R. Ussatis Aberle
Debate and Marketing Instructor
Debate Coach
Mandan High School
Mandan, North Dakota

Melissa Bennett
Forensics Coach
Frontier High School
Bakersfield, California

Kristine Besel
Communications Teacher
Worthington High School
Worthington, Minnesota

Rebecca Cash
English Teacher and Debate Coach
Lawrence North High School
Indianapolis, Indiana

Carolyn Dersen
Teacher
Hastings High School
Houston, Texas

Stephanie Fegan
A.P. English Instructor
Severna Park High School
Severna Park, Maryland

Beth A. Goldman
Director of Debate and Forensics
J.P. Taravella High School
Coral Springs, Florida

Jeanette Hardesty
Debate Teacher and Coach
Mill Valley High School
Shawnee, Kansas

Thomas R. Meyer
Business, Debate, Journalism, and
    Language Arts Teacher
Mater Academy Charter High School
Hialeah Gardens, Florida

Michele Mitchell
Debate Coach
Dodge City High School
Dodge City, Kansas

Holly T. Reineking
Debate and Speech Teacher
Kingwood Park High School
Kingwood, Texas

Jennifer Smith
English Teacher
Former Director of Forensics and
    Debate Coach
Westside High School Career Center
Omaha, Nebraska

Deadra K. Longworth Stanton
Language Arts Instructor
Mason City Senior High School
Mason City, Iowa

Shelley B. Tatum
Debate Coach
Lufkin High School
Lufkin, Texas

Susan Telehany
Assistant Director, Testing Coordinator
Ysleta Independent School District
El Paso, Texas

Jim Wakefield
Debate Coach
Ft. Lauderdale High School
Ft. Lauderdale, Florida

Rex Wiesenthal
Speech Instructor
Bel Air High School
El Paso Community College
El Paso, Texas

Contents

About the Authors

Mariann Fedrizzi is a teacher at North Star Academy in Marquette, Michigan. She taught speech, debate, and English in Houston for 24 years where her students brought home numerous honors as state and national contestants. Ms. Fedrizzi is a recipient of the Texas University Interscholastic League Sponsor Excellence Award.

Randy Ellis is a veteran debate teacher and coach. A two-time president of the Texas Forensics Council, Mr. Ellis is Spring High School's fine arts department chair where he has taught for 30 years. He was inducted into the Texas Forensics Association Hall of Fame in 2006.

DEBATE...Give your students a voice!

Based upon the authors' experience as successful high school debate teachers and coaches, *Debate* provides students with opportunities to research, write, and experience competitive debate.

Getting Started

Each chapter opens with a real-world feature that connects debate with real life.

Famous Debaters profiles debaters and their contributions.
- Hillary Rodham Clinton
- Clark Kent Ervin
- Michael J. Fox
- Gwen Ifill
- Abraham Lincoln
- Sonia Sotomayor

FAMOUS DEBATERS

Michael J. Fox

"*Medical science has proven time and again that when the resources are provided, great progress in the treatment, cure, and prevention of disease can occur.*"

As an award-winning actor, Michael J. Fox used his voice to say the lines that others wrote. He used his voice to convey the emotions of the characters he was playing. Today Fox puts his voice talents to another use as well. He is a spokesperson for his foundation, the Michael J. Fox Foundation. It seeks to raise funds and support research to find a cure for Parkinson's disease.

Parkinson's is a degenerative disease of the nervous system. Nerve cells misfire, and the sufferer loses control of movements. The cause is unknown. Nearly 5 million people worldwide suffer from Parkinson's, including former Attorney General Janet Reno and former Heavyweight Champion of the World, Muhammed Ali. It can even strike young people. Fox was diagnosed with young-onset Parkinson's disease in 1991, when he was thirty years old.

Fox began his professional acting career when he was fifteen and later starred in TV shows and movies. His best-known role was Alex in the TV sit-com *Family Ties*, and he became an international film star with the *Back to the Future* trilogy. After he was diagnosed with Parkinson's, Fox kept it a secret from the public for seven years. He finally acknowledged that he had the disease in 1998 and committed himself to campaigning for research.

To help find a cure for Parkinson's disease, Fox believes in the need for ongoing medical research. In 1999, Fox appeared before the Senate Appropriations Committee to plead for funding for medical research to find a cure for Parkinson's. The Michael J. Fox Foundation for Parkinson's Research is dedicated to raising awareness about the disease and raising funds for research. Fox has stated, "Medical science has proven time and again that when the resources are provided, great progress in the treatment, cure, and prevention of disease can occur."

Fox maintains a busy schedule of appearances on television talk shows and personal appearances to raise awareness about the disease. Fox still acts. He is a five-time Emmy Award winner, the most recent being given in 2009. His prime-time special *Michael J. Fox: Adventures of an Incurable Optimist* was based on his autobiography and expressed his incredible attitude about life.

In 2007, Fox delivered the keynote speech at the BIO (Biotechnology Industry Organization) International Convention in Boston. To the scientists in the auditorium, Fox said "Looking around this room, filled with an incredible reserve of brain power, scientific prowess, and excellent intentions, I've got to ask, 'How can we get this right?' because I can't help thinking about the cost of *failing* to get it right."

Think Critically

Michael J. Fox once said, "One's dignity may be assaulted, vandalized and cruelly mocked, but cannot be taken away unless it is surrendered." Do you agree with Fox? Why or why not?

Real People | Real Careers

Lisa Ling

"*her goal was to say one thing each day that would make people think, whether it made them cheer or made them throw things at their TV*"

Lisa Ling is a debater on the frontlines. As a broadcast investigative reporter, Lisa has interviewed, argued with, and defended her own ideas with people from approximately two-dozen countries. As a co-host on ABC's morning talk show *The View*, she has debated entertainment celebrities and political figures.

Lisa was born in Sacramento, California and began her career in broadcast journalism while still a student at Del Campo High School. At sixteen, she was chosen to be one of four hosts for the nationally syndicated teen news magazine program, *Scratch*.

At eighteen, she became a correspondent for Channel One News, a program that serves over eight million students in approximately twelve thousand high schools. She covered stories that ranged from drug trafficking in Colombia to her thirteen year old cousin's unsuccessful fight with liver cancer. She risked her life to investigate the civil war in Algeria and the refugee crisis in Albania. She shared tea and ideas with the Dalai Lama. In 1996, she participated in a joint investigation with *Time* magazine into a Russian company accused of smuggling nuclear weapons. She was the first American television reporter to interview the company's owner. She has reported from more than two dozen countries, including Afghanistan, Iraq, Colombia, Algeria, Cambodia, Vietnam, China, Japan, India, and Iran. Before she reached twenty-five, Lisa was named senior war correspondent for Channel One.

She joined ABC Daytime's popular morning talk program, *The View*. Ling sat alongside Barbara Walters, Meredith Vieira, Star Jones, and Joy Behar and gave the "twenty-something take" with a dose of modern age philosophy. The five women discussed relevant, everyday issues and shared their daily no-holds-barred opinions and lively colorful conversations. While Lisa enjoyed her stint on the program, and has returned for guest appearances, she felt the urge to return to the field and follow the stories of people's lives.

Lisa returned to broadcast journalism and became the host of *National Geographic Explorer*. Lisa has stated that her goal was to say one thing each day that would make people think, whether it made them cheer or made them throw things at their TV. She became a special correspondent for *The Oprah Winfrey Show*, which has featured many of Ling's investigative pieces, including a report on North Korea. Ironically, Lisa's sister Laura, who is also a reporter, was arrested and detained in North Korea while doing a story on North Korean refugees escaping into China. Lisa became a spokesperson for her sister and her sister's colleague, Euna Lee. Fortunately, both were released after the intervention of former President Bill Clinton. Lisa Ling is a creative, courageous journalist who can teach debaters and non-debaters about the power of curiosity, good questions, and an impassioned spirit.

Think Critically

How has Lisa Ling used debate skills to be a successful investigative reporter?

33

Real People Real Careers

provides a personal view of how debate is used in the workplace.
- Al Gore
- David Hankus
- Bobby Jindal
- Lisa Ling
- Condoleezza Rice
- Oprah Winfrey

Getting Started

Strong learning tools promote a variety of individual and group work.

Goals are clearly stated learning objectives to guide your learning.

Terms appear in bold and are defined in the text.

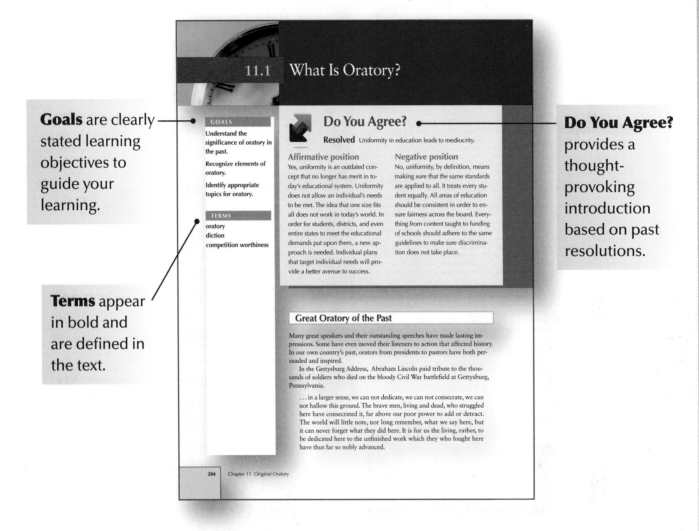

11.1 What Is Oratory?

GOALS

Understand the significance of oratory in the past.

Recognize elements of oratory.

Identify appropriate topics for oratory.

TERMS

oratory
diction
competition worthiness

Do You Agree?

Resolved Uniformity in education leads to mediocrity.

Affirmative position
Yes, uniformity is an outdated concept that no longer has merit in today's educational system. Uniformity does not allow an individual's needs to be met. The idea that one size fits all does not work in today's world. In order for students, districts, and even entire states to meet the educational demands put upon them, a new approach is needed. Individual plans that target individual needs will provide a better avenue to success.

Negative position
No, uniformity, by definition, means making sure that the same standards are applied to all. It treats every student equally. All areas of education should be consistent in order to ensure fairness across the board. Everything from content taught to funding of schools should adhere to the same guidelines to make sure discrimination does not take place.

Great Oratory of the Past

Many great speakers and their outstanding speeches have made lasting impressions. Some have even moved their listeners to action that affected history. In our own country's past, orators from presidents to pastors have both persuaded and inspired.

In the Gettysburg Address, Abraham Lincoln paid tribute to the thousands of soldiers who died on the bloody Civil War battlefield at Gettysburg, Pennsylvania.

> ...in a larger sense, we can not dedicate, we can not consecrate, we can not hallow this ground. The brave men, living and dead, who struggled here have consecrated it, far above our poor power to add or detract. The world will little note, nor long remember, what we say here, but it can never forget what they did here. It is for us the living, rather, to be dedicated here to the unfinished work which they who fought here have thus far so nobly advanced.

284   Chapter 11 Original Oratory

Do You Agree? provides a thought-provoking introduction based on past resolutions.

Photo caption questions help you connect to content covered in each chapter.

Why do you need to research both sides of an issue for debate?

What would be the purpose of eulogizing someone in an oration?

What are some of the roles played by students at a mock trial who are not on a competing team?

Special Features Enhance Learning

TURNING POINT

Brown v. Board of Education

On May 17, 1954, after years of legal debate, the U.S. Supreme Court issued an opinion that would change the nation's civil rights law. Brown v. Board of Education of Topeka, Kansas was a landmark reinterpretation of the Constitution's Fourteenth Amendment, which states "No state shall . . . deny to any person within its jurisdiction the equal protection of the laws."

This was not the first time the Court heard a Fourteenth Amendment case, nor was it the first case involving the civil rights of African Americans. In 1896, the Supreme Court had ruled in Plessy v. Ferguson that it was constitutional for railroads to provide separate seating for white and black passengers. The Court ruled that the facilities were "separate but equal" and held that Homer Plessy's rights were not violated by forcing him to sit in the blacks-only parts of the train.

From the late eighteen hundreds on, both southern and northern states had Jim Crow laws, that is, laws that mandated separate facilities for African Americans in many areas of public life. The states insisted that even though public services were segregated, they were essentially equal. By the 1950s, the "separate but equal" concept was being challenged in several states that enforced segregated education. Oliver Brown, of Topeka, Kansas, joined his case to appeals cases from four other states. Jim Crow laws in Kansas forced Brown's daughter Linda, then a third grader, to walk several blocks to catch a bus which drove her to a black-only school over a mile away. There was a whites-only school just a few blocks from her home. The plaintiff's lawyers would show that "separate but equal" did not apply to the unequal segregated schools and the education they provided to students. White schools had more money and better equipment. Black schools had far fewer resources.

Thurgood Marshall, the attorney for the plaintiff and later the first African-American Supreme Court Justice, asked the Court to revisit the Plessy decision's effects on segregation in public schools. The blatantly unequal facilities and resources in black-only schools clearly showed inequality.

Attorneys for the state argued for states' rights. State laws control education, and the federal government and Constitution cannot interfere. Since school attendance is based on where a student resides, forcing integration on segregated neighborhoods would impose a huge and unwarranted burden on the state.

Chief Justice Warren wrote the unanimous 9-0 decision in favor of Brown. He wrote, "We conclude that in the field of public education the doctrine of 'separate but equal' has no place. Separate educational facilities are inherently unequal."

Think Critically

How does the Court's decision affect education today?

320   Chapter 12 Mock Trial

By presenting influential historical connections, you will learn how classic debates have shaped the contemporary public forum.

Turning Point references noteworthy debates in history and poses questions to promote critical thinking.

- The Great Debates of 1960
- Wiley College Debate Team of the 1930s
- The United Nations
- Blogs
- Constitutional Amendment XIX
- Scopes Trial–1925
- Women in Broadcasting
- Civil Rights Act of 1964
- Town Hall Meetings
- Meet the Press
- "I Have a Dream"
- Brown v. Board of Education

You will learn debate etiquette while developing argumentation strategy.

You Be The Judge promotes the discussion of relevant ethical issues.

YOU BE THE JUDGE

The power to speak effectively and passionately and to move people with one's words can be used for good—or not.

Throughout history orators have used their skills to further their ends. Sometimes those ends were honorable; sometimes they were self-serving. In Shakespeare's *Julius Caesar*, Marc Antony uses his oratorical powers in his eulogy for Caesar to rile the Roman masses against his assassins. President Franklin Delano Roosevelt's inaugural address calmed a nation in the midst of the Great Depression when he reminded his listeners that they only thing they had to fear was fear itself. Winston Churchill's speeches inspired the English people to carry on during the darkest hours of World War II.

The term *demagogue* applies to a person who uses oratorical skills to appeal to people's emotions for the sole purpose of gaining power. Adolf Hitler was a demagogue.

Achieving skill in oratory carries with it a responsibility to use that skill and power wisely and honorably.

What Would You Do?

Suppose you listen to an oration given with terrific delivery and emotion. However, you know that facts cited by the speaker are wrong or twisted. Would you approach the speaker? What would you say?

Special Features Enhance Learning

FYI Pieces of evidence are often called "cards." This name originates from debaters who copied pages of books and cut the paper to show only the evidence that they wanted to use. Then they would paste the evidence to an index card.

FYI presents interesting facts and statistics to help you connect debate to the world around you.

Time Requirement Charts offer an organized view of the various forms of debate.

On March 28, 1925, the National Forensic League was born, the first honor society for high school debaters. It is currently the nation's oldest and largest high school debate and speech honor society.

Time Requirements for Lincoln-Douglas Debate		
Prep time	Three or four minutes	Prepare arguments before presenting the next speech. Because this is such a limited time, it should be used wisely.
Affirmative constructive	Six minutes	Affirmative debater presents the case that supports the resolution. All information that will be debated must be presented here.
Negative cross-examination period	Three minutes	Negative speaker asks questions of the affirmative speaker
Negative constructive rebuttal	Seven minutes	Negative speaker presents the negative stand regarding the resolution and presents a rebuttal to the affirmative's case. The key issues of the affirmative case must be attacked.
Affirmative cross-examination period	Three minutes	Affirmative speaker questions the negative speaker about his case
Affirmative rebuttal	Four minutes	Affirmative speaker points out the strengths of own case and tells why they are superior to strengths of opponent's case. Affirmative speaker then points out the weaknesses in opponent's case. No new evidence can be introduced in the rebuttal speech.
Negative rebuttal	Six minutes	Negative speaker's last chance to make an impression on the judge. First, just as with the affirmative rebuttal, the negative speaker emphasizes the strengths of own speech, as well as the areas of weaknesses within the affirmative case. Finally, the negative speaker tells why the judge should vote for him or her.
Affirmative rebuttal	Three minutes	Affirmative speaker's last chance to impress the judge. Must emphasize own strengths and opponents' weaknesses, and tell why the judge should vote for him or her.

eCollection Activity

Morals and ethics come into play in many Lincoln-Douglas debates. One moral debate that has been hotly contested for many years is the debate on capital punishment. Capital punishment, also known as the death penalty, is the legal infliction of death as punishment for violating a criminal law. It is reserved for serious crimes such as murder. Beginning in the mid 1960s, many states abolished their laws allowing capital punishment. In 1972, the Supreme Court ruled that the death penalty was unconstitutional as administered because it constituted cruel and unusual punishment. After changes were made by many states, the Supreme Court reinstated the death penalty in 1976. Fifteen states have eliminated the use of the death penalty.

Those who oppose the death penalty feel that if violates human rights. They also question the effectiveness of the punishment. Those who support the death penalty feel that the severity of their punishment matches that of their crime. They feel the punishment will discourage others from committing similar crimes.

To learn more about this debate, access www.cengage.com/school/langarts/debate and click on the link for Chapter 2. Find other arguments for and against capital punishment as well as other statistics.

eCollection Activity proposes Internet research exercises.

Ongoing Assessment

Engaging activities give you a chance to check your understanding of terms and content before moving to the next lesson.

Think Critically provides short answer exercises to reinforce concepts.

Research NOW! helps sharpen your research skills with practice activities.

Emphasizes Teamwork

Write NOW! exercises supply you with the practice you need to improve writing skills.

Speak NOW! offers exercises to give you the public speaking practice you need.

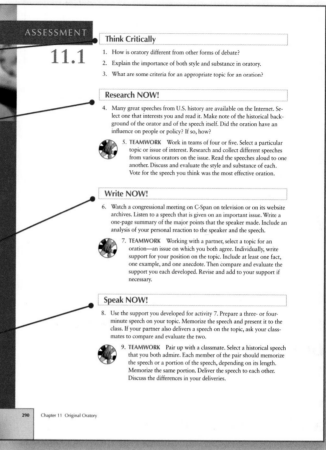

Think Critically

1. How is oratory different from other forms of debate?
2. Explain the importance of both style and substance in oratory.
3. What are some criteria for an appropriate topic for an oration?

Research NOW!

4. Many great speeches from U.S. history are available on the Internet. Select one that interests you and read it. Make note of the historical background of the orator and of the speech itself. Did the oration have an influence on people or policy? If so, how?

5. TEAMWORK Work in teams of four or five. Select a particular topic or issue of interest. Research and collect different speeches from various orators on the issue. Read the speeches aloud to one another. Discuss and evaluate the style and substance of each. Vote for the speech you think was the most effective oration.

Write NOW!

6. Watch a congressional meeting on C-Span on television or on its website archives. Listen to a speech that is given on an important issue. Write a one-page summary of the major points that the speaker made. Include an analysis of your personal reaction to the speaker and the speech.

7. TEAMWORK Working with a partner, select a topic for an oration—an issue on which you both agree. Individually, write support for your position on the topic. Include at least one fact, one example, and one anecdote. Then compare and evaluate the support you each developed. Revise and add to your support if necessary.

Speak NOW!

8. Use the support you developed for activity 7. Prepare a three- or four-minute speech on your topic. Memorize the speech and present it to the class. If your partner also delivers a speech on the topic, ask your classmates to compare and evaluate the two.

9. TEAMWORK Pair up with a classmate. Select a historical speech that you both admire. Each member of the pair should memorize the speech or a portion of the speech, depending on its length. Memorize the same portion. Deliver the speech to each other. Discuss the differences in your deliveries.

Abundant End of Chapter Assessment

Chapter in Review presents key chapter concepts for quick review.

Develop Your Debating Language matches terms with definitions to confirm understanding of key terms.

Chapter in Review

6.1 Use Defensive Negative Arguments

- In LD debate, the negative debate team builds a case. In CX debate, the negative debate team builds arguments. Use defensive negative arguments to challenge the significance of the harm stock issue, the inherent barrier of the inherency stock issue, and the solvency stock issue.

6.2 Use Offensive Negative Arguments

- Use offensive negative arguments to challenge the topicality stock issue. To challenge topicality, you must challenge the definition, identify the violation, establish the standards, and request the judge's vote.
- Use the disadvantages argument, consisting of a link, brink, and impact, as an offensive negative argument.

6.3 Use the Kritik

- A kritik is an offensive argument that challenges the philosophy behind the affirmative debate team's case.
- The language kritik and the knowledge kritik are the most common types of kritiks. A kritik consists of an observation, impact, and decision rule.

Develop Your Debating Language

Select the term that best fits the definition. Some terms will not be used.

a. attitudinal inherence
b. bias
c. brink
d. decision rule
e. disadvantage
f. fiat
g. field context definition
h. impact
i. knowledge kritik
j. kritik
k. language kritik
l. link
m. negative arguments
n. observation
o. philosophy
p. presumption
q. standard
r. structural inherency

1. Deals with laws, regulations, guidelines, and so on
2. The argument that if the affirmative debate team's plan is ratified, bad side effects will occur
3. Evidence that shows a connection to the affirmative plan
4. A system of concepts that forms an underlying theory of a topic
5. Idea that you are innocent until proven guilty
6. A guide to weigh the violation
7. An argument that establishes an all or nothing decision
8. An attitude, such as racism or feminism, exists and it is so entrenched that only a radical change will solve the harm scenario
9. An offensive argument that challenges a certain way of thinking
10. A major argument, similar to a contention
11. The meaning of a term in the "real world"
12. A prejudice toward a specific idea or cause
13. Claim that the action called for by the affirmative team's plan will initiate the disadvantage
14. An act of will that creates something without effort

x

Abundant End of Chapter Assessment
The assessments found at the end of every chapter give you the opportunity to test your knowledge.

Review Debate Concepts

15. How do you categorize negative arguments?
16. What is the most fundamental negative argument you can make?
17. Who is responsible for proving evidence?
18. What type of data does the affirmative debate team most commonly use?
19. As the negative debate team, how do you challenge the inherent barrier?
20. Is it harder to argue structural inherency or attitudinal inherency?
21. How do you challenge solvency?
22. Which stock issue can you challenge with an offensive negative argument?
23. What will the affirmative debate team do if you do not establish a direct link between your challenge and their case?
24. How do you establish that a topicality violation has occurred?
25. What are the standards that you can use to compare your negative position to the affirmative team's case and plan?
26. As the negative team, how can you offer the judges the opportunity to vote for you?
27. How would you categorize the disadvantages argument?
28. What should be in a disadvantages argument?
29. What does a kritik challenge?
30. How does a kritik change the direction of an argument?
31. What is the premise of a language kritik?
32. What is the premise of a knowledge kritik?
33. Why could the kritik argument be difficult for a judge?
34. What is a major argument that makes up a kritik?
35. What is an *a priori* position?

Make Academic Connections

36. **PROBLEM SOLVING** Read an Op Ed piece that could be used as an affirmative argument. What kind of negative argument could you build to oppose the position? Identify the negative arguments you could use.
37. **MATH** Affirmative arguments often use statistics. Look at a military conflict and identify statistics used to support or oppose the conflict. Write a one-page essay describing how the statistics were interpreted to support or oppose the conflict.
38. **ENGLISH** While learning about negative arguments, you encountered several words borrowed from other languages. Identify five additional

Review Debate Concepts provides questions that summarize key concepts to reinforce learning.

Make Academic Connections links chapter content to core subject areas such as social studies, language arts, and science.

words that originated in other languages. Provide definitions and examples of their use.
39. **HISTORY** Political parties are often on opposite sides of a debate. Select the Democratic or Republican party. Write a one-page essay about the party's formation. How has the party's philosophy changed or remained consistent since the party was established?
40. **CHALLENGES** Watch a televised commentary that supports a current topic. Identify the arguments you would use to oppose the commentator's position.

Research NOW!

41. Review the Scopes trial that occurred in 1925. Research the background and locate transcripts of the trial. What were the key philosophies behind the arguments of the prosecution and the defense? Offer a kritik based upon your research.

 42. **TEAMWORK** Working with a partner who selected the same side of the Scopes trial in the previous activity, evaluate the arguments made to support the side. Make a list of things you would have done differently.

Write NOW!

43. *Presumption* is a term used in debate and in legal situations. Write a one-page essay describing how the presumption of innocence affects debates and legal proceedings.

 44. **TEAMWORK** Working with a partner, examine a political speech given recently in your city or state. Look for evidence of bias in the speech. Rewrite the speech, removing any biased statements you found.

45. Select one of the resolutions provided at the beginning of each lesson. Write a one-page essay describing how you would build the negative arguments opposing the resolution.
46. Continue your research of the Scopes trial from activity 41 above. Review the findings that dismissed the ruling of the previous court. What was the impact of that final decision? Who, in your opinion, won the case? Write a short paper on your conclusions.

Speak NOW!

47. News is broadcast around the clock, but each news story is only a small piece of the broadcast. Therefore, many stories contain sound bites, portions of a longer speech. Identify several sound bites in today's news. Evaluate how the speaker delivered each sound bite. Practice delivering the sound bite. How does your delivery differ from the sound bite?

48. Find the text of a speech given by Bobby Jindal and a video of Jindal presenting the speech. Make a video recording of yourself presenting the speech and then watch the recording. Identify five ways that your presentation differed from Jindal's delivery. Which presentation was better? Why?

 49. **TEAMWORK** Funding is often important in political debates about new legislation. Working with a partner, investigate the funding planned to pay for a current piece of legislation. Deliver a brief speech supporting or opposing the funding planned for the legislation. Evaluate your partner's speech based on content and delivery.

eCollection Activity

The 1920s brought many changes to American life and culture, and many of those changes found their way into high school education.

Advances in technology brought about new possibilities in employment, and these possibilities required training. New courses were added to the curriculum in the sciences, industrial arts, home economics, and physical education to prepare students for a changing world. Students moved from rural to urban areas to attend schools that offered these courses. Increased enrollment required more schools and more teachers, teachers who received better training in new areas of instruction.

The controversies of the 1920s found their way into high schools as well. Religious debate was publicized with the Scopes trial but did not end there. Debate over funding for church-based schools raged in the 1920s. The Supreme Court overturned an Oregon law requiring all students to attend public schools, and the debate over funding continues to the present day. Other controversies such as the Red Scare, the worry about communism, made public schools as a place where citizens received training in civic responsibility.

Still, advances in instruction were introduced in the 1920s. The so-called Dalton Plan emphasized the value of individual projects conducted in the laboratory, and the Contract Plan also allowed for individualized instruction whose requirements were set down in a written contract signed by both student and teacher.

To learn more about the culture and issues of the 1920s, access www.cengage.com/school/langarts/debate and click on the link for Chapter 6. Choose one area of interest and locate informative articles on the subject. Write a one-page essay about your findings. Remember to provide citations for your information.

CHAPTER 1

Introduction to Debate

FAMOUS DEBATERS

Abraham Lincoln

> *Because of his eloquence in debates with Douglas, Lincoln gained national recognition. This recognition brought him the Republican nomination for president for the 1860 election, in which he soundly defeated Douglas.*

In 1858 serious issues were troubling the citizens of the United States: the forced labor of slavery versus the labor of free men, popular sovereignty, and the legal and political status of blacks in America. These issues were at the center of a series of political debates between the two candidates for the Illinois Senate: incumbent Stephen A. Douglas, who also was the leading choice for the Democratic presidential nomination in the election of 1860, and a little-known backwoods lawyer, Abraham Lincoln, who was trying to win the seat for the new Republican party.

Lincoln and Douglas traveled throughout Illinois, covering close to 10,000 miles and facing off in seven debates before crowds of up to 15,000 people. Debates were as important to the spectators of the time as they were to the debaters. Historians William and Bruce Catton wrote, "The people who flocked to hear Lincoln and Douglas were well informed on political issues and they did not take these issues lightly. They came primarily to affirm or reexamine party loyalties, to hear and weigh the opposing sides of a question that genuinely troubled them to see for themselves which of these able, forceful, oddly matched contestants had the better case."

Lincoln and Douglas held two different views on slavery. Douglas contended that slavery was naturally failing, was a local problem, and did not need national intervention. Lincoln claimed that slavery would expand into the nation's new territories. He thought the nation should react to prevent every laborer from being reduced to slavery. They also differed on the rights of black Americans. Douglas claimed that blacks were inherently inferior to whites stating, "I want citizenship for whites only." Lincoln also stated that he was not in favor of "bringing about in any way the social and political equality of the white and black races." However, he was adamant that black Americans were equal to whites and "entitled to all the natural rights enumerated in the Declaration of Independence, the right to life, liberty, and the pursuit of happiness. I hold that he is as much entitled to these as the white man….But in the right to eat the bread, without leave of anybody else, which his own hand earns, he is my equal and the equal of Judge Douglas, and the equal of every living man."

Lincoln lost his bid for the Illinois Senate seat. However, because of his eloquence in debates with Douglas, Lincoln gained national recognition. This recognition brought him the Republican nomination for president in the 1860 election, in which he soundly defeated Douglas.

Think Critically

Research the Lincoln-Douglas debates. How were the debates important to Lincoln's political career?

What Is Debate?

GOALS

Define debate.

List the people who were influential in the debate process.

Understand the significance of presidential debates.

TERMS

debate
informal debate
formal debate

Do You Agree?

Resolved When in conflict, the spirit of the law ought to take precedence over the letter of the law.

Affirmative position

Yes, circumstances and situations arise that put people in a position to make decisions that they otherwise would not make. This could be something as simple as driving over the speed limit to the topic of vigilantism.

Negative position

No, the letter of the law must be followed at all times. You cannot rely on personal interpretation to decide when a law will be obeyed.

Debate in Your Life

Debate takes place every day in all kinds of places. Debates can be heard in homes, offices, schools, and the halls of government. They also can be heard in shopping malls, churches, and hospitals. You engage in debate when you disagree with one or more people and try to persuade them to agree to your position. Debate is an important aspect of your life. It gives you the opportunity to make the best decisions possible based on the information you have.

Debate is defined as oral confrontation between two individuals, teams, or groups to argue reasons for and against a set position. These arguments follow a set form or procedure. Because debate is contentious by nature, you should expect to challenge your opponent's statements and to have your statements, opinions, and ideas challenged as well. *Persuasion*, which appeals to emotional responses, is a key element of the debate process. You will study several types of debate throughout this course: Lincoln-Douglas, cross-examination, and public forum. These are the most common forms of debate found at tournaments. Even though the goal is the same, each debate has its own format and set of rules.

Debate can be divided into two categories: informal and formal debate. **Informal debate** is a common occurrence with very little preparation or rules. It can take place anywhere. Examples of an informal debate are a group of friends deciding which movie to see or a child trying to persuade a parent to extend a curfew. In each case, there is an exchange of ideas for and against an issue between two or more people.

PHOTODISC/GETTY IMAGES

Why is debate important in everyday life?

Formal debates are quite different. They usually are scheduled and take place in a specified setting. People taking part in formal debates prepare extensively before the debates take place. The topic or resolution is established. There is a set of rules for the types of speeches given and the length of these speeches. Finally, the participants are dressed appropriately. A debate between political candidates is a type of formal debate. Other examples of formal debates include debates in Congress when making and passing laws and debates that occur during town hall meetings.

Debating is different from arguing. The one crucial difference is the aspect of listening. When you argue, you seldom are interested in the other person's point of view. You only want to express yourself. Debating requires you to listen to what the other person has to say. You then must respond to what has been said, not simply argue your position.

Early Influences on Debate

Debate has been going on for a very long time. The ancient Greeks are credited with inventing not only debate, but also the art of public speaking. For them, public speaking was an important part of *rhetoric*, the art of persuading an audience. The Greek orators Isocrates, Socrates, and Demosthenes, and later the Roman orator Cicero all made important contributions to debate.

Isocrates (436–338 B.C.) was one of the first people to affect education and debate. Isocrates was a lawyer and a teacher. He believed that rhetoric should be taught along with ethics and politics because rhetoric helped people to express their ideas. He believed that knowledge is tentative. There is no limit to what you can learn about a subject, and you can't know it all. Because you can't know everything all of the time, it is important to have good, informed opinions regarding the issues. Sharing these ideas helps to increase knowledge.

VASILIKI/ISTOCKPHOTO.COM

Why do you think virtue
is important in a debater?

Socrates (469–399 B.C.) is credited with setting the standard for Western philosophy. His teachings revolved around the nature of virtue. He believed that people do not deliberately do bad things, but instead they do what they think is the best thing to do at the time. Socrates taught that knowledge and virtue directly affect each other.

FYI Debates have been going on for a long time. In fact, there are those who believe that the debates which took place in early Rome established the premises and structure used in debate today.

Demosthenes (384–322 B.C.) is considered to be Greece's greatest orator. He had a superb command of language and knew how to use it. He wrote orations, letters, poems, political speeches, and speeches in courts of law. As a boy Demosthenes had a speech impediment and a weak voice. He was able to overcome these shortcomings and became a superb orator. Demosthenes paid close attention to all elements of delivery. He felt that gestures and voice were very important. Through close attention to delivery details, he was able to be more influential in sharing his ideas.

Cicero (106–43 B.C.) influenced both philosophy and politics. Born in the waning years of the Roman Republic, Cicero was a lawyer, politician, orator, and philosopher. The ideas Cicero put forth while he was a lawyer are still used. He believed it was important to look at an issue from all sides and to present and consider all information. He was open to new ideas and ready to confront new issues. This approach is used in debate today. In order to be able to write the best case, debaters must explore all sides of a proposition. They also must try to anticipate any arguments or premises that could be introduced in the course of a debate.

Debate has been an important element of governments throughout history. Many people have contributed to debate and oratory. Every political season produces another politician with exceptional speaking skills. It is safe to say that the list of influential orators and debaters will only continue to grow.

Debate Today

Because of presidential political campaigns, debates are more popular than ever. From the Kennedy-Nixon presidential debates to the Obama-McCain debates, candidates as well as the issues are dissected by the press and public alike.

There were four debates between Kennedy and Nixon during the 1960 presidential campaign. The first debate centered on domestic issues, while the second and third debate focused on China. The United States' relationship with Cuba was the topic of the final debate. Polling showed that more than half of all voters were influenced by the debates. Six percent said that their vote was a direct result of the debates.

This first nationally televised debate was watched by 77 million Americans. The format used in 1960 is still in use today. Presidential debates continue to be a source of information for the public.

During the 2008 presidential election, both parties hosted a series of debates between the candidates running for their party's nomination. Three presidential debates and one vice-presidential debate followed during the general election. Once again, millions tuned in to hear what the candidates had to say.

Research to learn more about the debates between Barack Obama and John McCain that led up to the 2008 presidential election. Who was the stronger debater?

AP PHOTO/CHARLES DHARAPAK

©BETTMANN/CORBIS

TURNING POINT

The Great Debates of 1960

During the 1960 presidential campaign, the Democratic candidate, Senator John F. Kennedy from Massachusetts, agreed to four debates with the Republican candidate, Vice President Richard M. Nixon. The first debate took place on September 26 in Chicago, Illinois. Howard K. Smith, a CBS news anchor, was the moderator. The format for the debates was an eight-minute opening statement, and then alternating questions from four panelists. The candidate had two and a half minutes to respond. This was followed by a rebuttal speech given by the other candidate. Not only was this the first debate between candidates of the two major parties, but it also was the first time presidential debates were televised.

The importance of the effect television had on these debates is significant. This was the first time the public could compare the candidates firsthand. Things did not go well for Richard Nixon.

In August, Nixon spent two weeks in the hospital because of a severely injured knee. As a result of this injury, Nixon had lost weight and was still twenty pounds underweight by the time the debates were held. Despite being very pale, he refused to wear any makeup. Nixon chose a gray suit for the debate which provided very little contrast with the background set.

Kennedy, on the other hand, had been in California campaigning during the early part of September. Even though he was already tan, he chose to wear makeup. In sharp contrast to Nixon, Kennedy wore a dark suit, making him stand out from the background. Kennedy also was coached on how to sit and what to do when he wasn't speaking. Kennedy appeared firm and confident.

The first debate centered around domestic issues. Kennedy was thought to be inexperienced, but he overcame this supposed weakness by focusing on his work in Congress. His style was strong and aggressive.

There is much discussion as to who actually won the debate. Studies show that voters who watched the debates on television thought Kennedy was the winner, while those voters who listened to the debates believes it was a draw. Everyone agrees that the debates changed the face of politics.

There were three more debates between Kennedy and Nixon, but the first was by far the most memorable. Their effect was far reaching. Italy, Finland, Sweden, Japan, and Germany followed by establishing debates for national office as well. The Great Debates of 1960 were the beginning of what has become a much-anticipated event in the presidential electoral process.

Think Critically

How have the presidential debates changed since 1960? What impact do the debates have today on presidential elections?

Think Critically

1. How is debate different from arguing? Why is debate preferable?

2. Compare and contrast formal and informal debate.

3. How do debates affect presidential elections?

Research NOW!

4. Many of Demosthenes' works are available online. Select one of his works. Read and evaluate it. How can his principles be applied to your life today? How do Demosthenes' principles hold up today?

5. Read the transcripts between any of the presidential debates since 1960. List the positions and the support given by each candidate for the topics that were debated. Decide who won the debate, and write a one-page paper giving specific details for the decision. Be able to tell which candidate gave the better answer and why.

Write NOW!

6. Attend a meeting of your school's student council. Pick a controversial issue that was debated at that meeting. Write a one-page summary of the issue you choose, analyzing both sides of that issue.

 7. **TEAMWORK**   Working with a partner, watch the video of any of the presidential debates. Follow the transcript and enact the debate in class. After the debate is complete, have students vote to pick a winner, giving reasons for their choices.

Speak NOW!

 8. **TEAMWORK**   Pair up with a classmate. Each pair should pick a presidential debate. From the debate, select a question that both candidates answered. Each member of the pair should memorize these speeches in order to present them in front of the class. Practice your delivery with your partner before your presentation.

9. Select a general topic and prepare a speech to give in class. The speech should be two- to three-minutes long. Have support to back up the main idea of the speech. Practice in front of a mirror before giving your speech to the class. Work on eye contact, making sure you are looking at everybody in class.

1.2 Debate Skills and Grooming for Debate

GOALS

Define the types of skills used in debate.

Understand the importance of grooming and appearance to success in debate.

TERMS

hearing
listening
articulation
pronunciation
vocalized pause
poise

Do You Agree?

Resolved Protection of the environment should take precedence over the development of natural resources.

Affirmative position

Yes, we only have so many natural resources left. It is important that we protect them for future generations. These resources are also important in our efforts to halt global warming.

Negative position

No, we are now in a position where we must develop our own oil resources. We should no longer depend on other nations to meet our oil needs. There are areas that will not upset the balance, and we should use the resources that are at our disposal.

Skills You Gain From Debate

You have to sign up for courses, and you would like to try something different. You read an article in the school paper about the debate team winning a trophy at a statewide competition. It interested you because the topics they debated—the environment, curfews, changing the age when you can get a driver's license—are topics that interest you. You argue about them with your parents and your friends, but you never quite feel like you get your point across.

There is a debate class, and you wonder about taking it. Can it help with other classes? What skills do you need to be a debater? You decide to investigate.

Reading Skills

Debate requires reading many different types of material in order to understand the debate topic and its issues. Weekly periodicals, newspapers, professional journals, websites, and law cases are a few examples of the types of materials that are invaluable for research. Reference librarians can acquaint you with the library's services and holdings, guide you to specific sources of information, and provide you with instructions about the library equipment available for use.

It is not enough to just read the articles and the stories. You also need to comprehend and retain the information. To achieve this, develop and use note-taking skills. Identify the key points found in an article. Then find areas of support or reason that validate the key points. Good note taking will save a lot of time. Make sure that your notes are always legible. You should be able to look at notes later and still understand what you wrote.

Listening Skills

Listening is the key to winning a debate. It is not enough to *hear* your opponent—you must *listen* to your opponent. There is a big difference between hearing and listening. **Hearing** is the act of recognizing sounds around you. **Listening** requires you to give meaning to the sounds you hear. It is a conscious act to comprehend and to be able to respond to others. Studies show that you only remember 25 to 50 percent of what you hear, but with practice and effort listening can be improved. These are the steps to becoming an effective listener:

- **Recognize a situation that requires critical listening.** During a debate round, you must focus wholly on what is being said in the round. Analyze each speech in order to form a thoughtful and effective response.

- **Tune in and pay attention.** Eliminate any distractions by focusing on the speaker. This is not the time to be thinking about your next speech. It is the time to hear and understand what is being said by your opponent. This skill will take effort on your part to develop, but it will play a large part in your becoming a successful debater.

- **Measure the value of what is being said.** Pick out the key points of the speeches. Not everything said in a debate is important, so it is up to you, the debater, to identify the issues that need to be addressed.

- **Defer judgment.** One of the biggest mistakes debaters make is to start formulating their argument while the opponent is still speaking. Because you have researched the topic, it is easy to anticipate what might be said in a round. However, your response must address the points presented in the round. Wait until the speaker is done to form the counterargument.

- **Check for understanding.** During the debate round, *cross-examination periods* provide the opportunity to question opponents regarding the information they have presented. This is the perfect situation to ask for clarification of the main ideas.

TRACK5/ISTOCKPHOTO.COM

One mistake debaters make is to formulate arguments while their opponent is still speaking. Why is this a problem?

- **Be an active listener.** An active listener is a person who is able to hear what is being said. Next, an active listener understands what is being said. This requires listening, evaluating, and comprehending. Finally, an active listener will be able to judge what has been said and apply it to the current situation. If you listen actively during a debate round, you will remember key points. If you listen actively while talking with friends, you will remember necessary information. Obviously, not every word you hear during the day or the debate round is important. An active listener is able to distinguish information that is important from the rest of what has been said.

Work on your listening skills every day. Improving listening skills will not only help you to be successful in the classroom or at a debate, but it also will help you to have a better understanding with friends, family, and people you interact with everyday.

YOU BE THE JUDGE

Ethics are the guiding principles of right and wrong. In debate there are specific dos and don'ts in developing your argumentation strategy. This begins with moral and ethical conduct in preparation for and during your debate competitions.

First and foremost, respect the people with whom you debate. Demonstrating respect for your opponents as well as your team will improve your image among the judges. It also will help you build stronger relationships among your team members.

Muhammad Ali was one of the greatest prizefighters of all time. Before stepping into the ring, he would masterfully manipulate his opponent's emotions with harsh talk, fierce stares, and frightening facial expressions. While this may be appropriate or even expected in the prize fighting arena, it is absolutely forbidden in debate competition. You will always have the temptation to psyche your opponent out with a glare, a rolling of the eyes, or cross-talk with team members during an opponent's speech. However, this shows a lack of respect and can be viewed as a distraction tactic to disarm and throw off the person speaking.

Being respectful is not only ethical, it also is a reflection of good manners and proper etiquette. In practicing respect, your nonverbal presentation is as important as your verbal message.

What Would You Do?

You arrive at your first competition. The team has prepared and is ready to debate. When you enter the room, you notice the other team sizing you up. They start snickering, whispering, looking at your team, and then looking back at each other and bursting out into laughter. Their coach smiles, and shoots your coach a competitive glare. How should your team react?

Critical Thinking Skills

Critical thinking is another skill that will help you become an effective debater. Critical thinking is the ability to review information from many points of view. Being fair-minded is the spirit of critical thinking. This means being objective in your evaluation of each viewpoint and drawing conclusions only after you have studied each point presented. Remember that in debate you must be ready to argue from both the affirmative and negative viewpoint. Be ready to substantiate each of your claims with evidence, cite your sources, and make a strong case. You also must be able to analyze all points of what is being presented. Critical thinking means not taking information at face value, but analyzing and interpreting the information that has been presented.

Writing Skills

Writing also is an important element of communication. Debate will help you to refine your writing skills. You will have many opportunities to write about a variety of topics. Three main types of papers are written for debate. The positions stated in the papers are fact, value, and policy.

- **Papers of fact** When researching topics, you will need to be able to prove various positions. You may have to prove that something did or did not happen. An example of this would be the statement, "Television has affected the way we view our presidential candidates." With research, facts can be found to support this. You could analyze the 1960 Kennedy-Nixon debates to confirm this statement.

- **Papers of value** The purpose of a paper of value is to show that one thing is better than another. When working with values, it is impossible to prove that one value is right and another value is wrong. However, it can be demonstrated or shown that one value is better than another.

IMAGE SOURCE/GETTY IMAGES

Why is it important to have good writing skills?

Take the statement, "All students should take four years of physical education." Not everybody will agree with this. Some people may think that this requirement can be met through areas like marching band. Others might feel the time would be better used in an academic class. Reasons must clearly articulate why the reader should agree with the statement.

- **Papers of policy**   A paper of policy suggests a change of the current situation or that action should be taken. An example of a statement of policy is "All high schools will require students to wear uniforms." This is a call to action. The paper will have to clearly state the advantages or disadvantages of requiring uniforms. It should also state why the action should be taken. An example of a reason why the schools should require uniforms could be safety. Some urban school districts require students to wear uniforms because it identifies anybody not dressed in the same manner as a visitor to that school.

While these are three distinct types of papers, a good paper will combine all three styles to present a strong position. You should incorporate these three styles into your own personal writing methods.

In writing these papers you effectively are writing speeches. Therefore, the language you use will be very important as well. Remember to use a variety of sentence structures, from simple to compound sentences. It also helps to vary the cadence, or sound, of the speech. This also is an opportunity to improve and expand your vocabulary.

After writing your speech, always practice reading it aloud. Practice in front of a mirror. Pay attention to your facial expressions, your posture, the tone of your voice, and the rate and pitch of your speech. Not only will this help to point out any areas of weakness, but you also will be able to detect grammar and punctuation errors. It also will indicate whether or not the speech flows smoothly. You always want to move effortlessly from one point to the next. If possible, videotape yourself debating your propositions. Analyze your strengths and weaknesses. Be sure to time your speeches. There is no better way to learn than to review your performance.

Speaking Skills

Speaking in front of a group of people or even just a couple of people requires certain skills. It is especially important for debaters to have good speaking skills. Good speaking skills will help you to formulate and articulate your arguments and responses. Articulation, pronunciation, volume, rate, grammar, vocabulary, correct word usage, and gestures are all key elements to effective speaking. Developing each of these skills will help you with your presentations and give you confidence as a speaker as well.

Speaking skills can be thought of as building blocks. Each one is important on its own, but together they create a strong foundation. Take a closer look at each of the key elements, or individual skills, that make up effective speaking skills.

- **Articulation** Poor articulation is the result of being a lazy speaker. This is very easy to correct, but it does take a conscious effort on the part of the speaker. Proper **articulation** is saying each syllable in a word correctly. Take the words *going to*. Listen to other students in the hallway and you will hear some of them saying *gunna*. The problem isn't that they don't know how to pronounce it correctly. Those speakers simply are not taking the time to say each syllable.

Poor articulation is not a problem in casual conversation. However, when you are trying to make an impression on a judge in a debate, it is important to have proper articulation.

FYI Three out of every four individuals have a fear of speaking in public. In a survey of the top ten things people feared most, the fear of public speaking was number one, ranking ahead of the fear of flying, fear of terrorism, and even the fear of death.

- **Pronunciation** It is not enough to simply say each syllable correctly. You must know how to pronounce it correctly. **Pronunciation** refers to saying the word correctly. It has a direct affect on a speaker's credibility. It is difficult to persuade somebody that you know what you are talking about when you are mispronouncing names and words. Take a look at the following name: *Mackinac City*. Unless you are familiar with this particular city, it would be easy to mispronounce it. The correct pronunciation is *ma-ka-naw*. If a word is unfamiliar, look up the pronunciation in a dictionary or ask somebody who is familiar with the word. Never guess.

- **Vocalized pauses** The sounds you sometimes utter while speaking, such as *um*, *er*, and *uh*, are called **vocalized pauses**. The trick is to become aware of how frequently you do this while making a speech. Points often are deducted off your speech in class, or worse, in a formal debate where the number of points deducted can mean the difference between winning and losing.

©MICHELLE D. BRIDWELL/PHOTOEDIT

Why is it important to impress a judge with good speaking skills?

- **Grammar**   Always use good grammar when speaking in front of an audience. Using good grammar will help you create a positive first impression with your competitors, and, more importantly, with your judges. Once you have created a first impression, it will be difficult to change. Debates are considered formal speaking events, and, therefore, good grammar is required. While you should use good grammar in everyday speech as well, it is extremely important in debate competitions.

- **Volume**   How loudly or softly you speak is the volume. You want the judge and your opponent to be able to hear everything you say. There are some factors relating to volume to consider when speaking. First of all, how big is the room? You would adjust your volume if you were speaking in an auditorium compared to a classroom. You do not want to blast people out of the room with your voice, nor should they have to strain to hear you. People's body language will give you feedback about your volume.

- **Rate**   How quickly or slowly you speak is the rate. The acceptable rate for delivery varies between the different types of debate. You should speak at a rate that makes it easy for the judge and opponent to understand what you are saying. Speaking too fast is a common problem. Taping practice rounds can help identify many of these problems as well as help to alleviate them.

- **Gestures**   Movements of the hands, arms, and body that help to express and emphasize an idea or a point are gestures. Gestures can be effective during a debate because they can help you to illustrate the key points that you want the judge to remember or notice. Gestures should be used sparingly. You must be careful to not let a gesture become a habit. It will no longer be effective as a tool for emphasis. Instead, it will become a distraction. Practicing speeches aloud in front of a mirror can be an effective tool to monitor your nonverbal communication.

- **Vocabulary and correct word usage**   Debate provides an excellent opportunity to expand your vocabulary. You will be required to read many different types of literature in the preparation of your cases. Record words you don't know. Look up the definition and the pronunciation of each word. Make sure you understand the meaning of the word and how it is used in the text. Then use the new word in your speeches. Become familiar with the word. By doing this for words you don't know, you will be able to enrich and increase your vocabulary skills.

- **Eye contact**   It is important to have a connection with your audience. In the case of Lincoln-Douglas debate, the judge is your audience. Speak to him or her. You are trying to persuade the judge that your arguments are the best in the round. By making eye contact with the judge, you will be able to tell when he or she agrees with a point you have made. You also will be able to tell which points you will have to explain again. Eye contact is another speech skill you can work on when practicing in front of the mirror. The more you can look up during a speech, the better relationship you will develop with the judge.

- **Poise**   The way you handle yourself during the round is called **poise**. Being prepared will help with poise because it will make you feel confident. Do everything you can to be aware of and eliminate anything that might make you nervous or uncertain. Try to focus on your own sense of purpose. Be confident by being prepared

Grooming and Appearance

The final area to discuss is grooming and appearance. Because debate is a formal event, it is important to dress for the occasion. You probably are familiar with the phrase "Dress for Success." This is critical in debate. Before you say your first word, you have made an impression on the judge. The style in which you dress, the way you walk into the room, and how you set up for the debate all tell the judge what kind of attitude you have about the event. It lets the judge know that you are serious about the debate.

What you wear and how you look should never distract from your performance. Shirts, pants, dresses, or jackets that are loud or flashy can be distracting. Clothing doesn't have to be expensive, but it should be clean and neat. Hair that is unbrushed or uncombed gives the impression that you didn't really prepare to appear in public. Your appearance should give the impression that, like every other aspect of your performance, you have put time and effort into your preparation. Your appearance should always show respect—for the judge, for your opponent, and, above all, for yourself and what you have to say.

Once the judge arrives in the room, the opponents can enter and set up for the debate. Take out your materials quietly and get them set up on the table. Take out your case, flow pad, pens, pencils, and stop watch. Once you are ready, quietly wait for the judge to start the round. The debate will begin when the judge identifies the competitors and their positions. Be patient. This is where your poise will be put to the test. Even though the actual round has not started, the judge has already begun to evaluate you.

By paying attention and practicing each of these skills, you will become the best speaker you can be. Being able to get your message across with ease is not only a debate skill, but a life skill as well. Pay attention to the small details and practice, practice, practice.

Why should your appearance always show respect for the judge and your opponent?

Think Critically

1. What is the difference between hearing and listening?

2. Why do your facial expressions and gestures matter while presenting your case?

3. What role does the way you dress play in making a first impression?

Research NOW!

4. **TEAMWORK** Working in small teams, discuss some of the great speeches that you have heard recently. Evaluate one of the speeches. Identify what made it a great speech. Analyze the content of the speech, the writing style, the grammar used, and the effect the speech had on the audience.

5. Select somebody you think is a good speaker. This can be a family member, a teacher, a person in the television industry, or a politician. Evaluate his or her speaking style. Write a brief paper explaining what makes this person a good speaker

Write NOW!

6. **TEAMWORK** Working with several other students, write a two- to three-paragraph paper on a topic of your choice. Present the paper to the group. Each member of the group should write a brief critique of the presentation. Select one thing that was done well and one area that could be improved. Share your critiques with your group.

7. Choose a controversial issue in your school or community. Write a two- to three-paragraph paper about this topic. Go back through the paper and underline words that are weak or ineffective. Use a thesaurus to find other options. Record these new vocabulary words on index cards. Build a vocabulary index to help improve the quality of your writing.

Speak NOW!

8. Give an impromptu speech on a topic of your choice between one- and two-minutes long in front of another student. Have your peer write down each vocalized pause that you use. Review the list and give the speech again. Any time you use a vocalized pause, start the speech over again. Repeat until you can give the speech without using any vocalized pauses.

9. **TEAMWORK** Prepare a panel discussion on the topic of your choice. Each panel member should research and write about one position of the topic. The panel will then present its findings to the class.

Do You Agree?

Resolved When engaged in a time of war, the United States government should be able to exercise censorship of the press.

Affirmative position

Yes, the government should have the absolute power to monitor what is being released to the public. In this time of high technology, our enemies receive the information just as quickly as does the public, which could put our troops in harm's way.

Negative position

No, the government must release information to the public that allows them to be informed regarding policies and actions of the government. This era of high technology enables information to be dispersed quickly and through a variety of means. The credibility of the government and the support of the public is directly affected by the news they are given

GOALS

Identify the different types of debate.

Be able to distinguish the differences in the styles of debate.

TERMS

resolution

Lincoln-Douglas (LD) debate

constructive speech

rebuttal speech

cross-examination (CX) debate

spreading

public forum debate

Student Congress

Responsibilities in Debate

You sign up for debate class. You are a little nervous because, as you sit and wait for class to begin, you discover that other students have already had experience as debaters. They discuss different types of debates that you have never heard of. As the teacher passes out the schedule of assignments, you discover that you too are about to become familiar with the many and exciting forms of debate.

There are two categories of debate: informal and formal. Informal debate goes on everyday in all walks of life. Formal debate is more structured. You, as a debater, will be taking part in formal debate.

Before any debate can take place, there must be a resolution. A **resolution** is the topic that will be debated. Resolutions, like the one above, are written in the form of a statement. The debater must analyze the statement and determine its intent. The resolution is then separated into two areas: the affirmative, which supports the resolution, and the negative, which disagrees with it. All debates, regardless of type, must start with a resolution.

There are different time limits and speaker responsibilities for the debates. It is important to know what these rules are before competing in a debate. The length of speaking time will determine how each speech is written.

As the debate continues, the speaker's responsibilities also change. Each speech has a specific goal to achieve. It is important to understand these rules in order to be successful. The rules should play a key part in planning and practice sessions.

Lincoln-Douglas Debate

Lincoln-Douglas (LD) debate is named for the seven debates that took place between Abraham Lincoln and Stephen Douglas in 1858. Lincoln and Douglas campaigned through different parts of the state of Illinois. They addressed issues that were important to the people. They were able to explain their points of view to the citizens. The debates were hugely popular and drew large crowds.

How is the audience reacting to Lincoln in this picture?

Format of Lincoln-Douglas

Lincoln-Douglas debate takes place between two people. One person is the affirmative, and one person is the negative. Lincoln-Douglas debate is considered to be a value debate. All of the topics will revolve around worth, usefulness, or importance. For instance, a resolution might focus on the value of public education versus private education. It will be hard to find somebody who doesn't think that education, in general, is important or has worth. In this case, however, the debate will focus on one type versus another and which one is better.

There are two types of speeches that are given in the Lincoln-Douglas debate. The first type is the **constructive speech**. This is an informative speech where the key points of the debate are presented. The second type of speech is a **rebuttal speech**. This speech is more persuasive. In this speech, you are pointing out to the judge the areas of strengths in your speech and the areas of weaknesses in your opponent's speech. There also is a cross-examination period where you can ask questions of your opponent.

THE ART ARCHIVE/CULVER PICTURES/WWW.PICTURE-DESK.COM

Time Periods for Lincoln-Douglas Debate

It is very important to pay attention to the time periods when you are debating. First, you want to make sure that your constructive speech fits within the time period. Second, you want to be able to attack all of your opponents' weaknesses and still have enough time to support your strongest issues in your rebuttal speeches. Make sure you know the lengths of time for each speech and the goals you must achieve in each speech.

Time Requirements for Lincoln-Douglas Debate

Prep time	Three or four minutes	Prepare arguments before presenting the next speech. Because this is such a limited time, it should be used wisely.
Affirmative constructive	Six minutes	Affirmative debater presents the case that supports the resolution. All information that will be debated must be presented here.
Negative cross-examination period	Three minutes	Negative speaker asks questions of the affirmative speaker
Negative constructive rebuttal	Seven minutes	Negative speaker presents the negative stand regarding the resolution and presents a rebuttal to the affirmative's case. The key issues of the affirmative case must be attacked.
Affirmative cross-examination period	Three minutes	Affirmative speaker questions the negative speaker about his case
Affirmative rebuttal	Four minutes	Affirmative speaker points out the strengths of own case and tells why they are superior to strengths of opponent's case. Affirmative speaker then points out the weaknesses in opponent's case. No new evidence can be introduced in the rebuttal speech.
Negative rebuttal	Six minutes	Negative speaker's last chance to make an impression on the judge. First, just as with the affirmative rebuttal, the negative speaker emphasizes the strengths of own speech, as well as the areas of weaknesses within the affirmative case. Finally, the negative speaker tells why the judge should vote for him or her.
Affirmative rebuttal	Three minutes	Affirmative speaker's last chance to impress the judge. Must emphasize own strengths and opponents' weaknesses, and tell why the judge should vote for him or her.

Cross-Examination Debate

There are several key differences between Lincoln-Douglas debate and cross-examination debate. While Lincoln-Douglas debate is about values, **cross-examination (CX) debate** is about policy. The purpose of the resolution is to present a topic that requires change or action. The affirmative team is always a proponent of change, while the negative team is going to show that change is not needed. They also can provide a better plan as a solution to the problem. Consider the resolution that states the President of the United States should be elected by the direct vote of the people. The affirmative proposes a change or the abolishment of the electoral college as you know it today. The negative, on the other hand, shows how the current system best represents all people in all states.

There are two people to a team in cross-examination debate. Each person has very specific duties, and team members must work together to be successful. CX debate requires many hours of research to develop effective cases. The debate centers around the presentation of evidence which supports the plan that has been presented. This is a key element of this debate.

Because of the amount of evidence that is presented in CX, debaters tend to speak at a much more rapid speed than LD debaters. This is called **spreading**. It requires a debater to speak rapidly, while still being understood by the judge and the opponents. A conversational rate of speech should be used for Lincoln-Douglas.

The time format in CX is very different from that in Lincoln-Douglas debate. Each debater will give two speeches, one constructive and one rebuttal. Take a closer look at the time requirements for CX as shown in the table on the following page. Each team is given eight minutes for prep time. This time can be used in any manner you choose according to the needs of the team.

How is the format of a cross-examination debate different from that of a Lincoln-Douglas debate?

Time Requirements for Cross-Examination Debate

Prep time	Eight minutes	Prepare arguments before presenting the next speech. Because this is such a limited time, it should be used wisely.
First affirmative speaker	Eight minutes	Constructive speech—presents key elements of the case
First negative cross-examination period	Three minutes	Questions the opponent about the case
First negative speaker	Eight minutes	Constructive speech—presents key elements of the negative case and refutes the First Affirmative's speech.
First affirmative cross-examination period	Three minutes	Questions the opponent about the case
Second negative speaker	Eight minutes	Constructive speech—extends the negative case as well as refutes the affirmative case
Second affirmative cross-examination period	Three minutes	Questions the Second Negative Speaker about the case
Second affirmative speaker	Eight minutes	Constructive speech—presents any remaining information, attacks the negative case, and extends arguments
First negative rebuttal	Five minutes	Extends arguments and shows the weaknesses in the opponents' case
First affirmative rebuttal	Five minutes	Extends arguments and shows the weaknesses in the opponents' case
Second negative rebuttal	Five minutes	Final speech for the negative case and the last opportunity to persuade the judge to vote for the negative team
Second affirmative rebuttal	Five minutes	Last opportunity to persuade the judge to vote for the affirmative team

Public Forum Debate

Public forum debate is a relatively new event. The purpose of **public forum debate** is to promote audience and media-centered debate. It provides another opportunity to experience debate on a totally different level. Instead of trying to implement a policy or choose a superior value, public forum debate centers around perception. Evaluating the credibility and trustworthiness of a debater, for instance, could be a factor in the outcome of the debate. The resolutions in public forum debate tend to be very much "ripped from the headlines" and they change much more frequently than with the other debate forms.

The start of this debate is rather unique. The sides are decided by a coin toss. The team that wins the flip then can choose between two options. They can decide to go first in the debate or they can decide whether to be affirmative or negative. The other team then gets to decide the remaining option. For example, suppose that the team that won the toss chose to be the affirmative team. The opponents would then get to decide if they wanted to be the first or the second speaker.

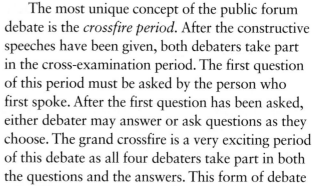
The most unique concept of the public forum debate is the *crossfire period*. After the constructive speeches have been given, both debaters take part in the cross-examination period. The first question of this period must be asked by the person who first spoke. After the first question has been asked, either debater may answer or ask questions as they choose. The grand crossfire is a very exciting period of this debate as all four debaters take part in both the questions and the answers. This form of debate was modeled after the television program *Crossfire*. Watching any political programming—whether it is Chris Matthews' *Hardball*, *Meet the Press*, or *Face the Nation*—will help you to understand this type of debate. It is easy to see how the moderators in these programs try to make specific points during the interviews. Just like in the television programs, it is very important to keep your cool while participating in the grand crossfire. During the crossfire period, the goal is to attack the weaknesses in your opponent's case. Another difference in the grand crossfire is that all four debaters are allowed to ask and answer questions during this period. The time periods are as follows:

Time Requirements for Public Forum Debate

Prep Time	Two minutes per team	
First Speaker Team A	Four minutes	Constructive Speech
First Speaker Team B	Four minutes	Constructive Speech
Crossfire	Three minutes	
Second Speaker Team A	Four minutes	Constructive Speech
Second Speaker Team B	Four minutes	Constructive Speech
Crossfire	Three minutes	
First Speaker Team A	Two minutes	Summary
First Speaker Team B	Two minutes	Summary
Grand Crossfire	Three minutes	
Second Speaker Team A	One minute	Final Focus—Persuasive Speech
Second Speaker Team B	One minute	Final Focus—Persuasive Speech

Student Congress

Student Congress is an event that continues to grow in popularity. Not only is it a fun and more relaxed style of debate, it also offers a realistic view of the actual legislative procedure. Instead of debating resolutions like you do in Lincoln-Douglas, cross-examination, and public forum debate, the goal of Student Congress is to pass legislation written either by you or your teammates.

Two types of legislation are written for Student Congress. The first is the *resolution*, which is a statement of recognition. An example of a resolution would be when a city wants to recognize somebody or something that has had an effect. For example, the city of Houston passed a resolution stating that a day would be set aside to honor the Houston Rockets for winning the National Championship. The second piece of legislation is a *bill*. Bills must have an action that is to happen and a penalty if the act is violated. Bills are written for a change in policy or to create a new policy. If you wanted to change the policy on tardiness in your school, you would write a bill that would state the reason why this is important. Bills are very specific and must follow the correct form in order to be introduced the congressional body. Sometimes the other students will like the basics of the bill, but want to make changes to it. This is done in the form of what is called an *amendment*. The amendment, like the bill, must be very specific as to what changes are to be made.

If you write a piece of legislation that has been selected for the Student Congress tournament, you will have the opportunity to give an *authorship speech*. This speech gives the background on the topic and gives the reason why it should be passed. Once the authorship speech has been presented, rebuttal speeches are given by the other members. Speeches rotate in an affirmative–negative manner.

While Student Congress is more relaxed than the other debates in structure, the manner in which students address one another is very formal. Students refer to one another as Senator or Representative. The entire Congress activity closely follows *Roberts' Rules of Order*, which provides rules and

©BILL ARON/PHOTOEDIT

How do the debates in a Student Congress resemble the debates that take place in the Senate or the House?

procedures for official deliberations and debates, while conducting the activity. Lively, energetic debates can take place during the sessions. These sessions are intended to imitate the actual meetings held by senators and representatives when they are trying to pass new legislation. Watch C-Span on television to see some sessions of Congress.

Like the other debates, Student Congress requires work and dedication on your part. It requires research first to find a topic that needs the attention of the legislative body. You then have to be able to present the problem area and tell how it is going to be corrected. Student Congress will be a worthwhile experience for the student who takes the time to prepare.

National Forensic League

Many states have different debate organizations that offer membership to schools and its students. It is always important to check to see what the rules for each debate event are, as they can differ from organization to organization. Time limits and topics are two of the things that should be checked for every tournament you attend. One organization, the National Forensic League, has done more to shape and define forensics and all of its activities than any other organization. *Forensics* is the official name for the art or study of formal debate. The National Forensic League has had a huge impact on debate events and continues to be a creative and inventive force.

In 1925, Bruno E. Jacob, a professor at Ripon College in Wisconsin, received a letter inquiring as to whether there was any type of honor society available for high school debaters. After doing some research, Mr. Jacob found that there were none. He then created a proposal and found that there was in fact, an interest, for this type of fraternity. On March 28, 1925, the National Forensic League was born. It is currently the nation's oldest and largest high school debate and speech honor society with members in all fifty states.

The National Forensic League has continued to grow and keep up with changes in technology. Debate rounds at the national tournament are now taped and can be viewed by students. The Internet has had an impact as well. It allows students and teachers to be constantly updated by visiting the web site provided for them

The National Forensic League continues to honor students' achievements. Certificates, pins, and honor cords symbolize the level of commitment by students. Most recently, the Academic All-American Award and the National Student of the Year Award have been added to the list of possible recognitions available to students.

The National Forensic League continues to provide opportunities for young people to enjoy forensic activities while encouraging and promoting the values of service, leadership, humility, integrity, and respect. National Forensic League members can be found in all fifty states, the U.S. possessions, and several foreign countries. It boasts more than a million members. Once you are a member, you remain a member for life. It is an organization that continues to promote excellence in the world of forensics.

Think Critically

1. Why is a resolution important to the debate?

2. What are three differences between Lincoln-Douglas debate and cross-examination debate?

3. How is a rebuttal speech different from a constructive speech?

4. Why does each form of debate have cross-examination periods?

5. What are two important roles played by the National Forensic League?

Research NOW!

6. **TEAMWORK** Should seniors have to participate in community service as a graduation requirement? Make a list of statements that support and negate this position.

7. On December 11, 1997, the Kyoto Protocol was officially adopted by initial signatory nations who were members of the United Nations Framework Convention on Climate Change. This landmark environmental treaty proposed a reduction in the emission of greenhouse gases. The United States opted not to sign this treaty. Research why the United States made this decision. Find three arguments that were used to support the adoption of the treaty and three arguments that were used to support not signing the treaty.

Write NOW!

8. **TEAMWORK** Consider the resolution "The federal government of the United States should substantially increase funding for education." In groups, write a one-page policy proposal that would affirm this resolution. The group also should provide supporting evidence that this policy proposal would result in better education for American children.

9. Write a one-page argument that negates the resolution "The United States should take a more aggressive stance towards North Korea."

10. Write a letter to the principal of the school explaining why the current curriculum needs to be changed. Have facts to support your statements.

Speak NOW!

11. Come up with an idea that you would present to your student government. Write and deliver a one- to three-minute speech designed to convince the government to adopt your proposal.

12. **TEAMWORK** Select a topic that is relevant today. In groups of two, debate the topic. One student should give a brief supporting the topic with the next student arguing against it.

1

Chapter in Review

1.1 What Is Debate?

- Debate is an essential process in homes, communities, and governments. It allows people to agree and disagree with one another.
- Debate can be both formal and informal.
- The history of debate is grounded in the philosophical traditions of Ancient Greece and Rome.

1.2 Debate Skills and Grooming for Debate

- Debate offers an opportunity to take part in academic competition, and it encourages development of essential life skills. By improving reading, writing, research, and speaking skills, your communication skills as a whole are greatly impacted.
- Debate requires listening skills. By listening to your opponent, you will learn to analyze, evaluate, and appropriately respond.

1.3 Types of Debate

- Several different types of debate are available at most competitions. Each type of debate is distinctive by its style and delivery. Find the type of debate that best suits you.
- The National Forensic League has helped to raise academic awareness regarding debate and public speaking. Not only has it provided opportunities for competition, it has also offered student recognition for service and scholarships to qualifying students.

Develop Your Debating Language

a. articulation
b. constructive speech
c. cross-examination debate
d. debate
e. formal debate
f. hearing
g. informal debate
h. Lincoln-Douglas debate
i. listening
j. poise
k. pronunciation
l. public forum debate
m. rebuttal speech
n. resolution
o. spreading
p. Student Congress
q. vocalized pause

Select the term that best fits the definition. Some terms will not be used.

1. Oral confrontation between two people, teams, or groups to argue reasons for and against a set position

2. Occurrence with very little prep or rules

3. Recognizing sounds

4. Topic that is being debated

5. Correctly saying each sound in a syllable

6. Team debate where the topics are policy oriented

7. Set of rules and preparation with a given topic

8. Audience and media centered debate

9. One-on-one debate centering around values

10. Informative speech which presents the key points

11. Way you handle yourself during a round

12. Activity where students attempt to pass legislation they have written

Review Debate Concepts

13. What were the main differences between Lincoln and Douglas's positions during the Illinois Senate race?

14. Give three examples of formal debate and of informal debate.

15. What were Isocrates' two major ideas that influenced debate?

16. What was Cicero's method of analyzing issues?

17. How was the presidential debate of 1960 different from previous debates? Why was this significant for the outcome of the election?

18. Name four skills needed to be a better listener.

19. Why is it important to be objective when debating?

20. Identify the key aspect of a paper of fact, a paper of value and a paper of policy.

21. Why is it important to practice reading your speeches aloud before presenting?

22. How is articulation different from pronunciation?

23. What is a vocalized pause?

24. What is a good way to see if you are speaking at an appropriate volume in a specific room?

25. Why is appearance important in formal debate?

26. What is the purpose of a resolution in debate?

27. What is a constructive speech? What is a rebuttal speech?

28. What are the resolutions in Lincoln-Douglas debate focused around?

29. What is the purpose of prep time during a debate round?

30. Why are speech times longer in cross-examination debate?

31. How are sides chosen in all public forum debates?

32. In Student Congress, how are resolutions different from bills?

33. What was Bruno E. Jacob's purpose in founding the National Forensic League?

Make Academic Connections

34. **PROBLEM SOLVING** Read an Op Ed piece from your local newspaper. What are the main arguments being made? What rhetorical devices is the author using to sway readers? Are the author's attempts at being persuasive effective? Why or why not?

35. **SCIENCE**   What are the steps of the scientific method? Why is the scientific method important? In what ways are the skills used in formal debate similar to and different from the scientific method?

36. **ETHICS**   Should all Americans be required to be organ donors upon death? Develop a list of reasons for and against this statement. Is it difficult to be objective while completing this assignment? Why or why not?

37. **HISTORY**   Research the dropping of the bomb on Hiroshima during World War II. Prepare arguments in support and against taking this action. Have a class discussion as to merits of both sides of the issue.

38. **CHALLENGES**   Read the "Letters to the Editor" in your local paper. These are letters responding to articles or Op Eds. Pick a series of letters about the same article. Find and read the original article and the letters that respond to the article. What objections do the letter writers have? Are the arguments made in refutation persuasive? Why or why not?

Research NOW!

39. The Lincoln-Douglas debates were a series of formal political debates between Abraham Lincoln and Stephen Douglas in a contest for one of Illinois Senate seats. Lincoln went on to lose the election to Douglas. The debates, however, helped propel Lincoln to national prominence. Find the text of their first debate held in Ottawa, Illinois. Write a brief synopsis of the major points that each candidate made in their opening speeches.

40. **TEAMWORK**   Pick a bill that is presently in front of the United States Congress. Have each member of your group research a different Congressperson's opinions on this piece of legislation. Each group should create a chart that summarizes their research and shows where their Congresspersons agree and disagree about that piece of legislation.

Write NOW!

41. Select or create a proposition that can be used for a debate. Briefly explain what you believe to be the best argument for the affirmative and the negative. Explain what type of debate this ought to be used for.

42. **TEAMWORK**   Choose a controversial issue in your school or community. Split the group in half with each portion of the group taking opposite sides on this issue. Each half will collaborate to write, with supporting evidence, a position paper in support of their position.

43. Draft a letter to the editor of a school or community newspaper in response to an editorial or opinion column published in a recent issue. Your letter should outline your position and supply supporting documentation.

44. Pick a newspaper article and read the first 6 paragraphs aloud. Read the article slowly focusing on articulation and pronunciation. Practice until you can read the paragraphs without making any mistakes, and then time yourself. Reread the article increasingly quickly while maintaining perfect articulation and pronunciation. Find the quickest time you can read the article with acceptable articulation and pronunciation.

45. Many actors practice diction by presenting Shakespearian sonnets. Pick any sonnet and practice reading it aloud. Present your sonnet in front of an audience.

46. **TEAMWORK**   Work in groups of four. One member of the group should read aloud a position paper he or she previously wrote while the other group members take notes. The other three members of the group will then have five minutes to cross examine the author about his or her paper. After the cross-examination period, the group should reflect on which questions were the most effective. Why were they effective? Which questions were weakest? Why were they the weakest?

47. Liberals and conservatives have vastly different views regarding the cause of the economic downturn of 2008. Imagine you are a political pundit. Develop a one- to three-minute speech advocating as either a liberal or a conservative. You are booked on AC-360 as a subject matter expert. Be sure to use effective rhetoric to try to sway the audience.

eCollection Activity

The Lincoln-Douglas debates took place in 1858. They were part of a much larger debate about the abolition of slavery. As early as the 1600s, leaders in individual colonies called for an end to the selling and owning of slaves. Samuel Sewall, a judge in the famous Salem witch trials, wrote *The Selling of Joseph*. This book was one of the first anti-slavery documents written in the North American colonies. Later, anti-slavery groups, such as The New York Manumission Society, called for the end of slavery. Important political leaders like Alexander Hamilton and John Jay did so too.

To learn more about these debates, access www.cengage.com/school/langarts/debate and click on the link for Chapter 1. Research the writings of the key figures noted above, or other important figures such as Frederick Douglass, Harriet Beecher Stowe, John Greenleaf Whittier, and the brothers Charles Henry Langston and John Mercer Langston. Pay attention to how these figures argued their case, and write a short essay on your findings.

CHAPTER 2

Lincoln-Douglas Debate

Real People | Real Careers

Lisa Ling

"her goal was to say one thing each day that would make people think, whether it made them cheer or made them throw things at their TV"

Lisa Ling is a debater on the frontlines. As a broadcast investigative reporter, Lisa has interviewed, argued with, and defended her own ideas with people from approximately two-dozen countries. As a co-host on ABC's morning talk show *The View*, she has debated entertainment celebrities and political figures.

Lisa was born in Sacramento, California and began her career in broadcast journalism while still a student at Del Campo High School. At sixteen, she was chosen to be one of four hosts for the nationally syndicated teen news magazine program, *Scratch*. At eighteen, she became a correspondent for Channel One News, which serves over eight million students in twelve thousand high schools. She covered stories that ranged from drug trafficking in Colombia to her thirteen year old cousin's unsuccessful fight with liver cancer. She risked her life to investigate the civil war in Algeria and the refugee crisis in Albania. She shared tea and ideas with the Dalai Lama. In 1996, she participated in a joint investigation with *Time* magazine into a Russian company accused of smuggling nuclear weapons. She has reported from more than two dozen countries, including Afghanistan, Iraq, Colombia, Algeria, Cambodia, Vietnam, China, Japan, India, and Iran. Before she reached twenty-five, Lisa was named senior war correspondent for Channel One.

She joined ABC Daytime's popular morning talk program, *The View*. Ling sat alongside Barbara Walters, Meredith Vieira, Star Jones, and Joy Behar and gave the "twenty-something take" with a dose of modern age philosophy. The five women discussed relevant, everyday issues and shared their daily no-holds-barred opinions and lively colorful conversations. While Lisa enjoyed her stint on the program, and has returned for guest appearances, she felt the urge to return to the field and follow the stories of people's lives.

Lisa returned to broadcast journalism and became the host *of National Geographic Explorer*. Lisa has stated that her goal was to say one thing each day that would make people think, whether it made them cheer or made them throw things at their TV. She became a special correspondent for *The Oprah Winfrey Show*, which has featured many of Ling's investigative pieces, including a report on North Korea. Ironically, Lisa's sister Laura, who is also a reporter, was arrested and detained in North Korea while doing a story on North Korean refugees escaping into China. Lisa became a spokesperson for her sister and her sister's colleague, Euna Lee. Fortunately, both were released after the intervention of former President Bill Clinton. Lisa Ling is a creative, courageous journalist who can teach debaters and non-debaters about the power of curiosity, good questions, and an impassioned spirit.

Think Critically

How has Lisa Ling used debate skills to be a successful investigative reporter?

The Resolution

GOALS

Recognize the importance of the resolution.

Understand the role of values in a Lincoln-Douglas debate.

TERMS

resolution
clash
framer
value
aesthetic value
moral value
political value
value premise
value criteria

Do You Agree?

Resolved When in conflict, the right to free press deserves a higher priority than the right to a fair trial.

Affirmative position

Yes, the press provides information that citizens have the right to know. This information helps people understand the legal system and form independent opinions about current trials. In some cases, the press even uncovers evidence that might not otherwise be found by the courts.

Negative position

No, an accused person has the right to a fair trial. The press sometimes reports biased, inappropriate, or even untrue statements that influence jurors, who then base their decision on those statements. Also, a fair trial cannot be guaranteed if the press reports evidence that might be inadmissible in court.

The Resolution

Your debate club at school is holding a debate on whether a school's right to search a student's locker outweighs a student's right to privacy. You've discussed the topic with other members of the club and realize that the debate will focus on values or morals rather than evidence. A debate like this can be argued using a Lincoln-Douglas format. Lincoln-Douglas debate focuses on reason and persuasion, and topics deal with values. Winners of this type of debate convince the judge that their set of values is more important than those of their opponents. Instead of a debate that focus on what is true, a Lincoln-Douglas debate focuses on what ought to be true.

Every debate begins with a **resolution**. The resolution gives you the topic of the debate that will be argued by two sides. The affirmative side must show that the resolution is true or best. The negative side must show that the resolution is not the most desirable position or solution. In Lincoln-Douglas debate, as well as in other types of debate, the resolution describes an opportunity in which the affirmative and negative **clash**, or present opposing viewpoints. Without clash, a debate can't exist. Instead, it becomes an exercise where two people simply present ideas. The affirmative and the negative sides should take very different approaches to the resolution.

Before you start researching the topic, thoroughly analyze the resolution. You must stay within the boundaries that are established by the **framers,** or the writers, of the resolution. The boundaries ensure that the debate is fair and competitive.

All resolutions begin with the word *resolved*. When something is resolved, it is determined or decided. In order to successfully debate your side of a resolution, you must make sure that you fully understand the resolution. First, make sure that you understand the key terms within it. Then, research both sides of the resolution.

Definitions

Even if you think you understand a resolution completely, you should look up the definitions of its key words. Remember that words can have more than one definition. As you prepare for a debate, you'll need to keep all the definitions of the resolution's words in mind. At the same time, you'll want to use those definitions that do not change the true intent of the resolution. Consider the following resolution and the basic definitions of its key terms.

Resolved: A just government should provide health care to its citizens.

Definitions:

- **just**   based on right, rightful, lawful
- **government**   the form or system of rule of a state, community, and so on
- **should**   ought; used to express obligation, duty, or an expectation
- **provide**   make available, give
- **health care**   the field concerned with the maintenance or restoration of the health of the body or mind
- **citizens**   members of a state or nation who owe allegiance to their government and are entitled to its protection

To understand the resolution as it was intended by the framers, you must interpret each word individually, and then interpret the statement as a whole. Two of the words, *just* and *should*, strongly imply the moral concerns of this resolution. The framers clearly show that they think that providing health care is a moral obligation. Remembering that a Lincoln-Douglas debate focuses on values, the affirmative side must persuade the judge that this moral obligation is important.

To further prepare for the debate, team members should consider the term *government*. To what body of government do you think the writers are referring? Local? State? National? A fairly reasonable assumption is that you will discuss national government, but you should think about the possibility of the involvement of other governments.

A good way to start defining key terms is to simply look up the words in the dictionary. However, the dictionary will give basic definitions only. To understand the words in a broader context, using an encyclopedia or other current print or online resources could prove to be helpful. Consider the term *health care* in the resolution given above. What does health care provided by the government mean? Will the government provide treatment only when a citizen is ill or does it include preventative care? Will government-provided health care cover only serious illness, or will citizens be able to visit a doctor for a simple cold or cough? What is the relationship between health care and health insurance, and how does that affect this statement? Will the quality of health care be better or worse if the government provides it? These and other questions are highly debatable. They must all be considered when debating this resolution.

Lastly, consider the term *citizens*. This term might be considered more straightforward than some of the others. If you don't already know, you might have to look past a dictionary to find the state or nation's definition of a citizen. To be considered a citizen, do you have to pay taxes? Is it required that you were born in a country to be considered a citizen? These facts about citizens may affect how you argue this resolution.

Having clear and concise definitions of the terms will not answer all questions you encounter, but the definitions will give you a better understanding of the resolution as a whole. They will also point you in the right direction for further research in supporting your arguments.

The affirmative and the negative may focus on different definitions and interpret them differently so that they fit their case. There are two things to remember when defining the words in the resolution. First, your definitions should be fair. Second, the definitions you choose should not change or alter the original intent of the resolution. Prepare arguments for each definition. Be ready to support your choice by showing how it relates to the true intent of the resolution. There is no such thing as being over-prepared for a debate.

How does the information in an encyclopedia differ from that in a dictionary?

Understanding the Concept of Values

A Lincoln-Douglas debate is based on values. What does that mean to you? **Values** are the ideals or principles held by a society or a person. When discussed, they usually provoke emotions and opinions. While a society defines a set of values, the importance of each value varies from person to person. For instance, consider the value of honesty. Overall, society holds this value in high regard. However, some people regard honesty as more important than others. If someone chooses to cheat on a test, do you think they have a higher or lower regard for honesty?

Determining Values of Individuals

Values differ in degree from person to person. This difference occurs because your values are often shaped by your environment and your experiences. If you were taught that getting high grades and doing well in school is important, you probably value education. On the other hand, education might not be highly valued by someone if good grades and learning weren't stressed at home. Two people can both value education, but the degree of importance to each individual will vary with experiences.

Experiences can also change your values over time. A person may not exercise because they don't place a high value on good health. An event, such as having a heart attack, might drastically change the importance of that value.

Common Categories of Values

Values can be divided into many categories. Among the most common are aesthetic, moral, and political values. Analyzing a debate resolution will help you determine which value is involved and will make writing your case that much easier.

Aesthetic values are values that appeal to beauty. Consider the following resolution.

Resolved: Protection of the environment should take precedence over the development of natural resources.

One argument that could be made by the affirmative side is that we must protect our last natural frontiers as they are part of the beauty of our natural landscape. These arguments are an appeal to aesthetic values. Would you rather look at a tree or a skyscraper? You are asking the judge and your opponent to make a decision based on the importance of this value.

Moral values deal with issues of right and wrong. Consider the following resolution.

Resolved: Terminally ill patients have the right to die when and how they choose.

The negative side could argue that (A) doctors have taken an oath to do all they can to save a life, not take a life, and should have the final say in a patient's care, (B) patients don't always know what is best for themselves regarding their medical care, and (C) no one has the right to take a life.

Claims A and B are factual. Claim C is based on moral beliefs. The decision requires a moral value judgment as to who has the right to end life. In a debate, the negative side will try to convince the judge that their moral value is superior to that of the affirmative side.

When the role of government is questioned in a debate, **political values** must be considered. Consider the following resolution.

> **Resolved:**   Allowing innocent people to be harmed is preferable to giving in to terrorists' demands.

The negative side could argue that the government has a duty to protect innocent people at all cost. The affirmative side could argue that giving into terrorists' demands once only encourages further acts, which would put more innocent people in harm's way.

Values in a Lincoln-Douglas Debate

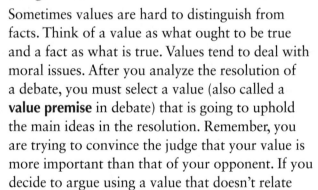

FYI One of the main topics of the original debates between Abraham Lincoln and Stephen Douglas dealt with the moral issue of slavery.

Sometimes values are hard to distinguish from facts. Think of a value as what ought to be true and a fact as what is true. Values tend to deal with moral issues. After you analyze the resolution of a debate, you must select a value (also called a **value premise** in debate) that is going to uphold the main ideas in the resolution. Remember, you are trying to convince the judge that your value is more important than that of your opponent. If you decide to argue using a value that doesn't relate well to the resolution, you'll have a hard time winning the debate.

Choices of values seem limitless, but some are more common than others in debates. Can you think of debate topics that might deal with some of these common values?

- **justice**   the quality of being just or fair; righteousness

- **freedom**   the right to enjoy the privileges of citizenship in a community

- **democracy**   rule of the majority

- **safety**   freedom from the occurrence or risk of injury, danger, or loss

- **equality**   the quality of using the same measure for all

- **progress**   forward movement

- **utilitarianism**   the greatest good for the greatest number

- **life**   the physical and mental experiences of an individual

- **quality of life**   condition of being

- **human dignity**   absolute and inherent worth that does not need to be acquired and cannot be lost or sold

- **societal good**   doing a deed that helps out the community around you, not just you

- **privacy**   the state of being free from intrusion or disturbance in one's private life

At times, your decision on what value to select for a resolution is clear-cut. Other times, the decision is not so obvious. For instance, assume you are arguing that the media should not be allowed to report on the personal life of a candidate running for a public office. What value might you use to support your arguments? Most likely, you would use the value of privacy.

Now consider a debate in which you are arguing for mandatory organ donation. That is, when people die, their families are forced to donate their organs to help others. Your choice of value is not as clear in this instance. You could support your arguments using the value of utilitarianism, progress, life, or even societal good. Be sure that you choose the value that you can best support and that has the fewest weaknesses.

Value Criteria

After you select a value, you need to determine the **value criteria**. The criteria are standards, ruler, tests, or measurements that judge the worth of your value. Criteria are necessary because values are vague, and not everyone agrees on how they should be measured.

To better understand the concept, you should come up with criteria for something other than a value. For example, what is your favorite restaurant? After you come up with an answer, ask yourself how you made your decision. In other words, what criteria did you use? Did you think about the taste, quality, or type of food it serves, its location, the speed of service, or other factors? These factors are the criteria you used to determine your answer. Now try to measure a value, for instance quality of life. What criteria would you use to measure the quality of life? Your answers may not come as quickly or as easily when you consider the criteria for measuring a value. However, providing the judge with a way to measure your value is important. Criteria also help you to show how the resolution and your case relate to your value.

Is a candidate's right to privacy more important than the media's right to free press?

COURTESY OF WILEY COLLEGE

TURNING POINT

Wiley College Debate Team of the 1930s

Many people think of the 1920s as "The Jazz Age," a time of freedom of expression in art and ideas. But the 1920s were also a period when segregation still flourished in many areas of American life, especially in education. A Supreme Court ruling allowed "separate but equal" institutions. Students at predominately black colleges found that they weren't allowed to compete in various activities with their counterparts from predominately white colleges. Among these areas was debate.

Such was the discovery of Melvin Tolson, a poet and scholar who arrived at Wiley College in 1923. Wiley had been founded in 1873 in Marshall, Texas, by Bishop Isaac Wiley. Tolson founded the Forensic Society of Wiley College to strengthen "mental alertness" in his students. At that time, coaches agreed upon topics just prior to the debate itself. Tolson's team read countless books and articles in preparation for debates. Tolson himself drilled his team members until their delivery was perfect. He was known to cross-examine debaters for over an hour.

At first, the Wiley team debated teams from other black colleges, such as Fisk, Morehouse, Howard, and Wilberforce. In time, Tolson's team debated teams from black universities several times the size of Wiley, always to packed auditoriums. The proceeds from these events helped pay the team's expenses. Ironically, despite their excellence, Tolson's team was not allowed to join the debate fraternity of Phi Kappa Delta because it excluded African-Americans. Tolson founded his own fraternity known as Alpha Phi Omega, which served black colleges and universities. By 1930, Tolson wanted to challenge racial attitudes and have his team debate students from predominantly white schools. He arranged a debate with law students from the University of Michigan. In 1934, Tolson debated the University of Southern California, the national champions and beat them. Even though Phi Kappa Delta sponsored the event, the team from Wiley was not allowed to claim the prize as, despite its victory, it was still excluded from the fraternity.

Tolson taught his students that the skills they learned in debate would be useful for the rest of their lives. Many of Tolson's debaters used those skills as prominent figures in the civil rights movement of the 1950s and 60s. Among these was James Farmer Jr., a founder of the Congress of Racial Equality and a passionate advocate for non-violent protest on behalf of civil rights. These views sometimes clashed with those of more militant leaders, such as Malcolm X. Farmer reported, "I debated Malcolm X four times and beat him. I'd think 'Come off it, Malcolm, you can't win. You didn't come up under Tolson.'"

Think Critically

Why do you think the Wiley College debate team was so successful?

Think Critically

1. What is unique about a Lincoln-Douglas debate?

2. What is important about a resolution?

3. What should you consider when selecting a value premise?

Research NOW!

4. **TEAMWORK** On your own, write the following words in a column: freedom, equality, utilitarianism, quality of life, and privacy. Analyze these values, and assign a number to each using a scale of 0 to 10 (0 meaning it has no importance to you and 10 meaning it is extremely important to you). Work with a group and compare and contrast your answers. Discuss why you think your values are similar or different.

5. Use a dictionary, encyclopedia, and/or other resources to define the terms in the following resolution.

   Resolved: Judicial decisions should be subject to recall.

Write NOW!

6. **TEAMWORK** Working in a group, select a current event that concerns a controversial issue and deals with a value. Write a resolution about it, and then compose a short paragraph that might be argued by the affirmative side. Write a second paragraph that might be used by the negative side.

7. Write one or two paragraphs stating the value premise that you would use to support the following resolution. Explain why you chose that value premise, and give the criteria under which the value premise should be measured.

   Resolved: Juveniles charged with violent crimes should be tried and punished as adults.

Speak NOW!

8. Choose a topic appropriate for a Lincoln-Douglas debate and create a resolution for it. Give a short speech stating the resolution, its value premise, and the criteria by which to measure the premise. Ask your classmates to comment on your ideas. Discuss with your class whether they agree that your value premise is the best one for the resolution.

9. **TEAMWORK** Working with two other classmates, decide who will argue the affirmative side, who will argue the negative side, and who will act as a judge. After you prepare arguments, conduct a short, informal debate in class. Ask the student judge who won and why.

   Resolved: The U.S. should make year-round school year mandatory.

GOALS

Describe the purpose of research in debate.

Explain why organizing research is important.

TERMS

jargon
credible
source

Do You Agree?

Resolved In a democratic society, felons ought to retain the right to vote.

Affirmative position

Yes, our justice system ensures that people who commit crimes will be punished. Once they have paid their debt to society, they should have all rights reinstated. A vote is an individual's way to let the government know how one feels about how we are governed. Each person's voice is important.

Negative position

No, voting is a privilege, not a right. We possess that privilege until we choose to give it up. Felons have refused to follow the very basic laws of society that govern all. Once the rules of society are broken, the social contract is broken. Losing the right to vote is part of the penalty one has to pay.

The Purpose of Research

Your debate class needs to prepare for the upcoming debate on the following resolution.

> **Resolved:** A school's right to search a student's lockers outweighs the student's rights to privacy.

Although you don't yet know if you'll be arguing the affirmative or negative side of the topic, you need to start your research. You think that you understand the resolution completely, and you have a strong opinion on the matter, so why do you need more research? You'll find that several reasons exist.

First, unlike facts, opinions are not right or wrong. You may be of the opinion that the school's right to search lockers outweighs the student's right to privacy. Another student may have the opposite opinion. No one is right or wrong, no matter how strongly you each feel about the issue. When debating, opinions hold no weight. You need to find solid facts, arguments, and supporting evidence. The only way to do this is to conduct research.

Next, no matter how much you think you understand a topic, research will almost always help you learn something you didn't already know. Whether it's an argument that you consider or new **jargon**, or language that relates to the topic, research will usually help you learn more about your subject.

Why do you need to research both sides of an issue for debate?

Last, strong research will impress the judges of the debate. Research helps you to gain a thorough understanding of your topic, which leads to confidence. This confidence will show as you present your arguments.

Gathering Appropriate Research Sources

Resolutions for Lincoln-Douglas debates change every few months. For that reason, current events often play a large part in the topics chosen for Lincoln-Douglas debates. Fortunately, you can usually find information about these current issues in recently published resources.

As you gather research, remember that you are trying to convince the judge that your set of values is more important than that of the opponent. The amount of research you'll need to find depends on how complex the resolution is. For instance, consider the following two resolutions.

Resolved: Human stem cell research should be banned.

Resolved: Students should not be allowed to use cell phones in school.

Researching Both Sides of the Topic

Once you find out whether you are arguing the affirmative or negative side of the resolution, your first instinct might be to find research that supports only that side. This strategy will not work well. To effectively debate a topic, you must understand both sides of an issue in great detail.

As you gather research, look for evidence that proves the strong and weak points of both sides of the argument. You will use the information that supports your side as you argue your own case. You will use the information that supports the opposing side when you argue against the points made by your opponent. In fact, if you know the strong points of the opposite side, you can prepare your counter-arguments in advance. This approach is an excellent debate strategy. Likewise, if you know the weak side of your own argument, you can plan your defense as well.

Sources and Credibility

In the past, only printed resources were available to help debaters. Many are still used today including specialty magazines, newspapers, journals, encyclopedias, and other books. You can use these sources to find facts, studies, and statements from authorities, statistics, research results, reports, and even transcripts of national debates. All of these can provide valuable information and ideas to help you prepare for your debate.

Today, the Internet is also a widely used source. Many students prefer its speed and convenience over traditional sources. You probably know that when it comes to the Internet, you must be careful what you believe. For every **credible**, or reliable, source many unreliable sources exist.

More Reliable Internet Sources
Lexus Nexus, JSTOR, and Project Muse
Sources found through the Google Scholar search engine
Many sites that end in .edu and .gov and some that end in .org
Unbiased news reporting sites

Less Reliable Internet Sources
Sites where the general public can contribute information (for example, wikipedia)
Articles with no author listed
Blogs
Papers, research, or articles written by students

What are the advantages and disadvantages of online researching?

When searching the Internet, you may actually find too much information. To narrow down your research, type descriptive keywords when using a search tool. For instance, if you type the words *drug testing* into a search engine, you may find millions of results. If you change your search words to *drug testing athletes* the number of results will decrease. Finally, if you type *drug testing high school athletes* your results will decrease even more. As you scan the results, watch for those that seem usable. Don't try to read every article you find. Instead, narrow down your choices by reading titles and topic sentences and then skimming the articles. Otherwise, you'll spend much longer than needed during the research phase.

Whether you use a printed publication or a website, ask yourself the following questions when deciding whether the source is reliable.

1. Who are the authors of the site?

2. What are the qualifications of the authors?

3. Is the information fact or opinion?

4. Could the authors be biased?

5. How old is the information?

6. Is the information useful to you?

Paying close attention to the reliability of sources is a sign that you are a careful reader and a thorough scholar. Your standards will give you confidence going into the debate itself.

Organizing Research

Ideally, you should organize your research as you gather it. However, you can still organize it after you have finished gathering. Organization will save you time in the long run. You won't spend five minutes searching for details of a fact every time you need it. It will also help you see how your data works together and in what order you can arrange it.

To start, choose a system for organization. Some popular methods include using index cards, a three-ring binder, or an expandable accordion folder. You may also choose to organize your research within computer files. After choosing your method, determine how you want to group the types of information you've found. For most debates, you'll want to separate arguments and research for the affirmative side from those of the negative side. Color coding your cards, papers, or electronic document file names can help.

FYI Pieces of evidence are often called "cards." This name originates from debaters who copied pages of books and cut the paper to show only the evidence that they wanted to use. Then they would paste the evidence to an index card.

If you choose to use index cards to help you organize, you may want to purchase multiple colored cards with writing lines on them. Use one color for your affirmative arguments and another color for your negative arguments. Write one argument at the top of each card. Below the argument list details and research you found to support the argument. Rather than writing paragraphs, bulleted points can be used. Bulleted points can be easily read, and they clearly separate different ideas. Clip the cards together or store them in separate envelopes. When you finish your cards, place them in the order in which you will present and number them. If you drop your cards, you'll be able to put them back in order quickly. You may also punch a small hole in the top left corner of each card. Then thread the cards in order onto a small ring, such as a circular keychain.

If you choose to use a three-ring binder or expandable accordion folder, record your data on paper instead of index cards. You can still use different colors of paper or ink to separate affirmative and negative arguments. Use tab dividers to separate papers placed in your three-ring binder.

YOU BE THE JUDGE

The Golden Rule tells you to treat others as you want to be treated. This adage has been around for many years but still applies today. When you come across situations that involve making ethical decisions, most people feel that the Golden Rule should be followed. It certainly applies before, during, and even after debates. You should treat your teammates, your judges, and especially your opponents with courtesy and respect, even if they do not do the same.

Unfortunately, not everyone acts courteously all of the time. During an address to Congress in 2009, President Barrack Obama refuted the idea that his health care reform plan would benefit illegal immigrants. As President Obama spoke, Congressman Joe Wilson shouted, "You lie!" The president, vice president, and speaker of the house, among others, were visibly shocked, and many in the room were upset at Wilson's outburst. Wilson later apologized for his inappropriate behavior, but his words and actions clearly broke the rules of courtesy and respect, especially during a formal meeting with some of the top leaders of the country.

Just as Wilson was out of place in his interruption, so is any interruption or discourtesy during a debate. Speaking out of turn, no matter how passionately you feel about an issue, is never acceptable. The same applies to name-calling, personal attacks on other debaters, shouting, or even discourteous body language. Even lesser offenses such as talking to a teammate or making unnecessary noise is considered rude and discourteous. Full attention should be given to the speaker.

What Would You Do?

You are in the middle of your affirmative rebuttal speech and your competitor starts shaking his head when you make a point. A moment later as you point out a weakness in his case, your opponent slams his fist on the table and calls your point ridiculous. How should you respond?

Label the pockets of the accordion folder to organize your sections. You can easily remove, rearrange, or add sheets of paper using either of these methods.

Using the computer to organize your research also provides a good method. You can use a word processor, spreadsheet, or database program. If using a word processor, you can create separate files for affirmative and negative arguments, or you can create one file and put different arguments on different pages. If your spreadsheet program allows it, you can create one workbook with two or more worksheet tabs. Each tab can contain a different type of argument. If using a database to hold your information, you can create a field that distinguishes the type of argument.

Whatever system you use to organize your research, make sure that you track the **sources** of your information. Sources are the materials from which you found information. They can be books, magazines, a website, or other resources. Ask your teacher what kind of information you need to note about each source. At the very least, write down the name of the source, the author, the page number (if applicable), the date it was published, and the date you found it. Make a list of your sources and assign an abbreviation for each. Then, as you write information on your cards or sheets of paper, mark the research with the appropriate abbreviation. Or, if you choose not to use multiple ink colors to track the type of information, you can coordinate ink colors and sources.

Why is it important to organize your research?

Think Critically

1. How important is the use of research versus the use of opinions when participating in a debate?

2. Why should you research both sides of a topic?

3. What is an advantage to color coding your research?

Research NOW!

4. Visit the National Forensic League's website at nflonline.org. Use the links on its home page to find current and past debate topics.

5. **TEAMWORK** Research the following resolution. Form a team of three students to research the topic. One student should research using only the Internet, the second student should only use books, and the third student should only use magazines and newspapers. After completing your research, compare and contrast the research methods.

Resolved: Stronger gun laws will not significantly reduce violence in America.

Write NOW!

6. **TEAMWORK** With a group of students, watch a debate on television or in person. Look for evidence of whether or not the debaters researched their topics. Write a one-page paper indicating whether the debaters used research, how well they used it, how you know they used it, and how it influenced your opinions of their statements.

7. Research a current debate or issue important in your state. Decide how you feel about the issue, and compose a letter to your state's governor about your thoughts. Incorporate the research you found, and make your letter persuasive. Ask your governor for specific action.

Speak NOW!

8. **TEAMWORK** With a partner, choose a topic appropriate for a Lincoln-Douglas debate, and brainstorm about arguments that could be used for the affirmative and negative sides. Assign a side to each of you and *without doing any research*, prepare a three-minute speech supporting your side. Present your speeches to the class. Afterward, research your sides and reevaluate your speeches. Add information that you found through research and rewrite your speech. Present your speeches again, and ask your classmates if they noticed a difference.

Do You Agree?

Resolved Limitations upon the content of student publications by secondary school administrators are justified.

Affirmative position

Yes, school administrators are ultimately responsible for everything that is published under the school's name. This includes student newspapers and yearbooks as well as literary works written in the classroom. School staff must ensure that every student feels safe and secure in a school environment.

Negative position

No, the concept of freedom of the press should extend to cover school publications as well. Students should be allowed to express and publish their opinions just as adults are. Extending this privilege in the school setting will provide students with real-life situations.

GOALS

Obtain a basic knowledge of debate tournaments.

Explain how debates are judged.

TERMS

round robin
cross entering
round
preliminary round
quarter-final round
semi-final round
final round
novice
junior varsity
varsity
ballot
speaker point
lay judge
panel

Tournament Basics

You've got a few in-class debates under your belt and you're starting to feel more confident of your skills. You've heard from some members on the debate team that they are entering a local tournament. Are you ready for this challenge? Learning more about debate tournaments can help you make this decision.

What You Need to Know About Tournaments

Tournaments are exciting events that provide opportunities for students to compete against one another. While it is exciting, it is also demanding. Preparing for and competing in tournaments is hard work. You will spend many hours researching, organizing, and writing your arguments. More time will be spent practicing your speeches and traveling to and from tournaments, which are often out of town. The actual debate can be very stressful as well. You'll speak in front of your opponent, a judge, and an audience. You'll have little time to prepare your counterarguments, so you'll need to know your facts. You will probably be nervous before every debate, but remember that nervousness isn't always bad. It can give you a boost of adrenaline that can actually improve your performance.

What would winning a debate award mean to you?

Along with the cons come a lot of great advantages of participating in debate tournaments. Debate tournaments can be extremely fun and rewarding! You have the opportunity to meet new, interesting people. The research and arguments allow you to gain knowledge of current and historical events that you might otherwise never learn. Debating also helps you learn and improve skills that will be important in your future. You learn the art of effective public speaking and persuasion—two skills that are valued in many careers. You also develop research skills that will help you in future classes and jobs. You gain confidence and respect for other people and other opinions qualities that others will admire. Last, participating in debate tournaments is rewarding, both from a personal and sometimes a financial aspect. Many winners of major tournaments are rewarded with academic scholarships.

You need to decide for yourself if the advantages outweigh the disadvantages. If so, you should look into tournament opportunities in your school or area.

Types of Tournaments and Events

Tournaments occur at many levels, ranging from local to regional to national. The National Forensic League has 106 districts that govern schools in all 50 states. The size, location, scope, and rules differ from tournament to tournament. You can usually find some of the details about the tournament in a tournament invitation. Many tournaments also publish details on websites. You should study the details so that you are well informed as to how a tournament will be run.

The number of competitors in an event can determine its format. Smaller tournaments may offer fewer events that larger ones do. Some debate tournaments are small enough that they use a **round robin** style. In this format, a total of six to eight teams compete. Each team debates all of the other teams, one at a time. After each round, teams rotate to compete against another team. For instance, if you enter a round robin tournament with seven other teams, seven rounds will be completed, and you will compete against each of the other teams. The winners of a round robin tournament are determined by the win-loss records.

Larger tournaments do not lend themselves to this format. Instead, they offer many direct competitions between two teams. Larger tournaments can allow many different types of events. Many large tournaments offer many of the following formats.

Student Congress	Original Oratory
Parliamentary	Dramatic Interpretation
Lincoln-Douglas Debate	Humorous Interpretation
Policy Debate	Duo Interpretation
Public Forum Debate	Poetry
International Extemporaneous Speaking	Prose
U.S. Extemporaneous Speaking	Impromptu Speaking

Some of the events differ from Lincoln-Douglas debates in that you compete with a team, rather than as an individual. Some tournaments allow you to enter more than one event. This variety can be a great experience. Entering in more than one event is known as **cross entering**. If you cross enter, tournament organizers will try to arrange the schedule so that your events do not conflict with each other. You'll need to make an effort to get to your events on time so that the tournament stays on schedule. If you are in two or more events, you should leave your first event as soon as it ends. Schedules are posted so that you know when and where you need to be. Symbols will indicate cross entries. For instance, the following partial schedule uses an asterisk (*) to indicate students who are cross entered. As you can see, M. Green is participating in two of the shown events—in Round 2 of oratory and Round 6 of domestic extemporaneous speaking.

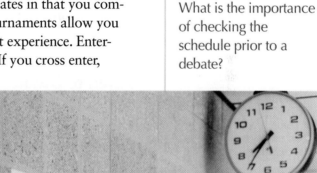

What is the importance of checking the schedule prior to a debate?

DIGITAL VISION/GETTY IMAGES

Oratory	Domestic Extemp
Section 3, Room 204	Section 4, Room 114
1. B. Ellis	1. J. Beaudry
2. M. Green*	2. S. Ortez
3. E. Roch	3. J. Shubat
4. K. Dillon	4. D. Engel
5. V. Tackman	5. B. Rademasher
6. T. Chen	6. M. Green*

Rounds of a Tournament

A **round** of a tournament is a series of timed speeches about one resolution. Although the number of total rounds of a tournament varies depending on the number of competitors and events, most tournaments have three or four *types* of rounds. The first round is called the **preliminary round** (or prelim round). All of the students entered in an event compete in a prelim round. In some tournaments, more than one set of prelim rounds are held. Students who win their rounds progress to the next round. Based on the rankings by the judge, the top students from each section of the prelim rounds get to move on to the next round, the **quarter-final round**. Likewise, winners of the quarter-final rounds progress to the **semi-final round**. During each round, students are placed in a new section and compete in front of a different judge. Once again, students are ranked from first to last with the top students moving on to the **final round**.

The final round has only one section. The top-ranked students compete for the last time. Students are usually awarded first through eighth place depending on their performances. The top three students or teams usually receive trophies, plaques, or other awards to signify their accomplishments.

Levels of Debate

You should not get frustrated if you lose a round or don't finish well in a tournament. When you enter a tournament, you will likely compete against those who have more experience than you. Everyone has to start somewhere, and many people who lose every round of their first few tournaments learn from their experiences. Many continue to become top winners in later tournaments.

Competitors are placed into a few categories. A **novice** is a person who is new to debate. Each tournament may have its own set of rules that define exactly who is a novice and who is not. Some tournaments simply state that if a student did not compete in debate prior to the current year, that student is considered a novice. Other tournaments might consider a student a novice if they are new to a certain type of debate but not new to debating. Before entering a novice tournament, check its rules to make sure you qualify.

Some schools and tournaments have a category of **junior varsity** (or JV). Typically, a junior varsity debater has passed the novice stage, but again, the rules can vary among tournaments. Some tournaments are intended strictly for JV and/or novices only. Varsity debaters may not participate in those tournaments.

The highest level of debaters is the **varsity** debater. According to most tournament rules, a varsity debater is a student who has passed the junior varsity stage. Also, if a varsity debater is working with a team during a round, the team is considered to be a varsity team. For instance, if a junior varsity member and varsity member are arguing together in a policy debate, they are considered a varsity team.

Tournament Judging

Typically, the debater who wins the most rounds wins the tournament. After every debate round, the judge casts a **ballot**. The ballot contains the names of the debaters, a place for the judge to write which side won, and a space to award **speaker points**. Speaker points allow the judge to evaluate the debaters' speaking and presentation skills. When judges determine speaker points, they are looking at your rate of speech, volume, articulation, eye contact, and other presentation skills. Many tournaments offer up to 30 speaker points per round. Although tournament guidelines vary, here is an example of how judges might be instructed to award speaker points. Any score below 16 indicates that a debater's presentation was inadequate or his or her behavior was inappropriate or disruptive. You will quickly learn the value of speaker points. When two or more competitors have the same number of wins, the speaker points break the tie.

Points	Rating of Skills
26–30	superior
16–25	average
0–15	poor or needs improvement

Only about ten percent of all students who compete at the local level advance to Nationals, the national competition sponsored by the National Forensic League. Students who compete at this level usually participate in a series of preliminary or prelim rounds. The results of a prelim round looks like this.

Name	School	Wins/Losses	Total Speaker Points
Campbell, J.	4	3-0	89
Ling, K.	13	3-0	86
Cirino, M.	9	2-1	90
Martin, L.	5	2-1	82
Rivard, T.	22	1-2	84

These lists show the students who qualify for finals and are known as are known as break lists. Notice that a number indicates the student's school. The students listed on a break list advance on to Elimination or Out Rounds. In an Out Round, speaker points are not awarded. Judges determine a winner and losers are eliminated or "out of the tournament."

Judges

Since judges decide who wins and loses each round, you may worry that they will be swayed by the resolution—especially in a Lincoln-Douglas debate that relates to controversial issues. What if you're arguing for capital punishment and the judge feels that capital punishment is unjust? Fortunately, judges are instructed to remain objective no matter what their personal feelings are. Remember that the judge is basing a win on who best presents their set of values as more important.

Besides determining the winning side, judges also need to track time for each speech. They will indicate when you have a little time to finish your speech and when time is completely up. Indicating that time is up is the only way the judge will communicate with you during the round. Judges will not ask questions during the rounds.

Two types of judges are used at tournaments. **Lay judges** are people from all walks of life that may not have any competition experience. Parents, neighbors, relatives, and teachers often volunteer to judge events. Without these lay judges, very few tournaments would be held.

You will find that the second type of judge, usually college students and others who have debate experience, tend to officiate varsity debates. At times, lay judges may also be asked to judge varsity events as well. While lay judges may not have been debaters themselves, they are still knowledgeable in the subject matter.

Most Lincoln-Douglas debates have only one judge, but some other events are decided by a **panel** of judges. Three or five judges usually make up a panel. An odd number of judges is often used to avoid a tie. Judges fill out their ballots independently. They do not confer with each other until the ballots have been turned in to the tournament official.

What are some of the responsibilities of a debate judge?

©JEFF GREENBERG/PHOTOEDIT

How to Win a Value Debate

A round in Lincoln-Douglas debate can be won by doing the following.

1. Proving to the judge that your value is the superior value in the round. You should be able to show how your case supports your value.

2. Proving to the judge that your case supports your value better than your opponent supports his value with his case.

3. Proving to the judge that your value best supports your case and your opponent's case better than his value does.

You will never be able to prove that your opponent's value is wrong. Values are neither right nor wrong. You can, however, use the above strategies to give the judge a reason to vote for you in the round.

Tournament Tips

The following tips should help you at a tournament in any competition.

1. **Be Prepared**

   Before and during the tournament, take care of yourself. Make sure you get plenty of rest and eat nutritious foods. Drink plenty of water to help your voice stay strong. Choose an appropriate, professional outfit to wear. On the morning of the tournament, gather all of the materials you need for the round. Take time to find the rooms in which you will be debating before the tournament begins.

2. **Be on Time**

   Be at your room five to ten minutes before the round is supposed to start. Wait outside the room until the judge arrives. If you are cross entered, go to the room where you are competing last and write your name along with the words "cross entered" on the board. That tells the judge that you will be there once you have completed the first event.

3. **Be Responsible**

   Check postings after each round to see if you have advanced. Make sure you have the correct room and the correct speaker position listed for each event. Speaking in the wrong room will result in a disqualification.

4. **Be Courteous**

   Listen to the other competitors. You should not be writing, talking, or doing anything else but paying attention. Not only is it considered to be rude behavior, but your judge will notice, leaving a poor impression. If you are cross entered, you should leave immediately after your presentation for your next event. If you are not cross entered, you should stay in the room to hear the other contestants. You can always learn something from every round.

FYI In 1992, President George H. W. Bush checked his watch during a town hall debate with candidates Bill Clinton and Ross Perot. Viewers took this gesture to mean that President Bush would have rather been somewhere else.

5. **Be Respectful**

Remember to thank the judge for his or her time. Compliment the other competitors and shake hands with them. Any comments made should be constructive.

6. **Be a Good Team Member**

Little things make big impressions. Remember to clean up the area where your squad has been. Treat the school you are visiting as if it were your own. Follow the guidelines that have been set forth by the host school. Do the simple things, and you will most certainly be invited to the tournament next year.

Tournaments are exciting, exhausting and nerve-wracking, but they are a great experience. Do you remember the slogan for a brand of potato chips that dares you to eat only one? The same can be said for tournaments. Once you have participated in your first tournament, you will want to compete again and again. Compete. Be successful. Have fun!

What are some ways to show respect for your opponent?

Think Critically

1. How does a round robin tournament differ from other types?

2. How does a judge's opinion on the topic of debate play into his or her decision in a Lincoln-Douglas debate?

Research NOW!

3. Visit the National Forensic League's website at nflonline.org. Use the links on its home page to find information about the next national tournament. Also, learn the history of the event. Last, search the site to find out about scholarships that are awarded after the tournament.

 4. **TEAMWORK** Find information on at least four high school debate tournaments. You can look for invitations, schedules, formats, rules, scoring, or other information. What are the similarities and differences among the tournaments?

Write NOW!

 5. **TEAMWORK** Working with a few other students, research what you would have to do to start a debate club at your school. Write a persuasive letter to your teacher about starting a club. Be sure to include why you want to start the club, how it would benefit students, and what needs to be accomplished. If your school already has a debate club, find out how you can enter tournaments. In this case, write a letter to your teacher about entering tournaments, how they would benefit students, and what needs to be accomplished.

6. Assume you help to run a debate club. Write a memo intended for new members to offer them tips on how to act during a tournament. Include tips on courtesy and respect as well as other behavior.

Speak NOW!

7. Consider the following resolution. Research the topic. Then break your classmates into groups of five or six and organize a round robin tournament. Other students or teachers may act as judges. Present your speeches during the debate rounds. After the in-class tournament, discuss your thoughts on this tournament format.

Resolved: All students attending public and private schools should be required to wear uniforms.

 8. **TEAMWORK** Working in pairs, write a resolution using a topic of your choice. Then write speeches for the affirmative and negative sides. Before you present your speeches, tell your classmates that they will act as the judges. Ask each of them to write on a separate sheet of paper your name and whether they think you won or lost the debate. Also, ask them to award you speaker points based on your presentation.

2

Chapter in Review

2.1 The Resolution

• The object of a Lincoln-Douglas debate is to convince the judge that your set of values is more important than those of your opponent. A resolution contains a topic of a debate that can be argued by an affirmative side and a negative side.

• You must choose a value premise for your debate and define criteria so that your premise can be judged.

2.2 Research

• Research allows you to better understand a topic and supply evidence to support your arguments. You should thoroughly research both sides of an argument using credible sources.

• Organizing your research allows you to quickly locate information and helps you arrange your arguments.

2.3 The Competition

• Tournaments vary in size and format. Many tournaments offer several events. Tournament structure is based on rounds. A round is a series of timed speeches about one resolution.

• Judges determine the winner of each round by casting a ballot with their vote and awarding speaker points.

a. aesthetic value
b. ballot
c. clash
d. credible
e. cross entering
f. final round
g. framer
h. jargon
i. junior varsity
j. lay judge
k. moral value
l. novice
m. panel
n. political value
o. preliminary round
p. quarter-final round
q. resolution
r. round
s round robin
t. semi-final round
u. source
v. speaker point
w. value
x. value criteria
y. value premise
z. varsity

Develop Your Debating Language

Select the term that best fits the definition. Some terms will not be used.

1. Entering more than one event at a tournament

2. Deals with the issues of right and wrong

3. Language that relates to a specific topic

4. Several people who judge a debate together

5. Places where you obtain research

6. Tournament style where every team debates every other team

7. To present opposing viewpoints

8. Person who is new to debating

9. Used to measure the worth of a value

10. Score sheet used by a judge

11. Series of timed speeches about one resolution

12. Writer of a resolution

13. Score awarded to a debater for presentation skills

14. The first round of a tournament

Review Debate Concepts

15. What is the role of a framer?

16. Why should you define the terms in a resolution?

17. The word *ought* is commonly found in a resolution for a Lincoln-Douglas debate. What does it imply?

18. What are aesthetic values?

19. List four values that might be cited in a Lincoln-Douglas debate.

20. How do you measure a value?

21. What do you need to prove to win a Lincoln-Douglas debate?

22. How can you tell if an opinion is right or wrong?

23. How can your knowledge of research improve your debate presentation?

24. How often do resolutions for Lincoln-Douglas debates change?

25. How can you prepare to argue against your opponents' points?

26. List at least four types of sources used for research.

27. What are three factors to consider when judging the reliability of information on a website?

28. Name at least two methods used to organize research.

29. List three benefits of debating.

30. How can you learn about details of a specific tournament?

31. List three events that might be offered in a tournament.

32. Compare and contrast a preliminary round to a final round.

33. Describe the different levels of debaters according to their experience.

34. Describe the high end and low end of speaker points usually awarded to a debater.

35. What are some of the duties of a debate judge?

Make Academic Connections

36. **SCIENCE**   Research the pros and cons of radio frequency identification (RFID) chips that can be implanted in humans. What kind of information could the chip contain? How might this benefit humans? How might it harm them? What are the ethical considerations? Write a resolution on this topic and briefly state arguments for the affirmative and negative sides.

37. **PHILOSOPHY**   What is philosophy? Use a dictionary, encyclopedia, or online resource to learn more about it. Then explain how it relates to debate.

38. **PROBLEM SOLVING**   Global warming has been a prominent international issue. Conduct research to find at least three potential solutions to the problem. Explain the feasibility of each solution.

39. **CHALLENGES**   Research to find a current controversy that is being argued in another country. Try to understand the controversy with consideration the degree that freedom is practiced in that country, remembering that rights and freedoms vary from nation to nation. Present both sides of the argument to your class.

Research NOW!

40. Research to find excerpts from the original Lincoln-Douglas debate. Be sure to find at least one excerpt from Lincoln's speech and at least one from Douglas's speech. What are your reactions to the speeches?

41. **TEAMWORK**   Work with a partner to research the topic of banning skateboarding in public places. One of you should use the Google search engine (google.com), and the other should use Google Scholar (scholar.google.com). Compare and contrast the types of results you find. Which site seems to have more reliable articles that could be used as evidence in a debate?

Write NOW!

42. Choose a topic suitable for a Lincoln-Douglas debate. Make sure that it is a topic that has not yet been used in your classroom activities. Write an original resolution for it, and define the terms of your resolution. Select a value and value criteria, and research for evidence to support both the affirmative and negative sides. Share all of this work, in written form, with an adult and ask his or her opinion of your work.

43. **TEAMWORK**   Choose one of the values listed in the chapter. In groups of three, brainstorm your initial ideas about the value. What does the value mean? What areas of life does it affect? What importance does society place on this value? How do you, as students, value it? Arrange your ideas into a logical order and write a two-page paper discussing some of your thoughts.

44. Interview a student, teacher, or other adult who has participated in a debate tournament. Ask them to describe the event to you in detail. Ask appropriate questions to learn details about their experience—not just what happened but how they felt about it. Organize the ideas and write a descriptive narrative of their experience.

Speak NOW!

45. Choose one of the tournament tips in the chapter and expand upon the idea. If possible, find evidence that supports the use of the tip. Come up with examples that demonstrate the proper and improper use of the tip. Give a five-minute speech to present your work.

46. Interview an adult who has worked as a judge at a debate competition. If you cannot find a debate judge, find someone who has judged another competition, such as a swim meet, a baseball game, a spelling bee, or a music competition. Ask them questions about judging. What did they like least and most about judging? What was the most difficult thing they had to do? Think of other related questions as well. Present your findings in class.

47. **TEAMWORK** Find a topic on which you and a partner disagree. Write a resolution on this topic. Then, assign yourselves to prepare arguments for the side that represents the *opposite* of each of your opinions. Research and prepare your cases separately and hold a short debate in your class. After your debate, discuss with your partner how you felt about arguing a side that you did not necessarily agree with in opinion. Was it more difficult to do? Did it help you understand that opinions do not hold weight in debates?

eCollection Activity

Morals and ethics come into play in many Lincoln-Douglas debates. One moral debate that has been hotly contested for many years is the debate on capital punishment. Capital punishment, also known as the death penalty, is the legal infliction of death as punishment for violating a criminal law. It is reserved for serious crimes such as murder. Beginning in the mid 1960s, many states abolished their laws allowing capital punishment. In 1972, the Supreme Court ruled that the death penalty was unconstitutional as administered because it constituted cruel and unusual punishment. After changes were made by many states, the Supreme Court reinstated the death penalty in 1976. Fifteen states have eliminated the use of the death penalty.

Those who oppose the death penalty feel that if violates human rights. They also question the effectiveness of the punishment. Those who support the death penalty feel that the severity of their punishment matches that of their crime. They feel the punishment will discourage others from committing similar crimes.

To learn more about this debate, access www.cengage.com/school/langarts/debate and click on the link for Chapter 2. Find other arguments for and against capital punishment as well as other statistics.

CHAPTER 3

Lincoln-Douglas Case Construction

PHOTODISC, ©FOTOSEARCH

FAMOUS DEBATERS

> *" You know, I have a long record of standing up and fighting. "*

In Congressional hearings and child welfare cases, in political debates and town hall meetings, at press conferences and summit meetings, Hillary Rodham Clinton has been a forceful public speaker and an expert debater. She has been a fierce advocate for children, the poor, and those in need of health care.

Born in Chicago, Illinois, Hillary Rodham attended Wellesley College in Massachusetts, where she was the first student commencement speaker. Her speech received a seven minute standing ovation, and may of her classmates predicted that she would be the first woman president of the United States.

Rodham went on to attend Yale University Law School, where she specialized in child welfare cases. She worked at the Yale Child Study Center where she conducted research on early childhood brain development. She also volunteered at the New Haven Legal Services, where she provided legal counsel for the poor. While at Yale, she met and started dating another young law student named Bill Clinton.

Many predicted that Rodham had a bright future in politics, but instead of staying in Washington, DC, she decided to marry Bill Clinton and move to Arkansas where he planned to pursue a political career. Hillary Rodham Clinton continued to write scholarly articles on children's law and cofounded the Arkansas Advocates for Children and Families. Clinton became the First Lady of Arkansas after her husband's successful run for governor. She served as chair of the Rural Health Advisory Committee, where she helped to expand health care facilities in some of Arkansas' poorest areas. After her husband's successful bid for the presidency, Clinton continued her fight for health care for the poor and legal protection for children. She hosted the first White House Conference for Teenagers in 2000.

After her husband finished his term as president, Clinton launched her own political career. She was elected senator from the state of New York in 2000. In 2008, Clinton decided to run for president.

Debates are one of the best ways for candidates to get their message out to the people and contrast their positions against those of their opponents. Throughout the course of her campaign, Clinton engaged in seven debates with her fellow contenders for the nomination. Clinton proved to be a tough debater. She stood firm on her record of advocating for women and children and expanding education and health care. She portrayed herself as a fighter and champion for the underdog, "You know, I have a long record of standing up and fighting."

While she lost her bid for the presidency, President Barak Obama appointed her as United States Secretary of State. She continues to argue passionately for human rights and international security around the globe.

Think Critically

What is unique about Hillary Rodham Clinton's experience of debate?

Hillary Rodham Clinton

GOALS

Know the order and time limit of each speech in a round.

Learn how to take and organize notes using a flow sheet.

TERMS

burden of proof
grace period
rebuttal
refute
dropped point
flow sheet
flowing
preflow

Do You Agree?

Resolved A victim's deliberate use of deadly force is justified as a response to physical abuse.

Affirmative position

Yes, situations occur where an individual may have to resort to the use of deadly force to protect himself or herself. People have the right to defend themselves, and there should not be consequences if one's physical being is in immediate danger. While laws are in place for the protection of people, they don't always work. Domestic violence, for instance, tends to escalate over time and no effective intervention from our legal system is available. In situations when a person is in imminent danger, deadly force may be the only way to protect oneself.

Negative position

No, deadly force is never the answer. We live in a civilized society where the offender is offered justice of a trial, not immediate execution sentenced by one person. Several agencies are available to people who feel they are in dangerous situations. The police should be notified. Shelters for battered spouses are available. Every alternative should be utilized instead of deadly force. Because there are a variety of resources available to victims of physical abuse, they will not be excused from any legal ramifications taken against them.

Speeches and Time Limits

You've entered a debate about mandatory school dress codes. You personally feel that dress codes are important, but you've been assigned to represent the negative side that argues against dress codes. How do you argue for an issue when you don't agree with it?

Every issue has two sides. Your responsibility is to be able to present both the affirmative and the negative sides in a clear and concise manner. At times, you have to argue a side of a resolution with which you do not agree. For instance, consider the men accused of planning and carrying out the September 11 terrorist attacks on the United States. The lawyers who defended these men may have believed their clients were guilty of the charges brought against them. They knew, however, that they had to provide the best defense possible for them. Our legal system is based on the premise that a person is innocent until proven guilty. Debaters are asked to do the same thing. Whether you agree with resolutions such as the death penalty or mandatory school dress codes, you must be able to present reasonable arguments supporting both sides.

Once you have completed the research for the resolution, you can begin your actual case construction. Each speech within a debate is unique in its own way. By taking a closer look at each speech, you will be able to recognize the differences among them.

The speeches during a Lincoln-Douglas debate are presented in a specific order, each with their own time limits, as shown in the table below. In this lesson, you will learn the order of the speeches and the general purpose of each speech. In the next two lessons, you will learn more details about each speech as it is given by the affirmative and negative sides.

Speech Name	Common Abbreviation	Time Limit
Affirmative Constructive	AC	6 minutes
Negative Cross-Examination	NCX	3 minutes
Negative Constructive Rebuttal	NC	7 minutes
Affirmative Cross-Examination	ACX	3 minutes
First Affirmative Rebuttal	1AR	4 minutes
Negative Rebuttal	NR	6 minutes
Second Affirmative Rebuttal	2AR	3 minutes

When you represent the affirmative side, you must show the judge why the resolution should be adopted or why you offer the best solution for the problem posed by the resolution. The affirmative must meet the **burden of proof**, the obligation to approve what is stated or disputed, in order to win the debate. Since the affirmative has the burden of proof, this side delivers both the first and the last speeches of the debate. As you can see from the table, both sides are given the same amount of total time to speak.

The time limits of all of the speeches are crucial to the debate. Some judges are willing to permit a **grace period**—additional time added to the original time allowance—to let you finish a thought or a speech. Judges will usually not extend a grace period beyond 30 seconds. Other judges will make you stop at the end of the original time. Your best policy is to assume that you only have the allowed time without a grace period. A debater who is prepared and has done all of the necessary work prior to the debate should be able to use all of the allotted time. Discussing your points in order of importance, starting with the most important, will guarantee that you don't miss key arguments due to time constraints. This could become the difference between winning or losing a round!

Affirmative Constructive Speech

The first speech of the Lincoln-Douglas debate, the affirmative constructive, is the only speech in the debate that can be completely prepared before the

Why is it important to practice your speech?

debate. In this speech, you show why the issue is significant and present all the major arguments in your case. You should also show how your value best upholds the resolution.

All of your arguments should be presented during this speech. Evidence—such as statistics, quotations, examples, studies, and reports—that support your arguments should be given. This speech is your only chance to submit this type of information. You will not be allowed to offer any new arguments after the affirmative constructive speech. If you try to enter new information after this speech, the judge will disregard it. Allowing new information past this point would place an unfair burden on your opponent and would take away from the structure of the debate round.

Plan your affirmative constructive speech so that it fills the entire six minutes allowed. Since this speech can be written ahead of time, this task should not be difficult. Time your speech in advance and practice it several times. During the actual debate, relax and avoid talking too quickly. If your speech is too short, the judge and your opponent will think that you have not prepared well. During this speech, as well as the others, face and speak to the judge, not your opponent.

Negative Cross-Examination

Once the affirmative has given the constructive speech, the negative side gets to question or cross-examine it. You can ask questions of your opponent during cross-examination periods. These questions can serve many purposes including the following.

- To challenge the affirmative's arguments

- To clarify meanings of key terms or arguments

- To obtain information that they missed

- To set up your next arguments

The negative cross-examination period should be used for questioning your opponent only. You will have time during your **rebuttal** speeches to counter the attacks and positions your opponent has presented. Questions should be well thought out and can sometimes be prepared prior to hearing your opponent's case. Remember that you only have three minutes to ask these questions.

Negative Constructive Rebuttal

Immediately following the negative cross-examination period, the negative side continues with its own negative constructive speech. In the first two or three minutes of this period, the debater should present his or her stand regarding the resolution. In most cases, this part of the negative constructive can be written in advance. During the remaining time of this seven-minute period, the debater should present a rebuttal, a reply to show fault with the affirmative's arguments and/or value. To present an effective rebuttal, you must attack each of the key issues of your opponent's case.

FYI In a court of law, the Sixth Amendment guarantees an accused person the right to confront, or cross-examine, witnesses who testify against him or her.

Affirmative Cross-Examination

The affirmative cross-examination is the second time the affirmative has a chance to speak. It is much like the cross-examination period of the negative side. The affirmative debater has three minutes to ask the negative side questions about its case. The questions serve the same purposes as those listed for the negative side.

First Affirmative Rebuttal

When you represent the affirmative side, you give two rebuttal speeches during the debate. The first rebuttal speech, which lasts four minutes, immediately follows the affirmative cross-examination. It should be used rebuild your case and attack the negative's case. You should emphasize why the strengths of your case outweigh the strengths of the negative side. Now is the time to **refute**, or prove false, the attacks against your case. Once you have addressed each and every argument that your opponent has offered against your case, you must then point out the weaknesses of the negative side. You must attack, or clash, with the negative. During this attack, try to raise questions in the judge's mind about every argument that the negative has presented. Remember that new evidence cannot be introduced in the rebuttal speech.

Negative Rebuttal

The next speech represents the negative's final chance to make an impression on the judge. In this six-minute speech, the negative side should respond to the attacks on its case and emphasize the strengths of the negative side. It should also repeat the weaknesses of the affirmative. The negative debater should also convince the judge that his or her side is the strongest. When you are representing the negative, you may only respond to arguments that you responded to in the negative constructive rebuttal.

Second Affirmative Rebuttal

This speech is the last one of the round and the last chance for the affirmative to make an impression on the judge. Because you only have three minutes to make a final impression on the judge, it is extremely important to use this time effectively and efficiently.

First, pick out the single greatest weakness in your opponent's case. You will want to tell the judge why it is not valid. Next, select one or two key points that show the strengths of your case. Again, stress to the judge why they are important and how they relate to the value and the resolution. Finally, remind the judge

1. How your case best supports your value

2. Why your value is better than your opponent's value

3. How your value best upholds the resolution

These points should be made clearly and with emphasis. They should also be succinct. Your main arguments have already been made, so now is not the time to extend them. You want to be sure that there is no doubt in the judge's mind that you have completely proven your case while showing why it is superior to your opponent's case.

Any point not argued in the first rebuttal speech cannot be brought up in a second rebuttal speech. It is considered to be a **dropped point**. A dropped point is simply any argument not addressed in the first rebuttal for the affirmative and the first constructive for the negative. The debater is responsible for making the judge aware that the point has been dropped. If an opponent tries to argue the point in a later speech, the debater must let the judge know that the point is no longer a "legal" argument. "Judge, my opponent dropped this argument in the negative constructive (or first affirmative rebuttal, whichever is applicable) and it cannot be considered in this debate." is one way to present it to the judge.

How can you show the judge that your arguments carry more weight than your opponent's?

©R. Gino Santa Maria, 2009/Used under license from Shutterstock.com

Even though the point should not be considered during the debate, you may still present an argument for it. Continue by saying "Even though the point should not be considered, I would like to offer the following arguments against it." Always take advantage of every opportunity to illustrate to the judge your skills as a debater.

Prep Time

Each debater is given a three to four minute prep time during a Lincoln-Douglas debate. You can ask to use this time any way you see fit during the round. Because this time is so limited, use it wisely. You may want to use it for one of the following purposes.

- Think of answers to opponent's questions

- Form rebuttals to opponent's arguments

- Decide on a strategy for your next speech

- Organize your ideas for your next speech

Since the affirmative's constructive speech should be pre-written, the affirmative should not use any of its prep time until after the first negative constructive. At that point, the affirmative might want to use some of its prep time to make sure it has attacks ready for each point made by the negative. Remember, any point that is not attacked in the first affirmative is considered to be a point for the negative. Both the affirmative and negative sides are encouraged to save much of the prep time for their final speeches—the negative rebuttal for the negative side and the second affirmative rebuttal for the affirmative side. These speeches represent the last chance you have to make an impression on the judge. Make sure to take time to organize your speech and emphasize the most important points.

When should you use prep time during a debate?

Flowing

The task of keeping your arguments and your opponent's arguments organized can be overwhelming. One of the most valuable tools you can use is a **flow sheet**. A flow sheet can be made from a piece of paper that you divide into columns or rows. It allows you to highlight and organize the main arguments and evidence of both the affirmative and negative. It also helps you prepare your rebuttals since you can group the information by argument. The process of taking notes on the flow sheet is called **flowing**.

Each debater can have his or her own style of flow sheet. Many prefer to use a legal-sized piece of paper, turned sideways and divided into the columns. Column headings can include Affirmative Case, Negative Case, Affirmative Counterarguments, and Negative Counterarguments.

Affirmative Case	Negative Case	Affirmative Counterarguments	Negative Counterarguments
Outline of affirmative team's case	Negative team's main points and evidence	Arguments or evidence used in rebuttal	Counterarguments by negative (line up with corresponding argument)

If you are the affirmative side, you can write your arguments into the first column of this flow sheet before the debate begins, called **preflow**. As the negative side presents, you can write that case and counterarguments in the appropriate columns. You can also jot down notes that help you or that minimize the opponent's arguments. Especially helpful is the ability to align the arguments and counterarguments side by side. For instance, if you were on the affirmative team supporting the use of school uniforms, one of your arguments might be that school uniforms save parents money because they don't have to buy as many everyday clothes. Another affirmative argument might be that it reduces conflict caused by socio-economic differences made obvious by clothing choices. You could write these arguments in the first column. As your opponent speaks, he cites a study from a teen magazine that one school uniform is twice as expensive as an average everyday outfit. You could write this information in the next column. Since it corresponds to your argument, write it so that it aligns in the same row as your argument. Since you think his research comes from an unreliable source, you might jot that down to help you in your rebuttal. Look at the partially-completed flow sheet on the next page to see how a debater might align the information.

Notice the abbreviations and symbols used in the sample flow sheet. Whether you use a flow sheet or another form to record your notes, you'll need to write quickly and concisely. Many students develop their own form of shorthand to help them take notes as they listen to their opponent's speeches. Consider writing only enough key words to help you understand arguments. For instance, you may leave out conjunctions, adjectives, and adverbs. Suppose a debater states the following: Dress codes reduce the ways that gang members can identify themselves. When students know a gang member is

Sample Flow Sheet

Affirmative Case	Negative Case	Affirmative Counterarguments	Negative Counterarguments
Saves parents money	Uniform costs 2x aver outfit: Cosmo Girl	Unreal source/one study vs. many	
socio-econ standing	Other ways ex: jewelry, shoes		

in the room, they are often intimidated and fearful. In shorthand, you could write: reduce gang ID; less intimidation/fear.

As you begin flowing, you'll make up shorthand symbols and abbreviations of your own. The following are symbols commonly used by debaters.

Symbol	Meaning
$\oslash$	not
>	greater than or better than
≠	two things are not the same
=	equal, is, or two things that are the same
Δ	change
↑	increase
↓	decrease
→	leads to or causes
NYT, 10/09	New York Times, Oct 2009
V	value
VC	value criteria
Ⓙ	justice
SCS	separation of church and state

Thorough knowledge of both sides of the case will help you tremendously. If you've researched well and know your opponent's arguments, you'll be able to formulate the wording and write them quickly. If you have organized your evidence on numbered index cards, you can even write the card number in place of a statement.

Understanding of the basics of speeches, how to use prep time, and flowing will help you in your debates. Now you need to think about the actual debate itself, where you will need to be organized, focused, and ready to think and speak on your feet. If you are to be a successful debater in a Lincoln-Douglas competition, you need to know how to use your time carefully and deliberately to construct a sound and thorough argument.

©SVLUMAGRAPHICA, 2009/ USED UNDER LICENSE FROM SHUTTERSTOCK.COM

The United Nations

In the closing days of World War II, President Franklin D. Roosevelt and other world leaders wanted to create an international organization dedicated to promoting and preserving world peace. They wanted a stronger and more stable organization than the failed League of Nations that had developed after World War I. In April of 1945, fifty nations gathered to draft the Charter of the United Nations (UN). The Charter was ratified the following October.

Now, virtually every nation in the world belongs to the UN. The organization fosters debate on an international scale. The topics include threats to international security, human rights, world health issues, and relief to refugees and victims of famine and other national disasters. Debates are conducted in Arabic, Chinese, English, French, Russian, and Spanish.

The UN is divided into five principal organs or divisions: the General Assembly, the Security Council, the Economic and Social Council, the Secretariat, and the International Court of Justice. Most of these divisions are located in the UN building that officially sits on international territory in New York City. The International Court of Justice is located at The Hague in the Netherlands.

Most debates result in a vote and a recommendation passed by the assembly. The Security Council, which consists of fifteen member states, passes resolutions which are binding agreements on all of the member governments. The Security Council has five permanent member nations: the United States, Russia, the United Kingdom, China, and France. The Security Council sometimes authorizes peacekeeping operations to halt hostilities within a war torn area, oversee elections, and provide assistance for reconstruction. Troops from member states, as well as other volunteers, provide assistance and support to restore and maintain peace.

The head of the United Nations is the Secretary General, a post President Roosevelt envisioned as a world moderator. The Secretary General is elected by the General Assembly after being nominated by the Security Council. The Secretary General usually serves one or two terms of five years. The Secretary General is the chief administrator of the United Nations, as well as a diplomat and negotiator in situations of international conflict. The Secretary General may not be elected from one of the five permanent member nations.

The UN oversees worldwide organizations that provide food and other means of valuable assistance to countries struggling with emergency situations. These organizations, such as the World Health Organization; the United Nations Educational, Scientific, and Cultural Organization; and the World Food Programme, have headquarters all over the world.

Think Critically

What do you think is necessary to successfully debate in the United Nations?

Think Critically

1. Why is it important to prepare your affirmative constructive speech so that it runs as close to six minutes as possible?

2. What must you do to give an effective rebuttal?

3. What is the purpose of a flow sheet?

Research NOW!

4. **TEAMWORK** Working in small teams, find one or two sample negative constructive speeches. These may be written by students, teachers, or other professionals. Evaluate the speeches, and as a group, discuss the format and effectiveness of each speech.

5. Research the following resolution from the point of view of the affirmative side. Determine your value and criteria to argue your case and decide what your three top arguments would be. Find supporting evidence for your arguments.

   Resolved: America is in decline as a world power.

Write NOW!

6. Select a debate resolution of your choice and choose one argument that will support the resolution. Write the argument word for word as you would present it in an affirmative constructive speech. Be sure to include your supporting evidence in the speech.

Speak NOW!

7. **TEAMWORK** Work with a partner and decide which of you will represent the affirmative and which of you will represent the negative for the following resolution. The affirmative should prepare a constructive speech and present it in class. The negative should prepare at least two cross-examination questions in advance. Then the negative should come up with at least two more cross-examination questions during the affirmatives speech. Last, the negative should ask the questions and allow the affirmative to respond.

   Resolved: In matters of collecting military intelligence, the ends justify the means.

GOALS

Know how to prepare an effective affirmative constructive speech.

List tips to help you in a cross-examination period.

Understand what should be presented in an affirmative rebuttal.

TERMS

contention
voting issue
crystallization

Do You Agree?

Resolved A just society ought not use the death penalty as a form of punishment.

Affirmative position

Yes, the death penalty should not be used in the United States or any society as a means of capital punishment. Too many variables exist—such as race and gender—that affect juries' decisions when it comes to the death penalty. The death penalty is also an inhumane punishment that should not be endorsed by a society that claims to be just. Last, it is not an effective means of deterring crime.

Negative position

No, the death penalty is a viable form of punishment. The fact that 37 of our states, a clear majority, have some form of death penalty supports the government's use of this punishment. Unfortunately, some crimes are so horrific, so incomprehensible, that no other form of justice is harsh enough. Justice must serve the victims and their families.

Affirmative Constructive Speech

Writing the affirmative case is much like writing a paper for your English class. It should be a complete presentation from the beginning to the end. Think of how you begin a paper. You probably create an outline. Your title indicates the overall subject of the paper. The main topics of the outline are listed using Roman numerals (I, II, III). The subheads of those main topics might be separated using letters (A, B, C). Similarly, you should create an outline for your case. In your case outline, your resolution is your title. The main topics are your arguments. The subtopics are the pieces of evidence that support them.

Like a paper that you write, writing the affirmative case is an ever-changing process. If you debate the same topic during two or more debates, you will find that in order to improve your case some information may need to be changed or deleted. You may also find that some arguments need more facts or statistics to back them. Just as you may edit a paper, you can continuously edit debate speeches to make them better. Successful debaters constantly evaluate and change their speeches as they learn from their mistakes and experiences.

The affirmative constructive speech contains three basic parts: the opening statement, the body, and the conclusion. You should time and practice your affirmative constructive speech so that you include all three parts. A suggested time breakdown for this speech is shown in the table.

Opening Statement	5 to 60 seconds
Body	5 to 5½ minutes
Conclusion	45 to 75 seconds

Opening Statement

Even though the opening statement, or the introduction, may be the shortest part of your affirmative constructive speech, do not underestimate its importance. As in many things in life, first impressions mean a lot. In sixty seconds or less, you must accomplish three things.

- Grab the judge's attention.

- State the resolution and define its terms.

- State the value and value criteria.

Grab the judge's attention. In order to get the judge's attention, you'll need to be original. Starting a speech with "I think that the death penalty is wrong" type of statement is definitely the wrong way to go. Consider using a quotation, interesting statistic, or unfamiliar fact. Make sure that the attention getter relates to the topic and supports the information that will be presented in the body of your case. Some sample attention getters for the resolution in the beginning of the lesson follow.

Resolved: A just society ought not use the death penalty as a form of punishment.

Photodisc/Getty Images

How can you catch the attention of a judge?

FYI *Bartlett's Books of Quotations* is an excellent source of quotes. It contains a collection of passages, phrases, and proverbs traced to their literary sources. You can find information at www.bartleby.com.

- **Quotations** "The Supreme Court can tinker with the death penalty guidelines all it wants, but patterns of implementation clearly show that who is killed and who is spared is determined largely by local culture—our way of doing things—and not by the law." –Sister Helen Prejean, author of *Dead Man Walking*.

In order to be effective, the quote should be from a reliable source. In this example, Sister Helen Prejean is a well-known Roman Catholic nun who actively campaigns against the death penalty. Her stand on this issue has been well documented. Her quotation directly relates to the resolution and one of the affirmative's main arguments.

- **Statistics** In 2008, 37 people were executed. These include 18 in Texas, 4 in Virginia, 3 each in Georgia and South Carolina, 2 each in Florida, Mississippi, Ohio, and Oklahoma, and 1 in Kentucky. All 37 were men and all but one died by lethal injections. The other was electrocuted.

These statistics point out to the judge that the death penalty is still being used today, often in southern states. It also gives specific information as to how the executions were administered.

- **Facts** Herman Lindsey. Ronald Kitchen. Daniel Wade. What do these men have in common? They are among the 137 inmates who were sentenced to death row in recent history, only to be later found innocent and released from prison. These 137 inmates lost years of their lives, sometimes spending up to 33 years in prison, for crimes that they did not commit—The Death Penalty Information Center.

The facts in this opening are not only informative but will be startling to most. They suggest that some of the inmates who were executed may have also been innocent. Using the names of some of those who were sentenced has a strong impact on the listener. They make the listener realize that they were real people with real names, not just statistics.

State the resolution and define its terms. Once you have the judge's attention, state the resolution. To avoid suggestions that you are trying to interpret the resolution to better serve your purpose, read the resolution word for word as it was written by the framers. Stating the resolution during the introduction also serves to remind the judge of the exact topic of the debate. Quickly define key words of the resolution, stating your source. For example, you can say, "The following definitions come from Webster's Dictionary."

State the value and value criteria. At the end of the introduction, state the value and the value criteria. A brief explanation should be presented telling the judge how they relate to the topic. For instance, using the death penalty resolution, you might state your value as justice or life. Your criteria might be the moral standard that killing is wrong.

Body

Immediately following the introduction is the body of your affirmative constructive speech. This section allows the most time, but often it won't seem like enough. In the body of the speech, you must build a case that upholds your value. The body is made up of contentions. A **contention** is a major argument. Each contention should be a self-contained argument and be able to stand on its own. You should have two or three pieces of support and evidence that defend the contention. Statistics, facts, quotes, examples, evidence, and logical reasoning are some of the ways to build a contention. Always give the reliable sources for your information to add to the credibility of your case. When presenting the information, it is important to continually remind the judge how it supports the resolution and your values.

Every affirmative constructive speech should have two or three contentions. Having a few strong arguments is more effective than several weak points with very little support. Think of a few strong arguments as "hitting the nail on the head." You can drive a nail into a piece of wood by striking it gently many times or giving it a few strong hits. Which is more effective and more impressive?

Another reason to have only a few strong contentions is time limitations. Always present contentions according to their importance to the case. The strongest point should be presented first with the weakest point last. Be sure to practice this and other portions of your speech over and over so that you know exactly how long it will take. Don't fall into the trap of speaking about one contention for so long that you miss the opportunity to present the others.

Why is it important to have a strong contention?

An example of one affirmative contention for the resolution regarding the death penalty is shown.

Example of a Contention

The Death Penalty is Racially Biased

It is undeniable that the ethnicity of a person accused of a crime directly affects not only the verdict, but more importantly, the penalty. According to the ACLU (February 26, 2003), people of color comprise 43 percent of total executions since 1976 where they comprise only about 25 percent of the population. Another report by Amnesty International ("Death by Discrimination—The Continuing Role of Race in Capital Cases" April 24, 2003) states that while African-Americans make up only 12 percent of the population, they account for 43 percent of current death row inmates. The National Coalition to Abolish the Death Penalty goes on to say that since the United States ratified the International Convention on the Elimination of all Forms of Racial Discrimination in 1994, the U.S. courts and legislation have failed to act decisively in the face of evidence that race has had an impact on capital sentencing. However, the numbers tell the story.

The race of the victim also has an impact on whether the death penalty will be given. Professor Baldus, a law professor at the University of Iowa and Professor Woodworth, a statistics professor at the same school, conducted a study in three-fourths of the states that allowed the death penalty. In 93 percent of those states, the race of the person murdered correlated with whether a death sentence would be given in a particular case. According to the Reverend Jesse Jackson (1996), "The death penalty is essentially an arbitrary punishment. There are no objective rules or guidelines for when a prosecutor should seek the death penalty, when a jury should recommend it, and when a judge should give it. The lack of objective, measurable standards ensures that the application of the death penalty will be discriminating against racial, gender, and ethnic groups." Clearly, this indicates that justice is not found here. The only way to eliminate the bias is to eliminate the death penalty. It is the first step in ensuring that these are objective criteria for determining not only right and wrong, but the depth of punishment as well.

In this contention, the use of quotations, statistics, and facts all help to show how racial bias affects the death penalty. The information in parentheses is not read during the speech. During the cross-examination period, your opponent may ask for the sources or dates of those particular items. You can look back through your speech in order to get that specific information. Finally, the last point made in the contention is to show the judge how this contention supports both the value and the value criteria.

Conclusion

Like the introduction, the conclusion is short but important. The introduction gives a first impression, but your last statements stick with the judge. Start your conclusion by summarizing your case by reminding the judge of your contentions. "Judge, I have shown how racial bias influences the death penalty. I have also shown…(list other contentions)."

Second, restate the value and value criteria and how it supports the resolution. "Justice is the supreme value in this round because it is the only way everybody will be able to get what is truly deserved and earned. This will be achieved by a set of objective standards to determine the rightness and wrongness of actions." Next, ask the judge to vote for you. "Judge, I urge you to vote affirmative." Finally, let your opponent know you are ready for cross-examination. "I am now ready for cross-examination."

Remember that once you have indicated that your have completed the affirmative constructive speech you will not be able to bring up any new arguments. Everything that you want to present to the judge regarding this topic should have been presented in this speech. The judge will ignore any new information that may be introduced at any later time during the debate. A well-researched and well-written speech provides the basis for a strong debate. In the next lesson, you will learn to prepare and present strong speeches supporting the negative side of the resolution.

YOU BE THE JUDGE

Former debaters often speak proudly of skills they've learned in debate that transfer to their jobs and different aspects of their lives. One such skill is the ability to research and understand both sides of an issue. Even if they don't agree with one side, they usually still make an effort to understand the opposition's views.

You've probably heard of the injustices of other countries where their governments censor the media. In a country with free press, most people expect the broadcast media to report both sides of every story. When you read the newspaper or watch the news, you probably assume that you are learning all the facts of an issue. However, many analysts warn that this is not always the case. They point out many cases where the media is very biased in their reports to the public.

What Would You Do?

Using the knowledge you've obtained, how do you feel about this issue? Do the media have a duty to report both sides of the story with equal coverage or do they have the privilege to lean towards one side or the other?

Affirmative Cross-Examination

After the negative cross-examines and delivers its constructive rebuttal, you get a turn to ask questions about the negative case. Like the negative side, you can ask questions that challenge or clarify the opponent's arguments, obtain information you missed, set up your next arguments, or question the logic used in your opponent's case.

Think about using the following tips as you cross-examine your opponent. Some of the tips also apply to the period where your opponent is cross-examining you.

- Prepare some questions in advance of the debate. Thorough research and knowledge of both sides will aid you in this process.

- As your opponent presents his or her case, write new questions on your flow sheet. Use the flow sheet during your cross-examination to remind yourself what you wanted to ask.

- Although you are asking questions of your opponent, be sure to face the judge. This procedure is standard for Lincoln-Douglas debates.

- While you are asking questions and while you are answering your opponent's questions, stay calm. It's easy to get flustered or upset, but staying calm will impress the judge and may rattle your opponent.

- Don't ask open-ended questions. Try to ask questions that can be answered with a simple yes or no and a brief response. If your opponent tries to give a lengthy answer, stop him or her. Otherwise the answer will take up much of your allotted time.

- When answering questions, give direct, honest answers.

How can a flow sheet help you during rebuttals?

aldomurillo/iStockphoto.com

Affirmative Rebuttal

As soon as you finish your cross-examination, you begin your first affirmative rebuttal. This speech is considered by many as the most difficult speech in the debate. It allows you only four minutes to refute the negative's remarks against your case and to point out the weaknesses and faults of your opponent's case.

Your flow sheet will be a great tool during your rebuttal. Since you cannot predict all of your opponent's comments, you cannot completely prepare for rebuttals in advance. Your best plans include noting arguments to respond to on your flow sheet and knowing the case well. Knowledge of both sides of the argument is crucial at this point. You need to think of responses without paging through your notes for answers.

When you address the attacks against your case, address them in the same order that your opponent uses. Do not ignore any attacks. That tactic will cause you to lose points. Sometimes you might have to concede a minor point, but that's okay.

You can challenge your opponent's arguments in two ways. You can attack the argument or evidence used or you can attack the soundness of the opponent's logic. If one point doesn't really lead to another and your opponent is trying to make that connection, don't be afraid to point it out. Be professional when describing errors in logic. Make your opponent's errors known, but don't dwell on them.

Following your first rebuttal, the negative side presents its last rebuttal. Then you have the chance for one final rebuttal—the second affirmative rebuttal. In a sense, you get the last word in the debate, so use it wisely. Because of the importance of this speech, use some of your prep time to organize your thoughts. Appearing unorganized or unsure of yourself at this point can be disastrous to your case.

In this final rebuttal, you need to accomplish the following.

1. Quickly emphasize your opponent's greatest weaknesses. Rebuild your attacks by negating any defenses that your opponent brought up in the negative rebuttal.

2. Rebuild your position by addressing any major weaknesses pointed out by your opponent in the negative rebuttal.

3. Present the arguments that will convince the judge that you have won. Significant arguments that show you are winning and that give the judge reasons to vote for you are voting issues. **Voting issues** are arguments, not general ideas, which prove why you should win the round. **Crystallization** occurs when you state your voting issues. It gives the judge information to put all of the arguments together so that he or she can decide who won the debate. During crystallization, sum up the debate, address the most important arguments, and offer voting issues.

4. Ask the judge to vote for you.

Think Critically

1. The more contentions you have in a speech, the better. Is this statement true or false? Explain your answer.

2. Why is the first affirmative rebuttal considered the most difficult speech to make?

3. What is the difference between crystallization and voting issues?

Research NOW!

4. **TEAMWORK** Assume you are debating whether the maximum speed limit in your state should be raised. With a partner, conduct research to find the maximum speed limits in at least four states. Then try to find statistics that correlate speed limits to automobile accidents.

5. Visit www.bartleby.com and explore the website. List at least three categories of topics that you can search. Then find a quotation that could be used in a debate about liberty.

Write NOW!

6. **TEAMWORK** With a small group of students, examine the sample contention used in this lesson. Identify each supporting detail. List the details and indicate if each is a quotation, statistic, fact, study, or other category. Then, write a brief explanation of whether your group finds each detail effective in supporting the contention.

7. Now that you've learned more details about preparing speeches for the affirmative, revisit the contention that you wrote in activity 6 in lesson 3.1. Use the knowledge that you gained from this lesson to expand and improve your writing. Add an opening statement as well. If you did not complete that activity, write a new affirmative opening statement and contention with supporting details on a topic of your choice.

Speak NOW!

8. Assume you are representing the affirmative side for the following resolution. Write and present an introduction that includes an opening statement, the resolution, definitions, the value, and the value criteria. After all presentations have been given, hold a classroom discussion on why some introductions were more effective than others.

Resolved: A victim's deliberate use of deadly force is justified as a response to physical abuse.

Do You Agree?

Resolved Liberty is more precious than law.

Affirmative position

Yes, we have fought wars as long as anyone can remember for the right to be free. Liberty must be defended even if it means breaking the law. Freedom from constraints encourages society to flourish.

Negative position

No, laws are essential to sustain liberty for all. There must be clear guidelines as to what is and is not acceptable. Laws do not stifle a society, but instead help a society to provide the liberties desired by all.

GOALS

Identify the purpose of cross-examination questions.

Understand the two parts of a negative constructive rebuttal.

Describe the purpose of a negative rebuttal.

TERMS

road map
line-by-line presentation
signpost
preempting

Negative Cross-Examination

You've entered a tournament and won your first round. In that round, you represented the affirmative side of the resolution used in the last lesson. In the next round, you are assigned to represent the opposite side.

Preparing to argue the negative side of the resolution is much like preparing the affirmative side. Obviously, your contentions will contradict those of your opponent, but the case preparation is similar. Your negative case will have a value, value criterion, definitions, and contentions.

As you learned, the affirmative constructive speech is always the first speech of a Lincoln-Douglas debate. When you represent the negative, your first chance to speak occurs during the negative cross-examination period. This period is used strictly for asking questions of your opponent. The questions can serve any of the following purposes.

- To challenge the affirmative's arguments

- To clarify meanings of key terms or arguments

- To obtain information that you missed

- To set up your next arguments

Many debaters fail to take advantage of this important opportunity. However, an experienced debater will prepare for the cross-examination period just as one might prepare for constructive and rebuttal speeches. You should prepare some of the questions in advance, especially those used to set up your next arguments. For instance, you might ask the affirmative if he or she thinks there is anything more valuable than life. If the opponent answers honestly,

the response will probably be no, that life is the ultimate value. Later in the debate you can remind the judge of the opponent's answer and use it to the advantage of your own case. Of course, when using this strategy, you should be fairly certain that you can predict your opponent's answer.

Other questions may be asked to challenge the affirmative's arguments. Thorough research will help you understand both sides of the resolution. It allows you to predict your opponent's main contentions and formulate questions about them in advance.

You need to control this cross-examination period. Do not allow your opponent to give long, rambling answers that use up your time. In order to avoid this problem, ask questions that can be answered with a yes or no or with a brief answer. Avoid questions that require in-depth answers. If your opponent insists on responding with a lengthy answer, you should do three things.

1. Say "Thank you, you have answered that question."

2. Continue with "My next question is…"

3. Proceed by asking your question.

How can your research affect the cross-examination period?

Do not be rude or abusive, but do be firm. Rude behavior will only make you look bad in the eyes of the judge.

Finally, be sure to use the information you have received during the cross-examination period in your rebuttal. The cross-examination period can be a very effective tool that can give you an advantage during the round. Take the time to prepare for it. Be sure to question classmates during practice rounds as this will be a good time to see which questions work for you. A good question will pay big dividends!

Negative Constructive Rebuttal

Following the negative cross-examination period is the first actual speech given by the negative side. You may notice that the time allowed for the negative constructive rebuttal is a bit longer than that allowed for the affirmative constructive speech. The reason is that this speech actually contains two parts. The first portion is the negative constructive speech, which is much like the affirmative constructive speech. The second part allows for a rebuttal speech. Some Lincoln-Douglas debate formats allow you to choose the order of presentation of these two parts. However, most debaters tend to present the constructive portion first. This portion is pre-written so the debater will know exactly how much time this portion will take, whereas the length of the rebuttal can vary.

The total speech time for this portion is seven minutes, and the constructive portion should last two to three minutes. If you allow much more, you may not have enough time for a thorough rebuttal.

Negative Constructive Speech

The negative constructive speech should follow a format similar to the affirmative constructive speech. Like the affirmative, the speech should begin with an opening statement that catches the judge's attention. The use of quotes, startling facts, or statistics is still appropriate. For instance, a negative debater arguing the death penalty resolution could open with the following statement.

FYI Instead of reading a quotation from note cards, some debaters use a more dramatic approach–reading the quote directly from a book or another source. This technique may add credibility and emphasis to your quote.

> The Bible says "an eye for an eye and a tooth for a tooth." Apparently, the federal government, the U.S. military, and 37 states agree. They all think that the death penalty is a just punishment for those who have committed horrific crimes such as murder.

After your opening statement, repeat the resolution. If you disagree with any definitions of key terms given by the affirmative, argue your disagreements at this point. Then state the value on which you believe the resolution should be argued as well as its criteria. When arguing the negative, you may agree with the affirmative that the value is justice or life. However, your criteria might point to justice brought to the victim and the victim's family instead of the criminal.

Like the affirmative, the next part of your constructive speech— the body—contains your contentions. Your contentions should clash with the affirmative. Also like the affirmative, having a few strong contentions is more effective than having a lot of minor ones. Each contention should be backed by supporting evidence. Time may only allow you to present one or two contentions, so choose your strongest ones. Which two of the following four contentions would you consider the strongest?

Brian A. Jackson/iStockphoto.com

How can reading from a source affect your statement?

1. Some criminals have committed such vulgar crimes that they have earned the ultimate punishment that society has to offer.

2. If we don't use capital punishment, our justice system places a lesser value on the lives of the victims than on the lives of the criminals.

3. Society not only has the right, but the duty, to act in self-defense of the victims.

4. Existence of the death penalty deters crime.

No right or wrong answer exists. Choose your contentions based on how well they relate to the resolution, how strongly they support your value and value criteria, and how much sound evidence you have to support them. Each contention should be backed by supporting evidence as shown in the last lesson. After the body of your speech, present your conclusion by briefly summarizing your contentions. A sample negative constructive speech is shown below. The rebuttal portion of the speech is not shown as it would vary greatly depending upon arguments used by the affirmative.

Sample Negative Constructive Speech

Opening Statement	According to C.S. Lewis, "If deterrence is all that matters, the execution of an innocent man, provided the public think him guilty, would be fully justified." It is because I agree with C.S. Lewis that I negate today's resolution. **Resolved:** A just society ought not use the death penalty as a form of punishment.
Value/Criteria Statement	I would like to offer the value of life and the social contract as my criteria.
Observation	It should be noted that the death penalty can only be imposed once a person has gone through the legal process.
Contention 1: Capital Punishment Has a Deterrent Effect on Crime	It is erroneously thought that criminals do not fear death because they do not take time to think about the consequences of their acts. Their actions alone show this to be untrue. How many times has a criminal surrendered and dropped to the ground when faced by a police officer at gunpoint? Criminals have the same feelings of fear as their victims. Edward Koch, former mayor of New York City said, "Had the death penalty been a real possibility in the minds of…murderers, they might well have stayed their hand. They might have shown moral awareness before their victims die…Consider the tragic death of Rosa Velez, who happened to be home when a man named Luis Vera burglarized her apartment in Brooklyn. "Yeah, I shot her," Vera admitted. "…and I knew I wouldn't go to the chair." Furthermore, studies show that the death penalty does in fact act as a deterrent to murder. Naci Mocan, an Economics professor at the University of Colorado at Denver found in studies done in 2003 and 2006 that each execution results in five fewer homicides while each death sentence that is reduced to a lesser sentence results in five more homicides. Mocan stated: "Science does really draw a conclusion…There is no question about it. The conclusion is there is a deterrent effect. The results are robust. They don't really go away. I oppose the death penalty. But my results show that the death penalty (deters)–what am I going to do? Hide them?" Another study done in 2003 by professors at Emory University concluded that each execution deters an average of 18 murders. By entering into the Social Contract we agree to abide by all rules governing us. We are also aware of the penalties should those rules be violated. The death penalty also exemplifies the value of each and every life.

Contention 2: Capital Punishment vs. Life Without Parole	Those who disagree with the death penalty argue that a life sentence is just as much of a deterrent and protects society. This is not always true. Consider the following.
	Case Number 1 — In 1973, Dawd Mu' Min was serving a 48 year sentence for the murder of a cab driver. In 1988, he escaped a road work gang and stabbed to death a storekeeper named Gladys Nopwaskey during a robbery. He got $4.00. Mu' Min won't harm anybody else; he was executed by the state of Virginia on November 11, 1997. This is little compensation for Gladys Nopwaskey's family.
	Case Number 2 — In 1966, two boys were shot to death. Even though a Fort Worth jury ruled that Kenneth McDuff should die in the electric chair, his sentence was commuted to life in prison. In 1989, McDuff was released from prison because Texas prisons were overflowing. Under pressure from the federal judiciary, the prison population was reduced. He then went on a murdering rampage, killing at least nine more people. He was finally caught and executed in November 17, 1998.
	There are too many factors that can affect a life sentence. Laws change, people change, and parole boards change. It is our duty to protect innocent people from these violent offenders. The death sentence will ensure that criminals don't harm more victims.
At this point, the negative would present the rebuttal.	I would now like to address my Opponent's case.
Final statement	As you can see judge, the only way to protect our citizens from these brutal acts is to enforce the death penalty. Please vote negative in today's round. Thank you.

Rebuttal

Now that you have presented your position, the time has come to attack the affirmative's case. The purpose of the rebuttal is to show fault with the affirmative's arguments and/or value. Refer to the notes you took on your flow sheet during the affirmative's constructive speech to remind yourself of the opponent's contentions. Give the judge a **road map**. Tell the judge exactly what you are going to refute.

> "Judge, I am going to start with my opponent's value and criteria. Then I am going to address contentions 1, 2, and 3."

The judge will likely refer to his or her own flow sheet to follow your rebuttal and document your statements. Presenting your counterarguments point by point in the order that your opponent presented them is known as using a **line-by-line presentation**. This method adds organization to your presentation and ensures that you will not skip an argument.

Next, present problems or arguments against every one of your opponent's contentions. To make yourself as clear as possible, use the four steps of refuting.

Courtesy of National Forensic League, www.nflonline.org

What is the best way to begin a rebuttal?

Step 1 Signpost

Identify the claim you are refuting. In the debate, your opposition has probably brought up many arguments. **Signpost,** or clearly signal with words, to identify which of those arguments you are refuting.

Example My opponent argued that the death penalty is an inhuman punishment that should not be endorsed by a society that claims to be just.

Step 2 State

Make your counterargument. After you identify your opponent's argument, state your response to it.

Example However, the death penalty has been determined a humane punishment by many state courts as well as the U.S. Supreme Court.

Step 3 Support

Refer to your research. Show that your counterargument is better than your opponent's argument by introducing evidence and/or explaining your justification.

Example In the 1976 case of Gregg v. Georgia, the U.S. Supreme Court ruled death by lethal injection did not violate the Constitution's ban on cruel and unusual punishment, and thus was not inhumane. When challenged again in 2008, the U.S. Supreme Court upheld the same ruling. Thirty-seven states permit the death penalty. None of those states have declared it inhumane. Due to the nature of crimes that death row inmates have committed, Dr. Jay Chapman, inventor of the lethal injection used in most states, declares, "I think that execution by the method we've set up is far too humane for many of these people because of the things I've seen they've done to their victims."

Step 4 Summarize

Explain the importance of your argument. Summarize to contrast your argument with your opponent's and show how yours is stronger.

Example A just society, such as that of the United States, has repeatedly evaluated the humanity of the death penalty. No matter what evidence the opposition offers, you cannot refute the fact that it has been found to be a humane punishment.

Utilize your time well in order to argue all affirmative contentions. If time does not allow, don't elaborate too long on any one contention. Any affirmative contention that you do not address at this time will be considered a dropped point and will be awarded to the affirmative. Once your time is up for this speech, you will not be allowed to bring up new issues or argue a contention that you did not have time to argue.

If you have time remaining after presenting all of your attacks against the affirmative case, return to your constructive case. In your own words, simply restate the main ideas of each of your contentions. Do not reread your case! This will only irritate the judge. If you have properly researched, written, and practiced your case, you will be able to explain the significance of each point of your case. Demonstrate to the judge that you are in control of your material. Show him or her that you can think on your feet and use time effectively. Your final statement should be to urge the judge to vote for you by simply saying, "Judge, please vote negative."

The "No Neg" Case

Recently, some debaters have started a trend in Lincoln-Douglas debate where a negative case is not presented. This is called a "no neg" case. The debater does not present an alternative case for the judge to consider. Instead, the entire seven minutes of the negative constructive rebuttal is used to point out discrepancies and weaknesses in the affirmative case.

Using this strategy, two problems can occur. First, the judge has only one area to consider—the one that has been presented by the affirmative. This also limits the types of arguments that can be presented in the round. If you choose a "no neg" presentation, your opponent may point out to the judge that you haven't been able to offer another side to the resolution. Consider this resolution.

Resolved: Liberty is more precious than law.

Without presenting a negative case, you are limited to arguing the merits of liberty. How laws provide for this liberty can then be totally lost in this debate.

Second, by presenting a "no neg" case, you are allowing your opponent to suggest to the judge that you have been abusive in the round. The affirmative may declare that you have created an unfair burden in the round because you have not given them a case to argue against. It will be up to the judge to decide whether you are being abusive, but this may give the judge a reason to vote affirmative.

How should you use any remaining time in a rebuttal?

Negative Rebuttal

After your negative constructive rebuttal, the affirmative has a chance to cross-examine and then present their first rebuttal. Following those speeches is your negative rebuttal. This is your last chance to impress the judge. In this speech, you should do five things.

1. Revisit the affirmative case and show how its arguments are still flawed. Return to the affirmative arguments one by one in the same order that they were originally presented. Emphasize the fault, weakness, or inconsistency of each argument and compare your arguments to the affirmative with reference to the value criteria.

2. Respond to the attacks made against your arguments. Return to your negative arguments one by one in order and answer the criticisms against them. Explain why the affirmative's arguments are not effective.

3. Present the arguments that will convince the judge that you have won the round. Select the voting issues that advance your position.

Courtesy of National Forensic League, www.nflonline.org

How does participating in an LD debate teach you new skills?

4. If time permits, put yourself in the affirmative's place and anticipate the arguments they will use in their final speech. Address these arguments now so that they hold less weight when your opponent mentions them. Predicting and responding to an argument before the opponent brings it up is called **preempting** an argument.

5. Close by asking the judge to vote for you.

Representing the negative side of a resolution can be a difficult task. Following the guidelines and advice in this chapter will help you to improve your skills. Don't get frustrated if you lose your first few debates. With each speech you give, you will learn from your experiences and your skills will improve. Just remember that, by participating in these debates, you are learning critical thinking and organizational skills that you will be able to use in school and in life.

As you engaged in debate, you may have looked for sources to help you support your argument. While you may have had statistics and other factual material, you perhaps also wanted to use sayings and insights from famous thinkers. Reading the lives and works of great philosophers can help you do this.

Think Critically

1. What are the purposes of the negative constructive rebuttal?

2. How should you choose the contentions for your case?

3. Explain what a line-by-line presentation is and why it should be used.

4. In the sample negative constructive speech, does the debater effectively present all of the necessary parts?

Research NOW!

 5. **TEAMWORK** With a partner, research for tips and techniques for cross-examinations. You may look for tips and techniques as they relate to debates or in any field where cross-examination is used.

6. Think about the skills you've developed as you practice debate. Use the Internet to research careers where your skills will be valued.

Write NOW!

 7. **TEAMWORK** Write a list of at least 10 questions that deal with any topic. In your questions, include some that can be answered with a simple yes or no and a short explanation and others that require a lengthy answer. Then, trade questions with a partner. On your partner's list, indicate whether you think the questions would work well during a cross-examination. Discuss your opinions with your partner to see if you agree or disagree.

8. Pre-write one or two questions that you might use in the negative cross-examination period on the death penalty resolution. Then reread the sample contention in the previous lesson (page 78). Write one cross-examination question in response to this contention.

Speak NOW!

9. Consider the following resolution.

   Resolved: The minimum driving age should be raised to 18.

   The affirmative's first contention is that teenage drivers are particularly dangerous. Supporting evidence includes a study that shows that teens can be fearless and thrill seeking; taking risks that older drivers would not take. The affirmative also states that teens are influenced by peer pressure, which makes risky behavior more likely. Using the four steps of refuting, write and present a rebuttal against this contention.

Chapter in Review

3.1 Overview of the Speeches

- A Lincoln-Douglas debate consists of a total of seven separate portions. Both the affirmative and negative make a constructive speech, have a chance to cross-examine their opponent, and present rebuttals.
- Taking notes on a flow sheet allows you to track your arguments and the arguments of your opponent.

3.2 Affirmative Case Construction

- The affirmation constructive speech contains an opening statement that should catch the judge's attention, a body containing arguments and supporting evidence, and a conclusion that summarizes your case and asks the judge to vote for you.
- The affirmative cross-examination period allows the affirmative debater to ask the negative questions about its case.
- The affirmative rebuttals let the affirmative team refute arguments against its case and point out weaknesses of the negative case.

3.3 Negative Case Construction

- The process of preparing the negative case is much like that of preparing the affirmative case. Both sides must understand all of the affirmative and negative arguments. During the negative cross-examination period, the negative team asks questions about the affirmative's case.
- The negative constructive rebuttal allows the negative team to present its pre-written constructive speech and to attack the affirmative's case.
- During the negative rebuttal, the negative must convince the judge that they deserve to win the round.

a. burden of proof
b. contention
c. crystallization
d. dropped point
e. flow sheet
f. flowing
g grace period
h. line-by-line
   presentation
i. preempting
j. preflow
k. rebuttal
l. refute
m. road map
n. signpost
o. voting issue

Develop Your Debating Language

Select the term that best fits the definition. Some terms will not be used.

1. Point not argued in the first rebuttal speech

2. Process of writing your arguments on a flow sheet before a debate begins

3. Obligation to approve what is stated

4. Major arguments in a debate

5. Chart of rows and columns used to take notes about a debate

6. Reply to show fault with your opponent's arguments or value

7. Predicting or responding to an argument before the opponent brings it up

8. To clearly signal with words

9. Method of counter arguing in the order that your opponent presented its arguments

Review Debate Concepts

10. Why does the affirmative side speak first at a debate?

11. How should you determine the order of your arguments in an affirmative constructive speech? Why?

12. Describe the use of a grace period.

13. How does an affirmative construction speech relate to your value of a resolution?

14. During which speech do you present most of your evidence?

15. How is the negative constructive rebuttal similar to the affirmative constructive speech? How is it different?

16. What happens when you don't address one of your opponent's arguments in your first rebuttal?

17. What style of writing should be used on a flow sheet? Why?

18. How can outlining your case help you?

19. Why is the opening statement of a constructive speech important?

20. What are some common practices used for an opening statement?

21. Describe what is meant by a contention.

22. Should you prepare all or any of your cross-examination questions in advance? Explain your answer.

23. How can your flow sheet help you during a rebuttal?

24. What is usually the last thing you should say during your last speech?

25. What are some of the purposes of questions asked during the cross-examination period?

26. How should you act if during a cross-examination your opponent gives a long answer?

27. Should the negative side define the key terms in the resolution?

28. Explain the purpose of a road map.

29. What are the four steps of refuting? Briefly explain each.

30. What is a "no neg" case?

Make Academic Connections

31. **MATHEMATICS**   Research the history of the metric system in the United States. How commonly is it used? Is it likely to become the standard? What are the advantages and disadvantages of the metric system? Are Americans resistant to the system? Write a resolution about whether the metric system should become the standard system in the United States. With a partner, research both sides of the resolution and list contentions for each side.

32. **PROBLEM SOLVING** The United States has often been accused of using more energy than other countries, relative to population. Conduct research to affirm or deny this claim. If you affirm the claim, research further to find some viable solutions to the problem. If you deny the claim, conduct research to discover the reasons why other countries feel this way about the United States.

33. **HISTORY** Choose a war of your choice and research its causes. Could it have been prevented? Should it have been prevented? Were the results of the war worth the lives lost, the damage incurred, and the money spent?

Research NOW!

34. **TEAMWORK** Work with a partner to find a debate topic that affects you directly. Before conducting research, discuss your opinions on the topic. Research the topic, concentrating on the arguments for the side which you disagree with. Did the research allow you to better understand the other point of view?

Write NOW!

35. Consider the following resolution. Pre-write at least three questions that you might ask the affirmative during the cross-examination period.

> **Resolved:** High school students' confidentiality is of greater value than their parents' right to know. Assume that you are representing the negative side.

36. **TEAMWORK** With a small group, reread the sample negative construction speech in Lesson 3.3. Together, write questions for the affirmative cross-examination period and then outline a presentation for the affirmative rebuttal.

Speak NOW!

37. For a debate topic of your choice, write six potential cross-examination questions. Design your questions so that three are good examples and three are poor examples. Present the questions to your class and explain the advantages of the good examples over the bad ones.

38. **TEAMWORK** Partner with another student and choose a topic of debate. Research and prepare your case for a debate. Before you begin the debate, read your resolution and poll your classmates. Ask how many agree with the resolution and how many disagree. Present your entire debate and then poll the class again. Were any students persuaded by your arguments?

eCollection Activity

Lincoln-Douglas debates revolve around a value premise. Among popular values are those of justice, freedom, and societal good. A debate that could be argued on the grounds of any of these values is the debate of gun control. Specifically, strong debates are argued for and against the idea that private ownership of handguns should be banned in the United States.

Currently, gun laws vary by state. Each state has its own laws concerning handgun registration, waiting periods, background checks, possession, and child protection laws. State and federal decisions must consider whether laws violate the Second Amendment's right to gun ownership. A landmark decision in 2008 rejected the District of Columbia's ban on handgun possession, but the debate continues.

Those who favor private ownership of handguns contend that black market handguns, not legally obtained ones, are typically used in crimes. They feel they have a right to own a handgun for protection or other purposes. Those who oppose private ownership of handguns are concerned with the number of crimes committed using handguns and the safety of children in homes with handguns.

To learn more about this debate, access www.cengage.com/school/langarts/debate and click on the link for Chapter 3. Find other facts and arguments for and against the ban of handguns in the United States. Write a resolution and arguments for the affirmative and negative sides of the issue.

4.1

Philosophy

4.2

Fallacies and
Reasoning

CHAPTER 4

Philosophy and Fallacies

Real People | Real Careers

Oprah Winfrey

> *"One of the things I've learned is that the best way to enhance your own life is to contribute to somebody else's."*

Oprah Winfrey has been hugely successful in her life, and her success has enabled her to contribute to the lives of many others. Born to an unwed mother and raised for the first few years of her life by her grandmother, Winfrey had a humble start. Against all odds, she began her broadcasting career for a Nashville radio station while still in high school. By the age of 19, she became the first African-American woman to anchor the news at WTVF-TV. She was also the youngest anchor in the history of the station.

She moved to Baltimore to co-anchor the news and then co-host a talk show. In 1984, she left for Chicago to host WLS-TV's morning talk show. Her success was so great that within a year the show's name was changed, and *The Oprah Winfrey Show* was born. Since then, *The Oprah Winfrey Show* has been rated the top talk show for 23 straight seasons. By 2008, an estimated 42 million U.S. viewers watched the show each week.

Many attribute Oprah's success to her ability to listen attentively, speak passionately, and debate with her guests about key issues. She can pose tough questions and isn't satisfied with easy answers. In 2008, Duke University awarded Oprah with an honorary doctorate. The university's president told a story of how Oprah was nearly fired from her first real job because she could not detach herself from each story. This characteristic would obviously serve her well in her future.

Oprah's talk show is not her only success. She also founded her own production company, cable and radio channels, and a monthly magazine. She has produced and acted in films. Her web site, Oprah.com provides resources for women. It serves as a base for the Oprah Book Club. The club, with about two million members, has become the largest book club in the world.

Oprah has used her success and her access to large audiences to help others. Her compassion and generosity has helped her to achieve her goals of educating and empowering women, children, and families in the United States, South Africa, and around the world. She has donated millions to help promising students who have no money to continue their educations. She has built schools and given food, clothing, school supplies, and more to orphanages. She has contributed over $40 million to the Oprah Winfrey Leadership Academy for Girls in South Africa, which helps girls build skills to become future leaders for their country. Through her show, she raised over $80 million to support Oprah's Angel Network. The network establishes schools, scholarships, women's shelters, and youth centers. She has said, "One of the things I've learned is that the best way to enhance your own life is to contribute to somebody else's."

Think Critically

How do you think Oprah Winfrey defines success?

GOALS

Learn how to support arguments using both pragmatic examples and philosophical reasoning.

Understand the branches of moral philosophy and the characteristics of each.

TERMS

pragmatic example
philosophy
metaethics
divine command theory
moral relativism
egoism
altruism
normative ethics
consequentialist theory
ethical egoism
ethical altruism
utilitarianism
duty theory
categorical imperative
social contract
applied ethics

Do You Agree?

Resolved Laws that protect citizens from themselves are justified.

Affirmative position

Yes, situations can occur when individuals may be unable to make rational decisions regarding their own wellbeing. In these cases, individuals will benefit by having laws in place that will ensure their safety.

Negative position

No, people should always have the final say regarding their life. People who are the victims of Alzheimer's, cancer, or paralyzation as a result of an accident should be able to terminate their lives without government interference.

Supporting Arguments

You've received the following resolution for an upcoming debate.

> **Resolved:** When called upon by one's government, individuals are morally obligated to risk their lives for their country.

Off the top of your head, you can think of several arguments for this statement. Just as important as the arguments themselves, however, is how you defend your arguments.

All arguments in debate must be supported or they will not hold up during the round. One way to support an argument is to give **pragmatic examples** or examples that are practical. Using practical, real-life examples can serve you well in a debate because almost everyone can understand and relate to them. Consider the following resolution.

> **Resolved:** Liberty is more precious than law.

Most people understand what law is and understand the importance of law, but liberty can be interpreted in many ways. Associating the term liberty with a solid, practical example can make the resolution easier to defend. For instance, consider the liberty of freedom of speech. Now compare the specific liberty—freedom of speech—to laws. Many will now see your argument in a new light. Liberty has now been presented in a practical way where people can relate to it personally.

You should not support your arguments using only pragmatic examples. For every practical example for an argument, a counterexample exists. Instead you can use pragmatic examples along with philosophical reasoning to present a strong, solid case.

What Is Philosophy?

Socrates is considered the father of philosophy. Stories describe how the Oracle told him that he was the wisest person in Athens. He did not believe this and decided to question those he considered wiser than himself. He asked for explanations of truth, beauty, and justice, but he learned that no one he asked had time to think about these abstract issues. Their opinions of truth, beauty, and justice were not based on reason.

This led Socrates to begin to look for answers to these questions. Philosophers today do much the same as Socrates did. They ask questions such as: "What is the best form of government?" "What is the basis for moral action?" "What is friendship?" Philosophers often ask question about things that seem to have obvious answers. They question the beliefs and ideas that you may take for granted. For instance, a philosopher may ask, "What is truth?" The meaning may seem obvious to you, but a philosopher will examine many aspects of truth including facts, realism, and conditions of truth.

FYI In 399 BC, Socrates was put on trial for corrupting the youth and for refusing to recognize the gods of the state. He was found guilty and put to death by drinking a cup of hemlock, a poisonous herb.

Philosophy is defined as the investigation of nature, causes, and principles of reality, knowledge, or values based on logical reasoning. It is not based on experience or observation alone. To better understand this definition, think of "nature, causes, or principles of reality, knowledge, or values" as the most basic ideas. Rather than using practical examples (experience and observation) to support these ideas, philosophy uses logical reasoning.

Philosophers throughout time have offered a range of definitions of philosophy such as the

- Love of wisdom

- Search for wisdom

- Critical examination of ideas about yourself and the world

- Search for truth through reasoning

- Inquiry into the most fundamental questions facing human beings

The foundation of philosophy, like that of debate, lies in the art of investigating, examining, or arguing. Philosophers don't just ask questions. First, they try to understand the questions entirely—just as you try to fully understand a resolution. Then they try to answer the questions using reason. You will find that when philosophers answer one question, they are often led to another question.

Purpose of Philosophy

In Lincoln-Douglas debate, your purpose is to convince a judge that your value and arguments support the resolution better than your opponent's. Values and opinions are neither right nor wrong. Likewise in philosophy, few right or wrong answers exist. Instead, arguments are considered either better or worse than others. These arguments, backed by philosophical reasoning and practical examples, can help you support your debate case.

As an individual and as a society, you have certain beliefs that influence the way you live. Philosophy tries to examine your beliefs in hopes of improving your community and yourself. Philosophy also tries to understand fundamental topics by replacing opinions about them with knowledge. You can learn many things from studying philosophy. It can teach you to

- Question common knowledge and accepted wisdoms.

- Formulate new ideas of your own.

- Evaluate your own view as well as the views of others.

- Identify basic assumptions, develop a line of reasoning, recognize steps that lead to a conclusion, and determine if an argument is sound.

- Offer defenses against false statements.

You will find that the knowledge and skills you gain through philosophy will benefit you in debate.

A Guide to Studying Philosophy

As a debater, it is your responsibility to study philosophers' works so you will have a fuller understanding of their philosophies and how they apply today. When reading and studying philosophy, keep the following suggestions in mind.

1. **Read, Reread, and Read Again** Consider the audience for which a philosophical thesis was written. It takes time to get used to each style of writing. Some passages may have to be read several times before they make sense to you, but be patient.

2. **Find the Message** The purpose of the thesis is to present a central idea. Depending on the philosopher, the idea may have a positive or a negative connotation. Look for logical arguments through out the writings that support the main idea.

3. **Apply the Knowledge to Everyday Situations** While much of what you use in debate was written long ago, it can still be applied to your daily life. Look for examples that will help support your findings.

Branches of Moral Philosophy

Many great philosophers have written books discussing various aspects of society. Even though hundreds of years have passed, their ideas hold strong today. Aristotle, Plato, Thomas Hobbes, and Immanuel Kant are just a few of the philosophers studied and used in all types of debate. Their ideas and beliefs have been instrumental in shaping our views.

Much of philosophy used in debates deals with morals and ethics. The field of ethics, also known as moral philosophy, concerns matters of right and wrong behavior. Theories concerning ethics can be broken into three main categories: metaethics, normative ethics, and applied ethics. Although each category has distinct characteristics, they also have some ideas in common. For that reason, the lines between the categories can sometimes blur, allowing some philosophers and their ideas to fall into more than one category.

Metaethics

Metaethics explores two ideas. First, it asks what ethical principles mean. Metaethics tries to define goodness. It tries to determine how you can tell what is good from what is bad. Second, metaethics examines where you get your ethical principles. Are ethics eternal truths that can exist without humans or do ethics exist only because humans have created them? The first view holds that ethics or moral values exist in a spirit-like realm beyond humans. This implies that ethics never change and are universal—that is, they apply to all rational creatures, not just humans.

One theory that supports this approach is known as the **divine command theory**. This view believes that an all-powerful Supreme Being or God wills things and that they become reality. It states that God wills ethics as commands. For instance, God wills the ethic "murder is wrong" and gives moral intuitions to follow this command.

The second view holds that ethics only exist because humans have created them. This theory, called **moral relativism**, states that humans invented moral values. Under this theory, some people believe that certain individuals create their own moral standards. Others believe that morality comes from approval of one's entire society.

What motivates moral or immoral actions?

©SIMONE VAN DEN BERG, 2009/USED UNDER LICENSE FROM SHUTTERSTOCK.COM

Metaethics also tries to determine what motivates you to be moral. Even though you might understand what is right or wrong, why do you act on it? For instance, you may know that stealing is wrong, but what makes you not steal? Answers to these questions may include avoiding punishment, gaining praise, attaining happiness, being dignified, or fitting in with society. Some of these motivators include egoism, altruism, emotion, and reason as described below.

Egoism vs. Altruism Thomas Hobbes, a 17th-century British philosopher, maintained the idea of **egoism**. Egoism explains that your actions are prompted by selfish desires. Even if an action seems to be to be for the good of others, egoism tells you that there is a selfish motive behind it. For example, if a store owner strives to be honest and not cheat customers, it appears that he is doing so for the benefit of others. Egoism will explain that the store owner knows that honesty promotes more business, thus the store owner will act in an honest way to gain business (a selfish interest). Joseph Bulter, an 18th-century British philosopher, agreed that some actions are brought on by self interest. However, he also argued that other actions are prompted to show benevolence, or kindness, to others. This view of the instinct to show kindness towards other is called **altruism**.

Emotion vs. Reason   Other philosophers contend that moral ethics are based on emotion or reason. David Hume, another 18th-century British philosopher, argued that morals involve your emotions, not your power to reason. He states that you may have reasons that you agree with something, but reasons alone do not constitute a moral assessment. You must have an emotional reaction to make a moral decision of right or wrong. For instance, you may be able to list reasons why genetic engineering is right or wrong. However, until you express a personal emotion about the issue, you are not making a moral argument. On the other hand, Immanuel Kant disagreed with Hume. Kant, an 18th-century German philosopher, argued that moral assessments are the acts of reason, not emotions. Although emotions can affect your actions, you should resist their effects.

©GEK, 2009/USED UNDER LICENSE FROM SHUTTERSTOCK.COM

What is a moral argument for or against genetic engineering?

Normative Ethics

While metaethics looks at what moral principles mean and where you get these principles, **normative ethics** looks for *moral standards* that tell you what is right and wrong behavior. It examines how you ought to act, morally speaking. The main theories in normative ethics tend to fall into three categories: consequentialist theories, duty theories, and virtue theories.

Consequentialist theories contend that the result of an outcome determines the morality of an act. In other words, an action is morally correct if the favorable consequences of the action outweigh the unfavorable consequences. As shown in the table on the next page, three subgroups exist: **ethical egoism**, **ethical altruism**, and **utilitarianism**. Each differs by the person or group who is affected by the outcome of an action.

Theory	Premise	Example
Ethical egoism	An action is morally right if its consequences are more favorable than unfavorable *only to the person performing the action.*	A person sneaking into the front of a ticket line so that he is not late for a movie
Ethical altruism	An action is morally right if its consequences are more favorable than unfavorable *to everyone except the person performing the action.*	A soldier jumping on a grenade, sacrificing his life to save the rest of his unit
Utilitarianism	An action is morally right if its consequences are more favorable than unfavorable *to everyone.*	Setting speed limits to help ensure safety of all drivers

Utilitarianism is an especially important theme in many debates. Utilitarianism is a common value premise defined in Lincoln-Douglas debates. Utilitarianism refers to the concept that standard morality is determined by its usefulness. Jeremy Bentham was one of the first to introduce this concept. He believed that moral acts were decided by which ones gave the most pleasure and the least amount of pain. The question "What is the greatest good for the greatest number?" became the way to measure usefulness.

After reading Bentham's works, John Stuart Mill embraced his philosophy. While Bentham talked about the act, Mill refined the idea as a rule. Mill believed that an act should be considered morally right depending on the effect it has on all of the people involved. This would illustrate the greatest good for the greatest number. In his short work entitled *Utilitarianism*, John Stuart Mill wrote that right actions are those actions that create the greatest happiness for the greatest number of people.

Lawmakers use this same process when passing legislation. They must ask who will benefit from these laws. Do the benefits outweigh any possible negative effects? Because utilitarianism is used in everyday decision making, it is a philosophy that can be easily endorsed in debates.

Critics have brought up areas of concern when using utilitarianism. Utilitarianism should be used as an "end to justify the means." Who decides which end or action is right or moral? Hitler believed that he could create the perfect race. The means, or actions, he used to try to achieve it was the Holocaust. If you apply "the end to justify the means" concept, Hitler would be able to justify the Holocaust. The Holocaust was needed to achieve his end of "the perfect race." Clearly, Hitler's actions were neither right nor moral. In this case, the means did not justify the end.

Another area of concern with utilitarianism is protecting the rights of minorities. If the greatest good for the greatest number is the goal, where is the consideration for those left out? Inevitably, a group of people will not benefit. Who has the right to make that decision? For instance, if utilitarianism was used in the 1960s, would African Americans have won the right to vote?

Duty Theories

Also known as deontological, **duty theories** argue that that morality is based on basic duties or obligations and other's rights. For instance, if you adopt a dog, you probably feel that you have a duty to take care of the dog, even if taking care of it will cost you time and money. One theory, presented by Samuel Pufendorf, describes to whom you owe duties. The main categories are

1. **Duties to God**   Includes believing in the existence of God and worshipping God

2. **Duties to oneself**   Includes duties to take care of your soul and body

3. **Duties to others**   Includes avoiding wronging others, treating people as equals, and promoting the good of others

John Locke, a British philosopher, developed a duty theory that discussed rights of people. He argued that according to the laws of nature, one should not harm anyone else's natural rights. The natural rights, given by God, include the right to life, health, liberty, and possessions.

Immanuel Kant developed another rights theory called the **categorical imperative**. He argued that moral requirements are based on a standard of rationality. One rationally chooses the good and, therefore, one's choice is good for others as well. The categorical imperative is another look at the ends justifying the means. Immanuel Kant believed that people should not use others as a means to achieve an end because humans hold moral worth. Human dignity is violated when you use someone as a means. As was illustrated with the example of Hitler and the Holocaust, human dignity was violated, making the ends immoral.

Consider playing a sport to win. Some use rough play without much regard to the safety of other players to their advantage. Does the end result always justify the means?

Kant believed that by applying an action to everyone, a determination could be made as to whether the act was acceptable. Consider the example of speeding. If people were allowed to drive as fast as they wanted, there would be extremely dangerous situation on streets. By having speed limits, you can expect streets to be safe. When applying this law to everybody, the greatest number is protected. Because people value life, they will follow the driving guidelines. By using Kant's model, decisions can be made that will be in the best interest of society.

Another popular duty theory that was first expressed by Thomas Hobbes involves the idea of **social contract**. In early times, people existed in a "state of nature," where no rules governed them. In order to protect themselves from chaos, people started to band together as a society. A social contract is a real or hypothesized agreement between a citizen and his or her society. It considers the rights and responsibilities of each. Citizens give up some of their freedoms that they would have in the state of nature in order to receive the protection that a society offers.

The idea of social contract is popular in debating. When used in debate, the idea of society covers a broad range. Society may refer to an entire nation or a small group that one joins. For instance, you have entered a social contract by attending your school. You have certain obligations, such as to attend classes regularly and to comply with its rules. The society, in return, provides you with benefits such as providing a safe environment for learning and qualified instructors. This is just one of many social contracts that you have entered.

The social contract between the government and society works much the same way. You agree to give up some of your liberties and, in return, the government ensures us certain protections. Unlike the state of nature, the social contract provides agencies to protect people and to punish those who break the laws.

In debate, social contracts are used to determine how people should act. It is used to verify their rights and duties to society as well as the rights and duties of the society itself.

What other social contracts have you entered?

Virtue Theories

Instead of concentrating on learning rules or consequences that define moral conduct, virtue theories examine good habits of character that you should acquire. Aristotle and Plato are considered the founding fathers of virtue ethics. Plato emphasized the virtues of wisdom, courage, temperance, and justice. Aristotle contended that virtues are good habits that you acquire, but virtues fall inside the range of two vices. For instance, the virtue of courage falls between the extreme of too little courage (cowardice) and too much courage (rashness). The extremes are vices. Other examples of virtues include the following.

Action or Emotion	Vice (too little)	Virtue	Vice (too much)
seeking pleasure	insensibility	moderation	self indulgence
giving money	stinginess	generosity	prodigality
sense of worth	insecurity	self respect	arrogance

Applied Ethics

Applied ethics deals with controversial issues specific to a certain area of study, such as animal rights, environmental concerns, or nuclear war. In order to be considered an applied ethical issue, an issue must be

1. Controversial

2. A moral issue

Many issues can be moral issues but not controversial. Most agree that killing another person is immoral. This is a moral issue but not controversial. Other issues may be controversial but not moral. Current events sometimes fall under this category. For instance, a new tax plan presented by the government may be considered controversial, but it is likely not immoral.

Some examples of categories and specific issues are given below.

Bioethics Medical experimentation on humans Physician-assisted suicide Surrogate mothers Genetic engineering Using frozen embryos	**Business Ethics** Balance of work and home life Deceptive advertising Monitoring employees Drug testing in the workplace
Social Ethics Capital punishment Gun control Welfare	**Environmental Ethics** Preserving endangered species Pollution control Continued production of gasoline-powered vehicles

Both philosophical and pragmatic arguments are useful tools in debate. Read works by the philosophers. Become comfortable with their ideas. Incorporate them into your cases. Most of all, enjoy the world of philosophy.

TURNING POINT

Blogs

PHOTODISC/GETTY IMAGES

The term blog is a contraction of web and log. A blog is a website where an individual posts, or announces in writing, various types of information. Some who maintain personal websites might post everyday events of their lives in a log, like an online diary. This type of blog helps the blogger to keep in touch with friends and family members. Other blogs are posted by individuals that are interested in a particular topic. For example, a local news website might have a columnist or editor write a weekly blog about events and issues in its community.

Whether a blog is for personal or professional use, most are updated on a regular basis. The author adds new entries over time, and the entries are usually displayed with the newest entries at the top of the page and the oldest entries at the bottom. Also, most blogs allow readers to comment on the posts. Readers can post their own ideas and responses. Everyone who can see the original blog can also see all of the comments added by readers. The original blogger can then respond to comments. In a sense, a blog allows for an online conversation. Bloggers are not limited to expressing themselves with words. They can post pictures, videos, music and other audios, and links to other websites. As you read blogs, you should remember that they contain both facts and opinions.

Blogs have the advantage of reporting events as they are happening. In 2002, a blogger relayed a comment made by then Senate Majority Leader Trent Lott at a dinner in honor of Senator Strom Thurmond. Lott made the comment that the country would have been better off had Thurmond been successful in his run for the presidency in 1948. Many saw this comment as a subtle approval of segregation, a position held by Senator Thurmond during his campaign. While the comment was made at a public event that was covered by the media, Lott's comment received no coverage in mainstream news publications or programs. The comment spread among bloggers however, and the resulting furor over Lott's comments forced him to resign his position as Senate Majority leader.

Blogs have created a new forum for debate. You can find blogs that cover almost any area of debate, but in recent years political blogs that deal with presidential debates have increased in popularity. Now, many news websites post regular political blogs about presidential debates. Some even have live blogs, which allow narrators and viewers to comment on presidential debates in real time, as they are being shown on television.

Think Critically

Bloggers post both serious and sarcastic remarks. They often focus on the issues themselves but may also respond to points made by other bloggers. What type of behavior do you think is ethical or unethical while blogging?

Think Critically

1. How does reasoning with pragmatic examples differ from reasoning with philosophy?

2. What is the main idea behind utilitarianism?

3. How can the idea of a social contract be used in a debate?

Research NOW!

4. **TEAMWORK** With a partner, research the works for one of the philosophers mentioned in this lesson. Try to find some of the original text from the works. Is the language difficult to understand? Read it again and discuss your interpretations.

5. Research both sides of an applied ethic issue. You may use an example from this lesson or one of your own. Who does this issue affect? Why is the issue important?

Write NOW!

6. **TEAMWORK** With a partner, come up with an example of a social contract. Write a few paragraphs about who is a member of the group and what defines the "society" involved in that contract. Specify what duties, freedoms, and protections are expected, achieved, or lost as a result of the social contract.

7. Research the works of a philosopher not mentioned in this lesson. Read and reread the material. Write a report explains the author's writing style, the main idea of the work, and how you might apply the knowledge to everyday situations.

Speak NOW!

8. Think of a new example of ethical egoism, ethical altruism, and utilitarianism. Present your ideas in class and explain how each of your examples fits each category. Hold a class discussion about how each classmate's examples fit into categories. Do examples ever overlap categories?

9. **TEAMWORK** With a partner, think of a debate topic that can be argued using Immanuel Kant's theory of categorical imperative. To help you decide on an issue, think of whether the end justifies the means. Write a resolution, research your issue, and hold a debate in class with your partner.

Do You Agree?

Resolved The American media works against the best interest of the American Public.

Affirmative position

Yes, the American media has shown itself to be biased and have an effect on the opinions of the American public. They are in a position to influence the American public with their reports and coverage of events. In the 2008 presidential campaign, certain media were accused of using their coverage of campaigns to favor one candidate over another. It is possible that alleged slanted views would unduly influence voters.

Negative position

No, the American media has always been a vital force in informing the public. From the September 11 tragedy to the daily coverage in Iraq, Iran, and Afghanistan, the media has kept the public informed. The truth about the Watergate break-in and its long reaching effects were uncovered and reported by Carl Bernstein and Bob Woodward, two members of the media. The American media ensures that we are informed and assists in the checks and balances of our government's actions.

Logical Reasoning

You are participating in a debate about whether current music has adverse effects on teenagers. Your opponent supports one of his arguments by stating, "New music is clearly corrupting the youth of America. Music lyrics talk about kids killing police and taking drugs. It encourages teens to do these illegal things."

Your argument asserts that lyrics are written about these topics because that is what is happening in some places. The artists are not encouraging the actions but are writing about what is going on in society. You might argue that the reasoning used by your opponent is not logical. You can argue that his effect (violent behavior) is not a result of the cause (lyrics).

During a debate, one of the methods used to present and support your arguments is logical reasoning. **Logical reasoning** can be defined as statements that have been formed from sound thinking and proof of reasoning. Logical reasoning can be an explanation or a justification for a position made while debating. Review the following statements.

- A history test will be given tomorrow.

- Studying for the test will usually result in a higher grade.

- Most students who study for the test will do better than the students who do not study for the test.

It stands to reason that putting time and effort into understanding and comprehending information will help a student get a better grade on the test. It also makes sense to say that studying for the test will result in a benefit that will yield recognizable results. These statements are valid because you arrived at the conclusion through sound thinking and reasoning. Now, consider the following statements.

- A history test will be given tomorrow.

- Studying for the test will result in a higher grade.

- All students who study for the test will do better than the students who do not study for the test.

By slightly altering the statements, the meaning has changed. The logic of the statements has also changed. In the second statement, the omission of "usually" implies that studying will always make the difference. There are uncontrollable variables that you must consider when evaluating the reliability of the statement. How much time does each student spend studying? What material was studied? Was the studying done in a controlled environment? These are all important areas that should be considered.

The third statement has changed as well. Changing the word "most" to "all" implies that every student who studies will do better on the test than

Studying will usually improve performance on a test, but what other factors need to be considered?

every student who did not study. Some students may have paid more attention during class and not needed study time. Some students might have an easier time with test taking than others regardless of the amount of time devoted to studying. For these reasons, as well as other problems you might think of, some non-studying students may perform better than some studying students. This second set of statements is an example of illogical or flawed reasoning.

Inductive and Deductive Arguments

The main types of arguments are inductive arguments and deductive arguments. **Inductive arguments** give specific facts that lead to a conclusion or generalization. Look at this example of inductive reasoning.

* The weather this summer has been very warm.
* Strawberries grow very well in warm weather.
* This summer will be very good for strawberry picking.

Even though other factors are important, it is safe to say that the warm weather will have a positive effect on strawberries.

Deductive arguments differ when it comes to the conclusion. **Deductive arguments** begin with a general rule that is accepted as truth. From that rule, it makes a conclusion about something specific.

* Every student in debate class will argue both sides of the resolution.
* Maria is in debate class.
* Therefore, Maria will argue both sides of the resolution.

This argument begins with a general rule. From that rule it makes a conclusion about a specific student.

Arguments based on observations or experiences are usually expressed as inductive reasoning. Arguments based on laws, rules, or accepted principles are usually expressed as deductive reasoning. Often, you can express the same argument using either method as shown below.

Inductive Reasoning	Deductive Reasoning
a. On Monday, I threw a tennis ball into the air and it came back down.	**a.** The law of gravity tells me that everything that goes up will come back down.
b. On Tuesday, I threw a tennis ball into the air and it came back down.	**b.** If I throw this tennis ball into the air today, it will come back down.
c. If I throw this tennis ball into the air today, it will come back down.	

In order for reasoning to draw a correct conclusion, logic must be followed. If you state one or more true statements, they must justify the conclusion for the argument to be valid. Consider the following example.

- Mrs. Jones is considered to be a great cook.

- Mrs. Jones has a son.

- Mrs. Jones's son will also be a great cook.

The problem with the reasoning is obvious. Because Mrs. Jones is a great cook does not mean that her children will excel at cooking. It is true that Mrs. Jones is a great cook. It is true that Mrs. Jones has a son. Neither of these reasons, together or alone, is enough to support the conclusion.

Parts of an Argument

An argument contains three parts. They include the premise, the inference, and the conclusion. All arguments begin with a premise. The **premise** is the statement that sets up the argument. Premises are statements of fact (or assumed fact) that give reasons for believing the conclusion. The **inference** is a statement concluded from the premise(s). The **conclusion** is the final position agreed upon at the end of the argument. The conclusion is the final inference.

Sound arguments have valid areas of support and will help to reach the desired conclusion. Consider the following argument.

1. Lawyers earn a lot of money. (premise)

2. With a lot of money, a person can buy a nice home. (premise)

3. Lawyers can buy nice homes. (inference from 1 and 2)

4. I want to buy a nice home. (premise)

5. I should become a lawyer. (conclusion from 3 and 4)

How can advance research help you identify fallacies?

Inferences that are misleading are not considered to be sound. This type of information is associated with fallacies.

1. Baseball is the number one sport in America. (premise)

2. More people play baseball than any other sport. (inference)

3. Everyone in America loves baseball. (conclusion)

You cannot arrive at the conclusion that has been reached based on the information that has been provided. The inference made in statement number 2 does not follow logical reasoning. Therefore, the argument is not sound.

Recognizing Fallacies

A **fallacy** can be either a false statement or idea or an argument that is based on unclear or erroneous reasoning. Fallacies can affect the way the judge interprets arguments in a debate. As a debater, you are responsible for recognizing your opponent's fallacies and pointing them out. Once you identify your opponent's fallacy, you must be able to explain the problem with it. If you thoroughly research both sides of a resolution, you'll probably already have a very good idea of what your opponent's arguments will be. Using this information, think in advance about the reasoning your opponent is likely to use. From there, think about which fallacies your opponent could easily make. Then, listen closely to the constructive speech. Note any fallacies on your flow sheet so that you don't forget to expose them in your constructive speech (if you represent the negative) or in your rebuttal.

As a responsible debater, you should also avoid using fallacies in your own speeches. Although some less ethical debaters purposely use fallacies to deceive their opponent or the judge, you should not do so. If you use a fallacy, your opponent has the opportunity to discredit your argument and possibly your case. Evaluate your statements and your reasoning to make sure they accurately support your ideas. The addition or the removal of a single word can greatly change the meaning of a statement. Using fallacies can affect your credibility as a debater. Once you use a fallacy, a judge may be less likely to accept your position on a resolution. You will waste time defending the truthfulness and accuracy of the statements you have made.

Examples of Fallacies

The following examples of fallacies illustrate some of the most common ones you will encounter in debate. Familiarize yourself with fallacies so that you can better recognize flaws in arguments. Once you are able to discern which arguments are flawed, it will be easier for you to attack them.

Ad Hominem   Ad Hominem is Latin for "against the man." Rather than attacking an argument, this type of fallacy attacks the person speaking. During a round, your opponent says, "Judge, my opponent is only 14 years old. He doesn't know what he is talking about." Instead of attacking the case, the debater is attacking a trait or characteristic of his opponent. Do not make a debate personal no matter how strongly you feel about the topic. Instead, stick to the issues. Not only is this type of mistake pointless, but you also risk losing respect of the judge.

Appeal to Authority   An appeal to authority is questioning that a person is qualified to make a statement or is an authority in a particular area. For this reason, you should give an authority's qualifications when reading your evidence. Consider this statement: "Dr. Smith states that we will see an increase in flu cases this year." The statement does not tell us why Dr. Smith is qualified to make the prediction. She could be a doctor of psychology, which would not qualify her as an authority in the field of internal medicine.

YOU BE THE JUDGE

Most people agree that good sportsmanship is important, not only in sports, but in any type of contest. Debate is no exception. Ad Hominem is one fallacy that can be thought of as unsportsmanlike conduct. It is an obvious attempt to discredit another person. Unfortunately it is used in debate, even in professional politics.

An example of Ad Hominem was shown during the 1988 Vice Presidential debate between Senator Lloyd Bentsen and Senator Dan Quayle. Throughout the campaign, Senator Quayle had been criticized for his young age (41), limited service in the Senate, poor grades in college, and alleged attempts to avoid military service. A member of the panel asked Senator Quayle about his plan if he were to become president. Part of Quayle's answer included the following.

"I will be prepared not only because of my service in the Congress, but because of my ability to communicate and to lead. It is not just age; it's accomplishments, it's experience. I have far more experience than many others that sought the office of vice president of this country. I have as much experience in the Congress as Jack Kennedy did when he sought the presidency."

When Senator Bentsen was asked to respond, he did so as follows.

"Senator, I served with Jack Kennedy. I knew Jack Kennedy. Jack Kennedy was a friend of mine. Senator, you are no Jack Kennedy."

Senator Bentsen committed a fallacy with this statement. He implied that while Jack Kennedy was a great man, Dan Quayle was not. The audience and panel of questioners reacted with surprise and some with applause. A few moments later, Senator Quayle responded, "That was really uncalled for, Senator," evoking a similar reaction from the audience and panel.

This personal attack has become somewhat of a legacy in politics. The phrase "You are no Jack Kennedy" is now used to deflate people who think too highly of themselves.

What Would You Do?

During a rebuttal, your opponent launches a personal attack on you. Should you respond by denying the attack? Should you attack your opponent in a like manner? Or should you do as Senator Quayle did, simply stating that the comment was not appropriate?

Appeal to Tradition   This fallacy argues that because something has been done a certain way for a very long time, it should continue in the same manner. The Electoral College could be used as an example for this type of argument. Assume you opponent makes the statement, "The Electoral College has always been a part of our voting process, helping to decide who will be elected the president of our country. It is a part of our history. It should not be changed." Recent presidential elections, however, have shown that there are flaws in the system. Because something has been done the same way for a very long time does not mean that it is best.

Begging the Question   Begging the question is also known as circular reasoning. It occurs when conclusion of the argument is presented as a premise of the argument. Good reasoning should start with a statement and end with a different statement (a conclusion). The statement, "It makes no sense to deny evolution; it is a well-established fact of nature" begs the question. The truth of the status of evolution is the exact question of the issue, yet it is used as a premise.

Bifurcation   Bifurcation is also known as the Black or White argument. This type of argument gives an "either or" premise with no options between the two extremes. It states that you are either for something or you must be against it. Topics are just not that clear. The death penalty, for example, is a topic where different factors might be considered. Before deciding whether the death penalty should be sought, judges or juries usually consider the type of the crime committed, whether the accused is a repeat offender, or the age of the victim or criminal. If your opponent says that you are either for the death penalty or you are against it, he might be guilty of presenting a bifurcation argument.

Confusing Cause and Effect   Confusing cause and effect is also known as questionable cause and fake cause. This fallacy incorrectly assumes that one thing is the result of something else. Two things can happen together, but it does not necessarily mean that one caused the other. For instance, your opponent may state that cold weather causes illness. This statement is a case

What is the difference between a real cause and effect relationship and the fallacy of confusing cause and effect?

of confusing cause and effect. Although illnesses often are more prominent during cold weather months, cold weather does not actually cause illness. Bacteria and viruses cause illness. In a debate, you must show proof of cause and effect to use it as reasoning without committing a fallacy.

Composition   The fallacy of composition concludes with no justification that a property or characteristic of a part is also shared by the whole. For instance, one might argue the following: "Every player on our soccer team is an excellent player, so this team will be an excellent team." This argument offers no justification or proof of its truth. Even though the individual players are excellent, they may not work well together as a team.

Dicto Simpliciter   In common language, this fallacy is called stereotyping or sweeping generalization. It is often found when debating with moral and legal issues. It occurs when a general rule is incorrectly applied to a specific topic. The argument "Boys like football. You are a boy. You must like football." falls into this category. Genetics have nothing to do in deciding who is going to like sporting events.

FYI   Many fallacies have Latin names that portray their classical origins. For instance, dicto simpliciter translates to "from a maxim without qualification" or "from a universal rule." Non Sequitur translates to "it does not follow."

Hasty Generalizations   Hasty generalization is drawing a conclusion when there is not enough evidence to support it. It is also called jumping to conclusions. An example follows. "John has had five tennis lessons. John has not won a match yet. John will never be a good tennis player." Obviously, five lessons are not enough to be able to determine whether John will be successful as a tennis player. There simply is not enough evidence to support this conclusion.

Non Sequitur   When one line of reasoning does not follow another, it is a non sequitur. A conclusion of a non sequitur fallacy is supported by only extremely weak or irrelevant reasons. Consider the following example. "Nuclear disarmament is a risk, but everything in life involves a risk. Every time you drive in a car you are taking a risk. If you're willing to drive in a car, you should be willing to have disarmament." This line of reasoning is inappropriate because the two risks referred to do not equate.

Poisoning the Well   Poisoning the well is a preemptive attempt to discredit a person by making claims, which may be true or false, against him. The purpose of poisoning the well is to get people to reject anything said by the person before he or she has a chance to speak. If your opponent tries to discredit your source by saying, "Mr. Jones has taken part in several protest marches. He clearly has shown disregard for the law." then your opponent is committing this fallacy. Mr. Jones could have taken part in organized, legal marches, but he has now been portrayed as a rebel.

Post Hoc ergo Proctor Hoc   This comes from the Latin "After this, therefore because of this" and is also referred to as post hoc. When something happens before an event and is then assumed to be the cause of the event, it is considered to be post hoc. For instance, Jessie is in a batting slump. Her sister, Ashley, gives her a lucky penny to put in her shoe. Jessie's batting immediately improves. While the penny seemed to be "lucky," it had no effect on her batting skills. A penny does not have that power. To associate the penny with the improved batting would be to use a post hoc argument.

Red Herring When information is introduced during an argument that is irrelevant to what is being said, it is called a red herring. Its sole purpose is to distract attention from the real points. Consider this example: "It is true that a college education is important in today's work force, but look at the struggle women have had for years. How long did it take to get the right to vote? How long will it be before women are paid the same amount of money as men for the same job?" The discussion of the value of an education has now been derailed. While the other areas are certainly important, they do not have anything to do with the value of an education. The statements were thrown in to distract the judge from the real issue.

Slippery Slope This fallacy assumes that because one event has happened another event is inevitable. Usually, the steps that would be necessary to achieve a connection are eliminated. Consider this example. "The legal drinking age should not be lowered to 18. Before you know it, our jails will be full of young people." No proof is offered that the lowering of the legal drinking age would result in more crime. Nor are there intermediate steps that could lead from the first statement to the conclusion.

Straw Man This fallacy occurs when a position that has been presented is ignored. Instead, an inaccurate version of what has been said is introduced and attacked.

Person A President Smith said that young people should volunteer for public service in their community.

Person B I am working and going to school. Who will pay for my education if I am forced to do public service?

Person A's position has been distorted. Public service has been changed from volunteer service to mandatory service. This naturally changes the direction of the entire debate.

Many other fallacies are used besides the ones that have been introduced here. You will become a better debater if you can recognize the "traps" set for you by your opponent. Remember that it is just as important to eliminate fallacies from your arguments. Be sure to present and address issues without distorting them.

Logical fallacies even find their way into everyday conversation. "Love Is a Fallacy," a short story by Max Shulman in the book *The Many Loves* of *Dobie Gillis*, illustrates the problems one can get into when using fallacies as arguments. The story has been used to teach fallacies for years. A male college student narrates the story. He thinks of himself as highly intelligent—much more so than his roommate, Petey. In the story, he trades his father's raccoon coat to Petey in exchange for a chance to date Petey's girlfriend, Polly. During their dates, the narrator teaches Polly about logic fallacies. She happily accepts the conversations. One of their conversations is described as follows.

"What are we going to talk about?" she asked.

"Logic."

She thought this over for a minute and decided she liked it. "Magnif," she said.

"Logic," I said, clearing my throat, "is the science of thinking. Before we can think correctly, we must first learn to recognize the common fallacies of logic. These we will take up tonight."

"Wow-dow!" she cried, clapping her hands delightedly.

I winced, but went bravely on. "First let us examine the fallacy called Dicto Simpliciter."

"By all means," she urged, batting her lashes eagerly.

"Dicto Simpliciter means an argument based on an unqualified generalization. For example: Exercise is good. Therefore everybody should exercise."

"I agree," said Polly earnestly. "I mean exercise is wonderful. I mean it builds the body and everything."

"Polly," I said gently, "the argument is a fallacy. Exercise is good is an unqualified generalization. For instance, if you have heart disease, exercise is bad, not good. Many people are ordered by their doctors not to exercise. You must qualify the generalization. You must say exercise is usually good, or exercise is good for most people. Otherwise you have committed a Dicto Simpliciter. Do you see?"

"No," she confessed. "But this is marvy. Do more! Do more!"

Armed with these examples of fallacies combined with the material you learned in this lesson, you should now be able to support your debate arguments with more expertise.

What are some frequently used logical fallacies?

Think Critically

1. How can a slight change in a statement affect the logic of a statement?

2. What is the difference between inductive and deductive reasoning?

3. Why should you avoid using fallacies in your debate arguments?

Research NOW!

4. **TEAMWORK** Find the entire story "Love Is a Fallacy" in the book *The Many Loves of Dobie Gillis* by Max Shulman. Read the story and identify the fallacies used that you have not learned about. From the context clues in the story, discuss with your partner what you think the fallacies mean. Then research the fallacies to see if you were right. If you had previously read this story and understand all of the fallacies in it, conduct research to identify and explain at least two fallacies with which you are not familiar.

5. Entire courses are dedicated to the basics of reasoning with logic. Search the internet for college courses in logic. Specifically look for course descriptions and syllabuses. What kinds of topics are covered in these classes?

Write NOW!

6. **TEAMWORK** Each partner should choose a fallacy described in this lesson. Do not share your choice with your partner. Write a series of statements using an error described in the fallacy you chose. Trade statements with your partner and see if he or she can figure out which fallacy is committed. Discuss your answers and if time allows, repeat the activity.

7. Consider the resolution below. Write at least one affirmative or negative argument and support it with valid inductive or deductive reasoning.

Resolved: Smoking should be banned in public places nationwide.

Speak NOW!

8. Choose a debate issue in which you are interested. Using logical reasoning, prepare a statement that contains at least two premises, one inference, and a conclusion. Present your work to your class, identifying and explaining each statement as a premise, inference, or conclusion.

9. **TEAMWORK** With a small group, prepare and present a short skit that includes one or more fallacies. You may use the "Love Is a Fallacy" story as an example, although your skit does not have to be as long as the entire story. You may have a narrator and two or more acting characters. The skit may be serious or humorous.

Chapter in Review

4.1 Philosophy

- Arguments should be supported by pragmatic examples of observation and experience as well as the logical reasoning of philosophy. Philosophy questions common beliefs and ideas that we take for granted.
- Metaethics investigates what ethical principles mean and where you get them. Normative ethics examines how you ought to act, morally speaking. Applied ethics deals with controversial and moral topics in various fields.

4.2 Fallacies and Reasoning

- Logical reasoning, including deductive and inductive reasoning, uses sound thinking and proof of reasoning to justify statements.
- Fallacies result from untrue ideas and illogical reasoning. Debaters should recognize and point out fallacies in an opponent's arguments and avoid using fallacies in their own arguments.

Develop Your Debating Language

a. altruism
b. applied ethics
c. categorical imperative
d. conclusion
e. consequentialist theory
f. deductive argument
g. divine command theory
h. duty theory
i. egoism
j. ethical altruism
k. ethical egoism
l. fallacy
m. inductive argument
n. inference
o. logical reasoning
p. metaethics
q. moral relativism
r. normative ethics
s. philosophy
t. pragmatic example
u. premise
v. social contract
w. utilitarianism

Select the term that best fits the definition. Some terms will not be used.

1. Statement that is concluded by one or more premises

2. Belief that actions are caused by selfish desires

3. Investigation of basic ideas based on logical reasoning

4. Statement that sets up an argument

5. Agreement between a person and his society

6. Branch of ethics that examines what ethical principles mean and where they come from

7. Specific arguments that lead to a conclusion

8. Belief that things become reality because an all-powerful God wills them

9. Statements formed from sound thinking and proof of reasoning

10. Belief of the human instinct to be kind to others

11. Practical examples of observation and experience

12. Final position of an argument

13. Belief that ethics exist only because humans created them

14. Belief that morality is based on basic obligations and others' rights

15. Statements that start with a general rule that leads to a specific conclusion

16. Branch of ethics that examines how you should act morally

17. Kant's standard of morality

18. False statement or an argument that is based on poor reasoning

Review Debate Concepts

19. Name two purposes of philosophy.

20. How can you obtain a fuller understanding of writings of philosophy?

21. How is moral philosophy used in debate?

22. What are the similarities and differences between egoism and altruism?

23. How does David Hume think we achieve our moral ethics?

24. Compare and contrast consequentialist and duty theories.

25. How did Aristotle view virtues?

26. Under what branch of ethics does the issue of whether a family should be able to remove life support from a family member fall? Explain your answer.

27. What are the similarities and differences between an inference and a conclusion of an argument?

28. How might advance research help you identify fallacies in your opponent's arguments?

29. Consider the statements: "I met three women from Richmond, Virginia yesterday. They all live in mansions. All people from Richmond must be very wealthy." What type of fallacy is committed? Explain your answer.

30. Consider the statements: "The human body is made up of cells that are invisible. Therefore, the human body must be invisible." What type of fallacy is committed? Explain your answer.

31. Consider the statements: "Every time my hands and wrists hurt, it rains the next day. My pain causes the change in weather." What type of fallacy is committed? Explain your answer.

Make Academic Connections

32. **CHALLENGE**   Many advertisements commit logical fallacies in the claims that they make about their products. Find one and write a short summary of the kinds of logical fallacies you observed.

33. **ETHICS**   Research the pros and cons of using pesticides. With a partner, write a resolution, choose sides, and research arguments. Prepare your case and *purposely* build in at least two fallacies. Present a debate in class. During the debate, try to identify and argue your opponent's fallacies.

34. **PROBLEM SOLVING**   Research facts about the problem of music piracy. Write at least one set of statements about a solution or argument using inductive reasoning. Write a second set of statements using deductive reasoning.

35. **HISTORY**   Find a historical debate or issue that uses the concept of utilitarianism. Describe the issue and give your opinion of whether utilitarianism was the best measure of deciding whether or not a moral decision was made.

Research NOW!

36. Research to find detailed information on John Locke. Use the Internet, library resources, and other sources to look beyond the discussion of him in this chapter. Look for his writings in politics, religion, education, and more.

 37. **TEAMWORK**   Work with a partner to research at least five debate fallacies not discussed in this chapter. Find at least one example of each.

38. Use the Internet and other sources to find at least four definitions of philosophy. How do the definitions compare and contrast? Has the definition of philosophy changed over time?

Write NOW!

39. Make a timeline of well-known philosophers. You may use some or all of the philosophers mentioned in this chapter and you may use others that you've heard of or have learned about during your research. On your timeline, indicate the birth and death of each philosopher. Also include dates of their major accomplishments.

 40. **TEAMWORK**   With a small group, consider the effects of the grading scale used by your school. Among the most popular grading scales are a 10-point scale and a 7-point scale. Grades are determined by percentages as followed:

Grade	10-Point Scale	7-Point Scale
A	90–100	93–100
B	80–89	85–92
C	70–79	76–84
D	60–69	70–75
F	Below 60	Below 70

Using only pragmatic examples (real-life observations and experiences), write three arguments supporting the use of the 10-point grading scale.

41. **TEAMWORK** Using the information from the previous Write NOW! activity, use a combination of pragmatic examples and logical reasoning to support a 10-point grading scale. Discuss with your team members which methods (pragmatic only, logical reasoning only, or a combination of the two) best support your argument.

Speak NOW!

42. **TEAMWORK** With a partner or small group, choose two conflicting moral ethics theories from this chapter and research them further. Find details of each theory as well as solid examples. Act out a debate in support of the one theory as your partner supports the other. For instance, you could argue for the idea of egoism while your partner argues for altruism. As an alternative, your debate could center around Hume's emotion theory versus Kant's reason theory.

eCollection Activity

Many of the debates that you will argue will fall into the category of applied ethics. One current topic of applied ethics deals with how violence shown on television, in video games, and through other media affects the young people who watch it. Some argue that watching violence makes America's youth think that violence is okay. Does watching violence on television and video games encourage youth to act violently?

To learn more about this debate, access www.cengage.com/school/langarts/debate and click on the link for Chapter 4. Find facts and arguments about restricting exposure to violence through video games, television, and other media.

CHAPTER 5

Cross-Examination Debate:
The Affirmative Case

Famous Debaters

> " *An interest in politics helped Ervin become one of the nation's top high school debaters.* "

Clark Kent Ervin

Clark Kent Ervin got his name from his brother, Art, who named him after the mild mannered reporter who turns into Superman. Ervin was born a month premature, and despite overwhelming odds, he survived. The same drive and energy has stayed with Ervin all of his life.

Ervin is the director of the Homeland Security Program at the Aspen Institute. Prior to this appointment, he served as the first inspector general of the United States Department of Homeland Security (DHS) appointed by President George W. Bush. In May of 2006, Ervin wrote *Open Target: Where America Is Vulnerable to Attack*, a book that recounted his time at DHS and expounded his views about America's preparedness for terrorist attacks. In addition to his book, Ervin has written opinion pieces that have appeared in papers such as *The New York Times* and *The Washington Post*.

Ervin practiced private law in Houston, Texas, with two firms prior to his move into politics. For Ervin, the progression from law into politics came naturally. In school, he realized that learning how to debate and developing his speaking skills would be crucial for his law practice. An interest in politics helped Ervin become one of the nation's top high school debaters. "He could talk a dog off a meat truck," stated one of his teammates, Douglas Bacon. Becoming a member of the National Forensic League (NFL) taught Ervin skills that he needed to accomplish his career goals. Training in logic and argument were vital to his success in arguing cases in a court of law.

During his tenure at DHS, Ervin made great efforts to root out mismanagement and security flaws. Ervin wrote critical reports about the problems he discovered at DHS and found himself out of a job in December of 2004. ABC News reported that "Clark Ervin made himself very unpopular by issuing a series of stinging reports on security programs that he said had failed, officials he called inept, and fraud that he suspected."

Ervin also commented on the department's confusion and disarray during the aftermath of Hurricane Katrina in 2005. He felt that if the hurricane were a real-life rehearsal, then the response indicated that the nation was not prepared to deal with a terrorist attack of proximal dimensions. He said, "This is what the department was supposed to be all about. Instead, it obviously raises very serious, troubling questions about whether the government would be prepared if this were a terrorist attack. It's a devastating indictment of this department's performance four years after 9/11."

Think Critically

During Ervin's tenure at DHS, he wrote many expository documents outlining waste and mismanagement. Explain how his debate training might have aided his writing.

Clark Kent Ervin

Do You Agree?

Resolved The United States federal government should substantially increase social services for American citizens living in poverty in the United States.

Affirmative position

Yes, we live in the wealthiest nation in the world and there is no reason why we can't help Americans who are less fortunate. Through no fault of their own, America's elderly and children are often the hardest hit by economic changes and they are victimized by poverty. We should do more for these American citizens.

Negative position

No, I oppose any increase in social services. Our nation was built by those who worked hard and asked for little or no help from anyone. Over the past 50 years, too many individuals have become dependent on assistance and the time has come to reverse this trend. The services that exist now are sufficient and no increases should occur.

Differences between Lincoln-Douglas Debate and Cross-Examination Debate

Joining a debate team offers a variety of opportunities and challenges. For example, you can participate in a Lincoln-Douglas (LD) debate as an individual or you can participate in a cross-examination (CX) debate as part of a two-person team. Perhaps you will discover that you prefer the unique challenges of working with a debate partner more than facing down an opponent on your own. These two debate types have additional differences.

Fundamental Differences

A fundamental characteristic is a feature that defines the essential function of an object or an idea. There are three fundamental differences between an LD debate and a CX debate.

Focus The first fundamental difference between an LD debate and a CX debate is the focus of the debate. The founders of the LD format recognized a need for students to have an opportunity to debate questions of value because many value issues could not be debated under the CX format. An LD debate is often referred to as a *value debate* because the debaters focus on the worth, usefulness, or importance of the resolution. Value issues such as justice, privacy, and individualism are better debated under the LD format. The CX format was not designed to discuss issues of value. Rather, the CX format was created to discuss issues of policy. **Policy** is a specific action, implemented by government or society, which often requires changes in laws, rules, or legislation. Policy issues such as increasing the financial aid the United States sends to another country are better debated under the CX format.

Goal The second fundamental difference between an LD debate and a CX debate is the goal of the debate. The goal of an LD debate is to compare different values by focusing on which side is more or less appropriate under the circumstances without saying who is right or wrong. The LD format focuses on comparing abstract beliefs. In contrast, the CX format discusses concrete specifics. The goal of a CX debate is to propose a solution to a problem.

FYI The CX topic for 2009–2010 was: The United States federal government should substantially increase social services for persons living in poverty in the United States. The LD topic for November–December 2009 was: Public health concerns justify compulsory immunization.

Topic The third fundamental difference between an LD debate and a CX debate is the topic. Most schools debate the national topic in both LD debates and CX debates. The topics for LD debates and CX debates are published by the National Forensic League at www.nflonline.org. The CX debate topic is also published by the National Federation of State High School Associations at www.nfhs.org. All topics are frequently published by your state's debate organization. Starting in September, LD debates use a topic for only two months and then switch to a new topic. In contrast, CX debates use a single topic for the entire school year. The topic for CX debates is published in January of the preceding school year.

Fundamental Differences between LD Debates and CX Debates

	LD Debates	CX Debates
Focus	Debate a value.	Debate a policy.
Goal	Compare values.	Propose solutions.
Topic	Topic changes every two months; first topic starts in September.	Single topic used for a year; topic is announced in January of the preceding school year.

Structural Differences

A structural characteristic is a feature that defines the organization or composition of an object or an idea. There are three structural differences between an LD debate and a CX debate.

Number of Debaters The first structural difference between LD debate and CX debate is the number of debaters. The LD format is structured as one debater debating one debater. The individual debater in an LD debate is responsible for all of the duties required to prepare for and perform in the debate. The CX format is structured as a debate in which two team members debate two members of the opposite team. The two debaters on a CX debate team share the responsibilities for all the duties required to prepare for and perform in the debate.

Type of Arguments   The second structural difference is the type of arguments presented in the debates. The LD format requires that all arguments are value focused. The entire LD debate revolves around value comparison. Many of the LD arguments are abstract and focus on morals, ethics, and societal philosophies such as democracy. In an LD debate, issues such as possible legislation, funding, implementation, or solving the problem are never discussed. In contrast, the CX format requires arguments that are much more specific. CX arguments focus on the realistic feasibility of a policy. CX arguments look at the pragmatic, real world, causes and effects of an action by the government, private sector, or an individual. CX debate focuses on possible legislative needs, such as how much the suggested proposal will cost and how the money will be appropriated, who will enforce the suggested proposal and what will be the penalties for failure to adhere to the new proposal, and ultimately ask if the new proposal will actually solve the problem or create new problems that result in a negative impact.

Quantity of Arguments   The third structural difference between an LD debate and a CX debate is the quantity of arguments. In an LD debate, you are allowed to use evidence, but the real test of your arguments is your ability to use examples and emotional appeal to make your point. The volume of arguments in a CX debate is much larger and greater than in an LD debate. In a CX debate, you must support every idea with evidence. In a CX debate, you use examples and emotional appeal, but your evidence is most important. When you ask a judge or audience to support your ideas, you must give them creditable evidence from experts and knowledgeable sources. As a debater, in either LD debates or CX debates, you must listen carefully to the evidence that is presented to make sure that it is creditable and the source is knowledgeable. Later, you will learn how to organize your evidence and the best ways to structure your arguments.

Structural Differences between LD Debates and CX Debates

	LD Debates	CX Debates
Number of debaters	One debater faces one debater.	A team of two debaters faces a team of two debaters.
Type of arguments	Arguments revolve around value comparisons.	Arguments revolve around the feasibility of a policy.
Quantity of arguments	Use evidence, examples, and emotional appeal.	Support every idea with evidence.

Time Use in a CX Debate

A CX debate requires approximately 1½ hours, which includes approximately eight minutes of preparation time for each team. The exact amount of preparation time is determined by each tournament. Because teams can use the preparation time when needed, it is not scheduled into a particular location on the schedule.

Each debater is responsible for an eight-minute speech, a three-minute cross-examination (also known as a question-and-answer period), and a five-minute rebuttal speech. Each speech and cross-examination period has guidelines, specific duties, and responsibilities that you will learn about in the following sections.

The following table identifies the length of each stage, the title of each stage, and the responsibilities of each debater. For example, if you are the debater who presents the first affirmative constructive speech (A1), you also ask questions during the first affirmative cross-examination period and perform the first affirmative rebuttal speech. Your partner (A2) performs the remaining affirmative speeches and questions. If you are the debater who presents the first negative constructive speech (N1), you also ask questions during the second negative cross-examination period and perform the first negative rebuttal speech. Your partner (N2) performs the remaining speeches and questions labeled negative.

COURTESY OF NATIONAL FORENSIC LEAGUE, WWW.NFLONLINE.ORG

What is each debater responsible for in a CX debate?

CX Debate: Times and Responsibilities

Time	Responsibility	Debater
8 minutes	First affirmative constructive speech	**A1**
3 minutes	First negative cross-examination period	**A1** answers; **N2** asks
8 minutes	First negative constructive speech	**N1**
3 minutes	First affirmative cross-examination period	**A1** asks; **N1** answers
8 minutes	Second affirmative constructive speech	**A2**
3 minutes	Second negative cross-examination period	**A2** answers; **N1** asks
8 minutes	Second negative constructive speech	**N2**
3 minutes	Second affirmative cross-examination period	**A2** asks; **N2** answers
5 minutes	First negative rebuttal speech	**N1**
5 minutes	First affirmative rebuttal speech	**A1**
5 minutes	Second negative rebuttal speech	**N2**
5 minutes	Second affirmative rebuttal speech	**A2**

Types of Speeches

Eight speeches are presented during a CX debate. Regardless of your position on the CX debate team, you are responsible for two speeches. Examine the following descriptions to learn about the speeches that are the responsibility of each debater in a CX debate.

Constructive Speeches

The first four speeches are **constructive speeches**. In each constructive speech, the responsible debater constructs the position. Each constructive speech is eight minutes in length.

- **First affirmative constructive speech** This is the first speech of the debate. The debater identified as A1 in the CX Debate: Times and Responsibilities table is responsible for presenting the first affirmative constructive speech. This speech supports the policy.

- **First negative constructive speech** This is the second speech of the debate. The debater identified as N1 in the CX Debate: Times and Responsibilities table is responsible for presenting the first negative constructive speech. This speech presents the prepared arguments for the negative team, opposing the policy and the arguments that support the policy.

- **Second affirmative constructive speech** This is the third speech of the debate. The debater identified as A2 in the CX Debate: Times and Responsibilities table is responsible for presenting the second affirmative constructive speech. This speech responds to the negative attacks and supports the affirmative position by extending the original affirmative position.

- **Second negative constructive speech** This is the fourth speech of the debate. The debater identified as N2 in the CX Debate: Times and Responsibilities table is responsible for presenting the second negative constructive speech. This speech re-establishes the negative position and responds to the affirmative's attacks.

Rebuttal Speeches

The next four speeches are **rebuttal speeches**. The debaters narrow the debate during these speeches. The debaters may continue an argument established in the constructive speeches by giving new evidence, new examples, or new ways of explaining an already established argument. Debaters cannot add new argument. Each rebuttal speech lasts five minutes.

- **First negative rebuttal speech** This is the first rebuttal speech in the debate and the first rebuttal speech for the negative debate team. You may have noticed that the negative team has two speeches back to back. This is called the **negative block**. During this time, the debater identified as N1 in the CX Debate: Times and Responsibilities table extends the negative arguments that were established during the constructive speeches.

- **First affirmative rebuttal speech**   This is the second rebuttal speech in the debate and the first rebuttal speech for the affirmative team. During this time, the debater identified as A1 in the CX Debate: Times and Responsibilities table extends the arguments that were established during the constructive speeches and responds to the most recent negative arguments.

- **Second negative rebuttal speech**   This is the last negative speech. This rebuttal is designed to give the negative team one last opportunity to make its points about its arguments. This speaker, identified as N2 in the CX Debate: Times and Responsibilities table, must summarize all of the arguments against the policy and make the last appeal for a win in the debate.

- **Second affirmative rebuttal speech**   This is the last affirmative speech and the last speech of the debate. This rebuttal is designed to give the affirmative team one last opportunity to make its points about its arguments. This speaker, identified as A2 in the CX Debate: Times and Responsibilities table, must summarize the affirmative position supporting the policy and make a last appeal for a win in the debate.

Understanding the purpose of each speech will help you select the information that belongs in your speeches. In the next lesson, you will learn more about researching the policy that will be debated in your CX debate and organizing the information for your debate.

What may debaters do in a rebuttal speech?

Think Critically

1. What are the fundamental and structural differences between LD debates and CX debates?

2. How is time used in a CX debate?

3. What speeches are made during a CX debate?

Research NOW!

4. Clark Kent Ervin wrote several blog entries for *The New York Times* and several articles for a variety of publications. Read one of his blog entries or articles and evaluate his writing style. How did his participation in the National Forensic League affect his writing?

5. Read the transcript of a recent presidential debate. Select one of the topics discussed. Use the topic to write a resolution that could be debated in a CX debate.

Write NOW!

6. CX debate requires two debaters on each team. Selecting a partner is critical to your success as a team. List the characteristics you think are important in a debate partner.

7. **TEAMWORK** Working with a partner, compare the lists that each of you wrote in activity 6. Create a final list that includes only the characteristics that both of you think are important in a debate partner. Write a paragraph that describes how your interaction with a partner affected the characteristics you both think are important in a partner.

Speak NOW!

8. The constructive speeches in a CX debate last eight minutes. Select a book. Set a timer for eight minutes. Read aloud from the book for eight minutes. Count the words or lines of text that you were able to read in eight minutes.

9. **TEAMWORK** Pair up with a classmate. Without looking at the passage you read in activity 8, explain the content of the passage while your partner times you. Ask your partner to evaluate your presentation. The evaluation should include the amount of information you covered and the length of time you used to present the information.

10. **TEAMWORK** Identify a key social problem that has received extensive coverage in broadcast and print news. Formulate a policy in response to this problem and propose that policy in an eight-minute constructive speech. Ask an opponent to respond with a eight-minute negative speech. Ask for feedback from the class.

Do You Agree?

Resolved The federal government of the United States should substantially increase alternative energy incentives in the United States.

GOALS

Describe how to research a topic.

Understand how to organize your materials.

TERMS

brainstorming
research packet
evidence
brief
citation
plagiarism

Affirmative position

Yes, as a nation we need to commit to the use of alternative energy. Our society is addicted to fossil fuels and if we are to remain economically competitive, we must go green as soon as possible.

Negative position

No, our entire economic structure is based on oil. A rapid move toward any alternative energy would disrupt our economy. Incentives from the government are not the answer. The private sector must be the driving force if any changes in our energy programs are to take place.

Research the Topic

Regardless of the type of debate that appeals to you, research is key to your success. It is important to know your topic. Research helps you learn enough about your topic to make the concepts and the information a part of you. Remember, regardless of your personal biases, you must be able to argue the side of the debate that is assigned to you. How do you start researching your topic?

Identify the Topic

Information is everywhere. You can get information from sources such as the Internet, books, television, radio, and newspapers. You can also consult individuals, including your teammates, teachers, parents, and professionals involved in the topic of your debate.

First, ensure that you have the correct wording for the topic. Consult your debate coach or the National Forensic League's website, which identifies the debate topics. Verifying the correct wording saves time by preventing you from researching material that will not help you prepare for the debate.

After you have verified the correct wording of the topic, discuss the meaning of the topic with your teammates. This process is called **brainstorming,** an informal discussion in which you share as many ideas related to the topic as you and your teammates can conceive. This gives you a wide variety of ideas to research. Eventually, through your search for information, large topic areas will emerge. When these large topic areas emerge, you have the basis of research categories. For example, if the debate topic deals with renewable or alternative energy, you will find large topic areas related to solar power, wind power, and nuclear power. As you research, you can begin to collect the information you need to create your debate arguments. Now that you have defined your topic, you are ready to begin searching for information.

Purchase Research Packets

A wide variety of commercially created materials are available in the forms of briefs, books, workbooks, and **research packets**, which are materials compiled for debaters by universities, individuals, and research consortiums. Often, former debaters are involved in creating the materials. You can order these research materials at a cost, which ranges from inexpensive to expensive. To find these research packets, ask your debate coach, search the Internet, and talk to other debaters about the materials they use.

FYI Many online sources, particularly online journals or journal articles, provide a citation on the website. To find it quickly, use your browser menu's Search feature to search for *citation*. If you use Internet Explorer, open the Edit menu and select the Find on this Page option.

The advantage of purchasing a research packet is that the research is done for you. The disadvantages are that everyone who orders the same packet will have the same information and there are no guarantees that the information will be of the quality you want. Many schools order research packets and distribute the materials to everyone on the debate team. Each school will have its own policies concerning research packets and you should talk to your debate coach about your school's policies.

You can also use a purchased research packet as a map that shows you where you can search for information. You can go to the original source for more or different information. For example, if a research packet used information from a book, you can look in the book for additional information. The researchers may have found the best information or they may have missed something even better. Your search will provide you with a strong understanding of the topic and it may turn up something even beyond what is provided in the packet. Either way, you benefit by expanding your knowledge and understanding of the topic.

Search the Internet

The Internet provides a diverse and almost endless source of possibilities for research. However, enter cyberspace carefully. One of the problems with Internet searches is the lack of quality standards about the validity of the available information. As you search, ask yourself the following questions.

- Is this a reputable site?

- What are the author's qualifications?

- Do other articles support the information?

- When was the information produced? Is the article recent? Is there other information that is more current?

- What is the author's motive in creating and providing the information?

As you search for information and question the information you find, you will discover many excellent websites. From these websites, you will be able to find articles, images, slide presentations, and videos that will provide ideas you can use in your debates. As you continue to search for information on the Internet, you will improve your search skills. You might find more information that is better than the information the opposing debate team finds, giving you an advantage over your opponents.

© BOB DAEMMRICH/PHOTOEDIT

What must you remember when using an Internet site?

Read Books

Books have been written about every subject. Many nonfiction books provide an in-depth examination of issues that challenge our societies and explain the author's perspective. The value of these books is twofold. First, these books examine in much greater depth the issues relating to the debate topic. Second, your knowledge will expand extensively.

Peruse Periodicals and Newspapers

Periodicals and newspapers are excellent sources of information. These sources will cover virtually every subject related to the debate topic. Periodicals and newspapers are often the most recent and up-to-date publications available. Therefore, they are an excellent source of the most recent information about your debate topic. You can find many periodicals and newspapers online by searching for the publication's name. You can print many articles at very little cost. Be sure to ask the same questions about the quality of the article as you asked when searching the Internet.

Examine Government Documents

The United States government has sponsored vast amounts of research and collected a great amount of information. Most of this information has been documented and archived. Much of it is published on the Internet.

These documents are public record and they are available to the public at no charge. Depending on the topic, these records could provide valuable information and resources that you might not be able to find from other sources. However, many of these documents are lengthy and contain complicated information, so you may need to spend time finding and extracting the information you need.

Government documents are often filed under key terms. Become familiar with the key terms related to your debate topic so you can use the terms to find associated information. Use commercial search engines, such as Google, and use the search function on the government website to find the right information.

Organize the Materials

Now that you have started collecting evidence, you might ask, "Now what?" and "What is the best way to organize information?" Organizing your materials is as important as researching and finding the materials. You may have discovered excellent information, but if you cannot access the information it won't help you in the debate.

Sort and Organize Evidence

After you have collected the information, sort it into useful **evidence**. The purpose of evidence is to prove your position. Your evidence is your proof.

Once you have collected information from original research, divide the information into two stacks: affirmative and negative. After you separate your information, you will refine the information into evidence. To do this, remove any of the information you don't need. To collect and remove information, cut and paste information in a word processing document by subject. For example, if you were debating alternative energy incentives, you would create files of evidence by subject on specific aspects of different forms of alternative energy and possible incentives. The names of the files and their content will depend on the evidence you have found.

What is the benefit of using a brief?

If you purchased commercially prepared materials, they will already be separated into affirmative and negative categories and divided by subject. If you purchase these materials, you can add your evidence to theirs by creating folders to keep their evidence with yours. After you create all of the folders, you can reorganize the evidence into a **brief**, a collection of evidence about a single subject. Briefs make finding your evidence much easier and faster. During the debate, if your opponent makes a specific argument, you can pull out the folder that contains the information you need to respond.

Record Citations

Every piece of evidence must have a complete bibliographical **citation**. A citation enables you or others to find the source of your evidence. Therefore, a citation should provide all of the information needed to find a source, including the author's name, the title of the source, the publication date, and the publisher. The citation should include an Internet website if you used an online source.

A citation enables others to verify and evaluate your evidence. Arguments based on a weak source will be considered to be weak arguments. Citations also prevent **plagiarism,** the act of passing off someone else's words or ideas as your own.

When researching, you must develop the habit of recording the citation when you copy or print information that you might use as evidence. Evidence that does not have a full citation becomes useless.

When debating, it is not necessary to say the full citation aloud. You will often hear debaters say, "My card is from Smith in '09." The common practice is to state the last name of the author and the year. You must have the full citation, but you don't have to say all of the bibliographical information during the debate.

Update Evidence

As a debater, you never finish researching. The need for updated evidence is always a priority. After your files are created, you can efficiently update the files. As you find new evidence, add it to the files or replace existing evidence as needed.

Researching and organizing information relies on learning as much as possible about your debate topic. Learn more about your topic to discover potential arguments that might be helpful in a debate. Use your knowledge of the topic to organize your evidence into files or briefs that can be accessed quickly, even during a debate.

YOU BE THE JUDGE

Anyone who has been part of a debate team would agree that a unified team offers personal payoff. A unified team will help you feel good about your team, yourself, and what you are doing. In addition to bringing school pride, team unity gives the team a common goal and gives the team members the feeling of being part of something bigger than each individual.

Strong direction, clear expectations, honest communication, and a high level of trust make a healthy team. When these qualities are present in your team, you and your teammates will feel a strong sense of unity. You can promote this feeling by establishing clear goals and gaining commitment for them.

Clarify goals, roles, tasks, actions, deadlines, and expectations so that each team member can embrace his or her part and perform at his or her peak. Understanding who is doing what and when each task should be done gives the team an opportunity to ensure that everyone stays on track. Reward progress as well as achievements. Validate each team member's contribution to the team.

What Would You Do?

What would you do if roles and tasks assigned to each person were not clear? How would you communicate this to the team leader?

Think Critically

1. How do you research a topic?

2. How should you organize your information?

3. Why do you need a citation for all of your evidence?

Research NOW!

4. Read the resolution at the beginning of the lesson. Find one article on the Internet that provides information about the topic. Record a citation for the article.

5. Find a book that provides information about the resolution at the beginning of the lesson. Record a citation for the book.

6. Select a topic of social concern such as health care or the environment. Research to find out which government publication will inform you on the topic. Summarize your findings and present them to the class.

Write NOW!

7. Return to the article you cited in activity 4. Using the information in the article, write an affirmative constructive speech.

 8. **TEAMWORK** Working with a partner, combine each of your constructive speeches into a single constructive speech.

9. It is important to remember that different authors write with different biases. A bias may not necessarily be a bad thing, but it is important to know what that bias is and how it affects the author's writing. Locate two sources of information that present different points of view on a single topic. Your sources might be a government publication and a newspaper article, or two books with different perspectives on the same topic. Write a short compare-and-contrast essay that shows the different biases present in these sources.

Speak NOW!

10. Read aloud the combined constructive speech from activity 8. Record the amount of time required to read the speech.

 11. **TEAMWORK** Continue to work with your partner. Present the combined constructive speech while your partner times you. Ask your partner to evaluate your presentation. The evaluation should include the length of time you used to present the information.

12. Prepare a short presentation on the various sources of information that you have encountered while completing any of the activities above. Evaluate each source in terms of usefulness and bias.

Do You Agree?

Resolved The federal government of the United States should substantially increase its public health assistance to sub-Saharan Africa.

Affirmative position

Yes, public health assistance is neither political nor economic, it is humanitarian. As a superpower, we have the resources and we should offer medical help to African nations in need.

Negative position

No, our focus should be in our own nation. The United Nations, the International Red Cross, and other organizations are better equipped to provide assistance. Often, our financial aid winds up in the hands of leaders who, instead of helping their people, use the money to buy weapons and arms. We should not increase our aid to sub-Saharan Africa.

GOALS

Describe the stock issues in an affirmative case.

Explain how to build the affirmative case.

TERMS

stock issue
topicality
harm
significance
prima facie
inherency
inherent barrier
solvency
plan

What Are Stock Issues?

After collecting and organizing your evidence, you are ready to start building your case. How do you know what arguments you should make?

Stock issues are the four basic arguments used in every debate. They are the building blocks of affirmative case construction. Examine your evidence to determine how each stock issue applies to your evidence and how you can use the stock issues to present the strongest case for the affirmative position. When you begin writing the affirmative case, include all four of the stock issues to create your affirmative case. Stock issues act as a checklist to ensure that you have included the key elements necessary for a successful case. The stock issues are topicality, harm, inherency, and solvency (Think of the acronym THIS).

	Case	
Topicality		Harm
Inherency		Solvency

Topicality

A building block of every case is **topicality**, which addresses whether the affirmative case relates directly or indirectly to the resolution to be debated. To determine topicality when you are building an affirmative case, ask yourself if your case relates directly or indirectly to the resolution.

Many beginning debaters are confused about what is topical and what is not. As a debater, you must explore the various levels and nuances of the topic to find an area of the topic that you feel compelled to debate. The debate resolution narrows the debate to a topic. Your choices while building the affirmative case narrow the topic even more. Remember that no affirmative case can possibly cover the entire scope of the topic. In your affirmative case, choose an aspect of the topic and utilize that aspect in your affirmative case.

Articles related to topicality are posted on the National Forensic League website. Case area suggestions are offered and discussed. The resolution for the next school year is released each February. After the resolution is released, numerous articles, papers, and debate evidence are published. Some of the materials are free and some must be purchased. After you check out the resources at the National Forensic League's website and other sources, you can begin to narrow your case areas to those you think are defendable as topical. Your opponents will try to point out that your arguments are not topical or that you have stretched the scope of the resolution. Later, you will learn how to answer these attacks.

Harm

Another building block of debate is **harm**, which is an unwanted problem resulting from an action or inaction of the current system. The responsibility of the affirmative debaters is to focus the debate on a problem that exists in the present system that is not effectively being solved. The affirmative case lists, describes, and verifies with evidence the scope of the problem.

In some parts of the United States, the term **significance** is used in conjunction with the harm. Specifying that the harm is significant ensures that the subject of harm caused by the topic is large enough or important enough to warrant discussion.

> **FYI** Focus on the most significant harm that can occur as a result of the status quo. Audience members are affected more by catastrophes than inconveniences.

Use statistical information or testimony to explain effectively the scope and impact of the problem. Your evidence that explains harm should be current and timely. Old evidence is helpful for understanding, but it is not as powerful in a debate as more recent evidence. When explaining the harm, be sure to cite examples, statistics, specific government and nongovernment organizations, financial references, and names of leaders and important individuals.

To effectively persuade the judge, you need to create an affirmative case that the judge feels is **prima facie**, a Latin term that means "at first appearance." This means that your argument must be obvious or self-evident enough to convince the judge that you are correct before hearing any arguments from the opposing team. Remember to state the harm(s) in clear, straightforward language to establish a prima facie case, as well as to lay the foundation for your remaining arguments.

Inherency

Another building block of debate is **inherency**. Inherency addresses whether the status quo, or present system, can solve the harm(s). Of all of the stock issues, inherency is the most difficult to grasp because the term and the concept are new to most beginning debaters.

When you are building your affirmative argument, you choose a harm scenario and determine that the status quo cannot solve this harm through current programs. This is called the **inherent barrier**. After you establish the inherent barrier, you offer your own solution, called the *plan*. Establishing the inherent barrier and the inability of the status quo to solve the harm is crucial to the success of the affirmative argument.

Inherency is critical to your affirmative argument. The primary reason a judge would consider the affirmative team's plan is the inherency issue, which argues that the status quo cannot or will not solve the harm. After the inherent barrier is established, the debate takes on a truly competitive nature because both teams have the basis for the debate. The affirmative team argues that the status quo cannot solve the harm and presents the plan to solve the harm. The negative team argues that the status quo can solve the harm and that the affirmative team's plan to solve the harm is not needed or won't be effective.

Solvency

The final building block of debate is **solvency,** which addresses whether the affirmative plan can solve the harm. This stock issue is often the most debated of the four issues. Many negative teams spend the bulk of their constructive speeches trying to point out the flaws of the affirmative team's plan. The negative team argues that the plan will not solve the harm and the plan will possibly create more problems than we already face.

How does a debater build solvency?

To effectively establish solvency, you need specific evidence that shows that your plan will work. The evidence must be carefully researched and you need to show data, statistics, research, and case studies that prove your plan will be effective.

Since you can use theoretical arguments, you should research theoretical arguments as well. Many affirmative plans are based on an existing program that can be broadened or reworked to meet topicality requirements. After you create your plan, you will need to spend a great deal of time making sure that you can answer the potential attacks from the negative team.

COURTESY OF NATIONAL FORENSIC LEAGUE, WWW.NFLONLINE.ORG

Build Your Affirmative Case

You put the four stock issues together to build an affirmative case. Much like the parts of a machine, each stock issue works in unison with the others, and each has its own specific function. The following outline provides a basic format for your affirmative case. Adjustments to the format occur because the topic changes each year and, depending on the resolution, different stock issues are emphasized.

Step 1 Determine Topicality

Determine if your affirmative case relates directly or indirectly to the resolution. Remember that the negative team will challenge your case on topicality and inherency. You must prepare responses to these attacks and continue to support your position throughout the debate.

Step 2 Contention I—Introduce Harm Scenarios

In this contention, you introduce your most significant harm scenarios. This is your opportunity to explain to the judge the scope and impact of the harm. You need approximately two to three excellent pieces of evidence. This evidence provides stories, statistics, and testimony that illustrate the complexity of the harm scenarios.

Step 3 Contention II—Prove Inherency

In this contention, you point out the inability of the status quo to rectify the issues you introduced as harm scenarios. You need approximately two to three excellent pieces of evidence. This evidence provides specific examples of how the status quo has failed. Examples should include stories, statistics, dollar amounts, attitudes that prevent success, lack of governmental support, no specific plan of action, and so on. Be sure to show that the inherent barrier prevents the status quo from solving the harm scenarios now and in the future.

Step 4 Contention III—Establish Solvency

In this contention, you point out that the affirmative plan can and will solve the harm scenarios pointed out in Contention I. In Contention II, you proved that the status quo cannot solve the harm scenarios, which leaves the judge with the idea that there is no solvency. With this contention, you have the opportunity to give the judge an alternative to the failed status quo. You need approximately three to five excellent pieces of evidence that show how the affirmative plan will solve the harm scenarios. Some of the evidence may be theoretical. Try to have examples of how your plan has worked elsewhere or in a smaller situation, thus avoiding having only theoretical evidence.

A blend of theoretical and factual evidence is best. The focal point of solvency is, at the very least, to convince the judge that the affirmative plan is competitive with the status quo and, at the very worst, no worse than the current situation.

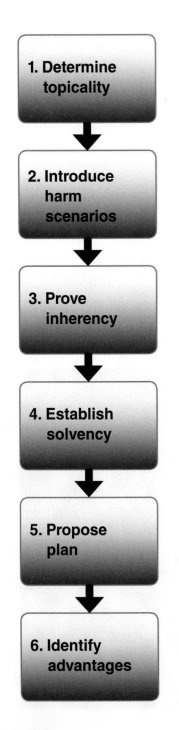

1. Determine topicality

2. Introduce harm scenarios

3. Prove inherency

4. Establish solvency

5. Propose plan

6. Identify advantages

Step 5 Propose Plan

The next component of the affirmative case is the plan. As an affirmative debater, you have the obligation and the opportunity to present an alternative to the status quo. Contentions I, II, and III are designed to prove that there is a need for change. The **plan** is a short paragraph that explains the change that you are suggesting. The following list identifies the mandates (parts) of a plan. Note: The importance of the mandates will change with each resolution.

PEEPO/ISTOCKPHOTO.COM

- **Implementation**   This is a brief description of what you want to happen, such as creating a new policy or program, eliminating an existing program or policy, making a new law, making a new rule, creating a new procedure, and so on.

- **Funding**   If your plan requires funding, you must specify the source of the funds, such as taxes, fees, reallocation of funds, and so on.

- **Enforcement**   Identify who will oversee your plan and offer the necessary directions for implementation.

- **Time frame (optional)**   Identify how long it will take to see results when the plan is executed. Describe the results. If the results are covered in another part of the case, a description is not needed in the plan.

What is the purpose of a plan?

Step 6 Contention IV—Identify Advantages

The final component of the affirmative case is advantages. As an affirmative debater, you are asking the judge to abandon the status quo for your plan. To effectively persuade the judge, you must offer the change, rationale for the change, a mechanism for change, and the benefits of the change. These are advantages. When the judge looks at your description of the status quo and your plan, you are offering a comparison. This comparative advantage gives the affirmative debate team an opportunity to point out specific benefits for choosing the affirmative arguments over the status quo. The structure is similar to Contentions I, II, and III offered earlier.

In this contention, you point out the advantages of choosing the affirmative plan over the status quo. You need approximately three to five pieces of excellent evidence. This is your last opportunity to make an impression on the judge and to reinforce the need for the change suggested in your plan. Comparing the affirmative case and plan to the status quo gives you the opportunity to show the judge specific reasons why he or she should vote for the affirmative debate team.

A well-constructed affirmative case can win a debate. Base your arguments on solid research and build your case with care. With the right evidence and a well-supported plan, you can enter a debate with confidence.

TURNING POINT

Constitutional Amendment XIX

The Nineteenth Amendment of the Constitution of the United States says, "The right of citizens of the United States to vote shall not be denied or abridged by the United States or by any State on account of sex." One simple sentence changed the face of democracy forever.

Although the amendment seems simple and obvious now, the road to ratification was long and rocky. The United States declared itself to be a nation in 1776. The Nineteenth Amendment was not ratified until 1920. For 144 years, women were not allowed to vote. Hundreds of years before the United States declared independence, women ruled as monarchs in England. And yet, in the United States, a nation born from the desire to free itself from oppression, women were not allowed to affect their government by an act as simple and important as casting a ballot.

During the Revolutionary War, Abigail Adams sent a letter to her husband, John Adams, who would become the second president of the United States in 1797. In it, she wrote, "If women are not represented in this new republic there will be another revolution."

After the Revolutionary War, women continued to press for suffrage through meetings and petitions. The first large suffrage demonstration was a women's rights convention in 1848. After the Civil War, suffragists argued that the Fourteenth and Fifteenth Amendments should be interpreted to allow women to vote. However, Susan B. Anthony was arrested when she tried to vote in 1872.

In 1875, Susan B. Anthony wrote the Nineteenth Amendment and it was introduced in the Senate in 1878. The amendment failed to pass the Senate four times—in 1878, 1914, 1918, and 1919. Although the amendment also failed to pass twice in the House of Representatives, it was finally passed by Congress in 1919.

The League of Women Voters, an organization that still exists today, worked tirelessly to urge the amendment's ratification by the required two-thirds of the states. The amendment was ratified August 18, 1920. At the signing ceremony, President Wilson gave the gold pen to Wood Park, who became the first president of the League of Women Voters. Finally, women had earned equal rights.

Think Critically

How has the Nineteenth Amendment affected your life?

Think Critically

1. Why are stock issues considered to be the building blocks of an affirmative case?

2. Why is the inherent barrier important when building an affirmative case?

3. How do you build your affirmative case?

Research NOW!

4. Read the resolution at the beginning of the lesson. Visit the National Forensic League website at www.nflonline.org. Search the website for information about the resolution. Summarize one article that you find.

5. Search the Internet for statistics about the amount of public health assistance that the United States gives to sub-Saharan Africa. Record the amounts given in different years. Record a citation for the information.

Write NOW!

6. Based on the resolution at the beginning of the lesson, make a list of items to research for each of the stock issues.

7. **TEAMWORK**   Working with a partner, compare your lists of items to research for each of the stock issues. Select one item, search for information about the item, and record the information you find. Remember to record the citation as well.

Speak NOW!

8. Using the information you found in the previous activities, give a brief speech about the information. Record the amount of time required for the speech.

9. **TEAMWORK**   Continue to work with your partner. Create a constructive speech that combines the information both of you collected. Present the speech to your partner. Ask your partner to evaluate your presentation. The evaluation should include the length of time you used to present the information.

10. Build an affirmative case in response to an issue that is important to your school. Use the steps that you learned in this lesson. When you have finished, ask for questions and feedback from the class.

Chapter in Review

5.1 Characteristics of CX Debate
- The fundamental differences between LD debate and CX debate include focus, goal, and topic. The structural differences between LD debate and CX debate include the number of debaters, the type of arguments, and the quantity of arguments.
- During CX debates, each team member has specific responsibilities that must be completed within time constraints.
- Each CX debate has four constructive speeches and four rebuttal speeches.

5.2 Research and Organization
- To research a topic, you must verify that you have the correct wording for the topic. Sources of information include commercial research packets, the Internet, books, periodicals, newspapers, and government documents.
- Sort and organize your evidence, recording a citation for each piece.

5.3 Build the Affirmative Case
- Build an affirmative case from the stock issues of topicality, harm, inherency, and solvency.
- To build your affirmative case, determine topicality, introduce harm scenarios, prove inherency, establish solvency, propose a plan, and identify advantages.

Develop Your Debating Language

Select the term that best fits the definition. Some terms will not be used.

a. brainstorming
b. brief
c. citation
d. constructive speech
e. evidence
f. harm
g. inherency
h. inherent barrier
i. negative block
j. plagiarism
k. plan
l. policy
m. prima facie
n. rebuttal speech
o. research packet
p. significance
q. solvency
r. stock issue
s. topicality

1. Materials compiled for debates by universities, individuals, and research consortiums

2. Act of passing off someone else's words or ideas as your own

3. Two negative speeches given back to back during a CX debate

4. Basic arguments used in every debate

5. Claim that the status quo cannot solve a selected harm through current programs

6. Large enough or important enough to warrant discussion

7. Building block that addresses whether the affirmative plan can solve the harm

8. Collection of evidence about a single subject

9. Complete bibliographical information

10. Specific action, implemented by government or society, that often requires changes in laws, rules, or legislation

11. Short paragraph that briefly explains the change that you are suggesting

Review Debate Concepts

12. What are the fundamental differences between LD debate and CX debate?

13. What are the structural differences between LD debate and CX debate?

14. How much time does a typical CX debate require?

15. During the debate, what are the duties of the A2 debater?

16. During the debate, what are the responsibilities of the N1 debater?

17. In a CX debate, why are the first four speeches called constructive speeches?

18. What is the purpose of the second negative rebuttal speech?

19. How do you identify your debate topic?

20. What are the advantages of purchasing research packets?

21. How do you determine if the information you find on a website is valid?

22. What are the benefits of using books in your research?

23. What is the benefit of using periodicals and newspapers in your research?

24. What criteria do you use to sort and organize your evidence?

25. Why should you record citations?

26. What is the significance of the acronym THIS?

27. What does it mean if an opponent says that your arguments are not topical?

28. Why is significance sometimes associated with harm?

29. During a debate, why is solvency frequently the most debated stock issue?

30. What is the sequence you follow in building your affirmative case?

31. What are the mandates of a plan?

32. What should be in the final contention to convince the judge that the affirmative debate team has proven its case?

Make Academic Connections

33. **PROBLEM SOLVING**   Read an Op Ed piece that could be used as an affirmative argument. What evidence is offered in the piece? What plan does the author offer? Is the Op Ed piece convincing? Why or why not?

34. **MATH**   Opinion polls are often conducted to gauge public opinion about a controversial issue. How can this statistical information be used to construct an affirmative case?

35. **ENGLISH**   Some pairs of words, such as *insure* and *ensure*, are commonly misused when speaking or writing. Identify and define five pairs of words that are often used incorrectly.

36. **HISTORY**   Select a ruling made by the U.S. Supreme Court. Read the majority opinion supporting the ruling that is produced by the Supreme Court. Identify the statements in the opinion document that could be used to create an affirmative constructive speech.

37. **CHALLENGES**   Local and national news commentators often present their opinions on television. Watch a televised commentary. Evaluate the commentator's content. Did he or she support the commentary with evidence? Did he or she present a reasonable plan? Evaluate the commentator's presentation as well. How does his or her presentation affect your impression of the content? Write a one-page evaluation.

Research NOW!

38. During court trials, witnesses are cross-examined by lawyers. How is this similar to and different from a CX debate? Prepare a summary of your findings and present it to your class.

39. **TEAMWORK**   With a partner, research key events that led to the passage of the Nineteenth Amendment, such as the Seneca Falls Convention and the National Women's Rights Convention. Identify key documents and persons involved with these events.

40. Political debates use a kind of cross-examination format. Try and locate a transcript of a recent political debate in your community or watch one on television. Evaluate how well each candidate proposes and defends his or her proposed solutions to pressing problems in your community.

Write NOW!

41. Your friend is joining the debate team. Write a one-page description explaining how to build an affirmative case.

42. **TEAMWORK**   Working with a partner, examine local political issues. Select and research one of the issues. Write the first affirmative constructive speech for a CX debate. Remember to record citations for the evidence you use in the speech.

43. Select one of the resolutions provided at the beginning of each lesson. Record citations for twenty potential sources of information about the resolution. Include websites, books, periodicals, and government documents.

44. Write a list of topics that you think would inspire interesting cross-examination debates. List how you think each side would build its case and what information each might utilize. Offer what rebuttals you think each side might offer. Read your list in class. Ask for questions and comments.

45. Select one of the resolutions provided at the beginning of each lesson. Without researching the topic, make a video recording of yourself talking about the topic and then watch the recording. What are your natural speaking habits when you are not prepared to speak about a topic? Identify five ways that you could improve your natural speaking habits.

46. **TEAMWORK** One of the most famous exchanges in election debates occurred between Lloyd Bentsen and Dan Quayle in 1988. Research to discover the famous exchange. Working with a partner, reenact the statements leading to the exchange and the actual exchange of words.

47. Who are your favorite speakers? Why are they your favorites? Deliver a short presentation on speakers that you know and admire. They may be still living, or you may know of their abilities through film, biographies, or histories. In your presentation, be sure to name the characteristic or characteristics you admire about these speakers, and how those qualities may have influenced your own style of public speaking and debate.

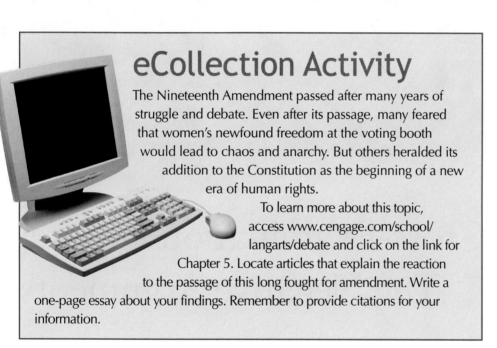

eCollection Activity

The Nineteenth Amendment passed after many years of struggle and debate. Even after its passage, many feared that women's newfound freedom at the voting booth would lead to chaos and anarchy. But others heralded its addition to the Constitution as the beginning of a new era of human rights.

To learn more about this topic, access www.cengage.com/school/langarts/debate and click on the link for Chapter 5. Locate articles that explain the reaction to the passage of this long fought for amendment. Write a one-page essay about your findings. Remember to provide citations for your information.

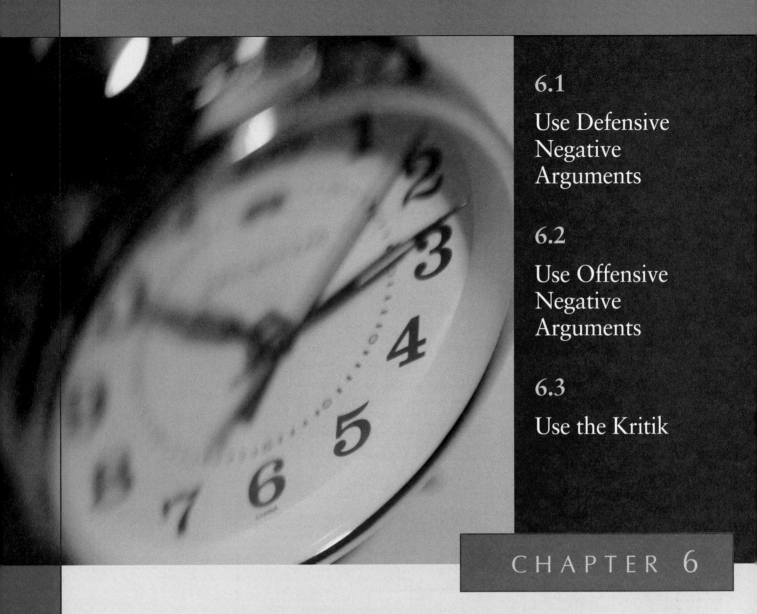

CHAPTER 6

Cross-Examination Debate:
The Negative Arguments

Real People | Real Careers

Bobby Jindal

"Under the spotlight of the world, with generosity from many and a clear call to common purpose…we have the opportunity to make lasting and positive change."

On January 14, 2008, Piyush "Bobby" Jindal was sworn in as the governor of Louisiana. At the time of his election, Jindal was the youngest governor in the United States, the only American of Indian descent to be elected governor, and one of less than ten persons of non-European background to be elected governor since the late 1800s.

After taking office, Jindal instituted ethics reforms in the first Special Session. In the second Special Session, taxes were eliminated to spur investment and growth of businesses in Louisiana.

Perhaps Jindal is best known for encouraging recovery in areas impacted by Hurricanes Katrina, Rita, Gustav, and Ike. In fact, Jindal has been credited for evacuating 1.9 million people, including 10,400 patients who were in hospitals and medical facilities, removing them from the path of Hurricane Gustav.

Jindal was born in Baton Rouge, Louisiana in 1971. After a stellar academic record, Jindal graduated from Brown University with honors in biology and public policy. He became a Rhodes Scholar at Oxford University in England. After working in the private sector, he entered the public sector by accepting an appointment as the secretary of the Louisiana Department of Health and Hospitals (DHH). As his career progressed, he gained national attention. In 2001, President George W. Bush appointed Jindal to serve as assistant secretary for the U.S. Department of Health and Human Services. Jindal resigned in 2003, returning to his home state to run for public office. He was elected to the House of Representatives in 2004 and reelected in 2006. In 2008, he became the governor of Louisiana. In February 2009, Jindal was chosen by the Republican party to deliver its official response to President Barak Obama's address before a joint session of Congress.

Jindal confesses that his self-chosen nickname came from his childhood when he was a fan of the popular television series *The Brady Bunch*. He identified with the character of Bobby, the youngest boy character on the show. While Jindal is known by his nickname, his legal name remains Piyush.

How did Jindal move from simple citizen to governor? Jindal worked hard and took advantage of opportunities that came his way. In other words, he is like any other American child who followed a dream to impact his world. As he stated at the beginning of his term as governor, "Under the spotlight of the world, with generosity from many and a clear call to common purpose…we have the opportunity to make lasting and positive change."

Think Critically

What can you learn from Jindal's example?

Use Defensive Negative Arguments

Do You Agree?

Resolved The federal government should require arbitration of labor disputes in all basic industries.

Affirmative position

Yes, our economy has become so complex that the traditional management/labor negotiation no longer works. Trained arbitrators would help solve many issues due to their unbiased positions. Emotional issues would be minimized through professionalism.

Negative position

No, the time-honored philosophy of the right to work is an American tradition. Workers have the right to join a union and to have the union leaders lobby for them. A process such as arbitration often empowers the arbitrator to create a compromise between the factions. This limits the voice of the worker.

Challenge Stock Issues

In Lincoln Douglas (LD) debate, when you are the negative debate team, you build a *case* just like the affirmative debate team. In cross-examination (CX) debate, you build **negative arguments** rather than a negative *case*. Your negative arguments should challenge the affirmative case.

Negative arguments can be separated into defensive negative arguments and offensive negative arguments. The affirmative debate team used the stock issues to build their affirmative case, so you will use the stock issues to challenge the arguments established by the affirmative debate team. Start by looking at the defensive negative arguments. Use defensive negative arguments to challenge three of the stock issues. These stock issues are harm, inherency, and solvency.

Challenge the Significance of the Harm Stock Issue

Perhaps the most fundamental negative argument you can make is challenging the affirmative team's harm issue. A harm is an unwanted problem resulting from an action or inaction of the current system. The affirmative debate team must establish that the harms are significant. You will challenge the significance of the harm.

First, consider the size of the harm presented by the affirmative debate team. As the negative debate team, your responsibility is to challenge the scope and importance of the harm stock issue.

The affirmative debate team presents evidence to create a scenario for the judge about the scope of the harms. While they are presenting their case, listen for statistics, numbers, and documentation—the tools that the affirmative debate team uses to create a scope for the judge.

The burden of proof is the responsibility of the affirmative debate team. The affirmative debate team uses a variety of methods to prove the harm scenarios to the judge. Use the following strategies to challenge the significance of the harms presented by the affirmative debate team to create your own scenario for the judge.

- **Statistics and Numbers**   One of the affirmative debate team's most common strategies is the use of statistics and numbers. These statistics and numbers can be very persuasive. If the affirmative evidence talks about issues such as unemployment or health care coverage and adds proportion through statistics and numbers, this can be overwhelmingly convincing to the judge. You must challenge these statistics and numbers by offering statistics and numbers of your own. For every statistic and number, a counter set of statistics and numbers will help you offer a different perspective. Your goal is to counter the affirmative position. If you cannot counter the position, establish some doubt in the judge's mind about the validity of the affirmative position.

©JAIMIE DUPLASS, 2009/USED UNDER LICENSE FROM SHUTTERSTOCK.COM

What must you remember when the affirmative team is presenting its case?

- **Evidence**   Examine the evidence used in the affirmative debate team's case. Remember the old saying, "If it sounds too good to be true, it probably is." Listen carefully to the evidence and challenge any that appears to be "too good." Ask for additional evidence. Do not allow the affirmative debate team to persuade the judge with poorly written and poorly researched evidence.

- **Bias**   A **bias** is a prejudice toward a specific idea or cause. A biased author attempting to persuade an audience might use one-sided information to encourage support for the selected cause. Bias can be difficult to detect. A bias could be motivated by politics, economics, or publicity. A public official might support a group or individual who donated money to his or her campaign. A researcher might produce slanted results to ensure that future research is funded. A company and its executives might issue statements to maintain a positive public image. Ask for additional evidence from unbiased sources.

- **Presumption**   A **presumption** is a belief that awaits further proof. The idea that you are innocent until proven guilty is a presumption. The affirmative debate team must clearly prove that you have been negligent and that you have done a poor job of dealing with the harm scenarios. The best way to show that you have been diligent is to provide evidence illustrating the success of the present system. Remember, you do not have to prove your diligence. You are innocent until the affirmative debate team proves otherwise. If the affirmative debate team provides evidence that enough money has not been spent for a certain program, provide evidence documenting the money that has been spent. If the affirmative debate team presents evidence that the harm scenarios are not a priority, provide evidence that explains the importance of solving the harms in the present system. Use evidence, examples, or testimony to counter any claim made by the affirmative debate team. You are not responsible for proving your innocence; you are only responsible for answering the specific attacks made by the affirmative case.

Challenge the Inherent Barrier of the Inherency Stock Issue

The affirmative debate team must establish that an inherent barrier prevents the present system from solving the harm scenarios. An affirmative case will attempt to create a scenario that claims the present system is doing nothing, doing too little, doing the wrong thing, or just doesn't care. Your argument should claim that the present system is working well, hasn't had the opportunity to solve the harm scenario, can adjust to solve the harm scenario, or does care and will solve the harm scenario if given the opportunity. Establishing the inherent barrier is key to the affirmative debate team's success. To be successful, you must demonstrate that an inherent barrier does not exist.

After establishing that an inherent barrier exists, the affirmative will claim that the present system and the barrier are inseparable. This claim is key to the affirmative debate team's success. It is equally key for you to show that solvency is possible while maintaining the present system. As the negative debate team, you will attempt to minimize the harm scenarios and then claim that if the harm scenarios exist, a new plan is not necessary because the present system can and will solve the harm scenarios.

The next step in arguing inherency is to determine if the barrier is structural or attitudinal. **Structural inherency** deals with laws, regulations, guidelines, and so on. Structural inherent barriers are the easiest to repair. If your position is that the affirmative debate team's claims have merit, then the present system can adjust as needed. You can demonstrate that the present system is flexible enough to solve the harm scenarios.

Attitudinal inherency is harder for the affirmative debate team to prove and, therefore, it is harder for you to create a defense against the claim. The affirmative debate team might claim that an attitude such as racism exists and it is so entrenched that only a radical change, which is offered by the affirmative case and plan, will solve the harm scenario. You must point out the efforts that are ongoing and claim that we, as a society, are moving in the right direction. It would be poor debating to claim that issues like racism do not exist, but you can claim that the present system doesn't support or legislate such attitudes and it is working to improve the situation. Primarily, you should claim that an inherent barrier does not exist. Therefore, a new plan is not needed.

What is the inherent barrier?

Challenge the Solvency Stock Issue

Solvency is the next stock issue that the affirmative debate team uses to build its case. Solvency is the claim that adopting the affirmative debate team's plan will solve the harm scenarios the team presented. As the negative debate team, it is your job to prove that the present system can solve the harm scenarios or that the affirmative debate team's plan will not solve the harm scenarios. Challenge the affirmative debate team's plan by examining general solvency, funding, time frame, implementation, enforcement, inherency, and fiat.

- **General solvency** Using a common sense approach is often the best way to start. Using words such as impractical, radical, and unrealistic gives the affirmative debate team's plan a bad image. The affirmative team will have to defend its position, which gives you a good start.

- **Funding** The affirmative debate team's plan should explain how they plan to pay for their proposal. You can claim that the plan is costly. It will cause tax increases, divert funds from other programs, increase the deficit, or unbalance the budget. All of these negative arguments cause problems for the affirmative debate team. Often, the affirmative team will claim that the plan costs nothing or that they will divert funds from current efforts in order to fund the plan. Listen to their explanation and question them if their explanation is unsatisfying. Ultimately, the plan must be funded. Attacking the funding mechanism is always important.

- **Time frame** Question how long the plan will take to create the affirmative debate team's list of benefits. Ask specifically for a time frame. Ask the affirmative team to verify, with evidence, how long the plan will require. If the time frame is too long, this becomes a good argument for your team.

- **Implementation** Ask the affirmative team who will implement the plan. For example, will the United States government, a government agency, or an international group such as the United Nations (UN) implement the plan? Ask if it will be self-regulated by individual governments. Asking the affirmative debate team to explain how the plan will be implemented gives you an excellent opportunity to point out the poor record of those implementing the plan.

- **Enforcement** Closely related to the question of implementation is enforcement. Ask who will make sure that the plan is followed. Will the same agencies or government groups that implement the plan enforce it? Make sure that the affirmative debate team explains this important detail.

- **Inherency** Solvency and inherency work together to create a checklist for your team. Closely examine the affirmative team's plan to see if the inherent barrier they identified is removed. If the affirmative plan solves the harm scenario by removing the same inherent barrier as the present system addresses, this becomes an obvious argument for your team. Simply point out that the plan targets the same inherent barrier addressed by the present system.

AP PHOTO/POOL, ALESSANDRO ABBONIZIO

Why would UN involvement be a violation of fiat?

- **Fiat** A **fiat** is an act of will that creates something without effort. Fiat is associated with debate because teams do not debate whether Congress would or would not pass the affirmative team's plan. It is assumed that Congress will pass the affirmative plan. However, the question of fiat remains an important negative position because you can ask if fiat is feasible. For example, we assume that Congress will pass the legislation, but if the plan is implemented or enforced by an international organization such as the United Nations or regulated by another nation's government, the legislation passed by the Congress would not have an effect. Therefore, you should ask if the affirmative team's plan is a violation of fiat. If a violation exists, this becomes another solvency attack for your team.

FYI Fiat is from a Latin term that means "Let it be done."

Ultimately, solvency is an important negative stock issue for both debate teams. The affirmative team must prove solvency and your team must challenge solvency by using any or all of the listed strategies.

All of the stock issues you have looked at so far are defensive negative arguments. To present offensive negative arguments, you will learn about addressing the stock issue of topicality.

Think Critically

1. What are the differences between how the negative side prepares for an LD debate and a CX debate?

2. Which stock issues are addressed by defensive negative arguments?

3. Who has the burden of proof in a CX debate?

Research NOW!

4. Bobby Jindal's home state of Louisiana has been affected by hurricanes several times. What has Jindal done to help Louisiana recover or to reduce the effect of future hurricanes on Louisiana?

5. The resolution in the beginning of Lesson 6.1 says that arbitration should be required. Use the Internet or other sources to find more information about arbitration and arbitrators. Describe the arbitration process.

6. Bias is an important element to recognize in any argument. Locate a transcript of recent Congressional proceedings. Look for key words and phrases in the use of description that indicate bias. Prepare a short summary of your findings and present it to the class.

Write NOW!

7. Attend a meeting of the student council. Identify the two sides of a controversial topic. Write a description of a solution proposed by one group.

8. **TEAMWORK** Working with a partner who selected the same proposed solution from the student council meeting, list the defensive negative arguments that could be used in a debate about the issue. Write a paragraph that describes how you would present your negative arguments.

Speak NOW!

9. It can be difficult to remain calm when you are challenging someone's arguments or being challenged about your own arguments. Write a one-page essay about a topic that is important to you. Be sure to practice reading the information to others.

10. **TEAMWORK** Pair up with a classmate. Take turns reading to your partner the essays that you wrote in the previous activity. Challenge the information in your partner's essay.

Use Offensive Negative Arguments

Do You Agree?

Resolved The United States should establish a system of compulsory service by all citizens.

Affirmative position
Yes, as Americans we live in the greatest nation in the world. One of our strengths is our citizens. Each of us should give our time and volunteer to strengthen our society.

Negative position
No, each citizen should decide how he or she will serve our society. Each person should have the freedom to serve or not. It is not the place of our government to mandate service.

GOALS

Use offensive negative arguments to challenge the stock issue of topicality.

Use the disadvantages argument to provide solid offensive negative arguments.

TERMS

standard
field context definition
disadvantage
link
brink
impact

CHALLENGE THE TOPICALITY STOCK ISSUE

You already learned to use defensive negative arguments to counter the stock issues of harm, inherency, and solvency. These arguments are considered defensive in nature because they defend the present system. To win a debate, it is not enough to defend the present system. You must attack.

Use the topicality stock issue to provide offensive negative arguments. The judge will weigh your offensive negative arguments against the affirmative debate team's case and plan.

After you hear the affirmative case and plan, you must decide if topicality is an appropriate option. If you choose to challenge the topicality stock issue, you must link your arguments directly to the plan, establishing a direct link from your argument to the affirmative debate team's case and plan. If you do not establish a direct link, the affirmative debate team will counter that your topicality position is generic. This response from the affirmative debate team will cancel out the topicality argument if you can't prove the link.

Topicality is the most complex and detailed stock issue. To effectively argue topicality, you must understand the issue and be able to explain each part of the topicality argument. Each part of the topicality issue serves a specific role that is equally important as any other topicality role. The four parts of a topicality argument are definition, violation, standards, and voting. You must structure your arguments to include options from each of the four parts.

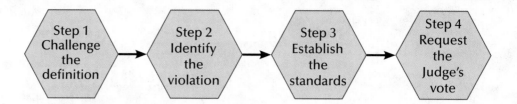

Step 1 Challenge the Definition

When presenting their case, the affirmative debate team offers the resolution and defines the key terms. The affirmative debate team chooses which terms in the resolution it thinks are important and defines those terms. It is very important that you listen to the definitions and the sources of the definitions. If you think that the affirmative has poorly defined one or more terms, this creates the first step in deciding if you want to argue topicality. To challenge the definition, you must offer a counter definition from a reliable source. Definitions can come from dictionaries, online sources, books, articles, or documents. When arguing topicality, you must establish the superiority of your definition. Be sure to use reliable sources. After challenging a definition, you identify the violation that occurred.

> **FYI** Use reputable sources for your definitions. The Merriam-Webster dictionary is available at www.merriam-webster.com. Encyclopedias and other reference sources are also available online.

Step 2 Identify the Violation

In this step, you establish that a topicality violation has occurred by comparing your definition to the definition provided by the affirmative debate team. Quote the affirmative team's plan and spell out the exact violation. It is necessary to compare the affirmative debate team's plan, the resolution, and your counter definition. This identifies the violation.

Step 3 Establish the Standards

In this step, you establish the standards for comparing your position to the affirmative debate team's case and plan. A **standard** provides a guide to weigh the violation. Use the following list to establish a standard in the topicality debate.

- **Best definition**   This standard argues that your definition is better than the affirmative team's definition. Provide a rationale that explains why your definition is better.

- **Field context**   Use this standard to define evidence in context rather than as it appears in a dictionary. A **field context definition** establishes the meaning of a term in the "real world." If you can establish a field context definition, your position is superior.

- **Education**   This standard argues that the narrow definition of the affirmative debate team's plan violates the educational value of debate. You argue that the affirmative debate team has limited the resolution too much, and has destroyed the opportunity to have a fair debate.

- **Bright line** This standard argues that the affirmative debate team's definitions have not offered a clear position. You argue that your counter definition offers a clearer position, which provides a clearer choice for the judge.

- **Ground** This standard argues that the affirmative debate team has defined the terms in a way that provides too many limits, preventing you from arguing against the affirmative case and plan.

- **Grammar** This standard argues that the affirmative debate team has provided definitions that are grammatically incorrect. This violation is difficult to prove, but it can be effective.

- **Limits** This standard argues that the affirmative debate team has provided definitions that have expanded the resolution beyond a reasonable limit. This violation causes you to cover issues that are beyond a reasonable limit.

- **Specific meaning** This standard argues that the affirmative debate team has combined the terms of the resolution, believing that it is fair to look at the resolution as a whole without looking at its individual terms.

Step 4 Request the Judge's Vote

After you have established your definitions, the violation, and the standard, the final step in arguing topicality is the voting issue. This is the chance for you to offer the judge an opportunity to vote for your team based on topicality. The voting issue can be framed in one of the following ways:

- **Fairness** This voting issue argues that the debate cannot be fair to your team. Argue that you prepared for the debate, but the affirmative debate team's case and plan are outside the limits of fairness.

- **Framers' intent** This voting issue argues that the authors of the resolution did not intend for the debate to extend this far outside the topic. The literature supporting the resolution does not include the affirmative team's position.

- **Tradition** This voting issue argues that the affirmative team's case and plan are outside the traditional limits of debate. This is difficult to prove, but it is effective if you can establish the issue.

- **Jurisdiction** This voting issue argues that the judge is limited to voting for topical cases only. When you argue jurisdiction, ask the judge to exclude the affirmative plan because it is not topical.

Each part of the arguments concerning the topicality stock issue is designed to challenge the affirmative debate team's case and plan. The affirmative team has the right to offer an alternative to the present system. You have the right to challenge the affirmative team's proposal. Topicality gives you an opportunity not only to challenge the affirmative debate team's plan, but also to offer offensive arguments of your own.

Use the Disadvantages Argument

The second offensive negative argument that you can offer is disadvantages. A **disadvantage** is the argument that, if the affirmative debate team's plan is ratified, bad side effects will occur. The affirmative team will offer advantages, which argue that benefits will occur if the affirmative plan is ratified. You will need to make offensive arguments of your own, such as the disadvantage argument.

After the resolution is released, many debaters begin to research and create disadvantages. These arguments guarantee that you will have negative arguments that you can use. It is impossible to know all of the affirmative cases that you could encounter; therefore, you should create loosely structured disadvantages that can be quickly adapted to various affirmative cases. Typically, affirmative teams will argue that the disadvantages are generic rather than unique. Your team should be prepared to answer the claims of the affirmative debate team.

Each disadvantage must include a link, a brink, and an impact. The following list will help provide the structure for the disadvantage, and it will give your team the opportunity to answer the claim of being generic.

- **Link**   The first component of the disadvantage is the link. The **link** is evidence that shows a connection to the affirmative plan. Your obligation is to establish a specific link to an action called for by the affirmative team's plan. The affirmative team will claim that it is generic rather than unique. You must show a direct connection. After you establish the connection, you can move on to the brink.

- **Brink**   The second component of the disadvantage is the brink. The **brink** argument claims that the action called for by the affirmative team's plan will initiate the disadvantage. You will use evidence to demonstrate that adoption of the affirmative team's plan will link directly to the disadvantage and the only way to avoid the disadvantage is to reject the affirmative plan. After you establish the brink, you can move on to the impacts.

- **Impact**   The third and final component of the disadvantage is the impact. To give weight to the idea of the disadvantage, you must show the negative **impact** (effect) of adopting the affirmative plan. The evidence you use should show the negative impact of the affirmative plan.

Providing disadvantages can give you the offense that you need to be successful. The disadvantages give weight to your negative arguments. To counter the offensive arguments of the affirmative debate team, you must have some offensive negative arguments. Disadvantages give you some solid offensive strength.

Why is it important to maintain credibility?

YOU BE THE JUDGE

Many people alter details in a story to make it sound more interesting. The size of the fish caught at the lake becomes bigger and the struggle to catch it more ferocious and hair raising. Perhaps it was only a small trout caught on a balmy summer day. But it makes for a better story if a storm gets added for dramatic effect. Listeners pay closer attention when they hear colorful details, and so other exaggerations such as the fish coming alive on the boat and trying to bite you find their way into the story. While most will recognize these details for what they are, creations to keep an audience interested, people still tolerate them with a smile. The "tall tale" is a revered form of storytelling, one practiced for generations in cultures and families up through the present day.

But in other situations, altering or exaggerating key details can be harmful to many people, especially the person who is responsible for the exaggerations. Court cases for both the prosecution and the defense can fail if cross-examination reveals that key details were exaggerated or distorted. Politicians lose votes and even positions when accomplishments from their past are revealed to be exaggerations of what they really did.

Credibility comes from a root word that means to believe. It is important to have credibility when speaking about a topic, especially one about which you want to appear to be an expert. Credibility is earned by having expertise that listeners trust. That trust is gained by being meticulous about presenting details. Be aware of the words and phrases that you choose to describe a situation. When making a generalization, make certain that you have the facts to back it up. When stating a fact, make sure that it is absolutely accurate.

What Would You Do?

You are on a school panel, listening to a friend argue for the need for more stylish band uniforms. Suddenly, you hear him describe an incident in which he states that you were cruelly mocked at a football game at another school, when in fact nothing like that happened. He finishes and hands the microphone to you. What do you say?

Think Critically

1. Which stock issue enables you to make offensive negative arguments?

2. Which terms does the affirmative debate team define?

3. What are the three parts of a disadvantage?

Research NOW!

4. Jargon is technical terminology or words that have a special meaning when used with a particular topic. Investigate a career that interests you. Identify and define five examples of jargon related to that career field.

5. Use the Internet to find at least five reputable sources of information about a career that interests you. Record the citations for the websites.

6. Listen to a proposal being made about a key issue, either in Congress, your community, or your school. Isolate the key terms on which the proposal rests and apply the standards that you learned in this lesson. See if the proposal is strengthened or weakened by your investigation.

Write NOW!

7. Use the jargon you defined in activity 4 to write a one-page essay about the career and why it interests you.

 8. **TEAMWORK**   Exchange essays with a partner. Verify that the citations and the jargon are used correctly in the essay.

9. Write a brief response to the proposal that you examined in activity 6. Either defend it or challenge it based upon your analysis of the key terms of the original argument.

Speak NOW!

10. Use the essay you wrote in activity 7. Read the essay aloud. Use your sources to verify the pronunciation of each jargon example.

 11. **TEAMWORK**   Pair up with a classmate. Take turns reading to your partner the essays written in activity 7. Challenge the usage or pronunciation of any jargon examples.

12. Read your essay for activity 9. Practice poise and conviction in your delivery. Invite classmates to question and comment on your presentation.

Do You Agree?

Resolved The jury system in the United States should be significantly changed.

Affirmative position

Yes, the concept of a jury of peers was at one time a cornerstone of American justice. However, the law has become so complex that it is time to revamp the jury trial system.

Negative position

No, our judicial system is the finest in the world. Problems do occur, but overall no other system works as well as ours.

PHILOSOPHY IN DEBATE

A **kritik** (pronounced like critique) is an offensive argument that challenges a certain way of thinking. Kritik questions the philosophy behind the affirmative debate team's case rather than challenging the case itself. Therefore, kritik can be described as a philosophical argument.

Philosophy is a system of concepts that form an underlying theory of a topic. Many large topics have been discussed by using a system of associated concepts, such as the philosophy of war, a philosophy of education, and even the philosophy of life. Obviously, all philosophies do not agree. Your philosophy of life may differ from others.

Some topics lend themselves to a philosophical investigation, which leads to philosophical arguments and debate. Thus, kritik, which challenges an underlying philosophy, can be viewed as an argument during a debate.

Basically, the kritik says that every affirmative argument has value, but it asks if we should debate the affirmative team's argument as such. Instead, a kritik argues that what should be debated is the philosophy that underlies the affirmative team's argument. Advanced debaters looking for a more challenging debate often turn to the kritik. It can be argued that the kritik challenges you to look differently at an argument. As the negative team, you can claim that an issue exists that is bigger or broader than the resolution and the broad issue must be dealt with before the affirmative plan can be considered. This approach focuses the debate on the larger issue, detouring around the affirmative team's much more focused argument. The kritik argument can be difficult to use.

Use the Kritik

FYI The use of kritik in debate is controversial. Before researching a kritik, verify that your debate coach supports the use of kritik.

To use a kritik successfully, you should become familiar with the kritik argument. It is important to know the types of kritiks, the hazards of using a kritik, and the structure of a kritik.

Types of Kritiks

Many types of kritiks are available for your use. The language kritik and the knowledge kritik are two of the more common types.

- **Language kritiks** The basic premise of the **language kritik** is that the language used in the affirmative case is harmful. It argues that the power of the language selected by the affirmative debate team was misunderstood. Language that is sexist, racist, ambiguous, or inflammatory can create an atmosphere in which the affirmative plan cannot be successful. As the negative debate team, you use a language kritik to offer a philosophical approach that challenges the language of the affirmative case, arguing that the language prohibits success and a discussion about language must take place before we could possibly solve the harm scenarios.

- **Knowledge kritiks** The **knowledge kritik** is based on the premise that we lack the knowledge to solve for the resolution. As the negative team, you suggest that, although the topic is important, we currently lack the information, education, or research ability to solve for the resolution. Therefore, the debate will focus on how to gain the knowledge needed to consider the resolution, and you argue that we are not where we need to

©JENKEDCO, 2009/USED UNDER LICENSE FROM SHUTTERSTOCK.COM

What must you remember when using the kritik?

be to realistically consider the resolution presented by the affirmative debate team.

Specific types of kritiks can include political and economic categories. Additional kritik types might include feminism, materialism, or other philosophical topics.

Hazards of Using Kritiks

As the negative team, when you commit to the kritik, you abandon traditional negative arguments. You cannot use other arguments with the kritik. For traditional judges, this can create the feeling that they do not have real arguments to consider. The kritik offers them a discussion, but no real options for solving for the resolution.

Another hazard is the old dilemma of putting all of your arguments in one basket; you win or lose based on one argument as opposed to the multi-argument attack of the traditional approach. When you use a kritik, it should be well-structured.

Structure the Kritik

Although there is more than one way to structure a kritik, the following construction is a good start. In this structure, the kritik begins with an observation, followed by impacts, and finally a decision rule.

- **Observation** To establish the kritik, you must establish an **observation**, which is a major argument, similar to a contention. The premise of the kritik is established through the observation.

- **Impacts** To help the judge understand the repercussions of the kritik, you will need to establish the basis of the kritik. The information offered will create the framework for the debate on the kritik.

- **Decision rule** The **decision rule** argument establishes an all or nothing decision. As the negative debate team, you are asking the judge to accept the kritik in contrast to the affirmative plan. This is referred to as an *a priori* position, which must be considered before any other position.

Before you try to use a kritik, remember that it is a one-way decision. You cannot make any additional arguments. Be sure that your kritik is well-structured and accurate before you start the argument.

What is a good way to structure a kritik?

COURTESY OF NATIONAL FORENSIC LEAGUE, WWW.NFLONLINE.ORG

Scopes Trial—1925

In 1925, one of the greatest legal debates of the twentieth century occurred in the small town of Dayton, Tennessee. That year, the Tennessee legislature passed the Butler Act, a law against teaching evolution or any theory that opposed the creation of man as stated in the Bible. Evolution was the theory published in Charles Darwin's book *On the Origin of Species* that all natural species had evolved over a long period of time. Many felt that Darwin's theories challenged the Bible's assertion that all creation occurred within seven days. The American Civil Liberties Union (ACLU) wanted to challenge the Butler Act and offered to defend anyone brought to trial for teaching the theory of evolution. They convinced John Scopes, a 24-year-old football coach and substitute teacher at the public high school to deliberately teach evolution. Scopes agreed to be the focus of a case to test the new law.

Scopes used a standard text that included Darwin's theory. He was arrested for including evolution in his curriculum. The resulting court case was billed as the trial of the century, but it became known as the "monkey trial" because many thought that the theory of evolution was on trial.

Many of the participants were already famous. Clarence Darrow was the attorney representing Scopes. Darrow was an agnostic who had gained a reputation as a defense lawyer representing labor figures. The prosecutor was William Jennings Bryan, a former Secretary of State and three-time presidential candidate. Bryan believed in a literal interpretation of the Bible. Bryan characterized the evolution theory as "millions of guesses strung together."

The trial lasted 11 days. The ACLU's original defense plan was to argue that the Butler Act violated a teacher's individual rights. As the trial progressed, however, the debate became centered on how to interpret the Bible. In a bold move, Clarence Darrow put William Jennings Bryan on the witness stand. The exchange became heated when Bryan insisted that Darrow quote the Bible word for word, instead of paraphrasing it. Finally, the presiding judge called a halt to the questioning and the case went to the jury.

After deliberating for nine minutes, Scopes was found guilty and fined one hundred dollars for teaching evolution. The Tennessee Supreme Court later set aside the conviction, ruling that the jury, not the judge, should have determined the fine.

Think Critically

Today, people still debate creationism versus evolution. What was the final effect of the Scopes trial?

Think Critically

1. What type of kritiks are described?

2. What are the hazards of using a kritik?

3. What is the structure of a kritik?

Research NOW!

4. Use the Internet to explain why this type of argument is called a kritik.

5. Search the Internet to find more information about a kritik.

6. Select a public proposal and analyze it in terms of its philosophy. What are the basic ideas upon which it is founded? Try to distill them and summarize them for the class.

Write NOW!

7. Select language kritik or knowledge kritik. Write a one-page essay describing how you would apply one of these kritiks to the resolution at the beginning of the lesson.

8. **TEAMWORK** Working with a partner, compare the essays you wrote for activity 7. Combine your work into one essay or, if you chose different kritiks, select the best essay and make improvements.

9. Write a kritik based upon your analysis in activity 6 above. Consider whether or not the underlying philosophical ideas are too large for the original proposal.

Speak NOW!

10. Use the essay created in activity 7 to read aloud. Focus on clearly pronouncing all of the words.

11. **TEAMWORK** Read the essay from activity 7 to your partner. Evaluate your partner's presentation and suggest improvements. Focus on the speaker's body language during your evaluation.

12. Deliver the kritik you wrote for activity 9 to the class. Invite questions and comments.

6

Chapter in Review

6.1 Use Defensive Negative Arguments

- In LD debate, the negative debate team builds a case. In CX debate, the negative debate team builds arguments. Use defensive negative arguments to challenge the significance of the harm stock issue, the inherent barrier of the inherency stock issue, and the solvency stock issue.

6.2 Use Offensive Negative Arguments

- Use offensive negative arguments to challenge the topicality stock issue. To challenge topicality, you must challenge the definition, identify the violation, establish the standards, and request the judge's vote.
- Use the disadvantages argument, consisting of a link, brink, and impact, as an offensive negative argument.

6.3 Use the Kritik

- A kritik is an offensive argument that challenges the philosophy behind the affirmative debate team's case.
- The language kritik and the knowledge kritik are the most common types of kritiks. A kritik consists of an observation, impact, and decision rule.

Develop Your Debating Language

Select the term that best fits the definition. Some terms will not be used.

a. attitudinal inherence
b. bias
c. brink
d. decision rule
e. disadvantage
f. fiat
g. field context definition
h. impact
i. knowledge kritik
j. kritik
k. language kritik
l. link
m. negative arguments
n. observation
o. philosophy
p. presumption
q. standard
r. structural inherency

1. Deals with laws, regulations, guidelines, and so on

2. The argument that if the affirmative debate team's plan is ratified, bad side effects will occur

3. Evidence that shows a connection to the affirmative plan

4. A system of concepts that forms an underlying theory of a topic

5. Idea that you are innocent until proven guilty

6. A guide to weigh the violation

7. An argument that establishes an all or nothing decision

8. An attitude, such as racism or feminism, exists and it is so entrenched that only a radical change will solve the harm scenario

9. An offensive argument that challenges a certain way of thinking

10. A major argument, similar to a contention

11. The meaning of a term in the "real world"

12. A prejudice toward a specific idea or cause

13. Claim that the action called for by the affirmative team's plan will initiate the disadvantage

14. An act of will that creates something without effort

Review Debate Concepts

15. How do you categorize negative arguments?

16. What is the most fundamental negative argument you can make?

17. Who is responsible for proving evidence?

18. What type of data does the affirmative debate team most commonly use?

19. As the negative debate team, how do you challenge the inherent barrier?

20. Is it harder to argue structural inherency or attitudinal inherency?

21. How do you challenge solvency?

22. Which stock issue can you challenge with an offensive negative argument?

23. What will the affirmative debate team do if you do not establish a direct link between your challenge and their case?

24. How do you establish that a topicality violation has occurred?

25. What are the standards that you can use to compare your negative position to the affirmative team's case and plan?

26. As the negative team, how can you offer the judges the opportunity to vote for you?

27. How would you categorize the disadvantages argument?

28. What should be in a disadvantages argument?

29. What does a kritik challenge?

30. How does a kritik change the direction of an argument?

31. What is the premise of a language kritik?

32. What is the premise of a knowledge kritik?

33. Why could the kritik argument be difficult for a judge?

34. What is a major argument that makes up a kritik?

35. What is an *a priori* position?

Make Academic Connections

36. **PROBLEM SOLVING**   Read an Op Ed piece that could be used as an affirmative argument. What kind of negative argument could you build to oppose the position? Identify the negative arguments you could use.

37. **MATH**   Affirmative arguments often use statistics. Look at a military conflict and identify statistics used to support or oppose the conflict. Write a one-page essay describing how the statistics were interpreted to support or oppose the conflict.

38. **ENGLISH**   While learning about negative arguments, you encountered several words borrowed from other languages. Identify five additional

words that originated in other languages. Provide definitions and examples of their use.

39. **HISTORY**   Political parties are often on opposite sides of a debate. Select the Democratic or Republican party. Write a one-page essay about the party's formation. How has the party's philosophy changed or remained consistent since the party was established?

40. **CHALLENGES**   Watch a televised commentary that supports a current topic. Identify the arguments you would use to oppose the commentator's position.

Research NOW!

41. Review the Scopes trial that occurred in 1925. Research the background and locate transcripts of the trial. What were the key philosophies behind the arguments of the prosecution and the defense? Offer a kritik based upon your research.

   42. **TEAMWORK**   Working with a partner who selected the same side of the Scopes trial in the previous activity, evaluate the arguments made to support the side. Make a list of things you would have done differently.

Write NOW!

43. *Presumption* is a term used in debate and in legal situations. Write a one-page essay describing how the presumption of innocence affects debates and legal proceedings.

   44. **TEAMWORK**   Working with a partner, examine a political speech given recently in your city or state. Look for evidence of bias in the speech. Rewrite the speech, removing any biased statements you found.

45. Select one of the resolutions provided at the beginning of each lesson. Write a one-page essay describing how you would build the negative arguments opposing the resolution.

46. Continue your research of the Scopes trial from activity 41 above. Review the findings that dismissed the ruling of the previous court. What was the impact of that final decision? Who, in your opinion, won the case? Write a short paper on your conclusions.

Speak NOW!

47. News is broadcast around the clock, but each news story is only a small piece of the broadcast. Therefore, many stories contain sound bites, portions of a longer speech. Identify several sound bites in today's news. Evaluate how the speaker delivered each sound bite. Practice delivering the sound bite. How does your delivery differ from the sound bite?

48. Find the text of a speech given by Bobby Jindal and a video of Jindal presenting the speech. Make a video recording of yourself presenting the speech and then watch the recording. Identify five ways that your presentation differed from Jindal's delivery. Which presentation was better? Why?

49. **TEAMWORK** Funding is often important in political debates about new legislation. Working with a partner, investigate the funding planned to pay for a current piece of legislation. Deliver a brief speech supporting or opposing the funding planned for the legislation. Evaluate your partner's speech based on content and delivery.

eCollection Activity

The 1920s brought many changes to American life and culture, and many of those changes found their way into high school education.

Advances in technology brought about new possibilities in employment, and these possibilities required training. New courses were added to the curriculum in the sciences, industrial arts, home economics, and physical education to prepare students for a changing world. Students moved from rural to urban areas to attend schools that offered these courses. Increased enrollment required more schools and more teachers, teachers who received better training in new areas of instruction.

The controversies of the 1920s found their way into high schools as well. Religious debate was publicized with the Scopes trial but did not end there. Debate over funding for church-based schools raged in the 1920s. The Supreme Court overturned an Oregon law requiring all students to attend public schools, and the debate over funding continues to the present day. Other controversies such as the Red Scare, the worry about communism, made public schools as a place where citizens received training in civic responsibility.

Still, advances in instruction were introduced in the 1920s. The so-called Dalton Plan emphasized the value of individual projects conducted in the laboratory, and the Contract Plan also allowed for individualized instruction whose requirements were set down in a written contract signed by both student and teacher.

To learn more about the culture and issues of the 1920s, access www.cengage.com/school/langarts/debate and click on the link for Chapter 6. Choose one area of interest and locate informative articles on the subject. Write a one-page essay about your findings. Remember to provide citations for your information.

CHAPTER 7

Cross-Examination Debate: The Competition

FAMOUS DEBATERS

> **" Ifill 'always knew' that she wanted to be a journalist. "**

In a long and distinguished career as a journalist, Gwen Ifill has often used debate skills to advance her career. Perhaps this was most evident when she moderated the vice presidential debates in 2004 and 2008. As an investigative reporter and as a respected talk show guest and host, Ifill knows how to pose and answer tough questions. She was the White House correspondent for *The New York Times* and a local and national political reporter for *The Washington Post*. She has also been a reporter for the *Boston Herald American* and the *Baltimore Evening Sun*, where she began to focus on politics. In Baltimore, she began to gain experience in front of the television camera. Ifill hosted a news program for a local public television program.

Ifill switched from newspaper reporting to television reporting when she joined NBC News. She became NBC's chief congressional and political correspondent. She began appearing as a guest on political television. Her political expertise, poise, and humor made her a popular guest on programs such as *Meet the Press* and *Washington Week*, a PBS show that discusses public affairs.

PBS was impressed with her abilities. In 1999, PBS hired her for two of its news discussion programs. For *NewsHour with Jim Lehrer*, she was a senior correspondent. She interviewed key political figures and reported political news and events. She also filled in for Lehrer from time to time, gaining the experience to host a news program.

She is the moderator and managing editor of Public Broadcasting's *Washington Week* and senior correspondent for *The NewsHour with Jim Lehrer*. On *Washington Week*, the best journalists in Washington discuss the major stories each week. With all of these responsibilities, Ifill also became the best-selling author of *The Breakthrough: Politics and Race in the Age of Obama* in 2009.

How did Ifill prepare for this career? She was born in New York in 1955. Ifill "always knew" that she wanted to be a journalist. In 1977, she graduated from Simmons College in Boston with a degree in communication. She gained her first practical experience in journalism at *The Boston Herald* through an internship program while attending college.

Since starting her career, Ifill has won a host of honorary degrees (15 at last count) and she has received several awards for broadcasting excellence. She has also been honored by the National Press Foundation, *Ebony* magazine, the Radio Television News Directors Association, and American Women in Radio and Television. Ifill has served on the board of several organizations, including Harvard University's Institute of Politics.

Think Critically

How has Ifill used her communication skills to build a successful career as a journalist?

Gwen Ifill

GOALS

Describe the role of each team member.

Describe how and when each team member should speak.

TERMS

rebuttal

kick

demeanor

Do You Agree?

Resolved Pharmaceutical companies should not be allowed to advertise their products directly to the consumer.

Affirmative position

Yes, direct advertising is harming the public's health. Pharmaceutical companies should be able to inform only professionals, such as pharmacists and doctors, of their products. They should not advertise directly to consumers who do not have the knowledge to evaluate the product's advantages and disadvantages.

Negative position

No, America has a market economy. Pharmaceutical companies should be able to purchase advertising as needed to increase profits. They should be able to compete like any other company.

What Do You Do?

You have learned how to build an affirmative case and negative arguments. Now it is time to put together everything you know about CX debate.

Remember that CX debate is a team activity that has a set structure and established rules. To effectively work together, you must understand your role in the debate, what your teammate expects from you, and when you should speak.

In CX debate, two teams of two debaters argue opposite sides of a single issue. Each teammate has the opportunity to present his or her position about the topic, present a rebuttal to the opposing team's position, question one member of the opposing team, and answer questions from one member of the opposite team.

First, you will learn to identify what you do in each role. Then, you will look at how your responsibilities fit into the structure of the debate.

First Affirmative

The two members of the affirmative team are the first affirmative (A1) and the second affirmative (A2). The two members of the negative team are the first negative (N1) and the second negative (N2). If you are A1, you are responsible for the first affirmative constructive speech, which presents your team's case and plan. Immediately after you present your case, you are questioned by N2. Later, you cross-examine N1 after his or her presentation and, finally, present a rebuttal speech.

First Affirmative Role	
First affirmative constructive	Present the case and plan.
First negative cross-examination	N2 cross-examines you.
First affirmative cross-examination	You cross-examine N1.
First affirmative rebuttal	You support your case and respond to negative arguments.

- **First affirmative constructive speech**   You present your team's case, plan, and the primary explanation that establishes your team's goals in relation to the resolution. This speech supports the resolution. It is the first speech in the debate.

- **First negative cross-examination**   N2 cross-examines you. Be prepared to answer questions about the content of your presentation.

- **First affirmative cross-examination**   You cross-examine N1. Questions should be specifically focused on the arguments presented by the negative team. Ask specific questions about the stock issues, disadvantages, counter plan, or kritik. These specific questions will help set up the arguments that A2 will present.

FYI The name of a cross-examination period is based on its sequence and which debate team asks the questions. For example, the first negative cross-examination period is the first questioning period in which a member of the negative team asks the questions.

What are the first two speeches in a CX debate?

- **First affirmative rebuttal speech**   The word **rebuttal,** or to rebut, means to refute by evidence or argument. Use this opportunity to bring into focus your team's affirmative perspective. This speech continues the debate and brings to the surface your affirmative arguments. You can also offer a rationale to explain why your affirmative team is winning the debate.

Second Affirmative

The second affirmative supports and extends the affirmative case. If you are A2, you are responsible for the second affirmative constructive speech, which strengthens your team's case and plan. Immediately after you speak, you are questioned by N1. Later, you cross-examine N2 after his or her presentation and, finally, present the last speech in the debate.

Second Affirmative Role	
Second affirmative constructive	Rebuild the affirmative case and answer the main arguments presented by N1.
Second negative cross-examination	N1 cross-examines you.
Second affirmative cross-examination	You cross-examine N2.
Second affirmative rebuttal	You rebuild your case and respond to negative arguments.

- **Second affirmative constructive speech**   Answer the attacks presented by N1. Follow the sequence established by N1's constructive speech to keep the debate organized. Offer specific responses comparing and contrasting the negative position to the affirmative case and plan. If the negative team presents stock issues, respond by presenting evidence to support your original position. Plan ahead for potential attacks. If the negative team presents a disadvantage, respond by challenging whether the disadvantage is generic or specific. Compare your advantages to the disadvantages. If the negative team presents a counter plan, closely examine the link, brink, and impact of the counter plan. You want to show that the counter plan is less competitive than your plan. If the negative team presents a kritik, understand its language before you challenge its validity.

- **Second negative cross-examination**   N1 cross-examines you about the answers you gave to the main negative arguments in your second affirmative construction speech.

- **Second affirmative cross-examination**   You cross-examine N2 about the arguments in his or her second negative constructive speech.

- **Second affirmative rebuttal speech**   This speech is the last in the debate. If N2 **kicked** some arguments (used a strategic move to eliminate an argument that they originally advanced) in his or her second negative rebuttal speech, then you should ignore those arguments and focus on the remaining arguments. Be sure to rebuild the original position and respond to the negative attacks. Present the key arguments to win the debate. Summarize your team's case and plan, present the rationale explaining why your team should win, and request the judge's vote.

First Negative

If you are N1, you are responsible for the first negative constructive speech, which presents your team's arguments. Immediately after you present your case, you are questioned by A1. Later, you cross-examine A2 after his or her presentation and, finally, you present a rebuttal speech.

First Negative Role	
First negative constructive	Present your main negative arguments, such as challenging the harms and stock issues, and providing disadvantages, counter plans, or kritiks.
First affirmative cross-examination	A1 cross-examines you.
Second negative cross-examination	You cross-examine A2.
First negative rebuttal	You present and extend the negative arguments.

- **First negative constructive speech**   This speech is the first opportunity for the negative debate team to present arguments. There are different philosophies about what type of arguments you should present. Note that local traditions may limit or direct your efforts. Your first option is to attack the harm area presented by the affirmative debate team. You can do this by challenging the significance of the harm area or by questioning the validity of the harm. You can read evidence, question the sources of the affirmative team's evidence, or offer logical examples to challenge the harms. The value of this strategy is to create a doubt in the judge's mind about the validity of the harms. Your second option is to choose from the stock issues, disadvantages, a counter plan, or kritiks. You can argue all or part of this list. The philosophy for the negative team is to put enough arguments in the round to defeat the affirmative team. The sequence, quantity of arguments, and type of arguments will have to be decided in the round. As beginners, you should choose arguments that you understand and that feel comfortable to you.

- **First affirmative cross-examination**   A1 cross-examines you about the main arguments you presented in you first negative constructive speech. Expect questions that focus on the arguments you made in your first negative constructive speech.

- **Second negative cross-examination**   You cross-examine A2. Your questions should specifically address the affirmative responses to your main negative arguments.

- **First negative rebuttal speech**   This speech is the second half of the negative block and the first rebuttal speech. In this speech, you should present the other part of the negative position.

Second Negative

If you are N2, you are responsible for the first negative cross-examination, the second negative constructive speech, the second affirmative cross-examination period, and the final negative rebuttal speech.

Second Negative Role	
First negative cross-examination	You ask A1 questions about the case and plan that he or she presented.
Second negative constructive speech	Re-establish your negative position and respond to attacks.
Second affirmative cross-examination	A2 cross-examines you about your constructive speech.
Second negative rebuttal	Summarize all of the negative arguments and request the judge's vote.

- **First negative cross-examination**   You ask A1 questions about the case and plan that he or she presented in the first affirmative constructive speech. This is the first cross-examination in the debate.

- **Second negative constructive speech**   This speech starts the negative block. This is your last chance to introduce new arguments. Use this speech to re-establish the negative position and continue the debate. Specifically, you should deal with the original negative arguments presented by N1 in the first negative constructive speech and A2's responses to the negative's arguments. As the negative team, your arguments should be divided between you and your partner. Dividing the arguments allows much greater depth of analysis and refutation. This speech should also cover different issues from those your partner will cover in his or her constructive speech and rebuttal speech.

- **Second affirmative cross-examination**   A2 cross-examines you. The questions should be about your constructive speech, focusing on the arguments you presented.

- **Second negative rebuttal**   This is the final negative speech. Do not present any new arguments or issues. This rebuttal is your opportunity to kick an argument, dropping an argument you have already established. Some arguments have greater weight than others and are more likely to be used by the judge when deciding the winner. You want to emphasize these stronger arguments. Therefore, you should summarize your team's negative arguments, present the rationale explaining why your team should win, and request the judge's vote.

How and When?

The structure of a CX debate is determined by rules, but how you perform your role can help determine the winning team.

How to Present Information

The way that you present information helps your audience determine your sincerity and knowledge. You probably know someone who can make a joke without smiling, making you wonder if he or she is really joking or not. As a debater, you do not want your audience to doubt your sincerity or question your intentions. Your **demeanor**, or your outward behavior or manner, should reflect your sincerity.

Speeches   In CX debate, each debater gives two speeches—one constructive speech and one rebuttal speech. The first affirmative constructive speech is the only speech in the debate that is not affected by any other speeches or questions, since it is the first speech in the debate. Therefore, this speech should be well practiced and free of fluency errors. The speaker should be able to read quickly, but maintain a persuasive tone of voice. The reading should be of a noticeably high quality level that will let the judge and the opposition know that the speaker is prepared and practiced.

Cross-examinations   In CX debate, every debater cross-examines another debater once and every debater answers questions once. When you ask questions, you should present a demeanor that is polite and knowledgeable. When you answer questions, you must be well versed on the topic and able to answer the questions convincingly and quickly.

You also want to be ready to speak when it is your turn. Be familiar with the structure of the CX debate so you know when to speak.

COURTESY OF NATIONAL FORENSIC LEAGUE, WWW.NFLONLINE.ORG

What should your outward demeanor reflect while speaking? Why?

When to Present Information

The sequence for each part of a CX debate is dictated by the rules of cross-examination debate. Over the years, the duties of each debater and the sequence of the stages in a CX debate have been defined through trial and error.

Sequence and Time for a CX Debate		
Sequence	**Stage**	**Minutes**
1	First affirmative constructive speech	8
2	First negative cross-examination period	3
3	First negative constructive speech	8
4	First affirmative cross-examination period	3
5	Second affirmative constructive speech	8
6	Second negative cross-examination period	3
7	Second negative constructive speech	8
8	Second affirmative cross-examination period	3
9	First negative rebuttal speech	5
10	First affirmative rebuttal speech	5
11	Second negative rebuttal speech	5
12	Second affirmative rebuttal speech	5

A CX debate has 12 stages in which specific debaters perform specific tasks. The length of each stage is determined by the rules followed by that particular debate. This information is provided in the debate's description or rules in a format similar to 8/3/8/3/8/3/8/3/5/5/5/5. Because the stages are always in the same sequence, the numbered sequence identifies the length of each stage.

The length of each stage might differ between debates, but the ratio of each stage to the other stages will be similar. The longest time period is given to constructive speeches. Cross-examination periods and rebuttal speeches are given less time. For example, a debate may use 6/3/6/3/6/3/6/3/3/3/3/3. Time usage is critical. In many debates, the judge will not consider anything said after the time limit expires.

Preparation time is also critical to debating. During cross-examination periods that do not require your involvement, you can prepare for your next stage. If you are involved in a cross-examination period by asking or answering questions, remember that your partner is using this time to prepare. Use all of the allotted time.

Each team also receives a predetermined amount of preparation time that the team can use as needed. If additional preparation time is taken, the time is usually removed from the offender's speaking time.

Think Critically

1. What are the responsibilities of the first affirmative debater?

2. What are the responsibilities of the second affirmative debater?

3. What are the responsibilities of the first negative debater?

4. What are the responsibilities of the second negative debater?

5. What happens during a cross-examination period?

6. How many cross-examinations and speeches does each debater perform?

Research NOW!

7. Gwen Ifill is frequently televised. Watch several clips of her appearances or a full episode of a television show in which she appears. Describe her demeanor. What impression do you have after watching her?

8. Investigate the requirements for a degree in communication or journalism. Describe several required classes.

Write NOW!

9. Read the resolution at the beginning of the lesson. Research current pharmaceutical advertisements. Write a one-page summary describing your findings.

10. **TEAMWORK** Working with a partner, use the essay that you wrote in the activity 9 to create a case and plan supporting the resolution or create arguments opposing the resolution.

Speak NOW!

11. In front of a mirror, read aloud the summary you wrote in activity 9. What demeanor do you project?

12. **TEAMWORK** Pair up with a classmate. Present the summary that you practiced in activity 11. Evaluate your partner's demeanor while he or she is presenting the summary and as an audience member.

13. Imagine that you are an investigative journalist. Write a list of questions that you would like to ask Gwen Ifill. Ask a member of your class to role-play and pose the questions as you would in a real interview situation. Afterwards, ask for comments and feedback from the class.

Do You Agree?

Resolved The United States should continue to participate in the United Nations.

Affirmative position

Yes, because some nations continue to be an international threat, the United Nations is the only group that has the hope of successfully containing such a threat. The United States cannot fight issues like terrorism alone. Only collectively can we have a chance of success.

Negative position

No, the United Nations continues to be inept and unsuccessful in fighting problems such as terrorism, world hunger, and disease. The United States would be better served to go our own way.

Presentation Skills

You enter the room for your first debate. Your hands feel clammy. Either there's a small earthquake or your knees are shaking. It's too late to run, so you head toward your team's area. In just a few minutes, your study, hard work, and practice will be put to the test. As you walk, you remind yourself of the presentation skills you learned.

Many beginning debaters focus intently on their arguments, cases, and plans. They focus on trying to remember every detail. Instead, you should remember that debate is a communication activity. The judges and the other team must be able to understand what you are saying. Your thoughts must be spoken effectively and concisely.

The old saying that "practice makes perfect" holds true for debate as well as many other activities. If you are a member of the affirmative team, practice your case and plan the secondary responses. If you are a member of the negative team, practice your disadvantages, counter plans, and any other arguments you will use often.

As the judge and the opposing team hear your arguments and watch your actions, they develop their perception of your ability. You want this perception to be positive. Often, the perception you establish is as real as any of your arguments, and it can make a big difference in the judge's decision. Practice gives you confidence and poise as you present. Reading your materials out loud often gives you the familiarity that helps you give a clear and polished presentation. Skills such as volume control, pronunciation, word economy, persuasiveness, and professionalism are just as important as the details you have worked hard to remember.

Volume Control

One of the first and most important factors for effective public speaking is volume control. When speaking, make sure that you speak loudly enough for everyone to hear you. In debate, a softly spoken, timid presentation will affect the judge's perception of you as a debater. When you practice presenting your materials, speak forcefully and check your volume to make sure you are speaking effectively. Recording yourself is an excellent way of checking your volume.

Pronunciation

Perhaps one of the fastest ways to sabotage your performance is to mispronounce the words in your case and plan or your arguments. You must be able to clearly pronounce each and every word and be able to explain any word or term if questioned. Debate evidence is often written by government officials, experts, and college professors. When they publish their ideas, they might not consider that high school debaters will be quoting their words. They write for others in their field, professional publications, or research purposes. Their vocabulary will often be very difficult. When using their ideas, you must be able to say the terms and know what they mean. Before you debate, make sure you have become familiar with every new term and that you are able to use the terms effectively. Practice any terms that are difficult to pronounce.

©MONIKA WISNIEWSKA, 2009/USED UNDER LICENSE FROM SHUTTERSTOCK.COM

How can a dictionary help you to prepare for debate?

Word Economy

Choosing your words carefully and precisely is an effective tool for speaking in debate. All speeches and cross-examination periods have strict time limits. As you gain experience as a debater, you will begin to find ways to express yourself by using language more effectively. One of the skills that will aid you is the ability to say what you need to say with fewer words and greater precision. Often, a young debater will ramble, making it difficult for listeners to follow his or her train of thought. Word economy will help you keep your thoughts clear as you express your ideas in the debate.

One very helpful technique is to look at your arguments and determine which ones are easy to understand. These arguments can be expressed verbatim and they need little explanation. Therefore, you don't need to speak about these simple arguments very much. On the other hand, the arguments that are more difficult to understand will need to be explained. Practice explaining the difficult arguments and then try explaining these same arguments using fewer words. Remember that, in debate, the end result should be clear and concise. Avoid rambling and lengthy explanations whenever possible. Say only what needs to be said and nothing else.

Persuasiveness

Part of the foundation for any effective speaker is the ability to **persuade**, to move someone to a belief or a course of action. Ultimately debate is persuasive in nature. Your goal is to persuade the judge to vote for your arguments. The tone of voice you use should be persuasive. Your tone of voice should have an urgency of importance that the judge will recognize. Intellectually, you appeal to the judge through the use of evidence, examples, and emotional appeal.

The ancient Greeks spent a great deal of time discussing persuasion and its value in public speaking. Persuasion is still recognized as a crucial element in debate today. Different judges' experience levels vary and the use of persuasion is even more important with judges who are less experienced.

To be an effective speaker, you should use persuasion when delivering your ideas. Using specific emphasis, stressing key phrases and words, and using varying rates of delivery and volume are all effective persuasive devices. As a speaker, you will decide what works best for you. As you hone your skill, the ability to persuade will serve you well.

Professionalism

Every debater has an obligation to present ideas in the most professional manner possible. An attitude of **appropriateness**, suitable for the environment, is absolutely necessary when debating. Every debater will get caught up in the competitiveness of the round and every debater wants to win. These are not good reasons to abandon an attitude of professionalism.

In athletics, the term *sportsmanship* describes the desired attitude of respect and fairness. In debate, the term **professionalism** is used to describe the attitude of friendly competition. A key to professionalism is to avoid personal attacks. It is perfectly acceptable to attack the opponent's arguments, but it is never acceptable to attack your opponent. Terms such as *stupid, ridiculous, absurd,* or *idiotic* are never appropriate and they will cause your opponent to want to respond at the same level. Using professional language allows you to remain competitive, but avoids the personal attack that will turn a debate into an argument.

Keep in mind the image that you want to project to the judges. It is just as important as the words you say. No matter how debating changes in the future, your presentation style will always be important.

Delivery Styles in Debate

You can find as many different opinions about how you should debate as there are schools and coaches. The part of the United States you live in will dictate much of how you debate. Here, you will learn about two of the most popular delivery styles.

Traditional Delivery

Traditional delivery is the style of delivery that is deliberate and moderately paced. It is the familiar form of delivery that is more related to public speaking and it is considered to be more conventional. As a beginning debater, you will begin by learning traditional delivery and later decide whether spreading is more appropriate for your situation.

FYI Before competing, discuss your coach's philosophy about style and delivery. This is essential to work effectively as a team.

For students who are learning **extemporaneous speaking**, a type of impromptu speaking done with little or no preparation time, the pace of traditional delivery is similar to the pace of extemporaneous speaking. Word economy, discussed earlier, is especially important if you use a traditional delivery.

The coaches who prefer the traditional delivery style argue that it allows the judge to follow the debate more effectively. They also think that this skill is useful in the real world, while spreading is a specialized skill that is not usable anywhere else. Even if you use spreading, some debate rounds require the slower pace of the traditional delivery style due to the nature of the round.

What is "spreading"?

Spreading

The term **spreading** is used to describe a rapid form of delivery that allows the debater to value quantity and quality of information more than it is valued in a traditional form of presenting information. Debaters use spreading when they want to move quickly to get in more arguments and information. You must ask how fast is too fast and ask if it is necessary to go quickly at all.

Speed drills are activities that help you learn spreading skills. Spreading is an advanced skill that you should work on only after you have a strong understanding of debate.

In some parts of the United States, spreading is an accepted form of delivery, but it is not accepted in other parts of the country. The issue becomes more complicated because some judges accept spreading, but others do not. As a beginning debater, the ability to use spreading may not be beneficial in your immediate future. Discuss this issue with your coach and look carefully at the traditions in the region of the United States where you live and at the judges for whom you will be debating. The judging criteria used in your part of the country and your specific debate competitions influence the skills that will become most familiar to you.

YOU BE THE JUDGE

Because judges make decisions that affect others, they are held to a high standard of ethical behavior. In the legal profession, these standards are particularly high because decisions can mean life or death to those affected. The Judicial Conference adopted a code of conduct for U.S. judges in 1973. The latest changes to the code of conduct were made in 2009. The code of conduct has five basic canons.

1. A judge should uphold the integrity and independence of the judiciary.

2. A judge should avoid impropriety and the appearance of impropriety in all activities.

3. A judge should perform the duties of the office fairly, impartially, and diligently.

4. A judge may engage in extrajudicial activities that are consistent with the obligations of judicial office.

5. A judge should refrain from political activity.

In all kinds of judging, the judge's impartiality is critical to achieving fair results. Impartiality is important for judges in the courtroom and in the debate hall. Regardless of who judges your debate competition, the judge's impartiality is assumed.

What Would You Do?

In several recent competitions, you notice that one of the judges seems to favor a particular type of argument. Does this preference indicate that the judge is not impartial? Later, when you watch your team participate in another competition that has the same judge, the opposite team uses the type of arguments that the judge seems to prefer. What will you do if the opposing team wins? What will you do if your team wins?

Think Critically

1. What is the focus for most beginning debaters?

2. How can practice improve your debate skills?

3. How can you verify that your speaking volume is at the correct level when you are debating?

4. Why is word economy considered to be a debate skill?

5. How important are your presentation skills during a debate?

6. What are the two most popular delivery styles?

Research NOW!

7. Investigate the attitude toward the spreading delivery style in your area. Write a paragraph explaining the attitude to the delivery style. Record citations for your sources.

8. Read about the ancient Greek attitude toward persuasion in public speaking. Write a paragraph that describes their thoughts about persuasion in public speaking.

Write NOW!

9. Select an advertisement that is televised or printed in a magazine. Write a one-page essay that describes how the advertisement tries to persuade the audience to think or behave a certain way.

 10. **TEAMWORK** Working with a partner, write a television advertisement that persuades a viewer to think or behave a certain way.

Speak NOW!

11. Write down 10 terms that you have difficulty pronouncing. Listen to the correct pronunciation at an online dictionary. Practice saying the terms aloud in front of the mirror. Make note of the ways in which you can improve. Keep practicing until you can say the word perfectly every time.

 12. **TEAMWORK** Pair up with a classmate. For the class, perform the television advertisement you wrote in activity 10.

13. Prepare and deliver an eight-minute speech on television advertising. Make certain that you have a strong central idea and that you develop that idea with examples. Practice delivering your speech on your own until you only occasionally rely upon notes. Then deliver it for the class and ask for comments on your demeanor and delivery.

Do You Agree?

Resolved The federal government should establish, finance, and administer programs to control air and/or water pollution in the United States.

Affirmative position

Yes, as a nation we still lack a uniform effort to battle pollution. We have made significant improvements, but still have far to go. A unified national effort is the only choice.

Negative position

No, we have allowed the United States government to administer our efforts in fighting pollution and the efforts have failed miserably. We need a new direction. We need to do more ourselves rather than depend on the government.

Types of Judges

You know it's rude to stare, so you glance at the judge and try to absorb an overall impression. Judges have an important role in debate. In every debate, the two teams debate for a judge. The judges, who are assigned by the tournament, should not know the debaters. In time, some judges will recognize some of the debaters, especially if they judge often. The judges are instructed to evaluate each debate separately and they must not allow their opinions to influence their decisions. Judges' experience and capability will range. Each judge will render a decision, fill out the ballot, and offer comments about why the decision was made. Learning about judges, ballots, and oral critiques will help you perform at your best.

Judges come in all shapes and sizes. Their experience ranges from no experience to very experienced. Judges are expected to be at least high school graduates and they must be willing to listen impartially to the debate. Judges are authority figures. Keep an open mind about their comments and don't be intimidated by performing in front of them.

The tournaments you attend recruit judges from a variety of places. The host school needs a large number of judges and it might require that its students recruit judges. Students might approach many adults in an attempt to get enough judges for the tournament. The judges they recruit could include community judges, teachers, coaches, former debaters, and parents.

Community Judges

A **community judge** is an individual recruited from the community who volunteers to judge at the tournament. This type of judge has no experience and will have no expectation of what will happen in the debate. Sometimes, the tournament will provide an instruction sheet, a judging seminar, or ask students to explain what the judge should listen for in the debate.

When debating for this type of judge, a traditional delivery style will work best. Avoid rapid delivery or the use of debate terminology. The judge may not have many helpful comments at the end of the debate, but the judge will make a decision and, ultimately, every vote counts equally.

Teachers

When students from the host school recruit judges, they will probably ask their teachers to judge at the tournament. Teachers are accustomed to evaluating students, but they are not necessarily familiar with debates. On the other hand, teachers might have knowledge about the resolution because the topic falls within the subject they teach.

When debating for this type of judge, use a traditional delivery style. Avoid rapid delivery or the use of debate terminology because they are probably not familiar to the teacher. This judge may not have many helpful comments about debating, but every vote is equal.

Coaches

When students attend tournaments, their coach is sometimes required to judge. If your coach is assigned to judge, he or she will not judge students from your school. A coach from a different school might be assigned to judge your team. This is one of the best types of judges. This judge will be familiar with the topic and will know how to debate. You can relax and do your best

What can you learn from a judge's critique?

debating with this type of judge. Coaches will give you many suggestions and directions about your debating performance. This type of judge will be an excellent resource for improvement.

Former Debaters

Former debaters are recruited and sometimes paid to judge. Their expertise makes them excellent judges. Relax and do your best debating for this type of judge. For the rounds they judge, experienced former debaters are very helpful as judges. They know what to do. They will offer useful suggestions that can improve your skills.

Parents

The host school's students will also recruit their parents to judge. Sometimes reluctant, this type of judge is similar to the community judge. When debating for this type of judge, use a traditional delivery style. Avoid rapid delivery or the use of debate terminology because it might not be understood. This judge might not have many helpful comments. Remember that every vote counts.

Adapt to the Judge

Judges are randomly assigned, so you might encounter different kinds of judges during a tournament. Make sure that you adapt to the judge. You cannot expect the judge to adapt to you. After you recognize what type of judge has been assigned to you, customize your approach to the judge's level of expertise. Failure to adapt could cause you to lose or make your win more difficult. You may briefly and politely interview a judge before the round to ascertain his or her level of expertise. Some tournaments will collect information about the judge's philosophy and publish the information, which will aid you in determining how to adapt to the judge. The judge's philosophy about debate is often referred to as a **paradigm**. Regardless of the information

How can you customize your approach to a judge?

NEUSTOCKIMAGES/ISTOCKPHOTO.COM

provided, it is your responsibility to adapt to the judge and not the other way around. Every judge provides feedback by filling out a ballot. Some also provide an oral critique.

Ballots and Oral Critiques

Feedback is an essential part of improving your skills. Feedback from experienced judges might be more valuable than feedback from inexperienced judges, but it is up to you to learn from every debate. Ballots and oral critiques provide essential feedback.

Ballots

The form used by the judge to indicate his or her decision and write comments is called the **ballot**. The format is standardized. Although several different ballots may be used across the country, they are very similar. Each ballot provides a place for the judge to write comments about each debater and space to explain his or her vote. Some comments contain constructive criticism that can seem unkind. Focus on the constructive aspect and use it to your advantage. Hopefully, a ballot has many constructive comments and is an excellent learning device.

The ballot also provides a place for the judge to indicate **speaker points**. These points are awarded to each debater, usually on a scale that ranges from 15 to 30 points, with 30 points being the highest. The judge assigns points based on the performance of each debater. The points are used to help determine who advances to the elimination rounds. In the elimination rounds, the top teams continue to debate beyond the preliminary rounds. The ballots are returned to your coach during the tournament.

FYI The normal range for speaker points is 22–29. A score of 30 is usually reserved for "perfection." Usually, the team with the highest combination of points wins the debate. If the judge believes that the team with the lowest number of speaker points should win, he or she writes "LPW" on the ballot to indicate a low point win.

Oral Critiques

At the completion of the round, some judges offer verbal feedback. This is referred to as an **oral critique**. Although controversial in some parts of the United States, the oral critique can be useful to debaters. The judge may not be able to write everything on the ballot. A conversation after the round gives the judge and the debaters the opportunity to cover a great deal more about the round than the judge could cover on the ballot. The dilemma faced at many tournaments is that the oral critiques take time and this can affect the tournament schedule. Judges want to share their thoughts and the debaters want to hear them, but some coaches and some teams feel that these critiques are counterproductive.

Ballots and oral critiques provide excellent opportunities to learn more about debate and improve your skills. Many opportunities to improve your CX debate skills surround you every day. It is up to you to take advantage of the opportunities and to follow up with practice to improve your performance at your next competition.

©STOCKLIGHT, 2009/USED UNDER LICENSE FROM SHUTTERSTOCK.COM

Women in Broadcasting

Today, women are in prominent positions in broadcasting. They act in entertainment programs, host talk shows, and anchor the news. Behind the scenes, they write, direct, operate cameras, and run networks. This didn't happen overnight. Many women pushed the boundaries during their careers to provide the opportunities that are available today.

Mona Kent wrote every script for the *Portia Faces Life* radio soap opera from 1940 to 1951. The main character was Portia, who is a successful attorney and young widow with a child. Kent opened doors for other female writers—and female attorneys.

Martha Brooks hosted a radio talk show, *The Martha Brooks Show*, from 1937 to 1971. In the late 1930s, she began by writing, producing, and starring in live television shows.

From 1937 to 1958, Helen Sioussat was the director of Talks and Public Affairs for CBS radio. She managed 300 broadcasts annually, which covered topics as varied as education, civil rights, and government.

These three women are only a few examples of the female pioneers in broadcasting. On September 5, 2006, Katie Couric became the first woman to serve as the solo anchor of a weekday network evening news program. She is the anchor and managing editor of the *CBS Evening News with Katie Couric*.

Couric was not the first female television news anchor. Barbara Walters worked her way up the journalistic hierarchy. The NBC network hired Walters in 1961 as a researcher and writer for the *Today* show. Initially, she was assigned stories that were considered to appeal to female viewers. She requested additional responsibilities and within a few months, she received the assignment of travelling with Jacqueline Kennedy, who was the first lady at the time, to India and Pakistan. In 1964, she became a co-host of the *Today* show, although she was not given the title. Walters was officially identified as a co-host in 1974. In 1976, she joined ABC and became the first female co-anchor of a network evening news program. She also moderated a presidential debate in 1976. Since then, she has continued to be one of the best-known interviewers on television.

All of these women moved forward with bravery, intelligence, and determination. But they are only a handful of representatives. Many others created pathways into new careers, opening doors for today's women.

Think Critically

Some careers today are primarily held by members of a single sex. Would you have the courage to enter a field dominated by members of the opposite sex?

Think Critically

1. What are five types of judges?

2. What are the minimum requirements for a debate judge?

3. Which types of judges might not recognize advanced debate strategies?

4. Which types of judges are more experienced?

5. How do judges vote for a winner?

6. What is the purpose of awarding speaker points?

Research NOW!

7. Obtain a copy of a ballot that is used in your area. Identify the major categories on the ballot and the information a judge should provide.

8. Investigate to determine if spreading is used in local debates.

Write NOW!

9. Make a list of 25 adjectives and 25 adverbs that could be used on a ballot to describe a debater's performance.

 10. **TEAMWORK** Working with a partner, write instructions telling community judges how to judge a debate.

Speak NOW!

11. Use the instructions you wrote in activity 10. Practice delivering the instructions. Record your presentation. When you watch the recording, note any verbal errors or mispronunciations. List improvements you could make to the presentation. Make the improvements and record your presentation again.

 12. **TEAMWORK** Continue to work with your partner. Read the instructions you wrote in activity 10. Use a ballot to evaluate your partner's presentation and suggest improvements.

13. Prepare a presentation on the rise of women in broadcasting. Do some research in print and online resources and gather information about key figures other than the women who were discussed in the Turning Point found in this chapter. Try to illustrate your presentation with photographs or images from the time periods in which these women lived and worked.

Chapter in Review

7.1 Who Does What When

• The first affirmative, second affirmative, first negative, and second negative are team members who play roles in CX debate. When speaking in a CX debate, your demeanor should reflect your sincerity.

• The sequence for each part of a CX debate is dictated by the rules of cross-examination debate.

7.2 Presentation Skills and Styles

• Volume control, pronunciation, word economy, persuasiveness, and professionalism are important presentation skills.

• The two most popular delivery styles are traditional delivery and spreading.

7.3 Debate Judging

• Community judges, teachers, coaches, former debaters, and parents are common judges at CX debates.

• Ballots and oral critiques provide valuable feedback that you can use to improve your debate skills.

Develop Your Debating Language

Select the term that best fits the definition. Some terms will not be used.

1. To move someone to a belief or a course of action

2. Activities that help a debater learn spreading skills

3. Attitude of friendly competition

4. The judge's philosophy about debate

5. Points awarded to each debater

6. To refute by evidence or argument

7. Outward behavior or manner

8. Rapid form of delivery that allows the debater to value quantity and quality of information more than it is valued in a traditional form of presenting information

9. Form used by judge to indicate his or her decision and write comments

10. Suitable for the environment

11. Judge's verbal feedback at the end of a round

12. Individual recruited from the community who will volunteer his or her time by judging at the tournament

13. Use a strategic move to eliminate an argument that was advanced earlier

14. Type of impromptu speaking done with little or no preparation time

a. appropriateness
b. ballot
c. community judge
d. demeanor
e. extemporaneous
   speaking
f. kick
g. oral critique
h. paradigm
i. persuade
j. professionalism
k. rebuttal
l. speaker points
m. speed drill
n. spreading
o. traditional delivery

Review Debate Concepts

15. What are the four things that every team member is responsible for during a CX debate?

16. Who presents the affirmative case and plan?

17. Who is cross-examined by the second affirmative debater?

18. What should the affirmative team do if an argument is kicked?

19. What are the first negative debater's options during the first negative construction speech?

20. Who delivers the final negative speech?

21. How many speeches does each debater deliver?

22. How is the sequence in which each debater speaks determined?

23. During the debate, when do team members prepare?

24. What is the focus of most beginning debaters?

25. How does a judge develop his or her perception of you as a debater?

26. Why might your presentation contain difficult terminology?

27. Why is word economy important?

28. How can you demonstrate professionalism?

29. What are the characteristics of spreading?

30. Why do judges' experience levels vary so much?

31. Which types of judges probably do not have a good understanding of debate?

32. Which types of judges will understand debate strategy?

33. How can you adapt to a judge?

34. How are speaker points used?

35. How is an oral critique helpful?

Make Academic Connections

36. **PROBLEM SOLVING**   You are hosting a tournament at your school. List the adults you could ask to serve as judges.

37. **MATH**   Speaker points can be compared to grades earned for performance in a class. Create a table that contains three columns: speaker points, letter grades, and percentages. Fill out the table so that the number of speaker points is in the same row as the equivalent letter grade and percentage grade.

38. **ENGLISH**   Write a one-page essay describing the difference between a persuasive document and an objective document.

39. **HISTORY** Investigate the history of broadcasting. Create a timeline that identifies key moments in broadcasting.

40. **COMMUNICATION** Select a worthy cause. Investigate to determine how you could use your communication skills to help the cause.

Research NOW!

41. Op Ed commentaries are always identified as commentaries rather than news. Write a one-page essay explaining why this practice is followed by all reputable news agencies.

42. **TEAMWORK** Working with a partner, identify other activities in which team members work together toward a common goal. Describe how the team members rely on each other to succeed as a team.

Write NOW!

43. Watch a local news broadcast and a national news broadcast. Evaluate one reporter and the news anchor from each broadcast. Fill out ballots for the reporters and the anchors. Offer constructive comments to improve their skills.

 44. **TEAMWORK** Select a current local issue. Write a news story about the issue that could be broadcast on the local news.

45. Select a current local issue. Write two paragraphs that could describe the issue on a news broadcast. Write two paragraphs that could persuade others that one side of the issue is correct. How do the two versions differ?

Speak NOW!

46. Select a topic that is familiar to you. Write a constructive speech about the topic. Record the speech using the spreading style and record the speech using the traditional style. Watch both recordings. Write a paragraph that describes the different impressions an audience member would get from the different styles.

47. Watch the most recent episode of *Washington Week* (available on the Internet). Select a topic discussed on the show. Based on the information on the show, prepare a five-minute extemporaneous speech about the topic. Record your presentation. How does your performance compare to the performance of the guest on the show?

 48. **TEAMWORK** Use a news story you wrote in one of the above exercises. Make a video recording of each team member reading the report. Sit with your teammates to watch all of the recordings. Give an oral critique after watching each recording.

49. Most national news broadcasters do not have a strong regional accent. Watch a recording you made in a previous activity. How does your accent compare to most national broadcasters?

eCollection Activity

The use of steroids in professional sports became a hot topic when star athletes admitted that they took performance enhancing drugs during their careers. They believed that only the finish line mattered, not how they reached the finish line.

Anabolic-androgenic steroids, commonly known as steroids, have been used by professional athletes to increase muscle mass and strength. These athletes wanted to increase the number of homeruns they hit, the number tackles they could perform, or the distance they could throw. Many soothed their consciences by using that tired old phrase, "everyone else is doing it." Some argued that they couldn't compete with other athletes who took steroids if they did not take steroids as well. Instead of bravely stepping forward by stating that no one should take drugs to alter their natural performance, these professional athletes stayed quiet and took drugs too.

What are steroids? The full name tells you more about the drug. *Anabolic* indicates the growth of tissue. If you are trying to "bulk up," growing tissue doesn't sound too bad. *Androgenic* indicates a substance that promotes male characteristics. That starts to sound a little dangerous. Steroids are usually made from synthetically modified testosterone.

Testosterone affects a lot more than your throwing arm. It can cause baldness and severe acne. All of the changes aren't visible on the outside. Steroids can also cause tumors in your liver, increase aggressive behavior, inhibit your natural growth, and cause depression. You may be able to throw a ball farther, but will you care about how far you can throw the ball if you develop any of these medical problems?

Do your research and think before you decide to take a drug that might affect you for the rest of your life. To learn more about steroids, access www.cengage.com/school/langarts/debate and click on the link for Chapter 7. Write a one-page essay about your findings. Remember to provide citations for your information.

CHAPTER 8

Student Congress

Real People | Real Careers

Al Gore

> *"Gore's debate expertise has promoted his career to one of historical importance.*"

Al Gore has had two passionate interests for most of his life: politics and the environment. As a long time debater, he has argued passionately for them both. Gore grew up in a political environment. His father, Albert Arnold Gore, Sr., was a representative and then senator from their home state Tennessee. As a high school student, Al Jr. began to refine the skills that would serve him throughout his life. He led his school's debate team. During the summer, he worked on the family farm in Carthage, Tennessee, where he cherished closeness to the earth.

Gore went on to attend Harvard University, where his coursework ignited his passions. He took a course in climate science and became interested in the environment. After the assassination of Dr. Martin Luther King, Jr., Gore took a course in political science and became interested in politics. He decided to major in Government. But upon graduation, Gore's path took a different turn. Even though Gore was opposed to the Vietnam War, he enlisted in the army and served as a military journalist.

Gore was honorably discharged in 1971, but life had changed. His father had been defeated in his bid for reelection to the Senate in 1970. Gore worked the night shift for *The Tennessean* as an investigative reporter. By this time he had married his high school sweetheart Mary Elizabeth "Tipper" Aitcheson. Still searching, Gore attended Vanderbilt University Law School, but left before graduating. He had decided to embark upon a political career. Gore served in the U.S. House of Representatives for four terms, returning home almost every weekend to stay grounded in his constituents' priorities. He ran for Senator in 1983 and won, continuing on to serve for eight years.

While Gore served in the Congress and the Senate, he avidly debated the issues that concerned him, especially environmental protection and sustainability. This strong advocacy helped Gore to secure a spot beside then Governor Bill Clinton in the presidential race of 1992. They defeated Republican candidate George Herbert Walker Bush, receiving 43 percent of the vote to Bush's 37 percent. As Vice President, Gore attempted many reforms, such as increased energy consumption tariffs, foreign policy initiatives and international trade laws. In 2000, Gore ran for the presidency of the United States. He lost by less than five hundred votes.

After losing the presidential election, Gore returned to his concerns about the environment. His efforts to educate the public about global warming became the subject of a documentary called *An Inconvenient Truth*. In 2007, Gore was awarded the Nobel Peace Prize for his work to save the planet. Gore's debate expertise has promoted his career to one of historical importance. His ability to research the issues, argue for effective legislation, and speak passionately about his concerns has truly helped to make the world a better place.

Think Critically

What can a debater learn from Al Gore's career?

GOALS

Understand how Student Congress functions as a debate activity.

Understand legislation in Student Congress.

TERMS

Student Congress
chamber
committee
docket
bill
resolution

Do You Agree?

Resolved The President of the United States should be elected by the direct vote of the people.

Affirmative position

Yes, the time has come to allow the citizens of the United States to directly elect their President; an informed electorate can make the choice. When the Electoral College was first created, the need existed. The need has passed, and it is time to allow the citizens to elect the President.

Negative position

No, despite all of our advances, the citizens continue to lack the knowledge to effectively elect our President. The Electoral College is necessary to insure that our democracy continues to function. Perhaps someday it will not be needed, but not yet.

Student Congress as a Debate Activity

You are excited to hear that your debate class has been invited to participate in Student Congress. You learn that **Student Congress**, or Stu Co as some call it, is similar to the Congress in Washington, DC, except that it is smaller. Groups of students, usually between ten and thirty, are divided into **chambers**, sometimes called Houses or Senates. Just like the real chambers in Congress, you will have the opportunity to write and vote on legislation or laws passed by a voting assembly. When the Congress in Washington, DC, passes legislation, it is sent on to the President who signs it into law. In Student Congress, you will write and argue for your own legislation with the hope that, after a process of debate, it will receive a winning majority of votes from other student legislators.

Like other forms of debate, you will learn and hopefully master many skills as a legislator in Student Congress. You will expand your knowledge on a wide variety of issues and ideas. Student Congress gives you the opportunity to speak and argue for legislation that you have written, legislation that came from your own observations and concerns. You must be able to think quickly on your feet as you introduce and defend your own legislation, and as you argue for and against the legislation of other students. You must speak clearly and forcefully in front of what might be a fairly large audience.

Like other debate tournaments, there is a judge at Student Congress who will award points to speakers based upon their performances. Sometimes,

What is unique about participating in Student Congress?

a Student Congress can go several rounds that include prelims, quarterfinals, and semifinals. The very best debaters go on to finals, where they are given an imaginary situation that they must write legislation for on the spot.

Legislation in Student Congress

You are anxious to get started. Your teacher tells you that there are different formats for Student Congress, and it is important to learn what they are. In some instances, legislation is submitted beforehand to an event coordinator who, in turn, mails a packet of legislation to your school. In other cases, legislation is submitted once you arrive at the tournament site.

Committees

At Student Congress, students are assigned to **committees.** You will receive a registration packet with your committee assignment. Like Congressional Committee in Washington, DC, Student Congress committees are based upon different kinds of legislation.

- **Public Welfare Committee**   This committee deals with legislation relating to the public good. Topics such as fairness in housing, hiring for jobs, and health care protection are considered.

- **Foreign Affairs Committee**   International relations such as border issues and matters relating to defense are areas this committee is concerned with.

- **Ways and Means Committee**   This committee (also called Economics Committee) oversees legislation responsible for government spending, as well as the means of raising money to cover that spending.

When your committee meets, a chair is elected. A chair is usually an experienced debater. The event coordinator will give the committee all of the submitted legislation that falls under its jurisdiction. The committee sets an agenda, called a **docket**, of legislation to be debated and voted on.

Bills

Legislation at Student Congress always involves bills and resolutions. A **bill** is a proposed new law. Usually, a bill responds to what the author sees as a problem in some area of society.

Topics used for bills are as varied as topics in debate. Current issues and events make an excellent start for the subjects of bills. Looking to national and international events is also a good place to look for topics for bills. Whatever you choose, you should be well versed and knowledgeable about the subject of your bill. Be willing to do any research necessary on the topic. In choosing a subject for your bill or resolution, make sure that there are two sides, with potential for debate. As you choose subjects, look for issues that arouse strong opinions on either side. That will interest people in wanting to hear both sides and therefore ensure meaningful debate. To be successful in Student Congress, you will need to give an effective speech. Effective speeches come from strong opinions.

FYI The One Hundred and Tenth Congress met between January 3, 2007, and January 3, 2009. Members of the 110th Congress introduced nearly 14,000 pieces of legislation, more than any Congress since 1980, but only about 3.3 percent of the bills actually were signed into law, the lowest success rate since 1976.

Resolutions

A **resolution,** unlike a bill, does not become a law. Rather, it proposes a topic worthy of public consideration. Some resolutions in the Congress in Washington, DC, honor specific persons. These resolutions often declare a day to be set aside to honor someone who has distinguished himself or herself in the service of the community or the country as a whole. Other resolutions take a stand on a particular problem or situation. Think of a situation where you have taken a stand: "The menu in the cafeteria needs to be changed," or "The school library should have more recent periodicals." In both of these examples, you are not recommending a solution. You are simply stating that a problem exists and should be fixed.

A resolution before Congress is much like these examples except it is on a grander scale. The problems are serious and affect the lives of countless persons, both at home and abroad. Issues like famine, terrorism, racism, and genocide are all important subjects for resolutions. You are looking for those issues that we need to work towards resolving, but at this time we have not been able to solve. Resolutions are important ways to raise confidence in Congress. They show that legislators are aware of important issues and problems and are willing to take a stand. Start thinking about what kind of legislation you want to write and debate.

TURNING POINT

HULTON ARCHIVE/GETTY IMAGES

Civil Rights Act of 1964

Throughout the later eighteen hundreds and stretching into the first half of the twentieth century, African Americans were restricted by a series of state and local laws popularly known as Jim Crow laws. The name originated with a song and dance routine from the 1830s that mocked African Americans. Restrictions based upon literacy tests and property taxes prevented blacks from voting. Jim Crow laws allowed the segregation of schools, lunch counters, restrooms, beaches, and other places of entertainment.

Efforts to challenge these laws had gone on for nearly a century. In 1955, Rosa Parks refused to surrender her seat to a white person in the whites only section of a Montgomery bus and was arrested. In protest, Reverend Martin Luther King, Jr. led the Montgomery Bus Boycott to end segregation in the city's transit system. Throughout the early 1960s, protests and demonstrations drew more and more attention to the need for civil rights reform.

Efforts to pass civil rights legislation were challenged in 1957 and 1960, because of procedural complications in both the House of Representatives and the Senate. Efforts in the Senate in particular suffered from the use of the filibuster, a provision in Senate Proceedings that allows for unlimited speeches. One senator who opposed the Civil Rights bill of 1957 spoke continuously for twenty-four hours and eighteen minutes. While the bill passed, it had been amended beyond recognition and was largely ineffective.

In 1963, President John F. Kennedy went before the nation on television to propose a civil rights bill that he hoped would address the shortcomings of earlier legislation. Tragically, Kennedy did not survive to see the bill pass. His successor, President Lyndon B. Johnson worked tirelessly to see that the bill passed without being weakened by compromise. President Johnson wanted to link the bill to President Abraham Lincoln and the fact that the United States had just celebrated the one-hundredth anniversary of Lincoln's Emancipation Proclamation of 1863. Johnson declared in a White House press conference "I hope [the civil rights bill] is acted upon in the House before the members leave to attend Lincoln Day meetings throughout the nation, because it would be a great tribute to President Lincoln to have that bill finally enacted upon in the House before we go out to celebrate his birthday."

Think Critically

What are the advantages and disadvantages of compromise in passing legislation?

Think Critically

1. What is Student Congress? How is it different from other debates?

2. What are the different kinds of committees used at Student Congress?

3. What is a bill? What areas of concern do bills address?

4. How is a resolution different from a bill?

Research NOW!

5. Look into the National Forensic League website (nflonline.org) for more information about Student Congress. Look into the history of the event and famous debaters who have been written about.

6. Read recent issues of your local newspaper. Look for articles about legislation that was written, sponsored, or opposed by your local Congresspersons. Study their reasons for supporting or opposing the legislation. Be prepared to agree or disagree with the reasons.

Write NOW!

7. Write a letter to your senator or congressperson proposing a bill or resolution. State the problem or issue you wish to address, and why it deserves attention. If you are proposing a bill, explain how it would solve the problem. If you are proposing a resolution, state why it should be a matter of public consideration.

8. **TEAMWORK** Working with a partner, review the proceedings of the last month from the Congressional Record (gpoaccess.gov/crecord). Have one of you review the Senate proceedings, and the other proceedings from the House of Representatives. Write a summary of the kinds of bills and resolutions being debated. Report your findings to the class.

Speak NOW!

9. **TEAMWORK** Pair up with a classmate. Make a presentation on an issue that affects your local community. Explain why current laws are inadequate to deal with the situation. Have your partner argue the opposite position. When you are done, ask your classmates for their reaction.

10. Imagine that you are a candidate for Congress. Deliver a speech in which you state the kinds of concerns that you have for your community and the kinds of legislation you would like to see address those concerns. Ask for questions and comments and see how well you can think and speak on your feet. After you are finished, ask how many of your classmates would vote for you.

Do You Agree?

Resolved Governmental financial support for all public and secondary education in the United States should be provided exclusively by the federal government.

Affirmative position

Yes, the current method of funding for the states has bankrupted most of them. Currently, many states rely on property taxes. This means of funding is outdated and cannot keep up with the increasing cost of education. The federal government has a variety of resources and could more adequately fund education.

Negative position

No, with federal money comes federal control. We have enough of that already. Local governments will have a better understanding of the needs of local education. The federal government has a huge deficit at the present time. A greater role in funding would make that deficit worse. The federal government should not be the only means of funding for education.

GOALS

Understand researching for Student Congress.

Understand writing legislation for Student Congress.

TERMS

policy
article
whereas

Researching for Student Congress

As you start to think about what legislation you will write and defend, keep in mind that you want topics that will create a lively debate. Think about current issues in society that are important and effect many people. Pay attention to what you hear people talking about. Study newspapers and broadcast news reports. Focus your concerns as specifically as you can.

Once you have a clear idea about the problem or issue that you want to address, you are ready to begin your research. As you proceed, you may discover ideas that you had not thought of, and these can be incorporated into your bill or resolution. Or, you can use those ideas as you respond to the attacks on your legislation. Either way, you will benefit greatly from your efforts and your bill and resolution will be stronger.

You will also need to do research about legislation authored by other students. In some cases, your teacher will provide you with a packet of bills and resolutions that will be used at the contest. In other instances, you will learn about other legislation at the debate site. Whatever the case, in order to speak for or against legislation, you should be informed about recent issues and concerns relating to public welfare, foreign affairs, and economics or ways and means. Be prepared to speak with authority and conviction about the bills and resolutions before you.

Useful Sources

As you begin the process of researching your bill or resolution, you will want to limit your search to resources that show up-to-date thinking and scholarship. As with other types of debate, use journals, books, or online resources that are respectable. Make sure that they were published or produced by organizations such as libraries, universities, and organizations with solid reputations. Beware of biases. Beware of authors who don't cite sources and only seem to be offering their opinions. Look for facts, statistics, documented interviews, anything that will help to build your case. As you find articles that support your bill or resolution, be sure to print or copy the articles.

As you search for topics, especially if you are interested in bills or resolutions relating to foreign affairs, you will want to expand your search to research materials published outside of the United States. Many excellent topics are international in nature. As you research your bill or resolution, make sure to go online and read some international articles published in the *London Times* or the *Manchester Guardian*, for example. This type of research will give your bill or resolution a sense of international importance.

Organizing Your Research

It is important to organize your research so that you can look at it quickly if you need to. Collect all of the articles you copied or printed on your bill or resolution, and place them in a three-ring binder. As you debate your bill or resolution, you may need to verify your information for your opponents. If you have those articles in a binder, you can find them quickly and easily if needed. As you print out or copy the articles, make sure that you have the URL if it's an online source, or proper source information if it's printed material. This is necessary to prove the creditability of your bill or resolution. For quick reference, you may even want to highlight the parts of the article you used.

Why is it important to have current research when writing a bill or resolution?

©MONKEY BUSINESS IMAGES, 2009/ USED UNDER LICENSE FROM SHUTTERSTOCK.COM

Writing Legislation

You have probably heard political figures talk about their domestic policy, foreign policy, or financial policy. A **policy** is a plan of action designed to solve a problem. A bill is written to turn a policy into law. If you are writing the bill, you must remember that it is a plan being put into action. If you have ever had to propose an outing, you know that you always have to say what will happen and how much it will cost. Because a bill is a law, you also have to include who will carry it out or enforce it, and what penalties, if any, will be imposed on those who do not conform to what it requires. The wording of your bill should show that you have carefully planned these areas. The bill should explain the step-by-step process that will resolve the problem area you mean to target.

FYI When the Senate and the House pass a bill in identical form, it is then sent to the president for his signature. If the President signs the bill, it becomes a law. Laws are also known as Acts of Congress. Statute is another word that is used interchangeably with law.

Format for Writing a Bill

The format for a bill is very specific. It is usually broken into stages called **articles**. Articles break down the steps of a bill for easy reference. Some writers also number the lines of a bill for easy reference during debate. While the format of a bill may vary from tournament to tournament, the basic principles are the same.

Title of the Bill

Usually a bill is introduced by a formal statement that states that it has been debated in Student Congress.

Article I	State the new policy to be adopted in a sentence.
Article II	Define any terms or phrases that are key to the bill.
Article III	Tell the date on which the new law would go into effect.
Article IV	Name the government agency which will be responsible for putting the new law into effect.
Article V	Include any punishment for breaking this law.
Article VI	Explain how funding will be provided to put the new bill into effect.
Article VII	State that all other laws that are presently in effect that are in conflict with this new law would then be null and void, that is, no longer in effect.

Respectfully Submitted by
High School Name

Look at the following example and notice how the articles explain how the bill will be put into effect.

A Bill to Decrease Drug Use

Be it enacted by the Student Congress here assembled that:

Article I   Any person receiving a driver's license or having a license renewed shall be subject to a mandatory drug test at the renewal site.

Article II   A drug test will be defined as a urine, blood, and/or hair sample that a person will be expected to give.

Article III   This bill shall take effect immediately upon passage. Persons found to have a positive result for illegal drugs will not be allowed to receive or renew a license to drive.

Article IV   This legislation shall have full force of state and federal law, and shall be enforced by federal, state, and local law enforcement agencies.

Article V   Anyone found to have illegal drugs in their system will have the opportunity to test a second time for illegal drugs.

Article VI   A $10.00 fee will be added to each application for a license or renewal to offset the cost of the program. Additional funding will be allocated through each state's normal budgetary process.

Article VII   All laws in conflict with this bill will henceforth be declared null and void.

Respectfully Submitted by
Jefferson High School

Notice how each article has a specific purpose and uses concise and clear language to state that purpose. The bill is clearly and carefully organized. The author paid close attention to detail. Organization and details show that you have thought through the bill and prepared carefully. When writing the bill, make sure that you have a clear plan as to how you want to structure your sections.

The bill can be no more than one page. It must be typed and double-spaced. Before you submit a bill, read it out loud to hear how it sounds. You might want to ask a classmate to listen and offer feedback. Check it carefully for spelling or grammatical errors. Legislation that you write and submit for debate represents you. Therefore, like your own grooming and performance, it must be neat and free from error.

Format for Writing a Resolution

Usually, when you state an idea or opinion, you follow it with reasons. Often, you will introduce your reasons with the word *because*. When writing a

What elements should
a bill include?

resolution, you do the reverse. The resolution is written to encourage debate over issues that need to be considered for the public interest. The resolution will offer reasons for discussion first. This is called a *whereas* statement. **Whereas** means the same as because and introduces your reasons. At the end of the resolution, you will suggest the action that will become the focal point of the debate. This is introduced with the word *resolved*. The format for a resolution is very specific. As with a bill, some writers number the lines for easy reference during debate. Look at the format below. Notice how, in writing a resolution, whereas statements trickle down from one to the next, linked by the word *and*.

Title of a Resolution

WHEREAS   State the problem as you see it.

WHEREAS   Describe the wide range of effects of the problem stated in the first whereas; and

WHEREAS   Explain how the problem creates harm or danger.

Be It Therefore Resolved That   State your resolution on how the problem should be addressed. Include a call to action.

When you present a resolution before Student Congress, make sure that your topic is a serious one. Think of yourself as a spokesperson who is speaking for people unable to speak for themselves.

> # United Nations Resolution
>
> **WHEREAS** The United Nations was created over 50 years ago and has outlived its purpose; and
>
> **WHEREAS** The United Nations' solutions to problem areas such as Georgia, Afghanistan, Iraq, and Darfur were either slow, nonexistent, or ineffective; and
>
> **WHEREAS** The United Nations has monetary issues that prevent successful action.
>
> **Be It Therefore Resolved That** The United States should withdraw from the United Nations.
>
> Respectfully Submitted by
> Dickinson High School

Notice how each "whereas" has a specific purpose and how its language is very concise and clear. Notice also that the therefore statement is a clear call to action. Like a bill, a resolution can be no more than one page. It too must be typed and double-spaced. Like your own appearance and performance, it must be neat and free from errors.

A well-written bill or resolution will stimulate good debate, but in order to effectively argue for its passage, you need to understand the laws and policies of debate at a Student Congress.

What types of situations require a resolution?

Think Critically

1. How should you research for Student Congress?

2. Why is it important to be well organized for Student Congress?

3. What is policy? How is policy related to the writing of a bill?

4. How is writing a resolution different from writing a bill?

Research NOW!

5. Read current and back issues of your local newspaper. Look for articles about problems in your community. Choose one. Prepare a short summary as to why this particular problem deserves attention in the legislature.

6. Review legislation for the past year and note all resolutions that were passed. Do you notice any trends in what Congress wants to raise for consideration? Make a list and share your findings with the class.

Write NOW!

7. Imagine that you are a senator or congressperson from your state. Write a short description of your policy about education. Be sure and list what you would change and what you would keep about the way students are educated.

8. **TEAMWORK** Consult the Congressional Record and find a bill that is being debated before Congress. With a partner, analyze how the bill includes the elements noted in this section. Write a short paper on your findings.

9. Choose an issue that involves legislation with international interest. Do some research and compare articles from American sources with those from other countries. Write a paper comparing and contrasting those sources. Be sure to examine different biases and perspectives.

Speak NOW!

10. Find a bill that is currently being debated before Congress. Take a position, and argue to support, oppose, or amend the bill.

11. **TEAMWORK** Arrange a simulated version of a *Meet the Press*-type of program. Have two students portray senators on opposing sides of a piece of legislation. Have four students portray members of the press, and have one student portray the moderator. Let the remainder of the class be the audience. Base the program on actual current legislation. Let the "press" portray columnists or reporters from actual newspaper, magazines, or television networks. Stage a program in which the "senators" briefly state their positions and then respond to questions.

GOALS

Understand the use of parliamentary procedure at Student Congress.

Understand the criteria for judging at Student Congress.

TERMS

parliamentary procedure
Robert's Rules of Order
Presiding Officer
authorship speech
negation speech
amendment
motion
cross-examination
judge

Do You Agree?

Resolved All members of Congress, both House and Senate, shall serve no longer than two (2) consecutive terms.

Affirmative position

Yes, term limits would require those in Congress to make more effective use of their time. Term limits would allow for greater variety and fresh voices in Congress. If more citizens could serve in Congress, it would be a far more representative body.

Negative position

No, term limits are an unfair limitation on public service. Term limits punish the achievements of Congressperson by telling that, despite their achievements in representing their state or district, they can no longer serve it. Term limits also deprive the American people of the opportunity to ultimately decide who stays and who goes in Congress.

Parliamentary Procedure

Now that you have written a bill or a resolution, you are ready to actually participate in Student Congress. Like the Congress in Washington, DC, Student Congress has its own set of rules you must follow. Those rules center on how you must conduct yourself during debate. Unlike other forms of debate, Student Congress uses short speeches and periods of questions and answers. There are also rules specific to Student Congress, regarding organization of the contest, authorships of legislation, speeches and amendments, voting, and cross-examination after speeches.

To make sure that order is maintained, you use parliamentary procedure in Student Congress. **Parliamentary procedure** is a set of guidelines, which allows for discussion by using the democratic process. This means that every participant has the right to speak without any fear of reprisal. This is key to Student Congress, just as it is to the democracy of the United States. Student Congress creates an environment that allows for meaningful debate without interruptions or interference as long as parliamentary rules are followed. Parliamentary rules can be found in a variety of publications, but the most famous is ***Robert's Rules of Order***. You can also find specific information on the National Forensic League website.

Organization of the Contest

The participants will be organized by a seating chart, so you will need to look for your location. In some contests you will be given a placard. You will use the placard to show your name as well as when you want to be recognized to speak. The chamber will elect a leader who will call on competitors who wish to speak or ask a question. The leader is called the **Presiding Officer** or PO. The Presiding Officer will keep a precedence chart. This chart is used to keep track of who has spoken and who has not. If two students raise their hands to speak, the presiding officer will use the chart to determine who has precedence to speak. The precedence is based on the time span between speaking. Whoever has a longer time span has precedence. If neither student had spoken previously, then precedence would be given to whomever the Presiding Officer says should go next. If two students raise their hands to speak and one student had spoken twice while the other had spoken three times, the student with the fewer number of speeches would have precedence.

Speeches and Amendments

The first speech on a bill or resolution is called the **authorship speech**. This speech is guaranteed to the author or his or her representative. The speech is three or sometimes four minutes in length. The purpose of this speech is for the author to elaborate on the bill or resolution. The authorship speech for a bill gives the author the opportunity to explain the rationale and offer information that would not be part of the actual bill. The authorship speech for a resolution gives the author the opportunity to offer depth of explanation that time and space does not allow in the original resolution. The authorship speech should be prepared and practiced before the contest. Authorship speeches are then followed by a **negation speech**, which also may be three or four minutes long.

FYI In the United States Congress, a senator or representative known as a sponsor introduces a bill or amendment and is its chief advocate. The sponsor did not necessarily write the bill, which may have been written by a staff member, an interest group, or others.

Speeches for or against the bill then follow. Speeches are typically three minutes in length. A speech is divided into three sections.

- **Introduction**   Use your introduction to grab the attention of your audience. Begin with an anecdote, fact, or statistic that you recall from your research. End your introduction by stating whether you think the chamber should vote for or against the legislation before it.

- **Contentions**   These are the specific arguments for or against the bill or resolution. Again, use your research to support your contentions.

- **Conclusion**   Restate your contentions and, if possible, return to the fact or anecdote that you began with. At the end of your conclusion, open the floor for cross-examination.

Speeches sometimes propose **amendments**. Amendments allow for participants in Student Congress to amend or change either a bill or resolution. You may agree with a bill or resolution, but you think that part of the legislation

©TONY FREEMAN/PHOTOEDIT

What makes an effective speaker at Student Congress?

needs to be changed. You may amend to improve, but you cannot change the original intent. Amendments should be written out and given to the Presiding Officer at the designated time. If agreed upon, the amendment will be debated in much the same way as a bill or resolution.

Motions

Amendments are introduced through a **motion,** a declaration before the chamber meant to determine the direction of the proceeding. Motions usually require a *second,* another speaker to agree that the motion should be considered. Motions require a majority of votes to pass. Motions begin the debate on a bill. They also propose a move to *table,* or suspend discussion, take the bill from the table or resume discussion, call the question or vote, and adjourn the session. A motion may also be raised to correct an error in parliamentary procedure if one has occurred.

Motions in Student Congress

Motion	Meaning	Requires a Second	Vote Necessary from Chamber for Passage
Main Motion	This opens the session for debate.	Yes	Majority
To lay a bill on the table	This ends debate on a bill. Legislators may return to debate on a tabled bill if it is "taken from the table," or if there is enough time left in the session.	Yes	Majority
To take a bill from the table	This opens debate on a bill that has been tabled.	Yes	Majority
To call the previous question	This ends debate on a bill and calls for a vote.	Yes	Two-thirds majority
To recess	This takes time out from the proceeding. Motion must specify how long the recess should be.	Yes	Majority
To amend	This modifies a bill.	One-third approval	Two-thirds majority
To adjourn	This ends the tournament.	Yes	Majority

Cross-Examination after Speeches

After each speech, there is one minute allotted for **cross-examination** of the speaker. After the authorship speech, there is a guaranteed two-minute cross-examination period. Questions should be in reference to the bill or resolution and/or comments that have been made. After every other speech there is a guaranteed one-minute cross-examination period. You should ask a question for a specific reason and not just for the sake of asking a question.

Voting

After the discussion has been concluded, the chamber will be given the opportunity to vote on the legislation. The Presiding Officer can ask to see a show of hands, ask for a voice vote, or vote by secret ballot. Whichever way the Presiding Officer decides, you should vote every time. Voting is a member's ways of voicing his or her opinion. If you feel that the decision made by the Presiding Officer was biased or incorrect, you may challenge the decision and ask for a revote.

Judging

In addition to the Presiding Officer, Student Congress has an adult official who functions as a **judge**. In each chamber, the judge scores the speeches and makes recommendations as to who should advance to the next level or who should win awards. The judge also serves as parliamentarian, that is, he or she ensures that the rules are followed. Whenever a question arises about procedure, the judge has the final word.

Criteria for Judging

The judge assigns points for each speech. These points are based on the scorer's opinion of your speeches. The scorer assigns points ranging from 1 to 6 points with 6 being the best. Listed below are typical standards that a judge would use to evaluate a speech.

- **Eloquence**   Like in other debates, it is important to speak clearly and powerfully in Student Congress. Use clear and precise language. Vary your tone so as to emphasize the important points of your speeches.

- **Logic**   The points that you make must show that you have thought them through.

- **Organization**   Part of thinking through a speech is in its organization. A speech that has no clear organization loses its audience.

- **Extemporaneity**   It is a bad idea to read from your notes. In some contests, it is against the rules. It is also important to be able to bring up points made by other speakers, either opposing or defending them.

- **Questioning**   Key to being a successful debater in Student Congress is being able to think on your feet. This is especially important when responding

COURTESY OF NATIONAL FORENSIC LEAGUE, WWW.NFLONLINE.ORG

to questions from other speakers. A judge watches how confidently and thoroughly you respond to questions, hopefully strengthening your case.

At the end of the contest, the officials determine a winner and present awards. The speeches that you give and the points that you earn are key to winning an award or advancing to the next level.

How does a judge determine a winner at Student Congress?

YOU BE THE JUDGE

Honesty is a quality that most people value, but not everybody practices. Many cynics roll their eyes whenever they turn on the television or radio and hear a congressperson or senator speaking. They believe that politicians in general don't tell the truth. Politicians sometimes exaggerate details about their own performance just to get votes. Or, they leave out details about deals made or votes missed. For many people, to leave out truthful details is the same as lying.

Honesty is at the heart of a society's trust in its leaders. It is a principal of democracy that goes back to the time of the Ancient Greeks and Romans. Julius Caesar (100 BC–44 BC) was assassinated by a group of senators who believed that he wanted to declare himself king and therefore had lied about his political ambitions. More recently, members of Congress have been censured for lying about illegal deals and practices. It is the responsibility of Congress to call hearings in which leaders of business, health care, and the military, among others, are called to account for their practices. In order to have the moral authority to carry out these hearings, it is important that Congress itself have a perfect record of honesty and integrity.

As a member of Student Congress, it is important that you, too, maintain honesty and integrity in your dealings with others, be they friends, opponents, or judges.

What Would You Do?

A friend of yours delivers a speech that you know meant a great deal to him. You know that he worked hard to prepare, but his actual performance had problems. There were lots of vocalized pauses and he seemed to keep losing his place. After the tournament, he asked you how you thought he did. What do you say?

Think Critically

1. Why does Student Congress use parliamentary procedure?

2. What are the responsibilities of a Presiding Officer?

3. What is the structure of a speech in Student Congress?

4. What criteria does a judge use to evaluate speakers?

Research NOW!

5. Find a copy of *Robert's Rules of Order*. Choose a particular section and look over its procedures. Be prepared to summarize your findings.

6. Look at the Congressional record for debate on a recent bill. Pay attention to how the bill may have changed from its original version. Look carefully at any amendments and decide if they supported or changed the original intention of the bill. Give a short presentation on your findings.

7. Find a speech delivered recently in Congress. Read it over carefully. Then evaluate it according to the standards you have learned. Present your evaluation to the class.

Write NOW!

8. Write a short paper on what you think should be the qualities of a good Presiding Officer.

9. **TEAMWORK**   Find a recent bill in Congress and think about how you might amend it. Pay attention to the original intention of the bill and think about how your amendment supports or changes that intention. Then write a joint paper that proposes your amendment. Be sure and list reasons why you think the bill should be amended.

Speak NOW!

10. **TEAMWORK**   Pair up with a classmate. Choose a bill or resolution that you know is being debated in Congress. With your partner, prepare a three-minute speech in favor of the legislation, and a three-minute speech against it. Make sure that each speech contains an introduction, two or three contentions, and a conclusion. Practice your delivery with your partner and then deliver your speeches in class.

11. Give a short presentation on the importance of being able to speak your mind in a democracy. Include examples from history and current events.

12. Give a presentation in which you offer your evaluation of a recent speech you have heard delivered. Briefly summarize the speech, and then offer your assessment of the speech and its delivery.

8

Chapter in Review

8.1 Bills and Resolutions

- Student Congress, or Stu Co, is a unique debate activity in which students can write their own legislation.
- Students are often organized into committees based upon types of legislation. A bill is a piece of legislation that becomes law. A resolution is a piece of legislation that argues for an issue to become a matter of public consideration.

8.2 Research and Writing

- Use up-to-date scholarship when researching for your bill or resolution. Research the legislation of other students, so you can more effectively argue for or against it.
- Make sure the topic of your bill or resolution will arouse strong opinions and spirited debate. A bill should state how it will work by addressing how it will be funded and how it will be enforced. A resolution states the problem, explains its wide ranging influence, lists all dangers involved, and concludes with a call to action.

8.3 Participate in Student Congress

- Student Congress uses parliamentary procedure to organize legislative debates. Parliamentary procedure is based on a guidebook called *Robert's Rules of Order*.
- Judges oversee Student Congress debates and award points based upon a student's eloquence, logic, extemporaneity, and ability to think on his or her feet during cross-examination.

Develop Your Debating Language

Select the term that best fits the definition. Some terms will not be used.

a. amendment
b. article
c. authorship speech
d. bill
e. chamber
f. committees
g. cross-examination
h. docket
i. judge
j. motion
k. negation speech
l. parliamentary procedure
m. policy
n. Presiding Officer
o. resolution
p. *Robert's Rules of Order*
q. Student Congress
r. whereas

1. Grouping of debaters at Student Congress
2. Plan of action in response to a problem
3. Piece of legislation that becomes a law
4. A declaration before the chamber to determine the direction of the proceeding
5. Student leader at Student Congress
6. Adult leader at Student Congress
7. Set of rules and procedures for debate in a Congress
8. Guidebook used for debate in a Congress
9. That which introduces legislation for debate
10. Means of clarifying a piece of legislation
11. Group of Congress participants responsible for specific types of legislation

Review Debate Concepts

12. What is unique about Student Congress as a debate activity?

13. What are the three types of committees sometimes found at Student Congress? What are their functions?

14. What is a bill?

15. What is a resolution?

16. Why is it important to have up-to-date scholarship when beginning research on legislation?

17. What are the benefits of using research materials from sources outside of the United States. On what type of legislation would you use this research?

18. Why is it important to research the legislation of other students in addition to your own?

19. Summarize the usual procedure for organizing research at Student Congress.

20. Define policy and name three types. What is the relationship between policy and legislation?

21. Identify the key components of a bill.

22. How is the structure of a bill different from the structure of a resolution?

23. What set of rules are followed in Student Congress? On what are they based?

24. Describe the functions of a Presiding Officer at Student Congress.

25. How is a piece of legislation introduced?

26. Describe the components of a speech in a legislative debate.

27. What is the function of a cross-examination speech at Student Congress?

28. What is the function of an amendment? What must the relationship always be between an amendment and the original piece of legislation?

29. Describe four types of motions.

30. How does debate on legislation in Student Congress end?

31. Describe the function of a judge at Student Congress.

32. Identify the criteria used to evaluate debaters at Student Congress.

Make Academic Connections

33. **PROBLEM SOLVING** Locate the domestic policy of your senator or congressperson. Then find a copy of his or her voting record. Has he or she been true to stated policy? Why or why not?

34. **CHALLENGES** Locate a political advertisement for a Congressional candidate. Does the ad provide you with a clear sense of policy? What else would you like to see included?

35. **ETHICS** Should those in Congress be limited in the amount of money they can raise and spend on election campaigns? Why or why not?

36. **HISTORY** Research the passage of the Civil Rights Act of 1964. How adequate was the bill? Are there still issues that need coverage?

37. **CHALLENGES** Find a copy of your state constitution. Does it represent the needs of the people? Would you amend it in any way?

Research NOW!

38. Research the history of Student Congress. Note its growth in popularity in recent years.

39. **TEAMWORK** As a class activity, create a survey that can be distributed to other students in your school, designed to find out what concerns them about living in the United States.

40. Research the careers of current senators and congresspersons. Try to find examples of particularly successful legislators, that is, senators or congresspersons who have authored or sponsored legislation that has passed. Why do you think they were successful? Do some research into their background and see what influenced them as speakers and debaters. Summarize your findings and present them to the class.

Write NOW!

41. Imagine that you are the host of a political talk show. Select a Congressperson you would like to interview and write a series of questions that you would ask him or her.

42. Prepare a manual for successful debaters in Student Congress. Use what you have learned in this chapter, and whatever tips you have gained from your own experience. List any techniques you think would be helpful.

43. **TEAMWORK** Based upon your research in 42 above, propose legislation that would address the concerns of your classmates. Divide your class into committees and write the legislation. Each committee should elect a spokesperson to propose the bill. Allow time for cross-examination.

44. Draft a letter to the editor of your local newspaper, proposing a piece of legislation that you would like to see passed in Congress. Provide reasons for your proposal.

45. Write an editorial in which you comment on the state of modern debate. Make reference to any Congressional speeches or any other public hear-

ings that seem relevant. Offer suggestions as to how the general performance of debate could be improved.

46. Think of an issue or problem that you think needs to be addressed through legislative action. Imagine that you are going to write a bill to address that problem. Write a bibliography that would be helpful in preparing legislation. Than draft legislation that uses that research. Present your legislation to the class. Ask for questions and comments.

Speak NOW!

47. Research one of the great legislative debates from United States' history. Imagine that you are part of it. Deliver a three-minute speech that participates in the debate

48. Pose as a candidate running for political office. Ask other members of your class to pose questions. Afterwards, ask for feedback as to how well you could think on your feet and speak spontaneously.

49. **TEAMWORK** Divide into groups of four or five and conduct a discussion on what the group sees as necessary for Congressional reform. Appoint a spokesperson to summarize the discussion after you have gathered back together as a class.

50. Conduct a class discussion on the roll of freedom of speech in our democracy. Do we have enough? Do we have too much? Ask for examples for each position. Write key points on the board and summarize the debate when you are finished.

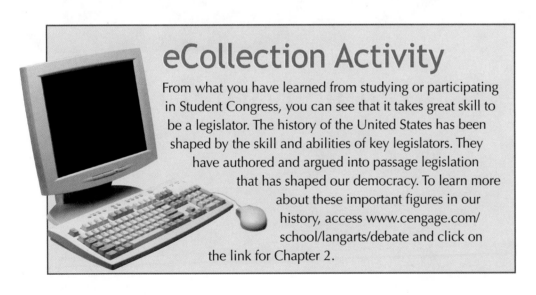

eCollection Activity

From what you have learned from studying or participating in Student Congress, you can see that it takes great skill to be a legislator. The history of the United States has been shaped by the skill and abilities of key legislators. They have authored and argued into passage legislation that has shaped our democracy. To learn more about these important figures in our history, access www.cengage.com/school/langarts/debate and click on the link for Chapter 2.

CHAPTER 9

Public Forum Debate

FAMOUS DEBATERS

" *I was going to college and I was going to become an attorney, and I knew that when I was ten.* "

Sonia Sotomayor

Sonia Sotomayor has truly lived the American story. She rose from humble beginnings to become a Justice of the Supreme Court, the first Hispanic to be so honored. Whether as a student, a lawyer, or a judge, Sotomayor has proven to be a fearless debater for justice for all peoples.

Sotomayor was born in the Bronx, New York, the daughter of Juan and Celina (Báez) Sotomayor. Both of her parents were from Puerto Rico. Sonia, her younger brother Juan, and her parents lived in a housing project in the South Bronx. Her mother worked as a telephone operator, and then as a nurse. Her father, who spoke no English, worked in a factory. Lively and intelligent, Sonia had to overcome serious tragedies at a young age. She was diagnosed with juvenile diabetes at age eight, and was required to take daily insulin injections. She continues to receive insulin injections even today. Tragically, Sonia's father died of heart failure when she was nine.

Originally, Sonia wanted to be a detective, but due to health concerns, her doctors suggested a different path. A fan of *Perry Mason*, a popular television series during the 1950s about a Los Angeles based lawyer, Sonia decided on her career. In a 1998 interview she stated, "I was going to college and I was going to become an attorney, and I knew that when I was ten."

Sonia was an excellent student. She entered Cardinal Spellman High School in the Bronx, a rigorous school that required a commute. Sonia worked part time, but still received top grades. She was class valedictorian at graduation. While at Spellman, she became a member of the debate team. Her debate coach inspired her to attend Princeton University as he had. At Princeton, she won the respect of classmates and teachers. One classmate remembers her: "She would stand up for herself and not be intimidated by anyone." At graduation, Sonia received the M. Taylor Pyne Prize, the highest honor that Princeton awards to an undergraduate.

Sotomayor went on to Yale Law School and used her debate skills as a lawyer and a judge. She was a fearless prosecutor for the New York District Attorney's office. She entered private practice, where she distinguished herself in commercial work, especially unfair competition practices. In 1992, President George H. W. Bush appointed Sonia Sotomayor to the District Court for the Southern District of New York. Once again, she proved to be a passionate defender of the law. In 1995, she ended the strike in major league baseball that had caused the cancellation of the World Series.

After serving for eleven years as an Appeals Court judge, a judge who reviews rulings from other courts, Sotomayor was nominated to serve on the Supreme Court of the United States. There, she continues to debate the issues that affect democracy for the American people.

Think Critically

What qualities have helped Sonia Sotomayor to succeed?

GOALS

Appreciate the unique aspects of Public Forum debate.

Know how to successfully participate in Public Forum debate.

TERMS

Public Forum debate
citizen judge
plan
crossfire
grand crossfire
status quo

Do You Agree?

Resolved In the United States, colleges and universities should be permitted to pay stipends to their Division I athletes.

Affirmative position

Yes, just as schools employ students to work in bookstores and other places that generate revenue for the school, they should be allowed to pay athletes for the services they provide. Athletics generate revenue, and students who promote the programs should be paid. The time spent training, practicing, and playing sports limits the time that athletes can devote to a job where they could earn money.

Negative position

No, most Division I athletes are already offered scholarships that pay for tuition, housing, dining, books, and more. Giving them a stipend on top of that would corrupt their work ethic and spoil the purity of the sport. Also, many schools would not have the financial means to offer stipends. Therefore, they could not fairly compete with other schools to attract top athletes.

Overview of Public Forum Debates

Your debate team is participating in a tournament that is offering an event called Public Forum debate. You've participated in Lincoln-Douglas and cross-examination debates as well as an Extemporaneous Speaking event. Do you want to try this event that is new to you? Do you have the skills to do it well?

Public Forum debates combine the speaking skills used in forensic speech events, such as Extemporaneous Speaking, with the research and argumentation skills used in other debates, such as Lincoln-Douglas debate. This relatively new NFL debate is one that strives to be informative and entertaining to the general public. It focuses on controversial issues that apply to the real world in current times. The resolutions are "stripped from the headlines" to provide up-to-date topics. In other words, the topics matter to the public.

Many consider Public Forum debates to be among the most fun and challenging events offered in NFL tournaments. They compare them to shows that hold debates on television. These shows, such as *Crossfire* and *The McLaughlin Group*, are popular because of their audience-friendly and fast-paced styles. They discuss topics that interest the common television viewer. Their guests present opposing views in an exciting, often dramatic, way. Although Public Forum debates might not be quite as exciting as these television shows, the crossfire portions of Public Forum debates can offer similar entertainment.

The challenge of Public Forum lies in the amount of time that the debaters have to present their cases. Debaters have only four minutes to present their arguments in constructive speeches and rebuttals, and summaries last only one or two minutes.

Public Forum vs. LD and CX Debates

Unlike Lincoln-Douglas debates, where individuals debate, Public Forum allows two teams, consisting of two members each, to debate a resolution. Similar to Cross-examination teams, the members must learn to work together in order to succeed.

Public Forum debate is unique in that it emphasizes speaking style over heavy research and evidence. Research must still be conducted and arguments must be supported by evidence. However, as a Public Forum debater you must be careful not to overwhelm or lose the judge by focusing too much on the evidence. A judge in a Public Forum debate is not a professional debate judge. Instead, the judge is an adult member of the community. This means that the judge may not know much about debate at all. Public Forum judges are sometimes referred to as **citizen judges** and are compared to a typical member sitting on an American jury.

When you debate in this forum, your speaking style will be more like the tone of a regular conversation. You will still need to make persuasive arguments that use logical reasoning. Since you don't know the background of your judge, your arguments and reasoning must convince a wide variety

COURTESY OF NATIONAL FORENSIC LEAGUE, WWW.NFLONLINE.ORG

How do Public Forum debates differ from other debates?

of audiences to vote for your team. Although LD debates also use a more conversational tone, they are like CX debates in that they can be difficult for the common person to follow. Public Forum uses less formal language with no jargon. This makes it easier for the audience to follow the debate.

The purposes of different types of debates differ. Lincoln-Douglas debates focus on the value of the resolution. Cross-examination debates focus on a plan to solve the problem. The purpose of a Public Forum debate differs from both of these. Public Forum focuses on promoting a position of the resolution. There is no burden of proof in Public Forum debates. In many other debates, the affirmative side has the burden of proof and the negative side can argue that they did not meet that burden of proof. In Public Forum, the affirmative must simply argue to explain why the resolution is true, and the negative must argue to explain why the resolution is not true. In fact, because there is no burden of proof, the negative side often presents their constructive speech before the affirmative does.

Related to burden of proof is the concept of offering a plan. A **plan,** as defined by the NFL, is a "formalized comprehensive proposal for information." In other words, it is a specific solution or proposal. Although Public Forum debaters may offer general solutions, they should never offer a detailed plan like that of a CX debate.

The last difference between the types of debate concerns cross-examination. Both LD and CX debates have cross-examination periods where the one person from one team questions a member of the other team. Cross-examination in Public Forum is referred to as **crossfire.** Like the other debates, crossfire involves two speakers—one from each team. Its unique aspect is that both debaters ask and answer questions during crossfire. The first person to ask

How does crossfire differ from cross-examination in other debates?

a question is predetermined, but after that point, either debater can ask a question at will. Even more unique is **grand crossfire**. In the grand crossfire period, all four debaters ask and answer questions at once.

History of Public Forum

Public Forum debate was first created during the 2002–2003 debate season. It was introduced at the 2003 nationals as a trial event. Public Forum became an official event during the 2004 nationals.

The event was originally named Ted Turner debate. It was named after Ted Turner who was the founder of the television station CNN. The debate show *Crossfire* was shown on CNN. Public Forum debate has also been known as Controversy debate in the past.

AP PHOTO/RIC FELD

How is Ted Turner related to Public Forum debate?

Resolutions

Since Public Forum debates focus on current events that can be understood by the general public, their resolutions must do the same. You might find Public Forum resolutions that deal with health insurance, the presidential election process, or standardized testing in public schools. You won't find resolutions about specialized topics such as complex scientific theories or historical issues. The general public wouldn't understand complex scientific theories and historical issues wouldn't deal

FYI Ted Turner was awarded an honorary membership to the National Forensic League. Turner's view on not quitting is summed up by his quotation, "We're not losing. We're just learning how to win."

with current events. Resolutions for Public Forum debates might involve some of the following areas.

Legal issues	Sports
Bioethics	Culture wars
Moral issues	Business
Entertainment	Transportation
Justice	Politics
Education	Military
Technology	Economics

Most Public Forum resolutions encourage debaters to argue whether or not a change should be made. Debaters must weigh the risk of change with the risk of the **status quo**—keeping things as they are. For example, consider the following resolution. Resolved: All young adults in every nation should be required to perform at least one full year of national service. The status quo is that young adults of every nation are not required to perform a year of national service. The affirmative side would argue that a change be made. They would explain why the change would result in an improvement over the current policy. The negative side would argue that the current policy (the status quo) is best.

Resolutions for Public Forum debates must also be narrow enough to allow for a thorough but short debate. With shortened constructive and rebuttal speeches, a typical Public Forum debate may last less than 35 minutes. Lincoln-Douglas debates tend to last a bit longer than this, but cross-examination debates can last up to an hour. In a CX debate, each team has an eight-minute constructive speech in which to present its contentions in detail. With only half this amount of time in a Public Forum debate, fewer contentions are usually argued with less detail.

The National Forensic League announces a new Public Forum resolution on the first day of every month, and the NFL National Tournament topic is announced on May 15 of each year. A committee, made up of a diverse group of people that are appointed by the NFL president, decides what the resolutions will be. The committee accepts ideas for resolutions by NFL members. Members can submit their suggestions though the website at www.nflonline. org. The committee selects resolutions based on various criteria. Some of the criteria considered are described below.

Timeliness	The topic of the resolution must be suitable for the current time. It should pertain to something that matters now or is happening now or within the very recent past.
Clarity of wording	The wording of the resolution is crucial. The resolution must be written so that it has a straightforward interpretation.
Perceived interest	Topics of debate must be interesting to both the students debating them and the general public. The committee will only choose issues that they think will grab the attention of the debaters and their audience.
Argument balance	The issue must allow for reasonable arguments for both sides. The strength, quality, and quantity of arguments must be fairly equal for both sides. If an issue is one sided, the team who argues that side has a distinct advantage, making for an unfair debate.
Availability of research	Since Public Forum deals with current events and recent issues, a challenge lies in easily obtaining research. For instance, if a debate issue involves the safety of a brand new vaccine, you won't likely be able to find books written on the subject. Instead credible online research must be available. You might also be able to find up-to-date research in magazines and newspapers.

Successful Public Forum Debating

In order to be successful in Public Forum debating, debaters must possess certain characteristics. First, you must have very strong, clear, and precise speaking skills. When you debate in Public Forum, your speaking skills are a big consideration. You should be careful not to talk too fast, too quietly, or in a monotone voice. You also should avoid using jargon that would not be understood by a citizen judge. If you make any of these mistakes, it may inhibit others from understanding your arguments. If an argument is not understood because of poor speaking skills, a judge may completely disregard that argument. The judge will also not penalize your opponent for not addressing an argument that was unclear due to speaking.

In addition to strong speaking skills, you must be able to organize your ideas and communicate your arguments in a professional manner. Poor speaking skills may influence the judge, as might an unorganized presentation of your case. Make sure that the judge can follow the flow of your arguments. Make sure that you use appropriate words and tone to professionally present your case. Remember that since the judge is not a professional debate judge, you must focus on communicating to all types of people. Your judge could be a nurse, a postal worker, a grandparent, a business owner, a janitor, or anyone else in the community. Find a way to organize and communicate your thoughts so that any type of person can easily understand them. Present yourself as an informed individual, but not as a showoff. Do not talk down to your judge, or be condescending in any way. Like all other forms of debate, it is extremely important that you show respect for your judge.

Which of these adults could act as a judge of a Public Forum debate?

Your delivery is as important as your speech. Try to relax. The better prepared you are, the more comfortable you will feel with your presentation. If you are unsure of your arguments, the judge may sense this through your delivery. Practice your constructive speeches and possible rebuttals many times. Enunciate your words and avoid "um's" and long pauses.

Critical thinking skills will help you successfully present your case. As you prepare your constructive speech, don't just list your contentions. Instead, analyze your data and explain why your contentions are important and applicable. Listen closely to your opponents' constructive speech and analyze their case. Consider their strengths and weaknesses. List the arguments that you can dispute and prioritize what you need to do to weaken their case. Your rebuttal time is short, so focus on the most important refutations. Remember success in Public Forum debating depends on the following.

- Speaking and delivery skills

- Using solid logical reasoning

- Analyzing your opponents' arguments, evidence, and entire case

- Presenting evidence but not being driven by it

- Presenting a clash

- Remaining calm and collected, especially during crossfire and grand crossfire

Public Forum debate is an exciting opportunity to engage in a lively discussion of ideas. It provides another opportunity to develop speaking, reading, and critical thinking skills. It is an opportunity to be engaged with the issues that affect today's world, issues taken from the headlines. Chances are, you debate these issues with members of your family or your friends. Now you have the opportunity to debate those issues in a challenging competition.

COURTESY OF NATIONAL FORENSIC LEAGUE, WWW.NFLONLINE.ORG

What are the keys to success in Public Forum debate?

TURNING POINT

Town Hall Meetings

AP PHOTO/TOBY TALBOT

The first recorded town hall meeting took place in Dorchester, Massachusetts in 1633. Since then, the local, state, and federal governments of the United States have always employed this interactive form of debate in deciding public policy. A town hall meeting is an informal public assembly where all are free to attend and voice their opinions. In early Dorchester, the purpose of the meeting was to see to the "good and well ordering of the affayres of the plantation." The purpose has remained much the same, all the way to the most recent Presidential election. It gives the people a chance to directly ask their future and current elected officials about policies affecting their communities, in a setting where the politician cannot avoid the question.

The town hall meeting allows politicians to hear the concerns and questions of their constituencies, which is why it has been successful. Real people at town hall debates can bring up issues that have personal importance for them like, "I'm working two jobs and can't afford healthcare." These are topics and questions that candidates cannot avoid and must answer directly and personally. In this way, candidates become more like real people themselves. Voters not only see the potential strengths and flaws of the candidates, they can also engage in constructive and meaningful debate with them. Hopefully, the candidates will listen.

The setting and format of town meetings have changed in recent years because of the advent of television and the Internet. In the recent Presidential debate between Senator John McCain and Senator Barack Obama, polling organization Gallup chose as the meeting's audience 100 to 150 undecided voters to ensure they represented all political affiliations. The audience's questions comprised the majority of those asked. Many questions also came from online submissions. The candidates had ninety seconds to respond and then an additional two minutes between them to discuss each question.

In the 1800s, Town hall meetings were instrumental in agitating for the grassroots support on which the anti-slavery movement relied. Henry David Thoreau expressed the town meeting's importance in 1854 when he said: "When, in some obscure country town, the farmers come together to a special town-meeting, to express their opinion on some subject which is vexing the land, that, I think, is the true Congress, and the most respectable one that is ever assembled in the United States." Today, because of modern technology, the town hall meeting has become an important way that everyday people can debate issues with public officials.

Think Critically

Why have Town Hall meetings become important to political candidates?

Think Critically

1. How does Public Forum debating differ from LD and CX debating?

2. How does the length of a Public Forum debate affect the resolution?

3. What type of sources do you usually use to research for a Public Forum debate? Why are these sources different than other debates?

Research NOW!

4. **TEAMWORK** With a partner, use the Internet to find more about Public Forum judging. What are the skills required? What guidelines are judges given? See if you can view sample ballots completed by judges.

5. Visit the National Forensic League website at www.nflonline.org. Navigate through the site to find current Public Forum debate resolutions.

Write NOW!

6. Consider the resolution introduced at the beginning of the lesson. Write a few paragraphs that explain how this would be presented in a LD and CX debate versus a Public Forum debate.

   Resolved: In the United States, colleges and universities should be permitted to pay stipends to their Division I athletes.

7. **TEAMWORK** With a partner, review newspapers and magazines from the last month. Find controversial topics that would interest the public and use the guidelines for Public Forum debate to write resolutions that address at least two different topics.

Speak NOW!

8. **TEAMWORK** Work with a group of three other students and choose a controversial topic that concerns your school or community that you think would make for an interesting crossfire. Assign two students to support each side of the controversy. Each group should take a few minutes to come up with a few arguments that support their side. In front of your class, take one minute per team to present your arguments. After you both present, perform a three-minute grand crossfire, asking and answering questions of the other team.

9. **TEAMWORK**   With a partner, prepare one argument each to advocate and reject the following resolution. Present your arguments and supporting evidence in class.

   Resolved: All young adults in every nation should be required to perform at least one full year of national service.

Do You Agree?

Resolved In the United States, the current system of federal income taxation should be replaced by a flat rate income tax.

Affirmative position

Yes, the flat rate income tax plan is simple and efficient. It would cut the time and cost of processing taxes and achieve fewer mistakes in calculations. Also, loopholes that currently allow giant corporations to unfairly avoid taxes would be eliminated. Last, the flat tax plan would eliminate double taxation on savings and investments.

Negative position

No, implementing the flat rate income tax would put an impossible burden on those in lower income brackets. It would also actually raise overall taxes for the majority of people. Last, if the new system was put in place, the IRS and tax preparation industry would collapse, leaving many unemployed.

GOALS

Understand how to make decisions related to the coin toss.

Obtain knowledge about the various speeches of a Public Forum debate.

TERMS

advocating

hard evidence

soft evidence

summary speech

final focus

You've decided that the skills needed for Public Forum debating match those of your debate club, so your team is going to go for it. Now it's time to prepare for the debate. The first thing you'll need to know is what type of speeches you'll be expected to make. Like other forms of debate, you'll be able to prepare some speeches in advance. Others will require you to predict your opponents' arguments and rebuttals so that you can argue against them. Like all debates, the more knowledge you have on the topic, the better chance you'll have of doing well. Before you learn about the speeches, you need to know about the importance of the coin toss in Public Forum debates.

Coin Toss

The decisions made during the coin toss in Public Forum debates make it unique. Before the debate begins, a coin is tossed. The team who wins the toss is allowed to make the first decision. They can either choose a side to argue or they can choose the order in which they speak. The team who loses the toss gets to make the decision not made by the first team. For example, assume the two teams are Team A and Team B. Team B wins the coin toss. This allows Team B to decide if they want to argue the affirmative or negative side of the

myhrcat/iStockphoto.com

How does the coin toss affect a Public Forum debate?

resolution *or* if they want to deliver their constructive speech first or second. Assume that they decide they want to argue the affirmative side. With this decision made, Team A then gets to choose whether they speak first or second. Assume that Team A decides they want to speak first. Each team has made one decision, but the team who wins the coin toss chooses which decision they want to make.

One effect of the coin toss is that, unlike other debates, the negative team may be the first to present their case. Since there is no burden of proof, having the negative team present first does not cause a problem. Since the negative side is simply trying to argue that the resolution should not be adopted and the affirmative is trying to argue that the resolution should be adopted, the negative's construction speech is not dependent upon the affirmative's constructive speech.

The coin toss adds uncertainty to the debate. It also means that both teams must fully prepare in advance to argue both sides of a resolution. Preparing arguments and evidence for both sides will also help you refute the arguments of your opponents.

You and your Public Forum debate partner will need to consider what strategies to use when making coin toss decisions. You probably won't make the same decisions every time. Your strategies may change depending upon the resolution. For instance, if you feel like you have a stronger case for one side and you win the coin toss, this may be your first consideration. In this case you might tell the judge that you want to pick what side to argue. In another case with a different resolution, you may feel that it is important that you have the last word in the debate. If you win the coin toss in this case, you may wish to choose speaking order instead. Whether you win or lose the toss, you will need to make one decision. Think about some of the following questions before making decisions.

- Do your arguments and evidence better defend one side of the resolution?

- Is your opponents' case likely stronger for one side of the resolution?

- Is one side more acceptable to the judge or to the general public? Even though the judge should put aside personal feelings, consider this question.

- Considering the resolution and/or your opponents' skills, would presenting first make a better impression on the judge?

- Considering the resolution and/or your opponents' skills, would having the last word have more impact on the judge?

After both teams make their coin toss decisions, one of the teams starts their constructive speech.

Speeches

Public Forum debaters present constructive and rebuttal speeches as they do in other debates. The speeches are generally shorter. Other elements, such as crossfire and grand crossfire are added. The following chart shows a summary of the speeches. This chart shows the order of the speeches when Team A is speaking first. Remember that this first speech could be an affirmative constructive speech or a negative constructive speech.

Speech Name and Team Members	Time
Prep Time	2 minutes per team to be used at any time between speeches
Constructive Speech—Team A, Speaker 1	4 minutes
Constructive Speech—Team B, Speaker 1	4 minutes
Crossfire—Speaker 1 from each team	3 minutes
Rebuttal—Team A, Speaker 2	4 minutes
Rebuttal—Team B, Speaker 2	4 minutes
Crossfire—Speaker 2 from each team	3 minutes
Summary—Team A, Speaker 1	2 minutes
Summary—Team B, Speaker 1	2 minutes
Grand Crossfire—All speakers from both teams	3 minutes
Final Focus—Team A, Speaker 2	1 minute
Final Focus—Team B, Speaker 2	1 minute

Prep Time

When you participate in a Public Forum debate, you and your partner will be given only two minutes of preparation time. You may use this time to consult with your partner. Together you may plan arguments, organize your thoughts, determine your own or your opponents' strengths and weaknesses, or discuss anything else about the debate. You may use the entire two minutes all at once, but you may wish to break it up into smaller increments. Save some of your prep time to use before your summary speeches and final focus.

Constructive Speeches

Each team is given four minutes to present their constructive speech. If you are arguing the affirmative side, you are **advocating** (or supporting) the position presented in the resolution. If you are arguing the negative side, you are opposing the position presented in the resolution. Consider the resolution presented at the beginning of this lesson. Resolved: In the United States, the current system of federal income taxation should be replaced by a flat rate income tax. The affirmative side will advocate the resolution, arguing that a

©Michael Newman/Photo Edit

Why is it a good idea to practice with your partner?

flat rate income tax should replace the current system. The negative side will oppose the resolution, arguing that the flat rate tax system should not replace the current system.

You should completely prepare your constructive speech in advance. If you wind up speaking first, you will present your speech exactly as you planned it. If you wind up speaking second, you will also most likely present your speech exactly as you planned it. Attacks of your opponents' speech are usually held until rebuttals, but the debater who presents the second constructive speech can decide to make last minute changes to include rebuttals of the opponents' constructive speech. Remember that your constructive speech represents the first impression that you make on the judge. Also remember that speaking and delivery skills are important in a Public Forum debate. For these two reasons, make sure you practice your speech until your delivery and timing are as perfect as you can make them.

Before the debate, you and your partner should determine who will present which speeches. The speaker who makes the constructive speech is required to participate in the first crossfire and make the summary speech. The other team member is responsible for delivering the rebuttal, participating in the second crossfire, and making the final focus.

Constructive Speech Team A Assume the coin toss decisions resulted in Team A presenting first. The first speaker of Team A starts by stating the resolution. He or she then makes an opening statement that catches the attention of the judge. If needed, he or she may quickly define terms in the resolution. Then the first speaker presents arguments and evidence for or against the resolution, depending on what was decided by the coin toss decisions.

Teams should focus on the quality of the arguments, not the quantity. Having a few solid understandable arguments with credible evidence will present a stronger case than a case that contains four or more weaker arguments. Each argument should be able to stand on its own rather than relying on or building on another argument. Since the speech lasts only four minutes and you want to focus on speaking in a conversational tone, use only your strongest arguments.

MERKURI2/ISTOCKPHOTO.COM

Use a variety of evidence to support your case. Both **hard evidence** and **soft evidence** should be used. Statistics, facts, and quotations from experts are examples of hard evidence. Persuasive stories, personal narratives, comparisons, and examples are soft evidence.

After Speaker 1 presents the arguments and evidence, he or she should close with a brief statement about the importance of the resolution to the public. Ask yourself why this issue matters to the general public.

Constructive Speech Team B   Next, Speaker 1 of Team B presents his or her constructive speech. Again, whether this speech supports the resolution or not depends on the decisions made during the coin toss. Usually the speaker for Team B presents a fully prepared four-minute speech. This speech should contain the same elements as Team A's speech. However, Team B may decide that they should change the speech in order to refute an argument made by Team A. This strategy is sometimes used when one of Team A's arguments directly clashes with one of Team B's arguments. Since the constructive speech cannot run longer than four minutes, Team B might need to remove one of their original arguments from their pre-written speech to make room for the change. After Team B presents their constructive speech, the crossfire round begins.

The resolution introduced in this lesson discusses the issue of a flat rate income tax. Why does this issue matter to the general public?

Crossfire

The first crossfire period allows Speaker 1 from each team to ask and answer questions about the cases. Both of the debaters who have already delivered constructive speeches should stand up at this point. If a podium is being used, they should stand near it. Otherwise, they should stand between the tables where their partners are sitting.

The debater that gave the first constructive speech—Speaker 1 of Team A in this case—will ask the first question. After that point, the debaters may ask each other questions in any order. Like cross-examination periods in other types of debates, students may ask questions that attack a weakness in their opponents' argument, further develop their own arguments, or clarify information. Speakers should be polite yet firm. Do not let your opponent take advantage of your politeness and ask all the questions. Make sure that you are firm enough to get some of your own questions asked as well.

Crossfire differs from cross-examination in other debates because both speakers ask and answer questions. In typical cross-examination, only one student asks questions and the other student provides answers. Crossfire allows for a discussion of issues during the round, not a simple question and answer period. It can be a very informative and interesting period, and it can add excitement to the debate. If used correctly, crossfire can help your case tremendously.

Rebuttals

After the crossfire period, each team presents their rebuttal speech. Team A will present first and Team B will follow. Speaker 2 of each team must make the rebuttals—not the same student who delivered the constructive speech.

Each team has four minutes to present their rebuttal speech.

Even though each student on a team is assigned different speeches, each student should know what their partner's speech includes. In fact, students should ideally outline, write, and practice all of the speeches together. This will allow their presentations to flow together in a logical order. Starting your rebuttal with a link to your partner's constructive speech adds a nice touch and demonstrates your organization.

FYI Our second president, John Adams, pointed out the difficulty of refuting solid facts with his famous quote, "Facts are stubborn things; and whatever may be our wishes, our inclinations, or the dictates of our passion, they cannot alter the state of facts and evidence."

Rebuttal speeches can serve many purposes. During your rebuttal you may want to address some or all of the following.

- **Attack opponents' arguments and supporting evidence.** Present evidence that reduces or destroys their arguments. Show inconsistencies or contradictions in your opponents' case.

- **Defend attacks against your constructive speech.** Present more evidence or an example that strengthens your argument and nullifies their attack. Give reasons why the opponent is wrong and then rebuild your own case

- **Extend a point that was discussed during crossfire.** The point can be either an attack or defense.

You can prepare some of your rebuttal in advance. Through research you conducted before the debate, you can predict some or all of the arguments that your opponent will use. Before the debate begins, you can prepare rebuttals against these arguments. One way to do this is to write each argument on a separate index card. On each index card, write ideas that refute that argument. Then, during the debate, pull out the index cards that contain the arguments that your opponent actually uses. Ideas for rebuttals are then at your fingertips.

If time allows, end your rebuttal with a brief summary of how your case is stronger than your opponents'. Then prepare for the second crossfire period.

Second Crossfire Period

The second crossfire period runs much like the first. In this period, Speaker 2 from each team participates. Speaker 2 from Team A asks the first question. After that, either debater may ask questions in any order.

Now that constructive speeches, the first crossfire period, and rebuttals have been made, the second crossfire debaters have more information to process. A lot of arguments and rebuttals need to be considered. Your team may find it more difficult to prepare in advance for this crossfire period. If you feel unprepared, you might want to consider using a little bit of your preparation time. Be sure to save some of your preparation time for the summary speech or for the final focus.

Summary Speeches

Summary speeches are similar to rebuttals, but they are much shorter. While your team had four minutes in which to present your rebuttal, the summary speech allows only two minutes.

In this short summary speech, you must focus on the most important aspects of your case and your opponents' case. You should summarize the top one or two important arguments that you are winning. You should also quickly attack a key argument of your opponent.

While you may not present new arguments at this point in the debate, you may present new evidence. Put a new spin on one of your arguments by presenting additional facts or statistics or tell a fresh story or new quotation that further supports your argument.

How does grand crossfire differ from other crossfire periods?

Grand Crossfire

The next period represents the most exciting part of the debate. Grand crossfire allows all four debaters to ask and answer questions at one time. Unlike regular crossfire, debaters should sit, not stand. All debaters should be able to see the judge from their seats. Grand crossfire will move quickly as the debaters only have three minutes to ask and answer questions.

The team that presented the first summary speech (Team A in this case) begins grand crossfire by asking the first question. After that point, any of the four debaters can ask questions in any order. Both you and your partner must be polite but assertive about asking questions. Don't let the other team dominate you with their assertiveness.

Teamwork plays an important role in grand crossfire. Know your teammate's and your own strengths and weaknesses and ask and answer questions accordingly.

Final Focus

Following the grand crossfire is the **final focus**. This important one-minute speech is also appropriately known as the "last shot." As this name implies, it is your last chance to tell the judge why you won the debate. Again, the team that presented their summary first will present their final focus first. The other team will get the last word in the debate.

The statements you make during the final focus should be persuasive. In most cases, you will want to repeat the single strongest argument and tell why it should represent the deciding factor. In some cases, you may reiterate two arguments, but keep in mind that you only have one minute. Arguments you may want to address in the final focus include the following.

- Stress an important argument that you are winning.

- Answer an important argument that you are losing.

- Prove that two of your opponents' major arguments have contradicted themselves.

- Turn an opponents' major argument around to show how it actually supports your case.

- Stress an argument that appeals to the judge.

If you think it is important to do so, you may present new evidence during the final focus. Like in the summary speech, new supporting facts, statistics, examples, and stories are allowed. However, the judge will ignore any new arguments that are made.

The judge votes on the issues that you and your opponent present in the final focus unless he or she feels that another argument presented earlier is more important. In a close round, the final focus may be the deciding factor for the judge. For this reason, try to objectively put yourself in the judge's place. What would you be voting on if you were the judge in this debate? Asking yourself this question may help you to succeed in Public Forum debates.

Think Critically

1. What are the consequences of the coin toss?

2. To what extent can you prepare in advance for a crossfire period?

3. How do summary speeches differ from rebuttals?

Research NOW!

4. **TEAMWORK** With a partner, search the Internet for a sample Public Forum debate between students. See if you can find a sample of an entire debate or at least each of the speeches discussed in this lesson. Especially focus on finding a crossfire period.

5. Find a video of an old *Crossfire* show and watch the episode. How does the structure of the debates on *Crossfire* differ from the structure of debates described in this lesson?

Write NOW!

6. Write an affirmative construction speech for the following resolution suitable for a cross-examination debate (8 minutes long) or a Lincoln-Douglas debate (6 minutes). Then write an affirmative construction speech for a Public Forum debate (4 minutes). Analyze your speeches and decide which is more effective. Attach a paragraph explaining your analysis.

   Resolved: The United States constitution should be amended to establish a mandatory retirement age for Supreme Court Justices.

7. **TEAMWORK**   If you were participating in a debate of the following resolution and won the coin toss, what would you choose to do? Write a specific choice you would make and justify your decision.

   Resolved: Awards for pain and suffering in medical malpractice cases should be limited to $250,000.

Speak NOW!

8. **TEAMWORK** With a group of three other students, choose a Public Forum resolution used in the past or write a new one. Ask your teacher to approve your resolution, and then break your group into two teams. With your partner, prepare an entire case for both sides of the argument. Present an entire debate in front of your class, including the coin toss.

Do You Agree?

Resolved Use of a cell phone should be prohibited while operating a motor vehicle.

Affirmative position

Yes, cell phones distract drivers and cause both major and minor accidents every day. In order to prevent accidents, drivers should give their full attention to driving and always have both hands on the steer wheel. A 2006 University of Utah study concluded that talking on a cell phone, including hands-free sets, is as dangerous as driving drunk.

Negative position

No, cell phones are not the problem here. Other distracters, such as talking to kids in the backseat, looking at a map or GPS, and eating cause more accidents. Are we going to ban these distracters as well? A University of North Carolina study found that cell phones were responsible for only 1.5 percent of accidents caused by distracters. Other distracters included changing the radio station and changing CDs.

Crossfire Behavior and Techniques

You've become more confident in your debating skills, but now you want to learn some details that will help you win more debates. You've seen experienced opponents, but you're not sure what they are doing that makes them successful. Subtle behaviors can help you become a more professional debater. Also, some techniques used during crossfire periods may help you to improve.

Appropriate Behavior during Crossfire

If you've seen or participated in debates, you know that excitement runs high at times. Debaters can feel so passionate about their side of an argument that emotions can get the best of them. Hopefully, your emotions will not cause you to act inappropriately. A key point to remember is that you should attack your opponents' case, but you should never attack or mistreat your opponent.

- **Don't be rude to your opponent.** Using disrespectful language, an offensive tone, or inappropriate body language are examples of rudeness. Never laugh or smirk at your opponent, no matter what statement or mistake they make. Keep your tone of voice at an appropriate, respectable level, and never shout at your opponent. Don't roll your eyes or use other rude body language, no matter how subtle it may seem. The judge will penalize any sign of rudeness. Use your best manners and treat your opponent with respect. Treat your partner and the judge with respect as well.

IONICA/GETTY IMAGES

Why might a judge stop a grand crossfire period?

- **Be firm but polite.** Crossfire and grand crossfire periods are short, so you'll be tempted to interrupt your opponent or try to **dominate,** or control, the discussion. You want to ask as many questions as you need to in order to make your point. However, you must learn to strike a balance between being aggressive and polite. Do be firm and slightly aggressive, especially if your opponent seems to be asking more question than you are able to ask. If your opponent is asking question after question, give your answer to one question and then immediately state that you would like to ask the next question.

- **Don't interrupt excessively.** The only time that you should interrupt or talk over opponents is when they are **filibustering**—giving a long answer or making a long speech with the purpose of delaying. Filibustering will cause a loss of points from the offender. You should almost never interrupt your partner, and don't do anything to make your partner interrupt you. You may make an exception to this rule during grand crossfire if your partner gets in trouble. If your partner is unable to answer a question, you can step in and help by answering it or deflecting the question with another question. Judges look at how you work as a team.

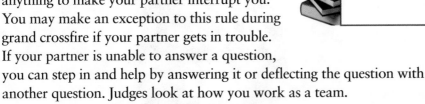
FYI Filibusters are used to delay or prevent the adoption of an action. The word stems from the Dutch word meaning "pirate." In debate, a filibuster is seen as a tactic to pirate or hijack a debate.

- **Pay attention to the rules of the debate.** Without being reminded, stand up during the first and second crossfire periods. Remain seated during grand crossfire, and make sure you can see the judge.

Judges will not ask questions during crossfire or any other part of the debate. However, a judge will stop a crossfire period if inappropriate behavior is being used by either team.

Crossfire Techniques

Just as appropriate behavior helps improve your chances of winning a debate, so do techniques. Speaker points are awarded during Public Forum debate, but they are awarded to the team—not individuals. If you don't work well as a team, you could lose these points and possibly the debate. Some techniques you can use during crossfire and grand crossfire follow.

- **Show the judge that you and your partner work well as a team.** Make a plan in advance on how you will handle the grand crossfire period. You'll have a lot of awkward moments if you and your partner always begin talking at the same time or if neither of you speak up when needed. You can try to determine in advance which partner will ask which questions and which partner will answer predicted questions. You may wish to create subtle signals that help you communicate with your partner. For instance, a slight nod of your head towards your partner could signal that you want him or her to answer a question because you don't feel prepared to do so. Another gesture could indicate that you would like to be the next person to ask a question.

- **Learn when to speak and learn when to listen.** If your opponents are digging a hole for themselves, let them. For instance, if one of your opponents is rambling in an unorganized manner, let him go for a little while. The judge will notice the lack of organization and count it against their team.

- **Don't let your opponent off the hook if they can't answer a question.** If you ask a question and your opponent remains silent because he is trying to come up with an answer, let it go for a while. Don't rush in to rephrase the question or ask another question. Let your opponent's silence become obvious to the judge.

How can your confidence level help or hurt you during a debate?

JHORROCKS/ISTOCKPHOTO.COM

- **Be sure to answer your questions with confidence and persuasion.** If you sound unsure, everyone will doubt that you are right.

- **Prepare in advance questions as well as answers to questions that you know your opponents are likely to ask.** Don't ask a useless question just for the sake of asking a question. Focus on questions that attack your opponents' case and ask questions that help your case.

- **Ask questions that only require brief answers.** Don't let your opponent drag out an answer to use up valuable time. If an opponent answers but then appears to be adding fluff, simply say, "Thank you. You've answered my question." to stop him or her.

- **Answer questions with brief, to-the-point answers.** Don't ramble on, but use the time to ask your own questions.

- **Don't rush your questions and answers.** You will sound desperate. Desperation does not persuade the judge and will make your opponent feel more confident.

YOU BE THE JUDGE

Standardized testing in schools. Universal health care. Military drafts. Dress codes. What is your first response when you hear these topics? If you're like many Americans, your first reaction is to judge the topic—to state if you are for or against it. When you first hear a new Public Forum debate resolution, your first thought might be the same. Before any arguments are considered and before supporting evidence is researched, you probably have an opinion that leans one way or the other about almost any resolution. Does this consideration affect you as you debate?

Perhaps you have been in situations where you needed to ask someone not to judge the topic. Maybe you didn't finish an assignment or project on time. Your teacher has emphasized timeliness and responsibility as important qualities in a student. You agree that those qualities are important. But your dog was sick and you were up all night with him. The topic is lateness, but the opposing argument is that sometimes, other circumstances come into play.

In debate, you sometimes have to argue against what you truly believe. You have to find ways to sound convincing to a judge. Perhaps in doing this, you discover other sides of an issue that you have never thought about before. Judges also have convictions, and sometimes, you will be arguing against them. It is hard to know when that happens, but when it does, you hope that your arguments will be convincing enough that he or she will set aside those convictions and listen to your arguments.

What Would You Do?

Think of a moral or core value that is extremely important to you. Now imagine debating the *opposite* side of this moral. Can you overcome your own opinions and argue against your beliefs? How do you accomplish this? Do you think it is difficult for a judge to do the same thing?

Teamwork

Throughout the Public Forum debate, you should demonstrate to the judge how you and your partner work well as a team. Sometimes you'll find a debate partner that you are in sync with almost without effort. Other times you'll need to work hard to become an effective team. Great teamwork is achieved when the accomplishments of the team surpass what the individuals could do alone. Think about what this means in terms of a debate.

Strengths and Weaknesses

The best team partners often complement each other. That is, your weaknesses tend to be strengths of your partner and your strengths tend to be your partner's weaknesses. You can take advantage of each of your strengths without overpowering each other. Consider your own strengths and weaknesses as well as your partner's.

- Name your top three strengths
- Name your top three weaknesses.

Together, ask yourselves some of the following questions.

- Are you better at asking or answering questions?
- Are you a better speaker or listener?
- Do you have strong research skills?
- Do you have strong organizational skills?

How can teamwork affect your performance in a debate?

COURTESY OF NATIONAL FORENSIC LEAGUE, WWW.NFLONLINE.ORG

- Can you think on your feet, or do you need to prepare in advance?

- Do you like to write arguments independently and then share them, or do you prefer to brainstorm with a partner and write together?

You may think of other questions that will help you identify your strengths, weaknesses, and work habits. Take inventory of the areas in which you both have weaknesses. Once you know where your team's weaknesses lie, you can work to improve your skills in that area. Once you know where your strengths lie, you can use them to your advantage. You can use this analysis to determine tasks that each partner should be assigned. For example, it may help you determine who should deliver which speeches. It could also help you determine who should ask questions and who should answer questions during grand crossfire.

Different students obviously have different personalities. If one partner has a more dominant personality, don't let this ruin your ability to work together. If you are the one with a dominant personality, focus on listening to your partner's ideas. Don't dominate your partner, especially during the grand crossfire. If you have a more timid personality, debate might bring out your strong side. Focus on offering your ideas and initiating questions.

Communication

Communication is key to effective teamwork. It involves both team members speaking and listening to each other. Communication brings a team together. Mistakes are often a direct result of poor communication.

Can people with different personalities find ways to work as a team?

Communicating with your partner is essential to successful debate. Together you must determine the goals of your team and present a unified front. You need to decide together what is most important and what is least important in the debate. Important factors range from deciding on what arguments to present in your constructive speech to determining the issue to concentrate on during the final focus.

Much of the communication between you and your partner will occur during the preparation phases before a debate. You should organize research together and outline, write, and practice your speeches together. As you practice, give your partner honest evaluations. Listen to your partner's advice as well. Remind each other if you need to slow your speech, change the flow of your arguments, stop using jargon or high-level language, or change the emphasis of points.

Some communication is also allowed during a Public Forum debate. Overall, you may not speak to your partner and you may not make signals to your partner while he or she is presenting a constructive speech, participating in a one-on-one crossfire, or making a rebuttal speech. During the grand crossfire period, you may communicate with all of the debaters on the floor, including your partner. You may wish to create signals to use between you and your partner for private communication. Before or after speeches, you should decide the best time to use your prep time. During prep time, you are free to speak with your partner.

Strategies, appropriate behavior, strong teamwork, and communication will help you succeed in Public Forum debates. Practice improving these skills each time you debate.

In what phase of a debate is communication between team members important?

Think Critically

1. What is the difference between dominating a crossfire discussion and filibustering?

2. How is teamwork emphasized in a Public Forum debate?

3. What is the importance of knowing the strengths and weaknesses of the individuals on a team?

Research NOW!

4. **TEAMWORK**   With a partner, research team building activities for small groups. Find at least three activities that you think would help a small group better work together. Try to find at least one activity that requires a team to do something with no verbal communication. What do you think the goals of the activities are? Do you think these activities accomplish their goals? How can you relate these to debate?

5. Find another video of a *Crossfire* or *The McLaughlin Group* episode. Compare the behavior of the hosts and guests to the behavior expected in Public Forum debate.

Write NOW!

6. **TEAMWORK**   With a partner, consider the following resolution. Think of two arguments to support the affirmative side and two arguments to support the negative side. Under each argument, list one example or fact to support it. Assume that you are arguing the negative side. Analyze the arguments, and write a list of questions that you might ask during crossfire. Then write a list of questions that the opponent might ask you.

    Resolved: Commercial airline pilots should be armed in the cockpit.

7. Copy the questions on pages 248–249. Write your answers to the questions. Use your answers to write a short paragraph describing the characteristics of your ideal debate partner. Write a second paragraph that explains ways that you could improve your weaknesses.

Speak NOW!

8. **TEAMWORK**   Choose a resolution that requires very little research, such as one that affects your school or your life. Work as a group of four to create a skit of a debate. Include the coin toss, construction speeches, and the first crossfire in your skit. Purposely build in performances of at least two inappropriate behaviors. See if your audience can identify your mistakes.

Chapter in Review

9.1 What Is Public Forum Debate

- Public Forum debate focuses on current controversial topics that interest the public. Crossfire allows two students, one from each side, to both ask and answer questions during the same period. Grand crossfire includes all four debaters.
- Strong speaking skills, delivery, and organization are emphasized over heavy research and evidence in Public Forum debates.

9.2 Speeches and Time Limits

- Public Forum debates begin with a coin toss that allows one team to determine whether to argue the affirmative or negative and the other team to determine speaking order.
- Like other debates, Public Forum utilizes constructive speeches and rebuttals, but crossfire, summaries, and final focus periods are somewhat unique.

9.3 Crossfire Techniques and Teamwork

- You should show respect to your opponents and the judge by following appropriate behavior during the debate. Planning and use of specific techniques can help you to succeed during crossfire.
- Knowing your team's strengths and weaknesses and improving communication with your partner will help you to improve your debate skills.

Develop Your Debating Language

Select the term that best fits the definition. Some terms may not be used.

a. advocating
b. citizen judge
c. crossfire
d. dominate
e. filibustering
f. final focus
g. grand crossfire
h. hard evidence
i. plan
j. Public Forum debate
k. soft evidence
l. status quo
m. summary speech

1. A period when two debaters cross-examine each other
2. Keeping a situation as it is without change
3. A short second rebuttal
4. Focuses on controversial current events that interest citizens
5. Supporting a position
6. Examples, stories, and personal narratives
7. To control a discussion or debate
8. A period when four debaters cross-examine each other
9. Adult member of the community that determines the winning team
10. Making a long speech to delay someone else from talking
11. Known as the last shot
12. Quotations, statistics, and facts
13. A specific solution or proposal

14. Why are Public Forum debate resolutions referred to as "stripped from the headlines?"

15. How are Public Forum debates similar to televised debate shows?

16. Explain a criticism of Public Forum debate.

17. Describe a typical judge of a Public Forum debate.

18. What are the differences in the purposes of cross-examination, Lincoln-Douglas, and Public Forum debates?

19. Why is it possible for the negative side to speak first in a Public Forum debate but not in other debates?

20. What happens during the first crossfire period?

21. Name two issues that could be debated in a Public Forum format. Do not use examples from the book.

22. How are Public Forum resolutions determined?

23. When related to resolutions, what does argument balance mean?

24. How do you use critical thinking skills in Public Forum debates?

25. What is the advantage of winning the coin toss in a Public Forum debate?

26. What is the longest speech presented in a Public Forum debate? The shortest? How long is each?

27. For what is prep time used?

28. Is the organization of the affirmative constructive speech the same as the negative constructive speech? Explain your answer.

29. Who determines what speaker on a team makes which speeches?

30. How does crossfire differ from typical cross-examinations in other debate types?

31. What is the difference between the first crossfire and the second crossfire?

32. How does grand crossfire differ from the other crossfires?

33. What is the purpose of the final focus?

34. Why are dominating and filibustering frowned upon in debate?

35. At what point will the judge be involved in crossfire?

36. Who can earn speaker points in Public Forum?

37. Why should you ask only questions that require brief answers?

38. How are mistakes related to communication between team members?

39. **ECONOMICS** Consider the resolution below. Research the affirmative and negative sides of this issue. Consider what types of questions you would ask and possibly answer during crossfire and rebuttals.

   Resolved: That the quantity of credit available to American consumers should be significantly reduced.

40. **GOVERNMENT** Consider the resolution below. Research both sides of this Public Forum resolution and write two arguments for each side. Discuss with a partner whether one side was easier to reason than the other.

   Resolved: Failed nations are a greater threat to the United States than stable nations.

41. **SCIENCE** Consider the resolution below. Hold a debate with classmates on this issue. Watch for inappropriate behavior and techniques made by the other team.

   Resolved: That the benefits of NASA's space exploration programs justify the costs.

Research NOW!

42. **TEAMWORK** With a partner, research to learn more about Ted Turner. What connections does he have to debate? What other achievements has he made in his life? What are some of his philosophies? Use several types of resources including at least one book, one magazine or newspaper article, and one online source.

43. Research to learn more about non-verbal communication. List examples of non-verbal communication. How does your conscious and unconscious non-verbal communication affect teammates, opponents, and judges?

Write NOW!

44. Find a topic that could be debated in a Public Forum debate. Write a resolution and write two arguments to support the resolution. Give at least one example of soft evidence and one example of hard evidence to support each of your arguments.

45. **TEAMWORK** With a partner, make a two-column table that lists each speech of a Public Forum debate in the first column. In the second column, list two or more strengths that you should have in order to effectively deliver each of the speeches.

46. On your own, consider the following resolution. Assume that you win the coin toss before the debate begins. Decide what decision you would make. Write a paragraph that states the decision and your reasoning for making it for this particular resolution.

Resolved: In a democracy, civil disobedience is an appropriate weapon in the fight for justice.

47. Consider the decision you made about the coin toss in activity 50. Think of a topic or resolution that would make you decide differently. For instance, if using the previous civil disobedience resolution you chose to argue the negative side, now you should come up with a resolution that would make you choose the affirmative side or would make you favor speaking order instead.

Speak NOW!

48. **TEAMWORK** With a partner, research past resolutions used by the National Forensic League. Find one or two good examples of how the resolution represented a controversial issue at the time. Present your findings to the class, providing details of the controversy.

49. Think about the use of the coin toss in Public Forum debates. Why is it used in Public Forum but not other debates? Is it fair? Answer these and other questions that you come up with and decide how you feel about it. Present your opinions to the class in an organized format. Focus on your speaking skills during your presentation.

eCollection Activity

Although Public Forum debates always focus on issues that are making the headlines, sometimes those headlines can serve to analyze events of the past.

One such example is the terrorist attacks of September 11, 2001. On this day, 19 members of an Islamic terrorist group executed a devastating attack on the United States. Thousands were killed as the terrorists crashed commercial airplanes into the Pentagon and the World Trade Center. The attacks destroyed the sense of security shared by many Americans. The U.S. government established new policies to reduce the risk of more attacks.

The war on terror may never end. Although the attacks occurred in 2001, the National Forensic League approved a resolution in June 2008 that focused on the tragedy of September 11. This resolution, Resolved: U.S. policies established after September 11, 2001 have substantially reduced the risk of terrorist acts against the United States, serves as an example of how history can be analyzed to make headlines.

Access www.cengage.com/school/langarts/debate and click on the link for Chapter 9. Find facts on the attacks of September 11 and research arguments about the success of the policies referred to in the resolution.

CHAPTER 10

Extemporaneous Speaking

Real People | Real Careers

Condoleezza Rice

> *"You have control, you're proud, you have integrity, nobody can take those things away from you.* **"**

One day in the early nineteen sixties in Birmingham, Alabama, an African-American woman was heading towards a dressing room with her small daughter. The little girl was holding a pretty dress that she was going to try on. Suddenly, a white sales lady stopped in front of them and pointed towards a storeroom. "She'll have to try it on in there," the saleslady said. The little girl's mother replied that, if the store was willing to take her money, she could try on the dress in a dressing room like everybody else.

The little girl was Condoleezza Rice, future Secretary of State. Growing up in the segregated South in the early 1960s made a huge impact on Rice's personal determination to succeed. Rice has said, "You have control, you're proud, you have integrity, nobody can take those things away from you." This work ethic and determination helped Rice excel in school and graduate from the University of Denver by the age of 19.

Continuing on with her education, Rice received a Master's degree in Political Science and a Ph.D. in International Studies. She was hired by Stanford University as a professor and lecturer in Political Science, where she was quickly promoted to the level of Provost (a professor with administrative duties within her field of study). She was the first African-American and the first woman to be elected to such a post.

While working for Stanford, Rice received a fellowship to study international affairs with the U.S. Joint Chiefs of Staff. This fellowship marked her entrance into politics. From there she quickly ascended the political ladder, working for the National Security Council, then as National Security Adviser to President George W. Bush, then as Secretary of State of the United States, the second woman to hold that position. A key figure in Rice's education was a specialist in international politics named Josef Korbel, who was the father of the first woman Secretary of State, Madeleine Albright. During her time in politics Rice worked on gender integration in the military, reunifying Germany, international diplomacy, and apportioning foreign aid to developing countries.

During her service in the Bush administration, Rice distinguished herself as a calm but forceful speaker. On many occasions she appeared before Senate committees to represent the administration and debate its policies. Rice consistently remained calm and focused, even under tough questioning from the senators. She appeared often on Sunday morning talk shows and news broadcasts, and once again was an effective debater and a poised and articulate speaker. As a scholar, teacher, and statesperson, Condoleezza Rice has been guided by the work ethic and determination given to her by her parents.

Think Critically

In what ways has Condoleezza Rice been an effective public speaker?

What Is Extemporaneous Speaking?

Understand the meaning of extemporaneous speaking.

Identify the different types of extemporaneous speaking.

Understand what happens at the contest itself.

TERMS

extemporaneous speech
extemp
Domestic Extemporaneous
   Speaking
Foreign Extemporaneous
   Speaking
draw

Do You Agree?

Resolved The possession of nuclear weapons is immoral.

Affirmative position

Yes, nuclear weapons present a danger to all living things. Not only is there the problem of human emotion, but human error presents a grave area of concern as well.

Negative position

No, the possession of nuclear weapons is vital to our society's well-being. The possession of nuclear weapons deters other countries from using aggressive tactics against the United States. Nuclear weapons are essential to providing safety and security for our citizens.

Extemporaneous Speaking

Everybody has had it happen at one time or another. You are asked to comment on a topic, give an explanation, or describe something. You did not expect it so you had nothing prepared, yet you managed to address the topic anyway. This is an example of an extemporaneous speech. An **extemporaneous speech** is one that has not been written out beforehand and is given on the spur of the moment. Rebuttal speeches in debate are good examples of extemporaneous speeches.

Extemporaneous speaking, or **extemp**, as it is often called, is an event that is offered at most debate tournaments. Most debaters, whether they are in Lincoln-Douglas or cross-examination debate, also compete in extemporaneous speaking. Extemporaneous speaking is very useful to learn. It will help you improve your speaking skills. You will be able to convey your knowledge on a topic to a judge or an opponent more effectively. Extemporaneous speaking teaches you to speak naturally and confidently.

Extemporaneous speaking will also increase your reading and analysis skills. It is important to keep up with current events in order to be successful in this event. You will want to read as much as you can in order to understand what is currently going on not only in the United States, but also in the world. This will also help in the preparation of your debate cases when the resolutions focus on real world issues.

The purpose of an extemporaneous speech is to answer a question that you have selected from three choices. Because you are selecting the question during a round at the tournament, you will have to prepare a speech during an allotted time period and then present it to the judge. An extemporaneous speech is seven minutes in length.

Types of Extemporaneous Speaking

Extemporaneous speaking is divided into two categories: **Domestic Extemporaneous Speaking** (also called U.S. Extemporaneous Speaking) and **Foreign Extemporaneous Speaking** (also called International Extemporaneous Speaking). You cannot compete in both categories because they are run at the same time. It is important to select the category with which you feel most comfortable and are most informed.

FYI Law firms typically hire costly trainers to help young associates prepare or improve their extemporaneous speech capabilities. Extemporaneous speaking is an important skill for trial lawyers.

Domestic extemporaneous covers all issues that pertain to the United States. Topics could include the economy, health care, judicial issues, or political campaigns. Foreign extemporaneous speaking deals with issues and policies of countries outside of the borders of the United States. There are times when a question could apply to both Foreign and Domestic extemp. For example, "What does the United States have to do to improve its relationship with France?" is just such a question. It could be found in Domestic extemp because it deals with policies established by our government. It could be considered Foreign extemp because it also deals with our policies regarding France, a foreign country. Look at the following questions. They are typical of the questions you could expect to see in an extemporaneous competition.

- **Domestic Question**   Will a comprehensive health care bill be passed soon?

- **Foreign Question**   Should North Korea be allowed to have a nuclear weapons program?

ANNEDDE/ISTOCKPHOTO.COM

What is the difference between Domestic Extemporaneous Speaking and Foreign Extemporaneous Speaking?

Topics always deal with current events. As a result, it is very important to constantly keep up on a daily basis with what is going on in the world.

The Contest

Contest rules for an extemporaneous competition can vary from tournament to tournament, and from state to state. Because the Super Bowl of speech tournament is the NFL tournament, the rules discussed in this section will be the same rules that are given and followed at the national tournament. Again, local and state tournaments may have different rules, so always be sure to check the rules for each and every tournament you attend.

The extemporaneous part of the tournament begins in the draw room. **Draw** refers to the process of selecting a topic. Time is especially important at this moment in the tournament. The draw starts thirty minutes before the speaking segment of the round. For example, if the first round in the morning begins at 8:00 A.M., the draw will start at 7:30 A.M. Once the draw starts, you should not leave the room until it is your time to draw. Speakers draw seven minutes apart.

Prior to the draw, you will be assigned a speaker position, which will tell you when it will be your turn to draw as well as when it will be your turn to speak. There will likely be postings to provide you with all of the necessary information. Study the posting carefully. You should know your section number and speaker position before going to the draw room. Postings generally provide the information shown in this sample posting.

> Domestic Extemp Section 7 Room 123
>
> 1. John Smith 7
> 2. Mary Black 12
> 3. Grace Bridges 14
> 4. Tina Pound 1

After looking at this posting, you know the following.

- The event is Domestic extemp.

- The section is number 7. The number of sections is determined by the number of students entered in the event. This number is important because topics are in an envelope marked with the section number on it. Drawing from the wrong section could result in being disqualified.

- Room 123 indicates the room where you will be speaking in front of a judge. All of the contestants in section 7 will be speaking for the same judge. There can be up to eight contestants in the room. Speaking order is indicated by the number in the left hand column. Grace Bridges is the third speaker in section 7. This also means that she will be the third person to draw topics in that section.

- The number following each name tells what school that student is competing for at the tournament. The numbers are assigned to the schools by the tournament director and will be the number for that school for all of the students who are entered. For example, Grace Bridges is competing for Lincoln High School. All of the students from Lincoln High School will have a 7 as a part of their code throughout the tournament.

The Draw

Quite often, because of the number of contestants involved, a draw is held in an auditorium. The person in charge of the draw makes a statement similar to "At this time, will all speaker ones please draw." The time for all speaker ones begins with this announcement. Speaker one now has thirty minutes to prepare a speech before delivering it before a judge. There will be envelopes set up with a sign-in sheet at the front of the room. The event and section number should be written on the sign-in sheet or the envelope. Because the draw for Domestic extemp and Foreign extemp usually takes place in the same room, it is very important that you make sure you are drawing from

1. The right event

2. The right section

3. The right speaker position

If any of these are done incorrectly, it can result in a disqualification.

Next, you draw three topics from the envelope. Again, the number of topics drawn can differ depending on the tournament you are attending. Be sure to check all of the rules, including the number of topics that can be drawn, before you enter the extemporaneous competition. Once you have pulled your three topics from the envelope, read each of them and select the one you are the best prepared to speak about. Don't waste time. Remember, the clock is ticking.

COURTESY OF NATIONAL FORENSIC LEAGUE, WWW.NFLONLINE.ORG

What information is given to you prior to a draw?

Suppose you pull the following topics.

- What do the Republicans have to do to rebuild their party?

- Will a new plan for health care be passed this year?

- What will it take for the economy to rebound from its present condition?

You have pulled three different topic areas: politics, health care, and the economy. You choose to do your speech on the economy. The sheet has been filled in with all of the required information. It is not necessary to write out the topic word for word. Key words, along with the topic number, are sufficient. This entire process should take no longer than two to three minutes. Less time spent selecting a topic will mean more time you have to spend preparing your speech. Remember, you cannot write out your speech, but you can think it through and make notes for yourself. After drawing your topic and correctly filling out the sign-in sheet, it is time to return to your seat to begin preparing your speech.

It is customary for the person in charge of the draw to inform students of the amount of time they have left before they must leave for their room. This is done at the same time new speakers are called to draw topics. The instructions given by the person doing the draw will be similar to the following.

7:30 A.M.   All speaker ones, please draw now.

7:37 A.M.   All speaker twos, please draw now. Speaker one, you have 23 minutes left.

7:44 A.M.   All speaker threes, please draw now. Speaker two, you 23 minutes left. Speaker one, you have 16 minutes left.

7:51 A.M.   All speaker fours, please draw now. Speaker three, you have 23 minutes left. Speaker two, you have 16 minutes left. Speaker one, you have nine minutes left.

7:58 A.M.   All speaker fives, please draw now. Speaker four, you have 23 minutes left. Speaker three, you have 16 minutes left. Speaker two, you have nine minutes left. All speaker ones must leave for their rooms now.

Note that at 7:58 A.M., speaker one still has two minutes left. This time is used to get to your room. Go directly there. Do not stop to speak to classmates, other competitors, or your coach. Any conversation could be interpreted as getting information or help. This would be grounds for disqualification.

You have 28 minutes before you will be told to go to your judging room. As you wait your turn to go and make your speech before the judge, you must outline what you want to say. Your preparation will go all the more smoothly if you have already conducted thorough research.

TURNING POINT

Meet the Press

Meet the Press has been one of the most important political debate shows in America. The show gathers politicians, commentators, and strategists from the whole political spectrum to engage in productive and informative public debate. President John F. Kennedy once called the show the "fifty-first state" because of its value to the American people. Since the show's beginning, almost every President, Vice-President, and Secretary of State has made an appearance on the program.

The longest running television program in world broadcasting history, *Meet the Press* began on radio in 1945. Journalist Martha Rountree devised a format for producer Lawrence Spivak of a weekly press conference for a guest or guests who would appear before a panel of three reporters. Rountree herself was the first moderator. In 1947, the program moved to the NBC television network.

By the late 1990s, the program had begun to slip in the ratings, and network executives feared for its future. They drastically changed the format. A single moderator who would ask questions to one or more guests replaced the panel of reporters. They hired NBC Washington Bureau chief Tim Russert to serve as moderator. Russert remained as moderator until his sudden death in June of 2008, longer than any other moderator in the program's history. Ratings soared, and *Meet the Press* became the highest rated Sunday morning talk show.

The table on the set of *Meet the Press* resembles a baseball field. The moderator sits at the most narrow point—home plate, while those who debate are spread along the first and third base lines. The moderator sits with his back to the camera, while the debaters face the camera as well as each other. The effect of this setup is such that the moderator represents the voice of the people, asking questions viewers themselves want answers to. It also creates the sense that those politicians involved in the debate answer directly to the viewers, the American people.

Since 2002, *Meet the Press* has featured a set of debates called the "Senate Debate Series." This series of discussions always happens during election season when incumbents and challengers battle for their states' Senate seats. In 2006, the Senate Debate Series pulled in 22.4 million viewers, an indication of just how important the art of debate, as well as this renowned program, is in our country. As the moderator announces at the end of the program, "If it's Sunday, it's *Meet the Press*."

Think Critically

Why do you think that *Meet the Press* is such a popular program?

Think Critically

1. Why is it beneficial to learn extemporaneous speaking?

2. What are the two types of extemp speeches?

3. What must you be clear about when checking a posting for an extemp draw?

4. What is a draw? What must a debater do there?

5. How should you use your time after you have selected your extemp question?

Research NOW!

6. Read issues of your local newspaper for the past month. What are the important domestic issues that have been written about? Make a list and present your findings to the class.

7. Watch broadcasts of the evening news of the major television networks. What international stories might lend themselves to topics for extemp speeches? Make a list and present it to the class.

 8. **TEAMWORK**   Brainstorm a list of topics for both foreign and domestic extemp speeches. Put your topics on the board and then try to weed out any that might not be interesting or provocative. Try to choose topics that you think will require challenging research and, ultimately, make for a lively and engaging extemp speech.

Write NOW!

9. Based on your research, write a series of questions that could be used as prompts for extemp speeches. Read your list to the class. Ask for reactions as to which questions they would choose for their speeches.

 10. **TEAMWORK**   Write a joint position paper on a matter of domestic or international importance. Brainstorm afterwards about the differences in preparing a written response as opposed to delivering an oral, extemporaneous one.

Speak NOW!

 11. **TEAMWORK**   Take turns with a partner developing responses to the prompts you wrote in number 6 above. Make a list of strengths and weaknesses you observed in each other's presentation and share after each has finished.

12. Practice delivering an extemporaneous speech on a general topic of your choice. Afterwards, make a list of what you felt went well and what areas of your delivery still need work. Share your list with the class and ask for comments.

13. Prepare a short presentation on why you think extemporaneous speaking is important to learn. Note the kinds of skills it requires and identify instances where the skills come in handy.

Do You Agree?

Resolved The American criminal justice system ought to place a higher priority on retribution than on rehabilitation.

Affirmative position

Yes, the relapse rate of criminals remains high. Once paroled, they are free to commit violent crimes once again. It is the responsibility of the criminal justice system to protect its citizens from habitual offenders. Retribution, when the punishment fits the crime, is not only just, but necessary.

Negative position

No, retribution is not the answer. By rehabilitating these offenders, they are shown how they can become productive members of society. Education and training in skills that are needed will help them to enter into society with a great success rate. It is the moral and ethical thing to do.

GOALS

Identify the research materials used for extemporaneous speaking.

Understand how to organize your materials in preparation for the tournament.

TERMS

annotation
tub

Research Materials

Even though this is an individual event, it truly takes teamwork to become successful at extemporaneous speaking. It is up to you and your squad to see that you have everything you need for the tournament. Using your time during practice sessions will not only help you with your speaking style, it will also help you see the strengths and weaknesses of your resource materials. By finding the areas that need improvement before the tournament, you will have a much easier time while competing.

It is easy to find materials to be used in extemp because the topics are always current. The questions are written straight from the headlines of the news. Watching national newscasts helps you to know what is going on in our country as well as other parts of the world. Newscasters are trained to break down a topic so that it can be easily understood. It is a good idea to take notes while you are watching. While the notes would not be allowed at a tournament, they can be used to inform you about specific topics as you prepare for the tournament.

It is also very important to read, read, read. You should read as many different periodicals as possible. It is always good to read material from opposing viewpoints on issues. *The New Republic, The Economist, U.S. News & World Report, Time,* and *Newsweek* are a few of the magazines available. *The Wall Street Journal, The New York Times,* and *The Christian Science Monitor* are some of the newspapers that make good sources for extemporaneous speaking. Always read your local paper. It will give you an insight into how your community is being affected by the issues of the day.

The Internet is also a valuable tool. It offers up-to-date stories and reports news as it happens. There are many sites that are available to you. You should always be looking for new sites that you can use. All of the national broadcasting stations offer Internet sites that carry up-to-the-minute reports of news that is happening around the world. Because of the nature of the Internet, the sites are always changing. Soon you will find sites that you think are the most beneficial to you. The Internet is extremely valuable when compiling information. Be sure and consult reputable sites from professional or scholarly organizations. Pay attention to any biases in any of the articles or editorials. Once you have compiled your research, you are ready to organize them into files.

> **FYI** Although newspaper circulation numbers have declined since the 1990s, due to increased competition from radio, television, and Internet, 70.3 million Internet users in the United States (one-third of the Internet population) read online newspapers.

The Files

The purpose of files is to provide reference materials before the draw period to help you organize your speech. In order to ensure fairness at the tournaments, guidelines are presented for all to follow. The National Forensic League is very clear about what is and is not acceptable for use during a tournament. While you may not know if you will attend the national tournament, it is a good idea to follow their rules. Failure to comply with the rules will result in a disqualification. Study the rules below that deal specifically with files.

The rules that determine the types of materials allowed into a competition are very specific. The only material allowed in the prep room is published books, magazines, newspapers, journals, and articles. These materials must be originals or photocopies of the originals. Any original article or copy must be intact and uncut. There can be no written commentary on that original or copy. In addition, extemp speeches, handbooks, briefs, and outlines will be barred from the prep room. Computers are also barred.

While computers are extremely helpful in creating your files, computers are not allowed in the extemp draw. You can, however, use the information you have printed from the Internet. All material that has been accessed from a computer must contain the copyright code. You will find this code at the beginning of the report in the credits. This will have a copyright symbol, which will indicate that it is computer copy of an original article.

When cutting articles, you must, once again, adhere to specific guidelines. NFL states that the original article must be intact or uncut. News articles should be kept as a whole article. Several problems can occur when articles have been cut and pasted. Paragraphs can be arranged to actually create a speech. Also, the original intent of the article can be altered by cutting and pasting. By omitting sentences or paragraphs from the original article, its entire meaning can be changed. This violates the spirit of extemp speaking.

How must articles appear in an extemp file?

There are a few exceptions to this rule however. Quotation books and political cartoon notebooks are both very popular with extemp contestants. Some contestants create their own catalogue of quotations that they can use for their speeches. As long as the quotations are not cut or changed in any way, they are perfectly legal. The quotations must be contained in a book format. Quotations that are pasted on cards could be placed in a speech. This would be considered to be an unfair advantage. Political cartoon notebooks are created when cartoons are cut, pasted, and organized alphabetically by topic. Any page with any handwritten description or explanation of the cartoon, other than a course cite, would be unacceptable.

Annotations, of any kind, are not allowed in the draw room. An **annotation**, according to *Webster's International Dictionary*, is "a note added by way of comment or explanation." Imagine a cartoon depicting the President of the United States holding a legal scale. On one side of the scale is etched the word Economy. Healthcare is shown on the other side. A student has written, "The president is trying to balance healthcare and the economy." The note written by the student would be considered to be an annotation. The entire notebook would be disallowed for the tournament.

Highlighting articles is another area of concern for extemp contestants. The NFL rule states "Underlining or highlighting in materials will be allowed if done in only one color on each article or copy." The use of multiple colors in an article could be used to aid the speaker in speech preparation. Pink, for instance, could indicate a quotation, while green could be used for statistics. This rule applies for all articles. Your squad should choose one color to be used by everybody. If you choose yellow, only those articles highlighted in yellow will be allowed. This rule, like all NFL rules, is meant to create an even playing field for all competitors.

The Tubs

Often, extemp materials are placed in large plastic **tubs**. These will be used to transport and store your materials in a preparation room at the tournament site. Domestic and Foreign extemp files should be kept in separate tubs. Most squads will have several tubs for each type of extemp to accommodate all of the files they have acquired. Because everybody should have contributed to the files, everybody should also be responsible for the tubs from the beginning of the tournament to the end of the tournament.

Organizing the tubs is the first step. All squad members should be familiar with the system you choose for filing articles. Hanging files are very handy to identify major topic areas such as economy, education, and healthcare. Topics can then be broken down into specific areas. Economy could have files that represent areas such as employment, retail sales, or the stock market. It doesn't matter how you organize the files as long as everybody understands the method used. Some squads put indexes on the front of the tubs indicating the areas that can be found in that tub. The index should only have topic areas listed. There should not be any description or notes other than topic headings in the index. An index system is helpful when you have multiple tubs at a tournament.

Why is organization important at an Extemp tournament?

COURTESY OF NATIONAL FORENSIC LEAGUE, WWW.NFLONLINE.ORG

YOU BE THE JUDGE

It is an item that appears in sports pages of newspapers or newscasts often. A player on a sports team misses practice. Later, the player is spotted at a fancy restaurant in another city. Sometimes it is difficult balancing your responsibilities as a debater with other interests. Responsibility is important when you are on a team. Practice and other responsibilities can be tedious, especially if you have other things you want to do. When you join any team, you are making a promise that you will do your best, not just for yourself, but for your other team members as well.

What Would You Do?

Imagine that your teacher has assigned a research project to prepare for an upcoming competition. Your team has broken up the assignment so that everybody has something that has to be done. That evening, you have a choice to watch your favorite baseball team play an important game or to work on the assignment. You know that your team is counting on you, but you really want to watch that game. How do you decide what to do?

Think Critically

1. How should you be watching newscasts in preparation for an extemp tournament?

2. What kind of research should be done to prepare for an extemp competition?

3. How should files be organized at an extemp competition? What kinds of materials are not allowed?

4. How are tubs used at extemp competitions?

Research NOW!

5. Read through newspapers and magazines such as *The New Yorker* and compile a collection of cartoons that could be gathered in a book.

 6. **TEAMWORK** Working with a partner, gather a list of relevant and interesting quotations. Gather your findings into a book and share it with the class.

Write NOW!

7. Prepare a bibliography of periodicals and websites that would be useful in preparing for domestic and foreign extemp speeches. Present your findings to the class.

8. Based upon your findings for activity 7, write a review of a select list of the periodicals and websites. Include any philosophies or biases that the source might have. Note any relevant features, such as such as short op ed articles or longer scholarly articles, the type of authors who write for the source, and anything you know about those who consult the source. Read your review to the class and invite questions and comments.

 9. **TEAMWORK** As a class, bring together all of the research that you have printed, copied, and gathered in preparation for the competition. Practice organizing and filing all of it in a manner that is clear and useful. Locate a plastic tub similar to those used in competitions. Place your materials in the tub and check your organization. Make any notes about how best to proceed when it comes time for an actual competition.

Speak NOW!

 10. **TEAMWORK** Consult your findings for activity 6 and divide the quotations into distinct groups based upon their differences. Present your quotations to the class and ask for comments.

The Speech

GOALS

Identify the parts of an extemp speech.

Practice an extemp speech.

Perform an extemp speech.

TERMS

grace period
source cite
attention getter
canned introduction
political notebook
transitional sentence
fluency break
vocalized pause

Do You Agree?

Resolved Showing disrespect for the American Flag is antithetical to fundamental American values.

Affirmative position

Yes, the American Flag is an important part of our heritage. It has been carried into battles. It has identified our ships, our troops, and our leaders. It flies over gatherings and is saluted before such significant events as the U.S. Open, The World Series. and the Super Bowl. The flag from Ground Zero has been carried proudly by firefighters as a reminder of 9/11. The flag is who we are as citizens of the United States of America. Quite simply, to be disrespectful to the flag by dragging it, spitting on it, or burning it is to shun the very values on which our country has been built.

Negative position

No, our American values are on display everyday. Our soldiers, who have fought for democracy throughout our history, demonstrate our true love and respect for our country. The firefighters who rushed into the Twin Towers to rescue fellow Americans displayed courage and bravery in a time of great uncertainty. From Henry Ford to Bill Gates, remarkable people have shown ingenuity, perseverance, and success in the field of business. These are American values. These values will continue to flourish. The flag, while a beautiful symbol, is simply material. Democracy, freedom of religion, entrepreneurships, and the freedom of speech are just some of the American values that make the United States great.

The Speech

You understand what extemporaneous speaking is all about. You have been working on the tubs to be sure you have good resources available to you at the tournament. Now it is time to learn how to construct an actual extemp speech. The extemp speech is seven minutes in length. Most tournaments allow a 30-second grace period.

A **grace period** allows you to finish your speech within 30 seconds of extra time allotment without a penalty. This is one reason why it is very

What does a source cite tell a judge?

important to be as prepared as possible. If you exceed the grace period by even one second, it can result in a disqualification. Like all of the other events, it is always a good idea to check the tournament rules set up by the host school. The exception to the grace period is the NFL tournament. You are allowed to finish your sentence and then must stop speaking regardless of how much of your speech is left.

An important element of the extemp speech is the source cite. A **source cite**, short for source citation, tells the judge what reference materials were used in preparing the speech. "According to an article in the July issue of *Newsweek…*" is an example of a source cite. Judges usually keep track of the number of source cites as well as the variety of resources given during the speech. They then use this as one of the factors to consider when choosing which competitors should advance to the next round. Novice extemp contestants should try to have three to five source cites per speech. Varsity extemp contestants should have five to twelve source cites.

Outlining the Speech

It is important to remember that, when making an extemp speech, you cannot use a prepared text. The purpose is to put together a speech within thirty minutes. You must prove to the judge that you are informed enough to answer the question you have chosen using research you have stored in your head. The entire purpose of extemp is to see how well informed you are on a particular topic. Your presentation will demonstrate your ability to answer the question and support your answer with credible information. Always give the impression that you prepared and knowledgeable about the topic.

Begin your preparation by constructing an outline. Collect your thoughts and organize them. That way, you will be organized when speaking. Remember, not only is the competitor judged on what he or she knows, but on how he or she delivers the information. The competitor is expected to know and understand the complexities of economics, healthcare, the environment, political reform, even entertainment. While it is challenging, extemporaneous speaking is definitely rewarding! A well-delivered extemp speech is a joy to judge and a thrill to accomplish.

The Introduction

Like every good speech, the extemp speech has three parts: the introduction, the body, and the conclusion. The introduction has four parts.

1. Attention getter

2. Restate the question

3. State your position

4. Transitional sentence

Each part of the introduction is very important. The introduction should be no longer than 1 minute to 1 minute and 15 seconds.

1. Attention Getter   The purpose of the introduction is to get the judge's attention. The **attention getter** should relate to the question you have selected. It should also set the tone for the speech. Quotations, rhetorical questions, anecdotes, jokes, personal stories, current events, canned introductions, and political notebooks are just a few of the devices that can be used as an attention getter. The choice is yours. It doesn't matter which method you choose as long as you introduce the topic in a manner that gets the judge's attention.

While most attention getters may be familiar to you, canned introductions and political notebooks are newer ideas. A **canned introduction** is prewritten. They are usually general in nature so that they can be easily applied to a variety of topics. They can be written by students at debate camps or by squads. While some coaches and judges like canned introductions, there are those coaches and judges who do not. There are advantages and disadvantages to using them. Ultimately, you must decide if it is right for you.

Because time is so limited, using a canned introduction allows you to work on other areas of your speech. You know the canned introduction, so it should already be memorized. Having used the canned introduction in practice rounds and at other tournaments, it should be a polished part of the speech. The canned introduction can also be a confidence builder.

There are also disadvantages to consider when deciding whether or not to use the canned introduction. You must be able to show how the attention getter relates to the question. Too often, competitors use canned introductions that have nothing to do with the rest of the speech. You also run the risk of presenting an intro to a judge that he or she has heard before. This removes the fresh and new aspect of your introduction. There is also the chance that you will perform in front of the same judge more than once during a tournament season. Using the same introduction repeatedly can leave a negative impression.

Political notebooks are tools that some squads use to help with their attention getters. A political notebook is a compilation of political cartoons that are arranged alphabetically by subject matter and contain complete source

TACOJIM/ISTOCKPHOTO.COM

What are the elements of a good introduction?

cites. In order for a political notebook to be an effective tool, you must work on keeping it updated. This should be done on a weekly basis. Before putting a cartoon in your notebook, you should study it. It will not help you unless you understand its message. Once you understand the cartoon, you should be able to describe it and its message in 20 to 30 seconds.

2. Restate the Question   Once you have given the attention getter, the next step is to *restate the question*. It reminds the judge of the topic of the speech. It does not have to be repeated word for word as it was written, but the intent of the question must not be altered in any way.

3. State Your Position   After stating the question, it is time to *state your position* and identify the main areas you will be discussing. Depending on how the question is written, a yes or no answer can be used. If a question is worded as

"Should our healthcare system by changed?"

a response could be

"Yes, our healthcare system should be changed. The uninsured, rising costs, and Medicare are areas that should be taken under consideration."

If the same topic asks

"What has to be done to change our healthcare system?"

the answer would be worded differently. A response could be

"In order to change our healthcare system, the increasing number of uninsured citizens, the rising costs involved, and the Medicare program must be addressed."

Both answers indicate that you agree that there is a problem within the healthcare system. The judge now knows how you are going to approach the topic and what key areas you will use as support for your answer.

4. Transitional Sentence   The last element of the intro is the transitional sentence. The **transitional sentence** indicates to the judge that you are done with the introduction. It helps to smoothly bring you to the next section of your speech. Transitional sentences can be the difference between a very good speech and a great speech. The following simple statement lets the judge know that you have completed the introduction and are now ready to begin the body of the speech.

"Before we can address the rising costs and Medicare, we must start with the many people who have no insurance."

The Body

The *body* of the extemp speech should be four to five minutes in length. It should have two to three main sections to support your answer. If you cannot think of at least two strong main sections to talk about, you should select a different question. You should be knowledgeable about the topic.

Present your areas of support in order of strength and importance. A popular structure for each section is *theory*, *application*, and *case study*. Use your sources to combine ideas and practical examples. Think of an idea or concept that applies to your question. Apply it to the specific situation you are speaking about. Back up that application with any source material you can think of. The most important section should be first.

The last sentence of each main section should always be a transitional sentence. A good transition from one main section to the next might be

"Now that we have discussed the uninsured, it is time to look at the rising costs."

The conclusion is the only area that does not need a transitional sentence.

The Conclusion

The *conclusion* is 30 to 45 seconds in length. The conclusion should

1. Tie back to the attention getter

2. Restate your position

3. Restate your main areas

4. Gently release the audience

Notice how the example below covers all of these areas.

1. A brief review of the attention getter is given.

2. "It is clear that the number of uninsured citizens, the rising costs of insurance, and the Medicare program must be addressed now…"

3. "In order to make the necessary changes to our healthcare system."

4. "A stable Health Care system will provide security for all."

It is short and to the point. Do not offer any explanations or examples. They should have been presented in the body. This conclusion wraps it all up neatly and makes it clear to the judge that you have finished speaking.

The Practice

Practice makes perfect. Practicing extemp speeches is essential. When conducting practice sessions, a tournament draw format should be simulated. Keep time and do not take more time than what is allowed at the tournaments. Do not ask for help or comments while you are delivering your speech. You will not be allowed to ask for or receive help at an actual draw.

Follow a time schedule. The sooner you start using time wisely, the better prepared you will be for the actual competition. Even though the draw time looks like you have 30 minutes, you are told to leave for your competition room at the 28-minute mark. A good guideline to follow is

1. Select your speech (2 to 3 minutes)

2. Prepare your speech (10 to 15 minutes)

3. Practice your speech (5 to 10 minutes)

Remember, you do not write out an extemp speech. Instead, you create an outline for your topic. You can make notes regarding your source cites. Some students choose to write out the transitional sentences. Once you have your outline completed, it is time to practice the speech. Students often look for a corner or a space in front of the wall where they can practice. Quietly say your speech aloud. A speech's time will change when being said aloud versus being read silently. It also lets you hear the flow of the speech. Continue to practice until you are told to leave the room.

Check the tournament rules regarding the use of note cards. Some tournaments allow you to use a 3 × 5 inch index card in a prelim round. They are not allowed in most final rounds. The NFL tournament does not allow them at all. It is best to practice without them whenever possible. The only things you will be allowed to take with you from the draw room will be the topic you selected from the envelope and a stopwatch.

© MICHAEL NEWMAN / PHOTOEDIT

Why is it important to practice your speech?

The Presentation

You have researched and practiced. You have chosen your topic and made your notes. Now you are ready for your actual speech at the tournament. When you get to your room, give your topic to your judge so that he or she knows the exact wording of your topic. There rarely will be anybody in the room besides you and the judge in the preliminary and semifinal rounds. The final rounds are exciting to watch, so there may be an audience at that time. Give your judge time to write your name and topic down before you start to speak.

Find a spot in the room where you feel comfortable and wait for the judge to indicate that he or she is ready for you to begin. Once you begin speaking, try to focus on vocal delivery, eye contact, fluency, and poise.

Your voice should be clear and controlled. Maintain a volume that is appropriate for the surroundings. Talk to the judge, not at him or her. Try to maintain a level of authority and confidence when you are speaking.

Eye contact will also help to reinforce confidence. Continue to look at your judge even if he or she is not consistently maintaining eye contact with you. Your judge may periodically glance at you. When he or she does, be sure to look at him or her.

Try not to fidget when speaking. Keep movements limited. Swaying, moving from foot to foot, and excessive hand gestures can be very distracting. You want your judge to focus on your message rather than your actions.

One of the most difficult hurdles for a novice extemp speaker to cross is fluency breaks. A **fluency break** is a pause in a sentence. **Vocalized pauses** such as "ah," "um," or "mm" are used to fill the void. They signal a break in thought as well. Too many fluency breaks will disrupt the flow of your speech. Practicing before the tournament will help to eliminate the number of fluency breaks you have in a speech. While it is extremely difficult to get rid of them altogether, you can keep them to a minimum.

At the end of the speech, thank the judge for his or her time and exit the room. The next speaker should be waiting outside the door.

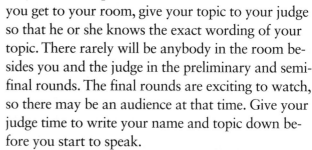

FYI In a national survey, about 40% of the online public state they can tell the difference between advertising and editorial content and indicated that online news is widely accepted as credible. People typically check domain names in making their judgment.

COURTESY OF NATIONAL FORENSIC LEAGUE, WWW.NFLONLINE.ORG

What are the elements of a good delivery?

Think Critically

1. What is a grace period?

2. What should an introduction contain in an extemp speech?

3. What is the function of a transitional sentence?

4. What structure should be used in outlining the body of an extemp speech?

5. What makes for an effective conclusion to an extemp speech?

6. What should you do to practice for an extemp competition?

7. What should you focus on while speaking at an extemp competition?

Research NOW!

8. Choose a political leader of local or national importance. Research a list of issues you would like to see discussed at a press conference.

9. **TEAMWORK** As a class, brainstorm a list of techniques that can help you to eliminate fluency gaps or vocalized pauses from delivered speeches. Try to be as specific as you can.

Write NOW!

10. Write a commentary on the quality of extemporaneous speaking that you have observed in press conferences or political debates. Note best and worst speakers and add suggestions for how speakers could improve their delivery.

11. Write a brief reflection paper on your experience as a public speaker. Acknowledge your strengths and weaknesses, and propose any strategies that you may have thought of to help you improve.

12. **TEAMWORK** As a class, write a joint description of your strengths as a team. After you are finished, review what you have written and discuss any areas where you might improve.

Speak NOW!

13. **TEAMWORK** Choose four members of your class to play the role of political candidates. Have the remainder of the class pose as members of the press and conduct a press conference. Have the press pose questions on local issues. Afterwards, have the press offer comments to the candidates on the smoothness and content of their responses.

14. Read an op-ed piece in your local newspaper and deliver a seven-minute response. Structure your response according to the format that you learned in this chapter. Make sure that your position is clear and well supported. Ask for reactions from the class.

Chapter in Review

10.1 What Is Extemporaneous Speaking?

- An extemporaneous speech is one that is not written out beforehand.
- A Domestic extemporaneous speech covers issues that pertain to the United States. A Foreign extemporaneous speech covers issues of countries outside of the United States.
- Students at an extemporaneous tournament begin the process at a draw where they learn the question they must speak to. Pay attention to all instructions about rooms and assignments.

10.2 Extemp Materials

- Keep up with current events to prepare for extemp. Watch the news and take notes. Look at newspapers, magazines, and websites. Only use those with respected, professional reputations.
- Organize your materials into files. Pay attention to the rules that tell you what kind of materials you can and cannot use at a tournament. Place all of your files in plastic tubs that you will bring to the tournament.

10.3 The Speech

- Every extemp speech has an introduction, a body, and a conclusion. An extemp speech is seven minutes long, with a grace period of thirty seconds.
- Practice before attending the tournament. Structure your practice sessions as if they were part of an actual tournament.
- While delivering your speech, your voice should be clear and strong. Maintain eye contact with the judge, and maintain poise at all times.

a. annotation

b. attention getter

c. canned introduction

d. Domestic extemporaneous speech

e. draw

f. extemp

g. extemporaneous speech

h. fluency break

i. Foreign extemporaneous speech

j. grace period

k. political notebook

l. source cite

m. transitional sentence

n. tub

o. vocalized pause

Develop Your Debating Language

Select the term that best fits the definition. Some terms will not be used.

1. Speech that is not written out before hand

2. Process of selecting a topic

3. Pre-written resource, often prepared by students at debate camp

4. Note added to comment or explain

5. Competition at which speeches are prepared just before delivery

6. Category of speeches whose topics pertain to the United States

7. An acknowledgment to a judge of a source used in a speech

8. Container used to store files

9. Period of extra time used to finish a speech

10. Moment that sets the tone in a speech

11. Compilation of political cartoons

Review Debate Concepts

12. What skills can you learn from extemporaneous speaking?

13. Summarize the difference between a Domestic extemporaneous speech and a Foreign extemporaneous speech.

14. What kinds of topics are always used at extemporaneous tournaments?

15. What is important about a draw at an extemporaneous tournament?

16. What information will the person in charge of a draw pass on to you?

17. On what should you base your choice for a topic in extemp?

18. Why is it important to watch news broadcasts before an extemporaneous competition? What should you do while watching them?

19. What should you pay attention to when using the Internet as part of your research?

20. Summarize the rules determining what materials may be brought into the prep room at a tournament.

21. How can quotations or political cartoons be used at an extemp tournament?

22. What do you need to remember about highlighting your research?

23. How should your team work together to organize files in preparation for an extemporaneous competition?

24. What should a good introduction contain for an extemporaneous speech?

25. What is the function of a transitional sentence in an extemp speech? What is the one place in an extemp speech where a transitional sentence is not found?

26. How should the body of an extemp speech develop your answer?

27. What should the conclusion of an extemp speech contain?

28. How should you practice delivering an extemp speech?

29. How do you actually deliver an extemp speech?

30. What should you focus on while delivering an extemp speech?

31. Why is it important to be specific about source cites? How many should you use?

32. What is the difference between a fluency break and a vocalized pause?

Make Academic Connections

33. **PROBLEM SOLVING** Many news stations or newscasts offer editorials. In these short segments, a spokesperson for the station or program offers a solution to a community, national, or international problem. Call your local station and find out times when one of these segments is going to be aired. Analyze the piece for the way in which the speaker focused on the problem and offered a solution.

34. **HISTORY** Research the role of the *disputation* in medieval universities. These were public debates in which students debated their teachers. Do you think that student-teacher debates should be a regular part of a school curriculum? Why or why not?

35. **CHALLENGES** Locate a transcript or video of a political debate. Notice how the candidates must speak extemporaneously in response to questions from reporters or the audience and in rebuttal to each other's responses. Take notes. Make a list of answers you found effective and state why.

Research NOW!

36. Research the background of extemporaneous speaking at debate competitions. Consult the website for the National Forensic League and other resources. Present your findings to the class.

 37. **TEAMWORK** As a group, watch a video of a recent presidential debate. Individually, make lists of your individual observations about the performance of each of the participants. Afterwards, compare notes about your observations. Include any observations or suggestions that you might make to a participant to help improve performance.

Write NOW!

38. Write a description of a recent debate or press conference that you watched. Describe in detail the performance of each participant. Note successful techniques such as humor, ability to recite evidence, or ability to focus on issues.

 39. **TEAMWORK** Choose an issue that you have seen debated on television, either on news programs or on televised debates from Congress. Divide into teams and take opposing sides of the issue. Have each side write a response paper. Make sure that each paper is well organized, structured to attract attention, and provides a persuasive argument for its position. Make sure that evidence is used to support that position. End with an effective conclusion. Read each paper in class. Ask for questions and comments.

40. Draft an op-ed piece for your local newspaper, addressing a national or international issue. Structure it as you would an extemp speech. Provide quotations or other means to attract attention, relevant evidence, and source citations.

Speak NOW!

41. Many times a newspaper will pose questions to its readers such as, "Should senior citizens over the age of 70 be allowed to drive?" Find a question such as this and deliver a seven-minute response.

When Susan B. Anthony was arrested for attempting to vote in the presidential election in 1872, she spoke out passionately, protesting her arrest and supporting women's right to vote.

Webster, Worcester, and Bouvier all define a citizen to be a person in the United States, entitled to vote and hold office. The only question left to be settled now is: Are women persons? And I hardly believe any of our opponents will have the hardihood to say they are not.

You may recognize this imperative: "Ask not what your country can do for you; ask what you can do for your country." It is from President John F. Kennedy's Inaugural Address. Kennedy's speech helped inspire thousands of young Americans to join the Peace Corps in service to their country and the world.

Those speeches all made an impression. Because of creative word choice, strong ideas, and impassioned deliveries, their impact has not diminished with time.

Your speeches can also make an impact. When you speak, you want to create a whole experience for your audience. Your listeners should not only be able to understand the ideas you present, but they should also be able to relate to you. They should trust you. They should be moved by you.

GEORGE SILK/TIME LIFE PICTURES/GETTY IMAGES

How can a speech such as President Kennedy's inaugural address affect listeners?

Elements of Oratory

In debate, CXers are given a resolution that they will debate for the entire school year. Approximately six times a year, LDers are given new resolutions that they will debate at the various competitions. Extempers are given three topics each round from which they select one to present to the judge. However, there is one event for which nobody tells you what to do in a round. The choice is completely yours. The event is Original Oratory. It is your opportunity to present a public speech.

Oratory Rules

According to the National Forensic League, competitive **oratory** is described as

an event in which the student writes, memorizes, and then delivers a persuasive speech arising from his/her personal feelings and convictions, or a source of irritation about some problem. No specific restriction as to the type of speech governs oratory. Although most orations are persuasive speeches, they may also be eulogies or inspirational speeches. Topics for the oration are selected by each contestant with the aid of coach or teacher. Not more than 10 percent or 150 words may be direct quotation. Extensive paraphrasing is also discouraged. The oration must be presented from memory. The oration must be between seven and ten minutes in length. Original Oratory offers the student an opportunity to develop skills in research and writing, to analyze his or her own values and to take a stand on important issues. It also teaches the speaker to develop logical proof, to memorize, to polish delivery and presentation abilities, and to rework and revise for excellence.

To ensure that your speech has no more than 150 quoted words, you or your coach must have a copy of your speech with you at every tournament, as well as a bibliography of source material you used. Highlight all quoted words. That way, if another coach or competitor challenges any portion of your speech, you will be able to produce a written copy as evidence that most of the words are indeed your own.

In addition to these guidelines, there are others you must follow in Original Oratory. Note cards, papers, or prompts by fellow students are not allowed during an oration. Costuming, or dressing to enhance the speech, is also forbidden.

A time limit, minimum of quotations, and prohibition on prompts and costumes are all restrictions on an oration. What does an effective oration include?

Style and Substance

Delivery is crucial for a public speaker. When you present your speech, you are evaluated—perhaps subconsciously by your audience but certainly consciously by the judge—on how effectively you speak and move. Poise, voice quality, and gestures are key elements of your oration. Your directness and sincerity are essential, and they should seem natural. Your **diction**, or choice of words, underlies your personal style.

Yet these elements of style and delivery are just one aspect of Original Oratory. A winning oration must have substance as well. The ideas you present are as important as the way you present them. In addition, your audience will look for support for your ideas. By including facts, examples, and anecdotes as support, you not only engage listeners, but you also win them over.

You and Oratory

Oratory provides you with many opportunities. It furnishes a platform for you to discuss issues that you feel are important and worthy of attention. You can present your views and support them to show why they are significant. You also have a chance to present your ideas with passion, conviction, and energy.

You've likely listened to speakers who went on and on about a topic that seemed of as little interest to them as it did to you. Speak about something that you feel passionate about and would like to share with others. If you are enthusiastic about your topic, you will *want* to do the research, write the speech, practice the speech, and perform the speech for others. If you are passionate about your topic, it will be much easier to make your audience passionate about it too.

The Oratory Topic

The biggest hurdle for orators often is finding a topic. Many students prefer to be assigned a topic rather than find one on their own. Other than your personal passion and interest in the topic, there are three general guidelines you should follow when considering a subject for a speech, especially one for competition.

- **First, is the topic important enough that the judge and the audience will want to hear about it?** If it is something that most people can relate to or feel a stake in, it will likely catch the audience's attention. The **competition worthiness** of the topic will go a long way in helping you deliver a successful oration. A topic such as pet grooming, while you may feel it is important, might not be able to keep everybody's attention for ten minutes.

- **Second, is the topic fresh?** There is no doubt that certain issues are important and often in the public eye. However, if a topic has been done many times by many students, there may be little that is new that you can say about it. Selecting a well-worn topic comes with the risk that your judge and audience may tune you out. Instead, look for a topic that is intriguing and innovative, or be sure you have some fresh, startlingly new ideas to share about a familiar topic. Step out of the box when you are planning your oration.

COURTESY OF NATIONAL FORENSIC LEAGUE, WWW.NFLONLINE.ORG

Why do you think passion about your topic is important?

- **Third, is the topic in good taste?** The last thing you want to do is to offend your judge or many people in the audience. If you are not sure if your topic is offensive, ask your coach, fellow students, or your parents. If even one person finds it offensive, you may want to reconsider selecting another topic. Offensive is not the same as controversial. A somewhat controversial topic can work because it stimulates thought and helps energize people.

FYI Fear of public speaking is one of the most common phobias that people have. Psychologists call it glossophobia (*glosso* comes from the Greek word for *tongue*). Certain techniques and practice, practice, practice can help overcome fear. One tip for overcoming anxiety is to select a topic that interests you so much that it takes your mind off yourself. Also, remember that 95 percent of all speakers—even experienced orators—feel some nervousness before a speech.

Purpose of Oratory

Oratory is generally persuasive speech. You try to persuade your listeners to take an action, accept a belief, or consider a situation from a different perspective. Many orations focus on a problem and then offer and explain a solution that you wish your audience to accept, but this is not the only acceptable purpose or format. You may simply want to alert your audience to a situation that deserves its concern. Or you might want to eulogize a person whose life you consider great or meaningful in some way.

Oratory can have many different purposes. Ultimately, as an orator you should seek to speak about your topic with, as the National Forensic League states, "some profit to your audience." If people are talking about your speech and your ideas after the round, you have done your job.

What would be the purpose of eulogizing someone in an oration?

TURNING POINT

"I Have a Dream"

AP PHOTO/FILE

Martin Luther King, Jr.'s "I Have a Dream" speech is still as powerful today as when Dr. King first presented it in 1963. It has been voted the top American speech of the 20th century by more than 100 scholars of American oratory.

King had traveled to the nation's capital to participate in the "March on Washington for Jobs and Freedom" for African-Americans. On the steps of the Lincoln Memorial, he spoke in front of almost a quarter of a million people. The speech he began to deliver was similar to one he had given before in Detroit. Much of the speech concerns the demand for equal opportunity and rights for African-Americans.

A Baptist minister, King had taken the phrase "I have a dream" from the Bible: "I have a dream that every valley shall be exalted." (Isaiah 40:4) Toward the end of his speech in Washington, gospel singer Mahalia Jackson shouted from the crowd: "Tell them about the dream, Martin!" Putting aside his text, King began to improvise.

> I have a dream that one day this nation will rise up and live out the true meaning of its creed: "We hold these truths to be self-evident: that all men are created equal."
>
> I have a dream that one day on the red hills of Georgia the sons of former slaves and the sons of former slave owners will be able to sit down together at a table of brotherhood.
>
> I have a dream that one day even the state of Mississippi, a desert state, sweltering with the heat of injustice and oppression, will be transformed into an oasis of freedom and justice.
>
> I have a dream that my four children will one day live in a nation where they will not be judged by the color of their skin but by the content of their character.
>
> I have a dream today.

John Lewis, who would later be elected to Congress from Georgia, was with Dr. King that day. After the speech, he went with King and others to the White House to meet with President Kennedy. According to Lewis, President Kennedy warmly congratulated King and said, "You did a good job . . . and you had a dream."

Dr. King's speech is an iconic moment of the civil rights movement in the United States. Civil rights legislation that was later passed included the Civil Rights Act of 1964 and the Voting Rights Act of 1965. You can watch and listen to King's "I Have a Dream" speech on the Internet.

Think Critically

What elements of the "I Have a Dream" speech affect you the most? Why?

Think Critically

1. How is oratory different from other forms of debate?

2. Explain the importance of both style and substance in oratory.

3. What are some criteria for an appropriate topic for an oration?

Research NOW!

4. Many great speeches from U.S. history are available on the Internet. Select one that interests you and read it. Make note of the historical background of the orator and of the speech itself. Did the oration have an influence on people or policy? If so, how?

 5. **TEAMWORK** Work in teams of four or five. Select a particular topic or issue of interest. Research and collect different speeches from various orators on the issue. Read the speeches aloud to one another. Discuss and evaluate the style and substance of each. Vote for the speech you think was the most effective oration.

Write NOW!

6. Watch a congressional meeting on C-Span on television or on its website archives. Listen to a speech that is given on an important issue. Write a one-page summary of the major points that the speaker made. Include an analysis of your personal reaction to the speaker and the speech.

 7. **TEAMWORK** Working with a partner, select a topic for an oration—an issue on which you both agree. Individually, write support for your position on the topic. Include at least one fact, one example, and one anecdote. Then compare and evaluate the support you each developed. Revise and add to your support if necessary.

Speak NOW!

8. Use the support you developed for activity 7. Prepare a three- or four-minute speech on your topic. Memorize the speech and present it to the class. If your partner also delivers a speech on the topic, ask your classmates to compare and evaluate the two.

 9. **TEAMWORK** Pair up with a classmate. Select a historical speech that you both admire. Each member of the pair should memorize the speech or a portion of the speech, depending on its length. Memorize the same portion. Deliver the speech to each other. Discuss the differences in your deliveries.

Do You Agree?

Resolved Decisions of the U.S. Supreme Court in criminal cases ought to reflect the values of the American people.

Affirmative position

Yes, the members of the Supreme Court are nominated and selected after carefully scrutinizing their stands on a variety of issues that concern the American people. By having a balanced court, it is more likely that the values of most will be represented. Because the decisions of the Supreme Court affect all of the American people, it is important to have judges who understand the concerns and desires of its constituents.

Negative position

No, the Supreme Court has one responsibility and that is to enforce and apply the Constitution as it is written. Those judges interested in rewriting or interpreting laws in a manner other than intended by the framers are not fulfilling their duties of the Court. The Constitution is the foundation of our country and should be the main influence in Supreme Court decisions.

GOALS

Understand methods for selecting and researching a topic.

Identify the various patterns for organizing a speech.

Recognize the importance of diction.

TERMS

topic statement
outline
rhetorical device
allusion
parallel phrasing
repetition

Topic Selection and Research

You've learned different criteria that you need to consider when selecting a topic. So where do you go to get ideas? Start with your coach. Your coach may have lists of topics for you to use. Write down three or more of the ideas that are the most appealing to you. It is possible that another student—either from your school or another team—may have already spoken on one of the topics. If so, you will want to know how recently the topic was used. Also, brainstorm with other students. Ask them what interests them and what they feel is important and relevant. Start a list of possible topics.

Listing Possibilities

You can add other topic ideas to the list of topics from your coach and fellow students. Many speakers and writers find it helpful to start big and end small when brainstorming for topics.

- **Global** Look at world issues to see if there is something currently going on that you would like to research and speak out on. Perhaps it is women's rights in foreign countries, climate change, or aspects of global economics. Watching the news on television, reading newspapers and magazines, and reading and watching the news on the Internet will lead you to possible topics.

- **National/Social**   Choosing a timely topic will ensure that you will be able to find plenty of material on the subject. Use news sources for possible high-interest, current event topics. High school dropout rates and mandatory public service are social problems that could interest you and an audience. Many of these areas require some government action as well as personal and family action to provide a solution to the problem.

- **Personal**   Is there a personal area that interests you? It might even be something as minor as a pet peeve that you have. List the interests that engage, fascinate, or irritate you.

Expanding Possibilities   In addition to the possible topics listed above, popular culture is also a resource for topics. Movies and novels can be an inspiration. For example, *Pay It Forward* is a movie that addresses one boy's idea of passing along good deeds. The movie is not only entertaining, it is also very inspiring. The idea of doing something nice for a stranger and expecting nothing in return would be an interesting topic. Anytime something profoundly touches you, it has the possibility of turning into an oratory speech.

Narrowing Possibilities   Once you have compiled a list, study it. Narrow it down to just a few topics—those you feel most intrigued and enthusiastic about—and then evaluate each one. If you think a topic may have been overused, eliminate it. Examine the significance of the topics. Your topic should resonate with your audience. Imagine yourself in a round with seven other competitors. Will your topic stand out? Select the topic that will help you to make an impression while being competitive.

Once you've decided on a topic, write it as a statement, not just a word or phrase. For example, rather than just "higher education," write "Higher education is a right and should be free to all qualified students." The statement will pinpoint your view on the topic and help focus your research. Finally, ask your coach to review your **topic statement**.

Research

Once you have decided on your topic, you are ready to start researching it. Research is key to writing a winning oration. Good ideas are important, but good ideas that are researched are essential to being successful in this event. Research your topic in depth. Find out all you can about all aspects of the topic. Be sure to investigate views that are different from yours. Do not be afraid to challenge current beliefs.

Brainstorming   An often overlooked research tool is one's own brain—the thoughts, feelings, and experiences that the speaker has involving the topic. Pick your own brain. Then pick others' brains. Talk to other students about your topic. Get their feedback, ideas, feelings, and experiences. Listen to what they have to say, and don't be afraid to ask why. The more in-depth their answers are, the better. Also, take accurate notes because you may want to ask one of your classmates a clarifying question at a later date.

Another valuable resource is your parents. Because they are older, they may have a different perspective on a certain topic. Parents obviously have many experiences that will affect their opinions. This information can be helpful when analyzing the problem and formulating a possible solution.

The Library   After generating ideas through brainstorming, visit your school library or the public library. Discuss your topic with the librarians. They will be able to suggest reference and other nonfiction books, periodicals, video materials, audio materials, indexes, and other matter that can help you in your research.

Take careful notes and document all your sources. Many students find it helpful to photocopy print material that they use as sources. This will also help you track quotations you want to use in your speech.

The Internet   Online resources can furnish valuable information for your speech, but you must be sure of the reliability of the source and the accuracy of the information you choose to use. Generally, .gov websites are reliable, as are many .org websites. Note the urls of websites you use. You may want to print out the pages that hold the specific information you plan to use because web pages are often taken down suddenly.

What library resources might be especially helpful when researching a topic for a speech?

IMAGES BY TRISTA/ISTOCK PHOTO.COM

Organizing Ideas in a Speech

Once you have researched your topic and gathered information, make an **outline** for your speech. An outline will help you organize your ideas and stay focused when you write your speech.

Introduction   Set up the introduction first. An introduction should include the following elements.

- **Attention Getter**   Begin with something that will grab your audience's attention, such as an anecdote, quotation, surprising statistic, example, or joke.

- **Topic**   State the thesis of your speech. Your topic statement and the way you deliver it will set the tone for the rest of your speech.

- **Roadmap**   Let the judge know what to expect. State why you chose the subject and why it is important.

- **Transition**   Wrap up your introduction. Provide a transitional sentence that will let the judge know you are ready to begin the main body of your speech.

Body   There are a variety of patterns you can use to organize your ideas when writing the body of your speech. One pattern usually works better than the others for a given topic.

- **Background-Problem-Solution Pattern**   Give a background of the problem to help listeners better understand it. Discuss the specific problem in detail. Present and evaluate alternative solutions. Then indicate and defend which solution is best.

- **Who-What-When-Where-Why-How Pattern**   Ask these six reporter questions regarding your topic. Choose two to five areas that you feel are the most significant. Develop these selected areas for the body of your speech.

- **Past-Present-Future Pattern**   Divide your topic into these three areas. Investigate the history of the problem. Examine the current situation. Predict how the situation will proceed into the future.

- **Pro-Con Pattern**   First present one side of an issue. Then present the other side. Select the side that supports your topic statement and gives reasons for supporting it.

- **Political-Economic-Social Pattern**   Divide your topic into these three areas. Present its political, economic, and social implications in detail. If one area has a stronger impact than the others, decide if you want to move from the area of greatest impact to the area of least impact, or from the area of least impact to the one of greatest impact.

- **Effects-Causes-Solutions Pattern**   First, explain why the topic is important and what effects are encountered because of the problem area. Next, discuss the causes of the problem. Finally, present possible solutions that will solve or alleviate the problem. Indicate and support the solution you feel is the best.

- **Topical Pattern**   Choose three areas of the topic to be discussed. Unlike the other patterns, the topical pattern allows more latitude as to approach. While this pattern may be more difficult, it rewards the speaker by allowing a creative, original perspective on the topic.

Conclusion   Even though the conclusion is the shortest part, it should not be overlooked. Take the time to develop a strong conclusion.

- **Revisit Your Attention Getter**   You may want to tie back to the opening attention getter. Show how it relates to the speech. Extend it with information you have given the audience in your speech.

- **Summarize Your Topic**   Restate your topic statement, and briefly review the main points you discussed that support that statement.

- **Release the Audience**   This is your last opportunity to make an impression. Leave your listeners with a strong statement. It may be witty, or it can "pack a punch," but it should be something that will make you and your speech stand out from the other competitors.

Expressing Ideas in a Speech

Research gives you the content—the substance—of your speech. Your expression of that content—your diction—helps create your style. It is just as essential as content for a winning oration.

FYI The English language has over 600,000 words, yet the average person uses only between 1,000 and 1,200 of them durng the course of a lifetime.

While the formats for extemporaneous speaking and oratory are similar, they differ in one important area. Extemp speeches are matter of fact and to the point. Oratory is an opportunity to use your language skills and command of diction. The National Forensic League includes this description of a successful competitive oration.

The composition should be considered carefully for its rhetoric and diction. The use of appropriate figures of speech, similes and metaphors, balanced sentences, allusions, and other rhetorical devices to make the oration more effective should be especially noted. Use of American English should be more than correct; it should reveal a discriminating choice of words and altogether fine literary qualities. It should be especially adapted to oral presentation.

Oratory enables you to use strong vocabulary. Instead of using a simple, general word, search for a more sophisticated way to say the same thing. Consider this statement

People see the world as confusing and fast moving.

Now replace the word *see* with a richer, more sophisticated word

People perceive the world as confusing and fast moving.

What type of vocabulary should be used in Original Oratory?

Making a simple change makes the sentence more interesting. A command of diction also adds precision to your communication. Look at the difference between some simple and enhanced words:

Simple, General, Low-Level	Enhanced, Specific, Sophisticated
show	illustrate
like	enjoy
old	aging
answer	reply

However, you don't want to go overboard with high-level, multisyllabic words. Too many will make your speech sound unnatural or even incomprehensible. Choose each word for its precision and its sound.

Rhetorical devices that make oratory effective include figurative language such as metaphors and similes. William Lyon Phelps, an English professor, once gave a speech in which he likened a book to a forest.

A good reason for marking favorite passages in books is that this practice enables you to remember more easily the significant sayings, to refer to them quickly, and then in later years, it is like visiting a forest where you once blazed a trail. You have the pleasure of going over the old ground, and recalling both the intellectual scenery and your own earlier self.

Allusions may be references to great literary classics or timeless myths, but they don't have to be. Ann Richards, speaking in 1988, alluded to the movie

Ann Richards referred to Ginger Rogers and Fred Astaire in a speech. How might an allusion to movie stars enhance an oration?

DIRCK HALSTEAD/TIME LIFE PICTURES/GETTY IMAGES

dance partners Ginger Rogers and Fred Astaire to underscore her point about the abilities of women.

> If you give us a chance, we can perform. After all, Ginger Rogers did everything that Fred Astaire did. She just did it backwards and in high heels.

It's important to note that Ann Richards did not originate that idea, but she was always careful to credit the person who told it to her.

Parallel phrasing is structuring related ideas in a similar grammatical way. President Barack Obama illustrated parallel phrasing in his keynote speech at the Democratic National Convention in 2004, as a senator from Illinois.

> That is the true genius of America, a faith—a faith in simple dreams, an insistence on small miracles; that we can tuck in our children at night and know that they are fed and clothed and safe from harm; that we can say what we think, write what we think, without hearing a sudden knock on the door; that we can have an idea and start our own business without paying a bribe; that we can participate in the political process without fear of retribution, and that our votes will be counted—at least most of the time.

Note how each major point of faith is expressed as a clause beginning with *that*.

Repetition can bring attention to your thesis while adding to the rhythm of your speech. Dr. Martin Luther King, Jr., stated "I have a dream" eight times in his speech that came to be called by those words.

On the sad event of the explosion of the space shuttle *Challenger* in 1986, President Ronald Reagan commemorated the crew with these words:

> We'll continue our quest in space. There will be more shuttle flights and more shuttle crews and, yes, more volunteers, more civilians, more teachers in space. Nothing ends here; our hopes and our journeys continue.

What effect did hearing the repetition of the word *more* have on you?

Write for Sound as Well as Sense

Parallel phrasing and repetition are elements of sound as well as content. They help create a flow and rhythm to your speech. They're important in written essays but even more so in speeches. Orations are, after all, meant to be heard. The sound of your speech can both please the audience as well as help emphasize your meaning.

As you are creating your speech, listen to the words that you're keying into the computer or writing on the paper. Choose words for their sound as well as their meaning. Use parallel phrasing and repetition. Structure sentences so that their lengths vary and they flow easily.

Revise and Fine-Tune

When you have finished the first draft of your speech, set it aside for a day or so. Then return to it and take a close look. First consider and, if necessary, pump up the content.

- topic statement
- organization
- support
- transitions

Next, read the speech aloud to yourself. How does it sound to you? How does it make you feel as you say the words? If necessary, fine-tune the sound.

- word choice
- sentence variety
- sentence flow

Finally, read and time your speech. Remember that it must be between seven and ten minutes in length. Be sure your pace is appropriate—not too fast, not to slow. If you find the speech is long, look for irrelevant or minor points to cut first; you don't want to undermine your speech by removing support for your thesis. If you need to add material, decide whether you really need to go back to your research notes for more support. You may just need to add an extra anecdote or two.

BROSA/ISTOCKPHOTO.COM

Why is revising and fine-tuning your speech essential?

Think Critically

1. How does writing your topic as a statement help?

2. Why is outlining a speech before writing it important?

3. What effect does the use of rhetorical devices such as parallel phrasing and repetition have?

Research NOW!

4. Select and read a famous speech on the Internet. If an audio is available, listen to the speech first and then read it. Make note of figures of speech and other rhetorical devices that you think are particularly effective or that struck you as a reader/listener.

5. **TEAMWORK** Work with several partners. Research and collect different speeches from various orators. Analyze the speeches for their organization of ideas. See if you can detect some of the patterns discussed in this lesson. Discuss and evaluate the effectiveness of the pattern of organization used in each speech.

Write NOW!

6. Choose an issue in your school or community. Write a three- or four-paragraph paper on the topic. Then go back through your writing and underline words that seem too simple or general. Use a thesaurus to find alternative words that are more precise and sophisticated. If you have already started a vocabulary index, record these enhanced words on index cards and add them to your index.

7. **TEAMWORK** Working with a partner, select a topic for an oration—an issue on which you both agree. Cooperate on doing research for the topic. Then choose different ways of organizing the ideas and write a paper presenting them. Share your papers with each other. Discuss which pattern of organization you each think was more effective.

Speak NOW!

8. Use the paper you prepared for activity 6. Look for spots where you might add parallel phrasing or repetition. Memorize the speech and present it to the class.

9. **TEAMWORK** Prepare a group speech on a topic of your choice. All of the team members should help research. Decide on a particular pattern of organization to use. One panel member should write the introduction, and another should write the conclusion. Each remaining member should write one section of the body. Practice speaking your section to the group, and review one another's sections for rhetorical devices. Present the final speech to the class.

GOALS

Identify techniques for rehearsing.

Understand the elements of delivery.

Know the procedures at an oratory presentation.

TERMS

body language
transitional move
volume
pitch
rate
pause
enunciation

Do You Agree?

Resolved Secondary education in the United States ought to be a privilege, not a right.

Affirmative position

Yes, the value of an education is priceless. Any student who continues to be a disruptive force in the classroom or threatens students and teachers does not deserve to remain in an educational setting. Students who are involved in illegal activities should also be removed from the school system. Not only are they abusing the educational system, they are interfering with the education of others. These students have now lost the right to attend public schools.

Negative position

No, education is a valuable tool that is and should be available to all. We stress the importance of education in order to be successful in life. Once we start mandating who can and cannot attend school, we become guilty of being discriminating. Who has the power or the right to decide who is to be denied? Education must be available to all.

Rehearsing

You've researched and written your speech. Now it's time to focus on rehearsing it for the presentation. Because no notes are allowed during your presentation, you must memorize the speech. Some students feel that this is the most challenging part of Original Oratory. If you consider this step to be learning your speech rather than memorizing it, it may not seem so daunting.

Memorizing: Learning Your Speech

When it comes to learning your speech, you will have to select a method that works best for you. There is no right or wrong way to do it. The one advantage to memorizing an oratory speech over anything else you may have to learn by heart is that you are the author of the work. You are familiar with the information and know the order of the ideas. This knowledge of the material should help when you are committing it to memory.

Here are two methods for learning a speech. You can try both and see which works best for you, or experiment with your own technique.

- **Section by Section**   One method is to start with the first section. Read it aloud several times and then say it aloud. Repeat it until you are comfortable with the content and can repeat it without looking at your paper. Once you have learned the first section, go on to the second section. Read it and say it, and then recite the first two sections. When you have learned the first two sections, go on to the third section. Always start with the first section when you recite the speech. This will help hold the speech together in your mind and connect the ideas from one section to the next. Continue with these steps until the entire speech has been committed to memory.

- **Whole Speech**   Read the entire speech aloud over and over, gradually removing the need to refer to your paper. Read the speech aloud to develop a rhythm. Eventually, you will remember your organizational pattern and key words and phrases as well as sections. This method helps you learn the speech as a whole rather than in parts.

Once you have learned the words to your speech, you're ready to practice it. You can practice at home in front of a mirror, especially for the first few times, but then expand your practice to include an audience of family or friends. As you practice, you may find that some parts of the speech work better than others, or perhaps some parts don't work at all. Feedback from your audience will help you determine this. Use your own feelings and feedback from others to help you polish and even rework the speech if necessary. Seldom is the first revised draft of a speech the speech that is given at a competition.

FYI Legend tells that Abraham Lincoln scribbled the Gettysburg Address on a napkin on his way to the ceremony. Actually, several drafts of the speech exist, as do reports that Lincoln edited the speech before delivering it.

Delivery

When practicing your speech, begin to incorporate the elements of delivery that will really sell it. Do not attempt to wait until an actual competition to pay attention to body language and voice. You may either forget to pay attention to them, or you will focus on them too much and may speak unnaturally or disrupt the speech itself. If you wait until a competition to note your body language and voice, your delivery will suffer. Judges are instructed to place great emphasis on delivery in their scoring, so you should too. That requires practice.

Body Language

Body language consists of all the ways your body can move and the positions you can strike that help convey the meaning of what you are saying.

   Posture   The way you hold your body when speaking reveals your feelings. Standing rigid and erect shows you are uncomfortable and will make your audience uncomfortable. Fidgeting or swaying tells people you are nervous. Slouching, slump-shouldered shows carelessness. If you stand straight, head up, shoulders back, arms hanging loosely at your side and occasionally gesturing, you come across as relaxed and confident.

Eye Contact   Eye contact is important in any presentation. It is essential in oratory. During competition, make sure you are aware of where your judge is sitting in the room. You want to gauge the judge's reactions as you proceed with your speech. Although the judge is important, do not focus solely on him or her. Be sure to look at members of the audience. You want them to take this journey with you, so be sure to include them.

Do not look at the floor or the ceiling when speaking. You're not going to find your speech—or your audience— there, and people will wonder what you're looking at. If you don't feel comfortable looking at individual people in the audience, find items in the room, such as books in a bookcase, that are at eye level. Even though you are glancing at the books, the audience members will have the illusion that you are looking at one of them. As you continue to practice and then give your oration throughout the year, making eye contact will likely become easier.

Hand Gestures   One way to emphasize words or ideas is with hand gestures. Hand gestures can and should be choreographed. Every time you practice your speech, make the same movements at the same point in your speech. Gestures should be simple, small movements that have a purpose. For example, an upraised palm can stress a matter-of-fact point you're making. Two upraised palms, accompanied by a shrug of the shoulders, signify a question.

Facial Expressions   Your face can help put an exclamation point on what you are saying. A smile is natural if you're telling a funny anecdote. A slight

What can a hand gesture convey?

frown shows concerns. Opening your eyes wide can stress that you're sharing a surprising fact. These are just a few examples of the facial expressions you can use to complement your speech.

Transitional Moves   Body language such as hand gestures and facial expressions are small movements. As you practice your speech, decide where to incorporate larger, transitional moves. A **transitional move** is going from one spot to another spot when you are moving from one major idea to another in your speech. There should be three to four transitional moves, depending on how many sections you have in your speech. These movements will help signal to the judge that you are moving to the next area of your topic. Transitional moves can complement transitional terms such as *first, next,* and *finally.*

Begin by standing in the front of the room. This is where you will start and end your speech. When you have completed your introduction, take two to three small subtle steps to your right. Be talking while you are moving. Continue with the first section of your speech.

When you are ready to conclude the first section and move on to the second, again take a few steps, but this time move to the left of your original starting position. You have a choice here. You can stay in this spot for the entire second and third sections of your speech, or you can move at the beginning of the third section. Try both ways with your speech to see what works best.

The last move is back to your starting position in the front of the room. This is where you will conclude your speech.

X 2nd position	X 3rd position
X 1st and 4th position	
Judge	
	Audience

Following this simple map will help reinforce your main ideas in the judge's mind. Practice these transitional moves each and every time you say your speech. Soon they will feel natural to you and look natural to a judge and audience.

Voice

As with your body, you can use your voice to help convey your ideas. Think of your voice as a tool. It has various characteristics that you can control and adjust to communicate effectively. Nothing turns off an audience more quickly than a monotone coming from the front of the room. Varying voice characteristics throughout your speech engages your listeners, making your speech more pleasing and therefore easier to listen to. Vocal variety also helps you emphasize your key points.

- **Volume** is the loudness of your voice. Speakers don't always realize that their own voice sounds louder to them than it does to their audience. In general, speak loudly enough to be heard by the farthest listener in the room. There can also be times when talking more softly or loudly can be used to emphasize certain words or ideas.

- **Pitch** is how high or low your voice is. Use a higher pitch than normal to communicate excitement or urgency. Use a lower pitch to show seriousness.

To see how varying the volume and pitch of your voice can affect meaning and impact, read each of these lines, saying the underlined word more loudly and at a higher pitch:

We ca<u>nnot</u> refuse to act.
We cannot <u>refuse</u> to act.
We cannot refuse to <u>act</u>.

- **Rate** is how fast you speak—the number of words you say per minute. In everyday conversation people tend to speak at a fairly fast rate. For a speech before an audience, a slower rate is generally needed. Then vary your rate within that slower pace to emphasize your ideas and emotions. Speed up a bit at emotional or exciting moments, and slow down at serious, thoughtful ones.

- **Pauses** are brief moments of silence between words or ideas. By pausing before a key word, you create a bit of suspense. Your audience zeroes in on what you will say next. When used appropriately and sparingly, pauses can say almost as much as words. But keep them brief and to a minimum, or they will lose their effect.

- **Enunciation** is the clear, distinct pronunciation of each sound and syllable in a word. It is essential when speaking to an audience. Slurring sounds and dropping syllables simply make it too difficult for your listeners to understand you.

Taping Your Delivery

Practicing your speech in front of an audience can give you valuable feedback. If possible, you should tape yourself practicing your speech, or—even better—make a video of yourself giving your speech. A video will help you see yourself as others see you and hear yourself as others hear you. It enables you to evaluate all the elements of your body language and voice. That way, you can make adjustments to improve your delivery.

The Presentation

When the time comes for you to present your oration in competition, be sure you are there on time. Punctuality is essential for making a good first impression on the judge.

Dress is another factor that can influence the judge. Your attire should be neat and clean. A T-shirt and jeans are too informal. Dress as if you are attending a special occasion, because you are.

There might be six to seven other students speakers in the Original Oratory room along with the judge. Be poised and in control.

When you are called upon to speak, give your code number to the judge. Also, ask if and how the judge will give you time signals about the length of your speech. You're allowed a 30-second grace period over 10 minutes. Go confidently to the front of the room. Do not speak immediately. Wait until the judge and the audience are ready to listen before you begin. Take a breath. Look around the room one more time. Then begin.

Points

The judge evaluates you on everything from the organization and ideas of your speech to your poise and vocal variety. Delivery is especially important. Speakers are ranked from first through eighth. Six is the highest number of points, awarded to the best orator in the eyes of the judge. Point totals decrease for each lower rank until 1. Top-ranked students may advance to the next round.

Why are poise and dress important in an Original Oratory competition?

Rank	1st	2nd	3rd	4th	5th	6th	7th	8th
Points Earned	6	5	4	3	2	1	1	1

The Written Critique

Ballots can differ from tournament to tournament, but the basic elements of oratory will be evaluated and contribute to the point score. The judge writes comments on the ballot that indicate areas that may need work or that did not fit well within the text of the speech.

The Oral Critique

An oral critique is a spoken analysis given by the judge. Because of the time is takes to give an oral critique, most judges and tournament directors prefer written critiques. Oral critiques are usually given in the final round.

An oral critique has several advantages over a written critique. An oral critique will be given soon after you have spoken. Your performance is still fresh in your mind as well as the judge's. It is an opportunity for the judge to suggest areas of improvement as well as to tell you what you did that left an impression. It also allows you to ask questions or clarification of any comments. Keep in mind that the comments are meant to help you. Do not take them personally. Do remember to thank the judge for his or her time.

Ballots as a Resource

Keep all your ballots from the different competitions in which you participate. They can be extremely helpful. Make a list of the comments made by the judges. If you see the same comment being repeated by different judges at different tournaments, that is an area you will want to address.

Is it necessary to change your speech after each competition? Should you make each and every change suggested to you? The answer to these questions is no. Your oration should, however, always be evolving. A great speech is a work in progress. Just ask Abraham Lincoln.

YOU BE THE JUDGE

The power to speak effectively and passionately and to move people with one's words can be used for good—or not.

Throughout history orators have used their skills to further their ends. Sometimes those ends were honorable; sometimes they were self-serving. In Shakespeare's *Julius Caesar*, Marc Antony uses his oratorical powers in his eulogy for Caesar to rile the Roman masses against his assassins. President Franklin Delano Roosevelt's inaugural address calmed a nation in the midst of the Great Depression when he reminded his listeners that they only thing they had to fear was fear itself. Winston Churchill's speeches inspired the English people to carry on during the darkest hours of World War II.

The term *demagogue* applies to a person who uses oratorical skills to appeal to people's emotions for the sole purpose of gaining power. Adolf Hitler was a demagogue.

Achieving skill in oratory carries with it a responsibility to use that skill and power wisely and honorably.

What Would You Do?

Suppose you listen to an oration given with terrific delivery and emotion. However, you know that facts cited by the speaker are wrong or twisted. Would you approach the speaker? What would you say?

Think Critically

1. What are the advantages of learning your whole speech as a unit rather than as individual sections?

2. What effect does varying your vocal characteristics during a speech have?

3. How might you make a good first impression on the judge at a presentation?

Research NOW!

4. Listen and watch a video of President Barack Obama's inaugural address on January 20, 2009. It is available on the Internet. Note his body language and vocal variety as he speaks. Make note of instances you find particularly effective.

 5. **TEAMWORK** Work with several students. Do online research to find audios of different speeches or famous lines from speeches by various orators (for example, Franklin Delano Roosevelt's "The only thing we have to fear. . . " or John F. Kennedy's "Ask not. . . ."). The library also may have audiotapes of famous speeches. Discuss and evaluate the delivery of each.

Write NOW!

 6. **TEAMWORK** Choose a partner to work with. Attend an Original Oratory competition together, or listen to orations given at competition. Some may be posted online or available on DVD. Study and evaluate the body language and vocal variety used by three speakers. Write an evaluation of each. Then compare and discuss your evaluations with your partner.

7. Choose an issue that you feel strongly about and write a three- or four-paragraph paper about it. Memorize it. Decide where and how you would use body language and vocal variety during an oral presentation.

Speak NOW!

 8. **TEAMWORK** Use the three- or four-paragraph paper you prepared for activity 7. Present your short speech to the class. Ask for feedback on your delivery from your classmates. Provide feedback to your classmates on their presentations.

9. Attend a school council or town council meeting when an issue that interests you is going to be discussed. Prepare a short speech beforehand that states your views. Rehearse it, keeping in mind body language and vocal variety. Then step up to speak at the meeting.

Chapter in Review

11.1 What Is Oratory?

- Oratory is speechmaking. Throughout history many great orators have made lasting impressions with their speeches.
- In Original Oratory the speaker chooses his/her topic and memorizes a speech of no more than 10 minutes. The elements of a successful oration are both style and substance.
- An appropriate topic for oratory is competition worthy, fresh, and in good taste.

11.2 Preparing Your Speech

- List possible topics, and then narrow the list to one that you feel most passionate about and that meets the criteria for an appropriate topic. Research for background and supporting facts is essential.
- Make an outline and choose a pattern of organization for the ideas in your speech.
- Because expression of ideas is key in oratory, use rhetorical devices and precise language when writing your speech.

11.3 The Presentation

- Learn, rather than memorize, your speech as a whole and practice it in front of a mirror and in front of others.
- Delivery is essential to scoring well, so use body language and vocal variety in your oration.
- Create a good first impression and use the judge's comments to improve your speech.

Develop Your Oratory Language

a. allusion
b. body language
c. competition worthiness
d. diction
e. enunciation
f. outline
g. oratory
h parallel phrasing
i. pause
j. pitch
k. rate
l. repetition
m. rhetorical device
n. topic statement
o. transitional move
p. volume

Select the term that best fits the definition. Some terms will not be used.

1. Choice of words

2. Figure of speech or other use of language that makes an oration more effective

3. Clear, distinct pronunciation of each sound and syllable in a word

4. Going from one spot to another spot when you are moving from one major idea in a speech to another

5. Reference to a classic, a myth, or popular culture

6. Loudness

7. How fast you speak; how many words you say per minute

8. The ways your body moves and the positions it strikes that convey meaning

9. How high or low your voice is

Review Oratory Concepts

10. What effect did President Kennedy's "Ask not" imperative have?

11. What is unique about Original Oratory compared to other competition events?

12. How much of a speech for Original Oratory may be direct quotation?

13. How long must an oration be?

14. What kinds of opportunities does Original Opportunity offer a student?

15. What are key elements of delivery in Original Oratory?

16. What three criteria should be considered when choosing a speech topic?

17. Where should you start when looking for a speech topic?

18. What are three general areas to consider when looking for a speech topic?

19. Name three resources you can use to do research on your topic.

20. What four elements should an introduction to a speech have?

21. What should you use to write the body of your speech?

22. What kind of vocabulary should you use in a speech?

23. Name two effects of repetition in a speech.

24. What does "write for sound as well as sense" mean?

25. Name two methods for learning your speech.

26. How can practicing in front of an audience of family or friends help?

27. Why should you practice body language and vocal variety?

28. How many transitional moves should you make during your speech?

29. What two qualities of your voice do you vary to emphasize a word?

30. What can you do to create a good impression with the judge before your oration?

31. How can judges' ratings be considered a resource?

Make Academic Connections

32. **SCIENCE/HEALTH** Your voice is the tool you use to present your speech. It is produced by air passing through your larynx, or voice box. Research to find out how breathing and posture affect the voice and how you can protect it. Also, explore relaxation techniques you can use before a speech to calm your voice and your nerves if necessary.

33. **MATHEMATICS** Figure your rate of speech. Use the Word Count function under Tools on a computer to determine how many words are in your speech. Time how long it takes you to deliver a speech. Divide the number of words by the time. If your speech is taking longer than the

allotted time, you can increase your rate of speech, but you should not exceed more than 170 words per minute. Cut content from your speech if necessary.

34. **HISTORY**   Research presidential inaugural addresses. Read several examples from George Washington to Barak Obama. Be sure and include some lesser-known ones, such as William Henry Harrison's, which was the longest inaugural address in American History. Choose the speech you feel was most effective and write an evaluation explaining why.

35. **SOCIAL SCIENCES**   Psychologists have studied body language and the meaning of various gestures and poses. Cultural anthropologists have noted how certain gestures mean different things to different groups of people. Research the meaning behind body language. List some gestures you might want to use during an oration.

Research NOW!

36. Motivational speakers are popular on television as well as in public appearances before large audiences. They speak on a wide range of areas, including personal growth, money and finances, careers, and sports. Use a speaker's bureau to identify a motivational speaker that interests you. Listen to a speech by the speaker. If possible, try to interview the speaker to inquire about tips and techniques for speaking in public.

37. **TEAMWORK**   Pick a national issue that is currently in the news. Have each member of your group research and collect a speech from a different orator on the issue—a congressperson or other politician or the head of an organization, for example. Read the speeches aloud to one another. Discuss and evaluate both the style and substance of each speech. Vote for the speech you think was the most effective oration.

Write NOW!

38. Select a person you would like to memorialize. It could be someone living or deceased, someone you know personally or not. Note the characteristics or actions of the person that move you to memorialize him or her. List facts, examples, or anecdotes you could include. Write a speech memorializing the person. Be mindful of using rhetorical devices.

39. **TEAMWORK**   Work with a partner. Choose a problem in your school or community. One partner should write one or two paragraphs describing the problem and its background. The other should write one or two paragraphs offering a solution. Work with each other to add rhetorical devices. Send your work as a letter to the editor to the school or local paper.

Speak NOW!

40. Use the speech you wrote for activity 39. Learn and practice the speech. Present it to the class.

41. Practice enunciation with tongue twisters such as "She sells sea shells by the sea shore" and "Thad threw three free throws." Enunciate vowel sounds by pronouncing word groups such as "cap, cop, cup" and "jest, gist, just."

42. **TEAMWORK** Work in groups of three. Decide on an issue of importance that has political, economic, and social implications. Each member should choose one of those areas and prepare a short speech on it. Work with one another to practice and evaluate your speeches. Present the speeches in a panel discussion of the issue.

eCollection Activity

The environment is a newsworthy issue that has stirred passion and conflict for years. When the United States established the Environmental Protection Agency (EPA) in 1970, the nation took the first step to address people's growing concern over air, water, and land pollution. The EPA has set standards for auto exhaust emissions, controlled pesticide use, and overseen toxic waste cleanup. In 1973 Congress passed the Endangered Species Act, which protects animal species from extinction caused by human economic growth and development.

Global warming, or climate change (which has become the preferred name), has been a concern for a number of years. The degree to which Earth is warming and the causes of this increase in temperature have been a controversial topic. Today, however, most scientists agree that the planet is indeed warming. The majority of people also believe that human activities have changed the makeup of the atmosphere and are therefore at least partially responsible for this temperature change. Disagreement exists about solutions to the problem.

Select an environmental issue that interests you. To research the issue, access www.cengage.com/school/langarts/debate and click on the link for Chapter 11. Decide on a specific position you wish to take on the issue. Use your research to write a speech about it. Present your speech to the class.

CHAPTER 12

Mock Trial

PHOTODISC, ©GETTY IMAGES

Real People | Real Careers

David Hankus

" To this day, Hankus believes his background in high school debate was instrumental in his professional success. "

David Hankus will always remember his high school debate experience. It provided him with a small community of good friends with like interests, and also helped hone his research, organizational, and speaking skills. His debating experience gave him the confidence to tackle the challenges he would confront in college, law school, and the real world.

When Hankus entered high school in the fall of 1978, he was one of approximately 750 students in his class. He recognized the importance of becoming involved in sports and other extracurricular activities as a way to connect with other students with similar interests. With a strong affinity for English, he thought he might want to pursue a career in law, and enrolled in debate class.

In the summer between his sophomore and junior years, Hankus attended a two-week debate camp at the University of Michigan. In the summer between his junior and senior years, he attended a three-week debate camp at Northwestern University. These summer sessions allowed him to meet students from across the country. He learned debating techniques and started on research that would carry him through the upcoming debate season.

Hankus had the same debate partner his junior and senior years. They attended the summer programs together. Based on their experiences at those programs, they helped shape what had been a marginally competitive fledgling program into a program which reached the state quarter finals their senior year.

In college and law school, his high school debate experience allowed Hankus to easily engage in the active classroom participation favored by the professors. In law school, he participated in moot court, a program designed to mirror actual courtroom experience. Once out of law school, he took a job at a large county prosecutor's office, which allowed immediate courtroom experience and built upon the oratory skills he first developed in high school debate. To this day, Hankus believes his background in high school debate was instrumental in his professional success.

Today David Hankus is an attorney who maintains a sole practice located in Troy, Michigan. He devotes his practice exclusively to representing the seriously disabled in federal administrative hearings before the Social Security Administration.

Think Critically

How did debate prepare David Hankus for his future profession?

DAVID HANKUS

GOALS

Understand a jury trial.

Describe the mock trial process.

TERMS

trial
defendant
advocate
prosecutor
defense attorney
alleged
plaintiff
judge
jury
verdict
witness

Do You Agree?

Resolved There are too many lawsuits and court cases brought in the United States because Americans are too litigious.

Affirmative position

Yes, for too many Americans the first response to any adverse or harmful situation is to sue whomever they think may be responsible in order to get financial compensation. They ignore their own responsibility for the harm experienced.

Negative position

No, most lawsuits are justified because too often governments, corporations, and individuals act self-interestedly, and ignore the harm their actions do to others. They should be made accountable and should pay for their negligence.

Jury Trial

In class one day, you have a guest speaker who is an attorney. She has come to speak about mock trials. You smile when you hear the term and wonder if a mock trial is some kind of comedy skit, meant to poke fun at the judicial process. As she explains, you learn that mock trials are quite serious. They are imitations of the kinds of trials that go on in courtrooms every day. Sometimes, real attorneys conduct a mock trial to test ideas about how to conduct a real trial. Law schools and colleges also use them, so that students can practice the skills needed to be an attorney. Mock trials are also an increasingly popular activity for high school and middle school students. Many bar associations, professional organizations for attorneys, sponsor these events. The National Mock Trial Association sponsors an annual national competition for high school students. In a mock trial, students recreate what happens in a jury trial. To learn about mock trials, you need to understand jury trials. At a mock trial, you will be playing many of the same roles with many of the same responsibilities.

A **trial** is a formal procedure where parties come together and present information before a judge and/or jury in order to achieve a resolution. There are two types of trials in the United States—criminal trials and non-criminal or civil trials. A criminal trial involves a violation of the law. A civil trial involves the violation of the rights of one or more persons. In a civil trial, the person or persons violated seek an amount of money as compensation. Often, a jury decides the outcome of both of these trials.

At the center of every trial is an event, or series of events, that in some way violated the law or the rights of others. The person or entity charged with this violation is a **defendant.** The United States legal system is based upon the fundamental idea that, even though a person may be charged with a crime, he or she is considered innocent until proven guilty in a court of law. In every trial, there are key roles that must be played. Usually, cases involving a criminal action are jury trials, because a jury ultimately decides the fate of the defendant. They decide if one side of the case has proven beyond a reasonable doubt, the guilt or innocence of the defendant.

Attorneys

In a jury trial, two attorneys, or lawyers, act as advocates for their side of the case. An **advocate** gathers as much information as possible to make an argument that supports his or her side.

A prosecuting attorney, or **prosecutor**, is the representative of government and makes the case that the defendant is guilty. The prosecutor argues the case for the state against the defendant. In a non-criminal court case, the plaintiff's lawyer acts as the prosecutor, trying to show that the person or entity being sued is guilty of the action as charged.

The **defense attorney** represents the accused party and gathers information that challenges the prosecutor's argument and shows why his or her client is innocent. The defense attorney then presents the information and arguments that show why his or her client is not guilty. In non-criminal cases, the defense attorney shows why, for example, a company is not responsible for harm **alleged**, or charged but not proven, against it. In non-criminal cases, the person who is suing another person or company is called the **plaintiff.**

The **judge** oversees the trial to make sure it is fair, and to make sure the information presented is in accord with the law and trial procedure (and allows or disallows it on this basis). The judge instructs the jury on the law and on what to consider when reaching a verdict. Some trials are argued before a judge only. The arguments are presented by both sides, and the judge makes the final determination regarding who is in the right and who is in the wrong. Most trials, however, are argued before a jury.

What is the role of the judge?

DIGITAL VISION/GETTY IMAGES

Jury

A **jury** is a group of twelve adult citizens who listen to everything that goes on in the trial, evaluate everything, and then reach a decision, or **verdict**. Attorneys for both sides question potential jurors and can disqualify or turn down a certain number of jurors they think will not judge the case fairly. For example, a potential juror who has had a bad experience using a product from a company that is being sued for damages would be eliminated because of assumed prejudice against the company. Attorneys are allowed a certain number of uncontested dismissals of jurors. That is, they can dismiss a few potential jurors without giving a reason.

Attorneys on both sides research to determine the profile of the ideal juror for their case. A profile may include the ideal juror's race, age, gender, income, occupation, or other characteristics. For example, if a young person is on trial, a defense attorney may dismiss older adults if research shows that they tend to believe that young people are often guilty of crimes. In some cases, the judge can disqualify a juror for cause. Generally, a certain number of alternate jurors are chosen, and these jurors must attend the trial just as the regular jurors do. A jury decides in favor of whichever side has proven beyond a reasonable doubt the guilt or innocence of the defendant.

A verdict is a statement of guilt or innocence or a decision about which of the parties is in the right. In a jury trial, the jury must base its judgment on written legal statutes, or laws. The judge informs the jury about what the law states and instructs the jury to deliberate on the basis of a particular law. A jury's verdict must be unanimous. If all jurors do not agree on a verdict, there is a hung jury. A hung jury often requires that a completely new trial take place, with a new jury.

What is the standard by which a juror must decide whether a defendant is guilty or not guilty?

Preparing for a Mock Trial

Typically, teams at a mock trial have eight students. Only six of the eight members participate in a round. The six students occupy roles that consist of three attorneys and three witnesses. A packet of information is sent out to the entire team several months prior to the competition containing information about the trials in which they will compete. That information includes the specific charges being filed, who those charges are being filed against, rules that must be followed during the mock trial, and various documents mean to help recreate the specifics of the case. Once the nature of the case is determined, you should decide which role you wish to play.

- **Prosecuting Attorney** The prosecutor presents information and evidence intended to prove that the defendant is guilty of the crime he or she is accused of.

- **Prosecution Team** The primary prosecutor almost always has a team of one, two, or more assistants who help with research and gathering information.

- **Defense Attorney** The defense attorney gathers and presents information and arguments intended to undermine the information presented by the prosecutor.

- **Defense Team** The defense team aids the defense attorney by doing research, gathering information, and generally helping the defense prepare its case.

- **Witnesses** In most trials, both the prosecution and the defense can call **witnesses**, people who can provide information that supports one side of the case. Witnesses swear under oath to tell the truth, and there are severe penalties for lying on the witness stand. Some witnesses are expert witnesses, such as doctors, who are hired to testify in court for one or the other side. In a mock trial, a team is allowed three witnesses.

Choose your role based on your strongest skills and remember that not everyone can play the role of an attorney. Other court roles may be played by students who are interested in learning about the legal profession but who are not members of the competing teams.

- **Judge** One student may play the role of the judge or three students may act as a panel of judges. (This role should not be confused with the adult who will evaluate the performances of the participants.)

- **Bailiff** One student may play the role of the bailiff, a courtroom attendant responsible for keeping order in the courtroom and overseeing the jury.

- **Court Recorder** One student may play the role of the court recorder, an employee of the court, who records everything that is said and done in the courtroom to create a formal transcript of the proceedings.

What are some of the roles played by students at a mock trial who are not on a competing team?

- **Jury** The jury is composed of twelve students who listen to everything that goes on in the courtroom and are then charged with using all this information to reach a verdict, or decide the case.

FYI In 2006, U.S. citizens filed 7,359,657 civil court cases. About 5.2 million were completed, either through arbitration, agreed settlement, or trial. About 1.5 million cases remain unsettled.

Students who play the judge(s) and jury should research these positions in regular court trials. If possible, they should research the role of the jury in the type of case that is being argued during the mock trial. They may want to read transcripts of actual trials of a similar type. Those who are not judges, attorneys, part of the attorneys' team, witnesses, the bailiff, or other actors in the trial can be part of the jury. It is common in a mock trial to engage everyone by having more than one jury hear and judge the case. It is also very interesting to see if different juries arrive at different verdicts, and their reasons for doing so.

Prosecution

The lead prosecutor and his or her team must gather as much information as possible about the case. This includes information about this particular case, as well as information about how similar cases were prosecuted in the past. They then must make the all-important decision about how to present their case. What will be their strategy for winning the court case?

- Will their case be based on hard evidence (for example, weapons with fingerprints)?

- Will their case be based on eyewitnesses, expert witnesses, or other testimony (for example, police investigations)?

- Will their case be based on undermining the character or reliability of the defense's witnesses? Or will they show weaknesses in the defense's arguments and/or evidence?

- Will their case be based on appealing to prior actions or illegal activities of the accused, or his or her bad character?

- In non-criminal cases, will their case be based on data and/or persuasive argument?

©BOB DAEMMRICH/PHOTOEDIT

Remember, it is the responsibility of the prosecution to prove the guilt of the defendant.

What is the responsibility of a prosecutor in a jury trial?

Defense

The defense team must interview the defendant to get as much information as possible about the defendant's involvement, or non-involvement, in the crime or incident. The interview should elicit what happened, witnesses the defendant knows who may help his or her case, character witnesses who can speak well of the defendant, and any other helpful information. Based on the interview, the defense team researches what happened, interviews potential witnesses, gathers evidence, and organizes as much information as they can get to prove their client's innocence. Then the defense team must devise a strategy for defending the client.

- The defense may show that their client has an alibi, that is, that the client could not have been present at the scene when the crime was committed.

- The defense may use their client's good character, or lack of previous arrests, to show that he or she is not capable of committing the crime.

- The defense may base its case on the lack of evidence presented by the prosecution.

- The defense case may rest on prosecutorial weaknesses. For example, unreliable witnesses, circumstantial evidence that doesn't constitute proof, or weak arguments made by the prosecutor may be used in a defense.

The defense must prove beyond a reasonable doubt that his or her client is innocent.

Once you have an idea of the kinds of cases you will be involved with, as well as who will occupy which roles on your teams, it is time to begin preparations in earnest. That preparation begins with gathering evidence for trial.

Brown v. Board of Education

On May 17, 1954, after years of legal debate, the U.S. Supreme Court issued an opinion that would change the nation's civil rights law. Brown v. Board of Education of Topeka, Kansas was a landmark reinterpretation of the Constitution's Fourteenth Amendment, which states "No state shall . . . deny to any person within its jurisdiction the equal protection of the laws."

This was not the first time the Court heard a Fourteenth Amendment case, nor was it the first case involving the civil rights of African Americans. In 1896, the Supreme Court had ruled in Plessy v. Ferguson that it was constitutional for railroads to provide separate seating for white and black passengers. The Court ruled that the facilities were "separate but equal" and held that Homer Plessy's rights were not violated by forcing him to sit in the blacks-only parts of the train.

From the late eighteen hundreds on, both southern and northern states had Jim Crow laws, that is, laws that mandated separate facilities for African Americans in many areas of public life. The states insisted that even though public services were segregated, they were essentially equal. By the 1950s, the "separate but equal" concept was being challenged in several states that enforced segregated education. Oliver Brown, of Topeka, Kansas, joined his case to appeals cases from four other states. Jim Crow laws in Kansas forced Brown's daughter Linda, then a third grader, to walk several blocks to catch a bus which drove her to a black-only school over a mile away. There was a whites-only school just a few blocks from her home. The plaintiff's lawyers would show that "separate but equal" did not apply to the unequal segregated schools and the education they provided to students. White schools had more money and better equipment. Black schools had far fewer resources.

Thurgood Marshall, the attorney for the plaintiff and later the first African-American Supreme Court Justice, asked the Court to revisit the Plessy decision's effects on segregation in public schools. The blatantly unequal facilities and resources in black-only schools clearly showed inequality.

Attorneys for the state argued for states' rights. State laws control education, and the federal government and Constitution cannot interfere. Since school attendance is based on where a student resides, forcing integration on segregated neighborhoods would impose a huge and unwarranted burden on the state.

Chief Justice Warren wrote the unanimous 9-0 decision in favor of Brown. He wrote, "We conclude that in the field of public education the doctrine of 'separate but equal' has no place. Separate educational facilities are inherently unequal."

Think Critically

How does the Court's decision affect education today?

Think Critically

1. What is a mock trial?

2. What are the responsibilities of a juror at a jury trial?

3. Compare and contrast the roles of a prosecuting attorney and a defense attorney in preparing for a case that goes to trial.

Research NOW!

4. **TEAMWORK** You are participating in a mock trial that involves vandalism at your school. What types of information do you need to either prosecute or defend the person accused of the vandalism? Prepare a list of the types of information you need.

5. **TEAMWORK** Have each person in your group research one item on the list in activity 4. Present your findings to the group. What information turned out to be most relevant and useful? How can you put all this information together to formulate a strategy for presenting your case?

Write NOW!

6. Find one or more articles in newspapers or magazines about a fairly recent court case. Write a summary of the case, including if possible the strategy of each side (the prosecution and the defense).

7. If possible, get a video from the library that is about a court case, for example, *Inherit the Wind, Twelve Angry Men*, or *Judgment at Nuremburg*. Write a summary of the trial, including the cases made by each side, the role of the witnesses, and the role of the jury.

Speak NOW!

8. **TEAMWORK** Work with a group to practice interviewing potential jurors for a trial involving vandalism at school. Use your questioning to determine the point of view of the potential juror. Each student should have a turn taking the role of the attorney and the potential juror. When you are done, discuss with the group which potential jurors would be favored by prosecutors and defense lawyers. Discuss why you judged the jurors in this way.

9. Jot down a few notes that you might use to describe your trial strategy in a court case. Explain your strategy aloud to members of a group, who will critique your notes and your presentation.

Do You Agree?

Resolved In felony cases, the testimony of a single eyewitness is insufficient evidence to convict in the absence of other concrete or scientific proof.

Affirmative position

Yes, studies have shown that eyewitness accounts are often unreliable, and several eyewitnesses may report seeing different things. Therefore in serious crimes, more concrete evidence should be required before a guilty verdict is reached.

Negative position

No, sometimes a single eyewitness account is the only evidence available to convict someone who has committed a terrible crime. If it can be shown that the eyewitness was in a position to accurately view the event, then that testimony should be sufficient to convict.

Evidence

As with debates, research is a key component to your preparation for a mock trial. Solid research helps you make your case and discredit the case of your opponent. Research for a mock trial is similar to research for a debate, but it is different as well. For a mock trial, your research must focus on the gathering and analysis of evidence.

Your experience with evidence has probably been limited to articles from journals or newspapers or facts taken from books or the Internet, whatever material you could find to help prove your point. **Evidence** at a trial is similar in that it must prove your point that the defendant is guilty or not guilty. It is different in that it involves **testimony**, the statements of individuals who were, in some way, involved with the case. Testimony is one person's version of events. How an attorney uses testimony is key to the outcome of a case.

Testimony as Evidence

In a mock trial, testimony is often given initially in affidavits. **Affidavits** are written statements that provide testimony from a person in some way involved in the case. Affidavits are signed by the person providing the testimony and sealed by a *notary public*, an official who affirms that the person signing is actually the author. Affidavits from witnesses or potential witnesses are included in the packet that a team receives prior to a mock trial.

Once you receive these statements, you must study them carefully and analyze how a witness's testimony could be used as evidence. You must determine whether the person's testimony helps your case because he or she supports the version of events that you want the jury to believe. If so, you probably want to call that person as a witness. If a person's testimony will damage your case, you need to think of a way to call their testimony into question so a jury won't believe it.

In addition to affidavits, a team receives other bits of information that help recreate the setting and events of the matter up for trial. Diagrams and maps typically are key elements of information meant to help the mock legal team understand the situation of the case. Once you receive these documents, the team needs to compare them with the affidavits and figure out how they can be used to complement a witness's testimony. They might illustrate events as described in an affidavit, and, if so, can be used to build your case. Or, they might call into question the testimony of a witness who is not favorable to your case. A map or diagram can be used when trying to call that witness's testimony into question. It is important to remember that evidence can only be used at trial if submitted for approval to the judge. Even witnesses require prior approval before they can be called to testify.

Testimony at Trial

Eyewitness accounts, descriptions of conversations or circumstances, may be used as evidence in a trial, not only as written in an affidavit, but in the sworn testimony of a witness in court as well. In certain respects, a witness at a trial can be the most important piece of evidence you have. Sometimes seeing a witness in person impresses a jury, either favorably or unfavorably, even more than sworn testimony that is written down. A witness's demeanor, tone of voice, and overall attitude can either credit or discredit him or her in the eyes of the jury.

©BOB DAEMMRICH/PHOTOEDIT

What is the importance of an affidavit in preparing your case?

©BOB DAEMMRICH/PHOTOEDIT

How are rules of evidence used at a trial?

It is important to remember that some types of testimony may be dismissed as evidence. The pertinent guidelines are the **rules of evidence**. Rules of evidence may vary according to the case and the court in which it is heard. In general, the rules of evidence are as follows.

- Leading questions are not permitted on direct examination. They are permitted in cross-examination.

- Evidence about the character of a party may not be given unless that person's character is an issue in the case.

- Refreshing the recollection of a witness, in which the attorneys help the witness remember, is allowed.

- The scope of cross-examination is limited to matters that were discussed during direct examination.

- Attorneys may impeach witnesses. That is, they may make the other side's witnesses appear to be unreliable and not to be believed.

- Hearsay is inadmissible as evidence. That is, statements that were overheard are not allowed.

- The opinion of a witness is not permissible as evidence, except for opinions about what the witness personally heard or saw. Expert testimony and professional opinions are usually accepted as evidence.

- Only evidence relevant to the case may be presented and admitted. Evidence that is relevant but that is unfairly prejudicial to one side in the case, that confuses the jury, or that wastes the court's time, is usually excluded or ignored.

An attorney who violates any of the rules of evidence will have his or her questioning disallowed and stricken from the court record. The opposing attorney will object to the question, and the judge will either sustain the objection, indicating that the question is in fact against the rules of evidence, or *overrule* the objection if it has no merit. Even if the opposing attorney neglects to raise an objection, the judge may step in to disallow a question that violates the rules of evidence.

For the most part, in a mock trial, you will be using evidence from witnesses as a key element of your legal strategy. In a real trial, you would also use other kinds of evidence. It is a good idea to learn these as part of your background in trial procedure.

Physical Evidence

Physical evidence includes those concrete objects or substances that are connected to the case, such as a weapon used in the commission of a violent crime, blood or blood-stained items, fingerprints at the crime scene, and items at a crime scene that belong to someone other than the victim.

Physical evidence in civil suits may include

- Written statements from experts, such as doctors, about injuries and their cause

- The object or model of the actual object that is alleged to have caused an injury

- Documents that show expenditures, intent, or other relevant information

For it to be accepted at trial, physical evidence must be in the same condition in which it was found at the scene or where it was discovered. If physical evidence has been contaminated by handling that leaves fingerprints or by other types of damage, alteration, tampering or manipulation, it cannot be used.

Attorneys for either side in a case may introduce physical evidence. However, certain steps must be followed.

FYI A grand jury is a body of jurors convened by a prosecutor to determine if there is sufficient evidence to proceed with a trial. The citizens sitting on a grand jury view evidence and hear sworn testimony. They determine if the evidence presented is strong enough to justify a trial.

- The item must be shown to the judge. The attorney must ask the judge to have it marked for identification by the bailiff or clerk.

- The item must be shown to the opposing counsel. The opposing attorney may object to admitting the item as evidence if he or she feels that it violates the rules of evidence (for example, has been tampered with in some way).

- The item must be shown to the witness(es), who must be asked to identify it and explain what it is.

- The item must be offered into evidence via a request to the judge, who must approve it.

- The judge must rule whether or not the item may be admitted as evidence.

Circumstantial evidence arises from facts that tend to prove other facts by inference. For example, two people are seen arguing violently. Then they part, but one of the pair is found murdered later on. Evidence of the fight may be admitted in court as circumstantial evidence incriminating the still-living arguer as the perpetrator of the murder. This person's guilt is inferred from the fact that he or she was seen arguing violently with the victim. It sometimes happens that an abundance of circumstantial evidence is used to convict the accused of a crime. Sometimes, though, juries refuse to convict on the basis of circumstantial evidence alone.

New Scientific Evidence

Since the 1990s, biologists and medical researchers have successfully mapped the entire sequence of nucleotides, or specific molecules that make up human genetic material. This genetic material, called **DNA** (deoxyribonucleic acid), is unique to every single person except for identical twins.

Increasingly, and especially in cases involving capital crimes for which the death penalty may be imposed, DNA evidence is required to establish guilt. Samples of DNA are taken from the crime scene and analyzed, or sequenced (the DNA's sequence of nucleotides is determined). If the DNA found at the crime scene matches the DNA of the accused, this is considered to be highly reliable evidence of guilt. Of course, it must be proven that the defendant's DNA was not at the crime scene for other reasons; for example, if the accused was a friend of the victim and visited often.

While you probably won't be working with the various forms of physical evidence, you do have lots of other evidence to work with. Once you have devised your legal strategy, it is time to go to court.

YOU BE THE JUDGE

"What do you know about this case?" is a typical question put to potential jurors. Attorneys, especially defense attorneys, are concerned that a potential juror has already formed an opinion about a case, especially if it has already received a great deal of media attention. In high profile cases such as murder, grand theft, embezzlement or other serious cases, several months may occur between the time a defendant is arrested and the time he or she is put on trial. During that time, the media may feature interviews with relatives of the defendant, the victim or victims, and other persons involved with the case. A defense attorney is often concerned that, because of this attention, a juror has already formed an opinion against the defendant. Sometimes, a defense attorney requests that the trial be moved to another area where media attention may not have been so extensive.

These concerns go back to the basic premise of the American legal system, namely, that a defendant is considered innocent until proven guilty. A prosecutor must prove guilt through evidence and witnesses. No conclusions should be drawn until both sides have had a chance to present their case. Even outside of a courtroom, it is important to remember that there are almost always two sides. It is important to hear both of them.

What Would You Do?

You are the captain of your debate team, and you are reviewing applications for next year's squad. A friend tells you that he knows someone who has applied. "Don't let him in," your friend says, mentioning the student's name. "He's a real slacker." What would you do?

Think Critically

1. What types of evidence does a mock trial team typically use?

2. What are affidavits? How should a mock trial team use them to prepare its case?

3. Why are witnesses a valuable source of evidence?

Research NOW!

4. Research to find out if the rules of evidence are different for a regular jury trial than they are for a mock trial. If they are different, explain how they are different.

5. One of the most complicated criminal investigations involves conspiracy, that is, planning to do something criminal. Research the rules of evidence allowed in a conspiracy trial. How do they differ, if at all, from the rules of evidence in a non-conspiracy case?

Write NOW!

6. Write a list of the types of evidence you would want to have if you were a defense attorney defending someone accused of breaking and entering a home and burglarizing it.

7. **TEAMWORK** Watch the movie *A Civil Action*. Take notes as you watch. Record everything the plaintiff's attorneys have to do to collect enough evidence to make their case. Share your list with the group and discuss your ideas about what occurred in the movie and what it indicates about civil law cases.

Speak NOW!

8. **TEAMWORK** Work with a group. One member suggests a situation that involves circumstantial evidence that might be presented in a trial. Another member responds by reformulating the evidence so that it is not circumstantial and inferred, but is actual and proven. Each person in the group should get a chance to suggest each type of evidence.

9. **TEAMWORK** Work with a partner to state a question that an attorney might ask a witness during a trial. One partner asks the question. The other partner states if the question is permissible in direct examination or only in cross-examination.

Do You Agree?

Resolved A witness's character and previous arrest record should detract from the validity and usefulness of that witness's testimony at trial.

Affirmative position

Yes, the testimony of a witness who has a history of lying should be suspect. A witness who has an arrest record shows contempt for the law, which is also a reason to disregard his or her testimony.

Negative position

No, just because a witness is not the ideal of an upstanding citizen, or has made mistakes in life, does not mean that in this case his or her testimony is dishonest.

Opening Procedure

The trial begins when the judge comes into court. Usually, a court official instructs everyone to stand. The official reads the names of the plaintiff and the defendant, as well as the charge filed against the defendant. The judge welcomes everyone to court and gives the instruction to be seated. Then the judge gives instructions to the jury. The judge usually instructs the jury to pay close attention to the evidence presented. This and only this can be used by a jury in determining a verdict. Finally, the judge instructs the attorneys to present opening statements.

Opening Statements

Both the prosecutor and the defense attorney make opening statements to the jury at the beginning of the trial. The purpose of the opening statement is to introduce the attorney to the jurors. The prosecutor describes the accused. The defense attorney describes the same person but from a different point of view, because the accused is his or her client. Each attorney explains to the jurors briefly what the case is about. The opening statement should not plead the case or introduce specific facts.

Prosecutor

The prosecutor gives the first opening statement. The opening statement should accomplish the following goals.

1. Introduces the prosecuting attorney.

2. Presents the facts of the case from the prosecutor's point of view.

3. Identifies which facts are the most important in the prosecutor's view.

4. Explains how these facts will be proven through evidence and/or testimony.

5. Concludes with an appeal for attention to the material and the arguments to be made during the trial.

There are certain things a prosecutor should avoid in the opening statement. An opening statement should avoid providing too much detail that may be confusing. The judge will reprimand you for this, as it is information that comes later in the trial. Exaggeration or overreaching certainty sounds arrogant. Remember, the defendant must be considered innocent until proven guilty. The burden of proof lies with the prosecutor. Likewise, the prosecutor's opening statement should not anticipate in an opening statement what the defense will say. This should be part of your strategy for cross-examining witnesses for the defense. Finally, avoid excessive walking around or gesturing in front of the jury. It is distracting and may make a jury uncomfortable.

©BOB DAEMMRICH/THE IMAGE WORKS

What should a prosecutor's opening statement avoid?

Defense Attorney

In general, the defense attorney's opening statement outlines the facts of the case from the defendant's point of view. The prosecutor cannot interrupt during the defense's opening statement. As with a prosecutor's opening statement, a defense attorney's opening statement has certain goals.

1. Introduces the defense attorney.

2. Presents the defense's theory about the case, and why, in general terms, the defendant is not guilty.

3. The defense may make a brief reference to facts that may weaken the prosecutor's case.

4. Provides a brief overview of defense witnesses and what they will add to the defense's case.

5. The defense concludes with an appeal for the jury to be open to its arguments and facts.

©DICK BLUME/SYRACUSE NEWSPAPERS/THE IMAGE WORKS

What should a defense attorney's introductory statement include?

As with the prosecution, the defense attorney's opening statement should avoid certain types of statements and behavior. In general, the defense attorney's opening statement should avoid stating or repeating facts that are not disputed by either party. It is a good idea to avoid exaggeration of any kind, especially about the innocence of the defendant or witnesses. The defense should not provide hints about the major arguments or witnesses that will be presented later. And, again, avoid excessive walking or gesturing.

Before the trial begins, attorneys for both sides have interviewed and selected witnesses whose testimony will support their case. Each side must advise the other of the witnesses who they will call into court to testify. Witnesses are called to appear in court to give testimony at a particular time. They are sworn to tell the truth. Lying under oath is **perjury**, a crime punishable in a real trial by jail time. Generally, the prosecution calls its set of witnesses first.

Presenting Evidence

The trial proceeds with the prosecuting attorney presenting evidence using direct examination of prosecution witnesses. The defense attorney cross-examines each witness in turn. When the prosecution rests, or has finished calling all its witnesses, the defense makes its case and calls defense witnesses. The defense attorney conducts the direct examination, and the prosecutor conducts cross-examination

Direction Examination

Direct examination is when the attorney who calls the witness questions the witness. In direct examination, the attorney knows what the witness will say and asks questions to elicit the information sought. Generally, the attorney has the witness introduce herself or himself to the jury. The attorney's questions elicit the witness's relationship to the case and the defendant.

In direct examination, questioning is directed at getting the witness to make a statement that supports the attorney's case. As the witness has been interviewed by the attorney doing direct examination, the attorney may use a list of prepared questions to examine the witness. Questions are usually crafted to get the witness to repeat or to elaborate on the information that helps the attorney's case. This helps the jury understand and remember the witness's testimony.

Attorney	Where were you on the night of October 7?
Witness	I was walking down Main Street.
Attorney	Did you see anything unusual that night?
Witness	Yes, I saw a car crash.
Attorney	Can you describe what you saw?
Witness	Yes. I saw a white car veer toward where I was walking and crash into a black car.
Attorney	Then what did you see?
Witness	I saw a man get out of the white car.
Attorney	If that man is in the courtroom now, could you point him out?
Witness	Yes, he's the man sitting over there at the defendant's table.
Attorney	Let the record show that the witness is indicating the defendant. How can you be sure that it was the defendant?
Witness	The front of the car was facing me, so I could see the man's face as he got out.

Direct examination must avoid **leading questions,** or questions that elicit a simple "yes" or "no" answer from the witness. If such questions are asked, the other attorney will rise to object to the question. The judge will **sustain,** or uphold, the **objection.**

Cross-Examination

Cross-examination is questioning by the attorney who did not call the witness. Cross-examination occurs after direct examination. Because both attorneys know who all of the witnesses are, the cross-examining attorney may also prepare in advance a list of questions for the witness. The attorney who is cross-examining a witness listens closely to the direct examination to catch any inconsistencies, flaws, or gaps in the witness's testimony or in the questions asked. In most cases, the cross-examination is done seriously. It may be harmful to one's case if the witness is ridiculed or made to look foolish. Then again, if the witness is clearly confused, a light and humorous form of questioning that undermines the witness's testimony may appeal to a jury.

Cross-examination must attack and raise questions about the witness's testimony. The attack is most often planned in advance and is part of the attorney's overall strategy for winning the case. The intent is to get the jury to question the reliability of the witness's testimony. This undermines the opposing attorney's case. A good cross-examination can upend the testimony to make it support the case of the cross-examining attorney. In cross-examination, leading questions are permitted, even encouraged. By eliciting "yes" or "no" answers and not allowing the witness to explain, the cross-examining attorney can raise important questions about the testimony in the eyes of the jury. **Impeaching** the witness by asking about past conduct, prior arrests, possible biases, and other accusations that diminish the witness's character are also allowed. However, cross-examination should follow from direct examination and not bring in extraneous facts.

Attorney	Why were you on Main St. so late on the night of October 7?
Witness	I was walking home.
Attorney	From where?
Witness	I was out with friends.
Attorney	What time was this?
Witness	Maybe eleven or eleven thirty . . .
Attorney	That's kind of late isn't it?
Witness	I don't know . . . maybe.
Attorney	When did you begin your day that day?
Witness	Maybe about five, five thirty . . .
Attorney	So, you were pretty tired, weren't you?
Witness	No, I . . .
Attorney	Was there a streetlight where the accident occurred?
Witness	There was a street light about 30 feet away, on the corner.
Attorney	So, there was no direct light at the site of the crash.
Witness	Well, no, but . . .
Attorney	So, it's possible that in the dim light, and having been up for close to seventeen hours, you might not have seen the face of the driver in the white car as clearly as you think.
Witness	No . . . I'm pretty sure that I saw. . .
Attorney	Thank you. No further questions. .

Objections

There are several types of objections that attorneys can make if they think the other attorney is asking impermissible questions or is in some way violating court rules. The attorney making the objection stands up and addresses the judge, saying "Objection, your honor," and then explains the objection. Both the prosecutor and the defense attorney can make objections. The judge decides if the objection has merit and can be sustained. If the judge decides the objection does not have merit the objection is denied. Both the prosecutor and the defense attorney can make objections. However, at a mock trial be careful how you use objections. Misuse will cost you points in your final evaluation.

Often Used Objections

Relevancy	The testimony is not relevant to the facts of the case.
Leading question	If asked during direct examination when it is not allowed ("Counsel is leading the witness.")
Improper character testimony	If the character of the witness is not relevant to the case.
Beyond the scope	If the questioning exceeds the scope of the case ("Counsel is asking matters that are beyond the scope of the direct examination.").
Hearsay	Hearsay is secondhand information (the witness heard something from someone else) and is generally not allowed in testimony.
Opinion	A witness's opinion may be disallowed if it is not relevant to the case.

Summations

After all the witnesses have been examined, both the prosecutor and the defense attorney speak directly to the jury, giving their summation of the case. The purpose of a summation is to reinforce one's point of view, or one's case, in the eyes of the jurors.

Many court cases are long and complicated, and tiring for the jury. The summation should be short and sweet, but punchy and effective. In a summation, the attorney should briefly review those facts in the case that support his or her point of view. The attorney may highlight the testimony of witnesses and evidence that supports the case. The attorney should highlight opposition witnesses who turned out to be less than convincing and explain why evidence does not conclusively prove the opposition's point of view. This part of the summation appeals to the jurors' ability to reason. A good summation may also subtly and effectively appeal to jurors' emotions. Attorneys may try to get the jurors to emotionally identify with the victim or defendant to influence how they see and evaluate the facts.

A summation must be brief and highlight those points and facts that support the attorney's case. It should be logical and to the point. A rambling summation, or one that reiterates every fact and bit of testimony already given, will likely bore the jurors, which will not win them to your side of the case. A summation usually ends with the attorney asking the jury to reach a verdict that supports his or her side of the case.

Final Judgments

After the jury returns its verdict, it is time for teams to be judged. Procedures vary, but usually a panel of judges evaluates each team. Evaluators award points from 1–10 to each attorney and witness, based upon his or her performance during each stage of the trial. These evaluations cover opening statements for the plaintiff and defense, the testimony provided by each of the witnesses, direct and cross-examination from the attorneys, and the closing statements made by each of the attorneys. A team will lose points for providing testimony that is outside of the specifics of the case, as well as for abuse of objections during the trial. Points may also be deducted for any inappropriate behavior by any of the participants. The team with the highest number of points is usually the team that wins the verdict, but not always. Ironically, a team may lose the verdict and still win the match!

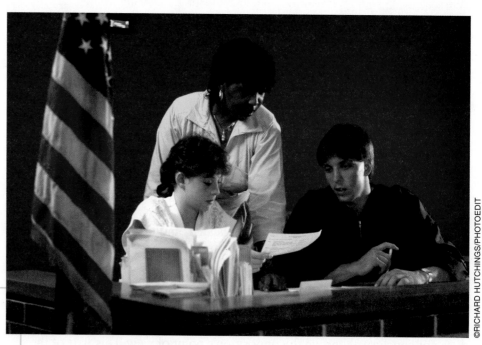

©RICHARD HUTCHINGS/PHOTOEDIT

How are teams scored at a mock trial?

Think Critically

1. How are the opening statements of the prosecutor and the defense attorney the same? How are they different?

2. What is the purpose of direct examination?

3. What makes an effective summation? What should be the relationship between an attorney's opening statement and his or her summation?

Research NOW!

4. Locate the transcript of an actual court case's opening statement(s) or summation(s). Choose one opening statement or summation to analyze. Note what the attorney stresses to the jury. Analyze the argument and the details used to support the argument. Note especially what the attorney says about the case that will be presented by the opposing attorney.

5. **TEAMWORK** Work with a group. Choose one trial to analyze. Have each member research examples of direct examination or cross-examination in that trial. Analyze the relationship between the direct examination and the cross-examination. Notice any differences in tenor, approach, or subject between the two types of questioning.

Write NOW!

6. Write a one-paragraph scenario about a court case that you, as attorney, are either prosecuting or defending. Then write down three questions you would ask an eyewitness regarding the case.

7. Write a short dialogue between a defense attorney and a witness in the case you imagined in activity 6. In the dialogue, include questions in which the attorney impeaches the witness's testimony.

Speak NOW!

8. **TEAMWORK** Work in pairs to write a direct examination of a witness that contains questions that would, in a court, elicit objections from the opposing attorney. Then each pair reads aloud the direct examination, with one student playing the role of the witness and the other the role of the attorney. The other pair of students listens to the role-play to note where they should object to a question. They should stand and say, "I object because . . ." and give the reason for the objection. Each pair takes turns reading and evaluating.

Chapter in Review

12.1 Concepts of Advocacy

- A trial is a formal procedure where parties come together and present information before a judge and/or a jury in order to achieve a resolution.
- Mock trial is a simulated trial in which competing teams play the roles of attorneys and witnesses. To prepare for a mock trial, attorneys and witnesses need to review the obligations of prosecutor, prosecution team, defense attorney, defense team, and witnesses.

12.2 Evidentiary Quest

- Attorneys and their teams must prepare evidence to use at trial. Evidence at mock trials usually consists of testimony from witnesses, diagrams, and maps.
- At a regular court trial, physical evidence is used. Physical evidence consists of concrete objects or substances connected to the case.

12.3 The Trial

- At a mock trial, the judge instructs the jury on how to conduct their responsibilities. Attorneys make opening statements.
- Attorneys examine and cross-examine witnesses, and make closing summations. The jury deliberates and hands down a verdict.
- Competing teams are scored according to their performance at each stage of the trial. Participants are scored on a scale of 1–10.

a. advocate
b. affidavit
c. alleged
d. cross-examination
e. circumstantial evidence
f. defendant
g. defense attorney
h. direct examination
i. DNA
j. evidence
k. impeaching
l. judge
m. jury
n. leading question
o. objection
p. perjury
q. physical evidence
r. plaintiff
s. prosecutor
t. rules of evidence
u. sustain
v. testimony
w. trial
x. verdict
y. witness

Develop Your Debating Language

Select the term that best fits the definition. Some terms will not be used.

1. Reliable information relevant to a case

2. Giving false testimony

3. The person accused of a crime

4. Supposed

5. The person suing another person

6. The attorney making the case for guilt of the accused

7. Questioning of the witness a lawyer calls to make his or her case

8. Someone who gives statements under oath relevant to a case in court

9. Stating or implying that a witness has a bad character

10. Twelve citizens who decide the outcome of a trial

11. A jury's judgment regarding guilt or innocence of the accused

12. An appeal to the judge to rule the opposing attorney's tactic inadmissible or against the rules of court

Review Debate Concepts

13. How does a mock trial differ from a real trial?

14. What are some of the key roles involved with a jury trial?

15. What do teams consist of at a mock trial? What are their responsibilities?

16. What are some of the other roles played by students who aren't on a team at a mock trial?

17. What is a defendant? What is the defendant's status during the trial regarding guilt or innocence?

18. Compare and contrast the roles, duties, and limitations in court of the prosecutor and the defense attorney.

19. What types of evidence is usually used at a mock trial?

20. What are two examples of physical evidence? How must physical evidence be handled? Why?

21. What is circumstantial evidence? Why is it sometimes unreliable in determining the guilt or innocence of the accused?

22. What are two important things attorneys should accomplish during their opening statements to the jury?

23. What is direct examination and who conducts it?

24. Contrast cross-examination with direct examination. What are at least two ways that cross-examination differs from direct examination?

25. Give one example of hearsay testimony and one example of impeaching questioning.

26. What is an objection? What is one circumstance in which a judge will sustain an attorney's objection?

27. What is a summation, and why is it so important to the outcome of a trial?

28. How are teams evaluated at mock trial? Who evaluates them?

Make Academic Connections

29. **CURRENT EVENTS/PROBLEM SOLVING** Choose one person or problem being covered in daily newspapers or on television news that you feel might be suitable for a court case because a person or entity is acting unlawfully. What did the person or entity do that you feel is illegal? What would your argument be for prosecuting this case? Explain how you would argue the case.

30. **TECHNOLOGY** Research and report on recent technological developments as they are used in the legal system. Write a one-paragraph description of each development and how it is used; for example, how computers and the Internet have affected legal investigations and court trials, especially regarding their use as evidence.

31. **SCIENCE**   How is science being used increasingly in court cases, particularly when scientists are called as expert witnesses? What scientific disciplines are most used in court cases, and how are they used? Choose one or two examples and show how the expert testimony of a scientist(s) affected the outcome of the trial.

32. **CHALLENGES**   Read the transcript of the decision in a Supreme Court case. Read both the majority opinion and the dissenting opinion. Evaluate both in terms of the argument made. Write your own evaluation of the arguments, explaining why you feel one is more persuasive, or correct, than the other. You may want to read the section of the Constitution on which the opinions are based.

Research NOW!

33. Use online or other resources to find transcripts of mock trials conducted at university or college law schools. Evaluate the opening statements, questioning, objections, arguments, and summations of each "attorney" in the mock trial. Was the case well argued? How would you have argued one side differently? Would you have acted differently if you had played the role of the judge?

34. How have jury trials sometimes caused changes in the law? Research a law or laws that were changed based on evidence or what occurred at a jury trial conducted on the state or federal level. Summarize why the events at the trial led to a rethinking and revision of the law.

35. **TEAMWORK**   What are the Geneva Conventions? Each person in the group should find out one of the following: What are the legal stipulations of the Geneva Conventions? How do the Geneva Conventions apply to U.S. law and legal process? How do they affect the rules of evidence in the United States and elsewhere? The group should then debate the current controversy in some quarters about the Geneva Conventions and their effect on the investigation of terrorism suspects in the United States.

Write NOW!

36. Select one court case that is currently being reported on in the newspaper or on television news. Read about both sides of the case. Write a letter to the editor of your local newspaper explaining your opinion about one aspect of the case.

37. **TEAMWORK**   Is there something going on in your community or city that you think should be legally changed? For example, are there people behaving in a way that you think should be unlawful? Are there laws on the books that you think should be overturned? Work with a group to learn all you can about

one issue. Then choose one side of the issue. Each group writes a summary of the issue and an explanation of their opinion about what should be done regarding the law, or lack of a law.

Speak NOW!

38. Research significant legislation such as reforming the U.S. health care system or reducing greenhouse gas emissions to allay global warming. Find out what the arguments are on both sides. Write a three-minute speech that you would present as an opening argument if the legislation that is enacted is challenged in court.

39. Locate one of the episodes of *Perry Mason*, which are available on DVD. Mason is a fictional defense attorney and the television series is a classic. Every week, Mason and his adversary, the prosecutor Hamilton Burger, faced each other in a courtroom. Take notes about the court proceedings. What irregularities, if any, did you notice in the actions of one or both attorneys? Can any of these actions be sanctioned based on the motive or the outcome? Deliver a short oral evaluation of the episode you chose.

eCollection Activity

In court cases, there is great pressure on both the prosecutor and the defense attorney to win the case for his or her side. This sometimes leads to one or the other attorney withholding evidence that will hurt his or her case while benefiting the opposition. Though such actions are technically illegal, they have frequently and secretly been used to influence court cases. Though this type of illegality is rare, such tactics are generally more prevalent among prosecutors, who, as goversnment employees, may see to it that evidence found by the police suddenly and "mysteriously" disappears and is never introduced at trial.

These rare but disturbing incidents have been discussed and debated among attorneys for years. Recently, the American Bar Association (ABA) has made its Rules of Conduct for lawyers far more explicit and punitive regarding the serious consequences for an attorney who withholds evidence. To learn more about this issue, access www.cengage.com/school/langarts/debate and click on the link for Chapter 12. Write a short paper summarizing your findings and present it to the class. Invite questions and comments.

GLOSSARY

A

Advocate in a trial, one who gathers as much information as possible to make an argument that supports his or her client, or one side of the case.

Advocating supporting the position presented in the resolution.

Aesthetic value a type of value used in a Lincoln-Douglas debate that appeals to beauty.

Affidavit a written statement used in a trial that provides testimony from a person in some way involved in the case.

Alleged a case or argument charged but not proven.

Allusions references to great literary classics or timeless myths that underscore topic points.

Altruism the idea that your actions are prompted to show benevolence or kindness to others.

Amendment changes proposed to a bill or resolution.

Annotation a note added for comment or explanation.

Applied ethics a branch of moral philosophy that deals with controversial issues specific to a certain area of study, such as animal rights, environmental concerns, or nuclear war.

Appropriateness suitable for the environment.

Articulation the act of saying each syllable in a word clearly and correctly.

Attitude inherence an attitude, or radical social belief, that becomes the basis for which the affirmation case claims the present system is doing nothing, doing very little, doing the wrong thing, or just doesn't care.

Attention getter quotations, rhetorical questions, anecdotes, jokes, personal stories, current events, canned introductions, and political notebooks used in a speech to grab the attention of the judge.

Authorship speech the first speech on a bill or resolution in Congress, usually three or four minutes long.

B

Ballot a judge's document that contains the names of the debaters, a space to write which side won, and a space to award speaker points.

Bailiff a courtroom attendant who is responsible for keeping order in the courtroom and overseeing the jury.

Bias a prejudice toward specific idea or cause.

Bill a proposed new law.

Binder a container similar to a notebook in which loose pages are fastened together.

Body language all the ways your body can move and the positions you can strike that help convey the meaning of what you are saying.

Brainstorming an informal discussion in which you share as many ideas related to a topic as possible, as well as your thoughts, feelings, and experiences with any given topic.

Brief a collection of evidence about a single subject.

Brink in a cross-examination debate, the second component of the disadvantage; it claims that the action called for by the affirmative team's plan will initiate the disadvantage.

Burden of proof the affirmative side's obligation to prove what is stated or disputed, in order to win the debate.

C

Chamber smaller groups of students participating in a Student Congress; sometimes called Houses or Senates.

Canned introductions a prewritten introduction to a speech used as an attention getter that is general in nature and easily applied to a variety of topics.

Categorical imperative a theory of moral obligation defined by Immanuel Kant that states that one rationally chooses the good, and, therefore, one's choice is good for others as well.

Circumstantial evidence facts that tend to prove other facts by inference.

Citation a bibliographical list of the sources of your evidence.

Citizen judge a judge at a Public Forum debate and meant to be a typical citizen, such as one that would sit on a jury.

Clash the two opposing positions in a debate, one affirmative and one negative.

Committees a specific group assignment in a Student Congress based on different kinds of legislation.

Competition worthiness the degree to which a topic or argument is suitable for a competition.

Community judge an individual recruited from the community who volunteers to judge at a tournament.

Conclusion the final position agreed upon at the end of an argument.

Consequentialist theory a theory that states that the result of an outcome determines the morality of the act.

Constructive speech an informative oral presentation of the debate's key points.

Contention another word for a major argument.

Copyright code a notation that indicates the original source for a book selection or article found online.

Court recorder an employee of the court who records everything that is said and done in the courtroom to create a formal transcript of the proceedings.

Credible being from a reliable source.

Cross-entering entering in more than one event.

Cross-examination period a guaranteed period after every other speech where specific questions can be asked of the speaker that refer to the bill, resolution, or comment he or she just presented.

Cross-examination (CX) debate a very well-researched and structured debate between two teams of two in which the topic is centered around policy.

Cross-examination speech a one-minute speech that follows each speaker in Student Congress.

Crossfire cross-examination in a Public Forum debate in which both debaters ask each other questions.

Crystallization the process of summarizing your voting issues or arguments for the judge so he or she can decide who won the debate.

D

Debate an oral exchange between two groups or individuals for and against a set position; the act of listening carefully to one's opponent and responding to what he or she has said is a crucial aspect that differentiates debating from arguing.

Decision rule an argument that establishes an all or nothing decision from the judge in which he or she accepts the kritik in contrast to the affirmative plan.

Deductive argument an argument that begins with a general rule that is accepted as truth.

Defendant the person charged with a violation of the law.

Defense attorney an attorney who gathers and presents information and arguments intended to undermine the information presented by the prosecutor.

Demeanor your outward behavior or manner.

Diction your choice of words.

Disadvantage an argument that if the affirmation debate team's plan is ratified, bad side effects will occur.

Divine command theory a belief that an all-powerful Supreme Being or God wills things and they become a reality.

DNA abbreviation for deoxyribonucleic acid; a genetic material that is unique to every single person except for identical twins.

Domestic extemp an extemporaneous speech that covers all issues that pertain to the United States, also called U.S. Extemporaneous Speaking.

Dominate control the debate or your opponent.

Dropped point any argument not addressed in the first rebuttal for the affirmations and the first constructive for the negative.

Duty theory a theory based on the statement that morality is based on basic duties or obligations and other's rights.

E

Egoism the idea that your actions are prompted by selfish desires.

Enunciation the clear, distinct pronunciation of each sound and syllable in a word.

Ethical altruism a theory based on the statement that an action is morally right if its consequences are more favorable than unfavorable to everyone except the person performing the action.

Ethical egoism a theory based on the statement that an action is morally right if its consequences are more favorable than unfavorable only to the person performing the action.

Evidence proof of your position.

Extemp another word for extemporaneous speaking, which takes place at most debate tournaments.

Extemporaneous speech a speech that has not been written out beforehand and is given on the spur of the moment.

F

Fallacy a false statement, something not true.

Fiat an act that will create something without effort.

Filibustering giving a long answer or making a long speech with the purpose of delaying.

Final focus an important one-minute speech, also appropriately known as the "last shot" or your last chance to tell the judge why you should win the debate.

Final round designates a round of a tournament where the top students from each semi-final round compete for the last time.

Flow sheet a sheet of paper divided into rows and columns where you can highlight and organize the main arguments and evidence of both the affirmative and negative.

Flowing the process of taking notes on a flow sheet.

Fluency break a pause in a sentence.

Foreign extemp an extemporaneous speech that covers all International issues, also called International Extemporaneous Speaking.

Formal debate a pre-planned, structured oral exchange between two opponents for and against one or more set positions.

Framers the writers of the resolution.

G

Grace periods additional time added without penalty to the original time allowance for a speech.

Grand crossfire a type of crossfire where all four debaters ask and answer questions at once.

H

Hard evidence statistics, facts, and quotations from experts used in a debate.

Harm a building block of debate, it's an unwanted problem resulting from an action or inaction of the current system.

Hearing the brain's act of recognizing sounds around you.

I

Impact the third and final component of the disadvantage, this argument shows the negative effect of adopting the affirmative's plan.

Impeaching asking about past conduct, prior arrests, possible biases, and other accusations that diminish the witness's character at a trial.

Inductive argument an argument that gives specific facts and leads to a conclusion or generalization.

Inference the statement concluded from the premise(s) of an argument.

Informal debate an impromptu exchange of ideas for and against an issue between two or more people.

Inherency a building block of debate, it's an argument that proves an inherent barrier exists.

Inherent barrier a reason for which the affirmation case claims the present system is doing nothing, doing very little, doing the wrong thing, or just doesn't care.

Internet computer-based resource containing websites used for researching topics.

J

Jargon a specific language that relates to a specific topic.

Judge an adult official that presides over a debate or Student Congress.

Junior varsity a category of debaters that is past novice but before varsity.

Jury a group of twelve adult citizens who listen to everything that goes on in the trial, evaluate it, and then reach a decision, or verdict.

K

Kicked when a team uses a strategic move to eliminate an argument that they originally advanced.

Kritik a defensive argument that challenges the certain way of thinking or philosophy behind the affirmative team's case rather than the case itself.

Knowledge kritik a defensive argument that is based on the premise that we lack the knowledge required to solve for the resolution.

L

Language kritik a defensive argument that is based on the premise that the language used in an affirmative case is harmful.

Lay judge a type of debate judge from all walks of life that may not have any competition experience.

Leading question a type of questions that elicits a simple "yes" or "no" answer from the witness at a trial.

Lincoln-Douglas debate a formal debate between two people in which the topic is centered around value; a debate, for example, over whether private or public education holds more value.

Line-by-line presentation presenting your counterarguments point by point in the order that your opponent presented them.

Link the first component of the disadvantage, it is evidence that shows a connection to the affirmation plan.

Listening the conscious act of applying meaning to what you hear.

Logical reasoning statements that can be formed from sound thinking and proof of reasoning.

M

Metaethics how you act, based on what moral principles mean and where you get these principles.

Mock trial a recreation of what happens in a jury trial.

Moral relativism a belief in moral philosophy that ethics exist only because humans have created them, therefore, morality is relative or consequent on one's own beliefs or the approval of others, and not to a fixed standard.

Moral value deals with issues of right and wrong.

Motion in Student Congress, a declaration before the chamber to determine the direction of the proceeding.

N

Negative arguments defensive and offensive arguments that challenge the affirmation case in a Cross-examination debate.

Negative block two negative speeches back to back given by the negative debate team.

Negation speech a three or four minute speech that directly follows the authorship speech.

Normative ethics how you act, based on moral standards that tell you what is right and wrong behavior.

Novice the lowest category for a debater, someone new to debate.

O

Objection when an attorney objects to, or argues against, a question or line of questioning.

Observation a major argument, similar to a contention, used to establish a premise for a kritik.

P

Panel more than one judge, usually an odd number of three to five judges to avoid ties.

Parallel phrasing structuring related ideas in a similar grammatical way.

Paradigm the judge's philosophy about debate.

Parliamentary procedure in Student Congress, a set of guidelines, which allows for discussion by using the democratic process.

Pause a brief moment of silence between words or ideas.

Perjury lying under oath.

Philosophy a system of concepts that form an underlying theory of a topic, investigation of nature, causes, and principles of reality, knowledge, or values based on logical reasoning.

Physical evidence in a trial, concrete objects or substances that are connected to the case, such as a weapon used in the commission of a violent crime, blood or blood-stained items, fingerprints at the crime scene, items at a crime scene that belong to someone other than the victim.

Pitch how high or low a voice is when speaking.

Plagiarism the act of passing off someone else's work or ideas as your own.

Plaintiff the person who is suing another person or company.

Plan a short paragraph that explains the change that is suggested.

Poise the way you handle yourself during the debate.

Policy a specific action, usually in response to a problem, implemented by government or society, which often requires changes in laws, rules, or legislation.

Political notebook a compilation of political cartoons that are arranged alphabetically by subject matter and contain complete source cites.

Political values type of value in which the role of government is questioned.

Pragmatic example an example offered to support an argument that is practical or real-life.

Preempting predicting and responding to an argument before the opponent brings it up.

Preflow affirmation side arguments written into the first column of a flow sheet before the debate begins.

Preliminary round the first round of a tournament.

Premise the first part of an argument that sets up the argument.

Presiding Officer the elected leader of a chamber who keeps a precedence chart.

Presumption a specific rule, like the idea that you are innocent until proven guilty.

Prima facie a Latin term that means "at first appearance."

Professionalism used to describe the attitude of friendly competition.

Pronunciation the act of saying a word correctly.

Prosecutor a representative of government who makes the case that the defendant, the person on trial, is guilty of the crime he or she is charged with.

Persuade to move someone to a belief or a course of action.

Public Forum debate a debate that combines the speaking skills used in forensic speech events, such as Extemporaneous Speaking, with the research and argumentation skills used in other debates, such as Lincoln-Douglas debate, and strives to be informative and entertaining to the general public while it focuses on controversial issues that apply to the real world in current times, "stripped from the headlines" to provide up-to-date topics.

Q

Quarter-final round designates a round of a tournament where the top students from each preliminary round compete.

R

Rate how fast you speak, the number of words you say per minute.

Rebuttal speeches that counter the attacks and positions that your opponent has presented.

Rebuttal speech a persuasive oral presentation of the strong areas in your speech and the weak areas in your opponent's.

Refute to prove the attacks against your case are false.

Repetition repeating a phrase to bring attention and rhythm to a speech.

Research packet materials compiled for debaters by universities, individuals, and research consortium.

Resolution the topic or issue to be debated or resolved, it does not become a law.

Rhetorical device language used to make your oratory effective; examples include figurative language, metaphors, and similes.

Road map a description statement for the judge of exactly what you are going to refute.

Robert's Rules of Order a famous publication that contains Parliamentary Rules.

Round a series of timed speeches about one topic.

Round robin a form of debate in which several teams compete against each other and the tournament is determined by the win-loss records.

S

Semi-final round designates a round of a tournament where the top students from each quarter-final round compete.

Significance a term used in conjunction with harm, ensures that the subject of harm caused by the topic is large enough or important enough to warrant discussion.

Signpost clearly identifying the claim that you are refuting.

Social contract a real or hypothesized agreement between a citizen and his or her society that considers the rights and responsibilities of each.

Soft evidence persuasive stories, personal narratives, comparisons, and examples used in a debate.

Solvency the final building block of debate, addresses whether the affirmative plan can solve the harm.

Source materials from which information is researched and gathered, such as books, magazines, and websites.

Source cite an important element of the extemp speech that tells the judge what reference materials were used when preparing the speech.

Speaker points an evaluation of the debater's speaking and presentation skills awarded during a debate based on the rate of speech, volume, articulation, eye contact, and other presentation skills; points are awarded to each debater, usually on a scale that ranges from 15 to 30 points, with 30 points being the highest.

Speed drills activities that help you learn spreading skills.

Sportsmanship the desired attitude of respect and fairness.

Spreading the act of speaking rapidly but clearly, often used in debates in which a lot of evidence is presented, such as a cross-examination debate.

Standard a guide to weigh an identified violation, used for comparing your position to the opposing team's case and plan.

Status quo keeping things as they are.

Stock issues the four basic arguments used in every debate: topicality, harm, inherency, and solvency.

Structural inherency a law, regulation, or guideline that becomes the basis for which the affirmation case claims the present system is doing nothing, doing very little, doing the wrong thing, or just doesn't care.

Student Congress a style of student debate similar to the Congress in Washington, DC in which the goal is passing legislation you or your teammates have written.

Summary speech a speech given by the prosecutor and the defense attorney directly to the jury to reinforce one's point of view, or one's case, in the eyes of those jurors.

Sustain to uphold.

T

Testimony a sworn statement from a witness.

Topic the subject matter for a resolution.

Topic statement a statement that pinpoints or summarizes your view on a given topic.

Topicality a building block for each debate that addresses whether the affirmative case relates directly or indirectly to the resolution to be debated.

Transition move during a speech, physically moving from one spot to another as you are moving from one idea to another.

Transitional sentence the last element of the introduction that indicates to the judge that you are done with the introduction and brings you to the next section of your speech.

Trial a formal procedure in which someone is proven innocent or guilty in a court of law.

Tubs in an extemporaneous competition, large plastic bins used to transport and store materials in the preparation room at the tournament.

U

Utilitarianism a theory based on the statement that an action is morally right if its consequences are more favorable than unfavorable to everyone.

V

Values the ideals or principles held by a society or a person.

Value criteria in a Lincoln-Douglas debate, standards, ruler, tests, or measurements that judge the worth of your value.

Value premises another term for value used in a Lincoln-Douglas debate.

Varsity the highest level category of a debater who has passed the junior varsity stage.

Verdict a statement of guilt or innocence or a decision about which of the parties is in the right.

Vocalized pauses words such as *um* and *uh* that signal a brief lapse in the thought process and disrupt the flow of a speech.

Volume the loudness of your voice.

Voting issue arguments, not general ideas, which prove why you should win the round.

W

Whereas a statement meaning the same as because, it introduces your resolution and reason for discussion.

Witness people who can provide information that supports one side of the case being tried in a court.